# CREOLE GENESIS, ATTITUDES AND DISCOURSE

Volume 20

John R. Rickford and Suzanne Romaine (eds)

*Creole Genesis, Attitudes and Discourse*

# CREOLE GENESIS, ATTITUDES AND DISCOURSE

## STUDIES CELEBRATING CHARLENE J. SATO

Edited by

### JOHN R. RICKFORD
*Stanford University*

### SUZANNE ROMAINE
*University of Oxford*

JOHN BENJAMINS PUBLISHING COMPANY
AMSTERDAM/PHILADELPHIA

TM The paper used in this publication meets the minimum requirements of American National Standard for Information Sciences — Permanence of Paper for Printed Library Materials, ANSI Z39.48-1984.

**Library of Congress Cataloging-in-Publication Data**

Creole genesis, attitudes and discourse : studies celebrating Charlene J. Sato / edited by John R. Rickford, Suzanne Romaine.
    p.     cm. -- (Creole language library, ISSN 0920-9026 ; v. 20)
   Includes bibliographical references and index.
1. Creole dialects. 2. Pidgin languages. I. Rickford, John R., 1949. II. Romaine, Suzanne, 1951-
III. Sato, Charlene J. IV. Series.
PM7831.C728     1999
417'.22--dc21                                  99-14907
ISBN 90 272 5242 4 (Eur.) / 1 55619 667 9 (US) (alk. paper)        CIP

John Benjamins Publishing Co. • P.O.Box 75577 • 1070 AN Amsterdam • The Netherlands
John Benjamins North America • P.O.Box 27519 • Philadelphia PA 19118-0519 • USA

# Table of Contents

PART C
**Attitudes and Education in Creole Communities**

# PART A

# Introduction

# Preface

John R. Rickford
*Stanford University*

Suzanne Romaine
*Oxford University*

This volume of papers is dedicated to Charlene ("Charlie") Sato in celebration of her rich but all too short life and her many contributions to the field of pidgin and creole studies. (See the biography and bibliography which follow this preface.) Our field is richer not only for her teaching, her academic research and publications, but also for her political engagement on behalf of speakers of pidgin and creole languages, those linguistically and sociopolitically significant varieties which arise in situations where people from different nations, ethnic groups and language backgrounds come into sustained contact, through trade, for instance, or on plantations fueled by slavery, indenture and immigration. While inspiring and challenging her colleagues, Charlie also influenced and encouraged a generation of younger scholars in her role as teacher and mentor, particularly through her establishment of a course on pidgins and creoles at the University of Hawai'i at Mānoa. (She was nominated for the university's Excellence in Teaching Award in 1985, 1986, 1987, and 1989.) She also played an active role in promoting the use and further development of pidgins and creoles in the public domain.

It is fitting that this volume contains more contributions on or in Hawai'i Creole English (HCE) — the variety which Charlie spoke natively and on which she worked extensively — than any other collection of pidgin-creole studies published to date. Our introductory section is rounded out by creative works by Eric Chock and Darrell Lum written in HCE. Part of Charlie's lifelong struggle to legitimize and enhance the status of HCE involved extending its use as a *medium* of communication, for instance in the novel section headings and notes ("Wea de ste?" "Sawri, aeh!" "Yu laik sabskraib o wat?") that were introduced in the *Carrier Pidgin* newsletter after she assumed its editorship in 1989, and she would have been pleased to see these contributions in HCE. She was very interested in the local literary movement in Hawai'i, and appreciated and promoted writers like Chock and Lum who used HCE in their writings. In their role as co-founders and co-editors of the literary journal, *Bamboo Ridge*, Chock and Lum, two of the best-known writers on the local literature scene in Hawai'i, in turn provided new opportunities for local writers to disseminate their work. In June 1997 they were both awarded the Hawai'i Award for Literature, a prize presented annually by the State of Hawai'i Foundation on Culture and the Arts and the Hawai'i Literary Arts Council in recognition of outstanding writers in Hawai'i.

## Pidgin-creole genesis and development

The first section of academic papers in this volume focuses on the genesis and development of pidgins and creoles, a topic of perennial interest in pidgin-creole studies, and one to which Charlie herself contributed, for instance in her (1985a) paper on linguistic inequality in Hawai'i.

*Bickerton*, drawing on recent recent research by Roberts (whose own paper follows) suggests that the early pidgin stages in Hawai'i involved considerably more language mixing, "driven solely by the desire to communicate," than was previously supposed. Based on this, and on evidence from Russenorsk, Chinook Jargon, and certain varieties in West Africa and the Caribbean, he proposes that pidginization might in general involve more of a "multilexical mess" and less of the systematic modification of a specific language than we normally assume.

*Roberts* draws on the considerable textual evidence of early HCE which she has amassed in recent years to explore the issue of whether similarities between HCE and the Atlantic creoles are due to diffusion from the latter to the former, reflecting in turn a shared West African substrate. After a careful examination of the development of each of the major Tense-Modality-Aspect (TMA) markers through the major historical phases of HCE — an examination which in the richness of its attestations for each historical phase is unmatched for other pidgins and creoles — Roberts concludes that such diffusion is unlikely to have taken place. The TMA system of HCE, with its unique habitual and completive auxiliaries (*stei* and *pau*, respectively, versus *de/(d)a* and *don* in Atlantic creoles) appears to be a local development.

*Drechsel* also considers the early language contact situation in Hawai'i, but casts a broader net, exploring sociohistorical and textual evidence that reduced or foreigner talk versions of the indigeneous languages of the Hawaiian Islands, the Marquesas, Tahiti, New Zealand and other Pacific territories were in use at least until the mid-19th century, both by Oceanic peoples and by Europeans and Americans. His focus on these native language contact varieties, which might even have constituted "a single Polynesian-based contact medium in use across much of the central Pacific" should help to redress the overemphasis on English and other European varieties in pidgin-creole studies.

With *Holm*'s paper, we turn our attention from Hawai'i and the Pacific to the Atlantic, although five non-Atlantic creoles are included to provide the crucial Atlantic/Non-Atlantic contrasts on which his major finding turns. The focus of Holm's paper, which draws on data from a larger study of comparative creole syntax involving seventeen other scholars, is the formal realization of the copula according to following grammatical environment, a recurrent feature in discussions of creole genesis. Holm and his collaborators show that despite some variation, the Atlantic Creole varieties, regardless of lexical origin (English versus French, for instance), are strikingly similar in their copula patterns, and the non-Atlantic varieties are quite different — most notably in not requiring a copula before an NP. This suggests that the primary influences on their development were their respective substrates, in the case of the Atlantic creoles, the Niger Congo languages whose copula patterns resemble theirs in several significant respects.

*McWhorter* is, however, quite sceptical about hypothetical substrate sources for Atlantic creole copulas, and in his paper he argues that Saramaccan *dε* (in Suriname, South America) represents an independent development rather than evolution from West African sources. Central to his argument is the fact that Saramaccan does not display the neat equative/locative split which many Caribbean English Creoles [CECs] and their West African substrate languages (like Ewe) do. The copula *dε*, although restricted to a locative or existential function in other CECs, has a much broader distribution in Saramaccan, and McWhorter argues on the basis of historical and comparative evidence that it represents independent grammaticalization from originally expressive uses of English adverbial *dε*. Moreover, this grammaticalization may have first occurred, not in Suriname, but in the 17th century English-based Gold Coast pidgin which he sees as the source of most CECs.

*Rickford's* focus is also on copula patterns in a CEC, in this case Jamaican Creole [JC], but his approach is quantitative, following paths laid down by Labov, Holm and Baugh in the 1970s and 1980s. In an attempt to go beyond the 1960 'Baba' Rowe data set which has provided the only quantitative perspective we have on copula absence in the JC continuum, and to fill the lacuna in quantitative studies of Caribbean copula absence, Rickford analyzes copula absence in two Jamaican speakers whom he recorded in the early 1990s. His results show that the effects of following grammatical environment are strikingly similar to those reported for African American Vernacular English [AAVE] speakers, even more so than in earlier comparisons by others. This typological resemblance reinforces the hypothesis that AAVE may itself have had creole influences if not origins.

*Mufwene*, in the context of a larger argument that Labov's accountability principle should be extended to diachronic and structural analyses of creoles, critiques a number of common assumptions about these varieties. The one on which he concentrates the most is DeCamp's assumption that the creole variety in Jamaica and other anglophone Caribbean territories was preceded by a pidgin stage and followed by a creole continuum produced by decreolization. For Mufwene, sociohistorical considerations argue against the development of pidgins during the initial homestead phases of New World creole communities, and insufficient sociohistorical evidence has been adduced in support of decreolization or debasilectalization. This is particularly so, he argues, in the case of the hypothesis that AAVE developed by decreolization from an earlier creole spoken throughout the American Southeast. In the spirit of accountability, Mufwene also argues against the assumption that creoles are structurally monolithic and totally different from their lexifiers.

The final three articles in this section focus on non-Anglophone varieties. *Parkvall* has in recent years argued that French Creoles derive from the diffusion of two ancestral French pidgins, one which formed originally in St. Kitts (and diffused to lesser Antillean teritories like Guadaloupe and Martinique), and one which developed in Senegal (diffusing primarily to Louisiana and Mauritius). In his paper for this volume, he considers the Senegal source, examining in detail the sociohistorical circumstances under which a French pidgin may have emerged there in the 17th and particularly the 18th century and under which it may have been transported to Louisiana and Mauritius. He also identifies several difficulties with Hull's alternative scenario that French Creoles derive from another West African source, based at Whydah.

*Lipski's* paper is a contribution to the reconstruction of the history of Afro-Caribbean Spanish. He examines, in particular, the importance of the transshipment of slaves and free laborers from one island to another, which increased the proportion of plantation workers who had already acquired other Caribbean creoles. The creole languages which aided in the formation of Afro-Caribbean Spanish varied according to time and place. Cuba, for instance, the largest sugar plantation colony, naturally received the widest variety of creole languages, including Haitian Creole, Jamaican Creole, Papiamento, West African Pidgin English, and Negerhollands.

*Schwegler* also considers Afro-Caribbean Spanish, but he focuses on internal linguistic evidence, in the form of pronominal *ele* (as used in Colombian Palenquero and among the Chota of Highland Ecuador) and *elle* (as used in Cuban/Puerto Rican Bozal Spanish). These forms, he argues, cannot be linked to a common Spanish source, nor to spontaneous, independent innovations in each region; instead, "they support the claim that in colonial times an Afro-Portuguese-based contact vernacular must have existed in many parts of Black Latin America." The sharing of "deep" grammatical features like these constitutes, he suggests, strong support for monogenesis, at least insofar as a common Afro-Portuguese source for New World Afro-Caribbean Spanish varieties is concerned.

## Attitudes and education in creole communities

The next section deals with attitudes to creole varieties, and with the related question of the place of such varieties in local schools, both of which were topics about which Charlie cared passionately and on which much of her research and writing focused. See, for instance, her 1989b paper, "A nonstandard approach to standard English," and her 1991b paper on sociolinguistic variation and language attitudes in Hawai'i.

The paper by *Eades* and *Siegel* relates some of the recent initiatives in education and the legal system which indicate a greater awareness and acceptance of Aboriginal English [AE] and creoles (including Kriol as spoken in the Northern Territory, and Torres Straits Creole) in Australia. Charlie would have been pleased to see these signs of a change in attitudes, both among speakers of these varieties, and among non-speakers, including teachers, lawyers, and others who work with AE and creole speakers. During her brief stay in Australia, Charlie took an active interest in these minority varieties and the rights of their speakers. At the Australian Linguistic Institute in 1994, she was co-organizer of a well attended workshop on pidgins, creoles and non-standard varieties in education. And at the time of her death she was involved in drafting a document about language policy in Hawai'i, inspired by developments in Australia. This followed the highly successful conference she helped organize in October 1994 on Language Rights in Hawai'i.

In his paper, *Grimes* looks at some of the linguistic and other components of local identity in Hawai'i as manifested in the HCE-speaking persona of Bu La'ia. In real life, Bu is a man named Kaui Hill, who owns a surfing shop in Kailua, on the windward coast of the island of O'ahu. Bu La'ia, however, is widely perceived as a person associated with rural ethnic Hawaiians who highlights in a humorous way issues of real concern to them. Grimes shows how the use of HCE identifies Bu as 'local' with a capital L, even though his is not the most basilectal variety.

The paper by *Romaine* documents some evidence of changing attitudes towards HCE and suggests ways in which linguists can actively contribute to such change. Attitudes towards HCE regularly become part of public controversy in Hawai'i, particularly when the annual achievement test results are announced. "Pidgin" is often blamed for the poor performance of Hawai'i's students on the verbal ability section of the Scholastic Aptitude Test (SAT). Romaine's data, spanning a period of four years, addresses attitudes to the use of HCE in the classroom. Although most respondents are reluctant to permit the use of written HCE, a slight majority think that spoken HCE should be allowed in at least some contexts at school.

Through her publications, workshops and related professional activities, Charlie influenced many people who never had the chance to meet her, such as Susan *Reynolds*, a classroom teacher at a rural school on the island of Hawai'i, who (in a personal communication to S. Romaine) acknowledged that Charlie's work had been an inspiration to her, "opening my mind and eyes to new possibilities in the field of education, and closer to home, in my own class-room.". Reynolds' paper reports some of her research on children's comprehension of HCE and standard English. Using a matched-guise instrument administered to all fifth grade public school classes on the island of Hawai'i, she found that students made twice as many errors on a listening comprehension test when their non-dominant language (whether HCE or standard English) was used.

*Pollard*'s paper shifts the focus from the Pacific to the Atlantic, providing an analysis of errors in English usage made by Creole English-speaking children on the Caribbean Examinations Council English examination at the Basic Level. She divides the errors into four categories — those associated with phonology/spelling, the lexicon, grammar, and idiom — and discusses possible sources of the errors in each category and instructional strategies for correcting them. Although she does not use the term, Pollard essentially uses a variety of the "Contrastive Analysis" advocated by Robert LePage for Caribbean English speakers back in 1968, and by others for speakers of African American Vernacular English in the 1970s and more recently. She emphasizes that the blanket teaching of English "Grammar" — popularly regarded as a panacea for the English language ills of Creole-speaking students — is likely to be much less effective than teaching that is informed by an understanding of students' vernacular language background and their error types.

## Creole discourse and literature

The final section involves studies of creole discourse and literature, areas of increasing attention within the field of pidgin-creole studies, and ones to which Charlie herself contributed, for instance in her (1982) paper on ethnic styles in classroom discourse and in her (1993b) annotated bibliography on narrative.

*Singler*'s paper, like the one by Andersen that follows it, could have fitted just as easily in a section on tense or temporal sequence marking as in one on discourse. Singler deals with the function of Vernacular Liberian English *feni/finish,* a completive marker similar in some respects to *don* in Guyanese Creole and African American Vernacular English. The relevance of discourse to the analysis of *feni* is particularly evident in the VLE basilect, where 82% of all its occurrences are in narratives, procedural descriptions, or hypotheticals, discourse types which are all structured along a time line. Noting that basilectal *feni* mostly serves to reinforce the chronological order of events already marked by the temporal order of narrative clauses, Singler suggests that this reflects a carryover from Kru languages. More generally, "discourse-based phenomena stand as especially salient sites for substratal influence upon creole languages." Singler also considers the perfect marking function of mesolectal *feni,* and its increasing pre-adjectival occurrence.

Critiquing the common practice of studying tense-aspect with constructed, isolated sentences, *Andersen* suggests that everyday discourse provides a richer picture of how tense-aspect markers serve speakers' purposes. The focus of his paper is Papiamentu present tense *ta,* which often occurs in past habitual and other non-present situations. Andersen argues that to understand the use (or non-use) of this and other tense-aspect markers, we need to understand the temporal frames which speakers and their listeners maintain in discourse. Examining seven contexts within which *ta* occurs — including dependent clauses, indirect discourse, the Historical Present, and hypothetical situations — Andersen shows how temporal frames set up by initial or main clauses and the perspectives from which speakers choose to view and narrate events (story time or speech time) allows for the use of present or no markers in past time and other situations.

In the four or five years before her death, Charlie was actively engaged in the study of discourse in HCE. One of her students, *Masuda,* examines in his paper the influence of substrate, superstrate and universals in the organization of HCE discourse. He identifies universal discourse processes as the source of topicalization structures in HCE, while a particular pattern of discourse organization he calls T[heme] S[cheme] R[heme] formation is due to transfer from Japanese substratum. The pattern of line predication organized around clauses, however, follows that of the superstrate, English.

*Winer* notes that Caribbean English literature, although considered a subtype of English literature, may contain Creole elements and references that limit its understanding and resonance by English readers. This leads her to question whether Creole writers and English readers can "be considered part of the same literary discourse community." Examining a poem by Derek Walcott, a short story by Olive Senior, and novels by Earl Lovelace and Robert Antoni, she explores ways in which Creole vocabulary, grammar, and rhythm serve to limit the English reader's ability to comprehend and resonate with literature in Caribbean English. The problem is compounded by the fact that English readers, beguiled by the many commonalities between Creole and English, may not be aware that they lack the sociocultural or linguistic knowledge which a full appreciation requires. More work is needed on creole discourse style, she suggests, to fully elucidate the problem.

**References: See "Biography and Bibliography," which follows.**

# Charlene Junko Sato (1951–1996)
## Biography and Bibliography

Suzanne Romaine
*Oxford University*

John R. Rickford
*Stanford University*

## Biography

Charlene Sato, known to her friends and colleagues as 'Charlie,' died peacefully on January 28, 1996, after a ten-month struggle with ovarian cancer. Charlie was born June 25, 1951, in Lahaina, Maui, and grew up in Wahiawa, on O'ahu. She was a graduate of Leilehua High School, the University of California-Berkeley (B.A. in Linguistics 1973), the University of Hawai'i at Mānoa (M.A. in English as a Second Language 1977, M.A. in Linguistics 1978), and UCLA (Ph.D. in Applied Linguistics, with a specialization in Second Language Acquisition, 1985). For fourteen years, she taught courses at the University of Hawai'i at Mānoa in pidgin and creole studies, second language acquisition, sociolinguistics, discourse analysis, linguistics for language professionals, and research methods in applied linguistics. She also served as Director of the Center for Second Language Classroom Research, and as Chair of the Ph.D. Program in Second Language Acquisition at the University of Hawai'i at Mānoa.

Many scholars in the field of pidgin and creole studies know Charlie from her publications and conference presentations on Hawai'i Creole English [HCE] and in her capacity as editor of the *Carrier Pidgin* newsletter from 1989–1993. Yet the study of pidgin and creole languages, especially HCE, was only one of her professional interests. Others know her for her work on second language acquisition, particularly interlanguage development, the topic of several major journal articles and her (1990) book. She was also interested in narrative, language policy, literacy and language acquisition in multilingual settings. Besides this volume, which celebrates her work in pidgin and creole studies, a festschrift edited by Thom Huebner and Kathryn Davis, *Sociopolitical Perspectives on Language Policy and Planning* — also published by John Benjamins — honors her work in some of these other areas.

Charlie was one of a handful of scholars who devoted their academic careers to the study of English in Hawai'i. Many of them are unfortunately dead: Elizabeth Carr, John Reinecke, and Stanley Tsuzaki. Like Reinecke, a school teacher and union organizer, whom she greatly admired, Charlie was a political activist. She co-authored with Aiko Reinecke a tribute to John Reinecke's life and work which appeared in the memorial volume dedicated to him (Sato 1987b). In it one can see many similarities in the issues and causes that shaped her life. A tireless fighter for social justice and the rights of working people, Charlie was a supporter of LACASA, the People's Fund, and other projects in Europe, Australia, and Japan, and an active member of the O'ahu General Membership Branch of the Industrial Workers of the World (the Wobblies).

Charlie's special contribution to the study of HCE lay in her emphasis on the role it played in local identity and culture in the face of opposing views which labeled — and continue to label it — 'broken English.' She testified before the Board of Education when it formulated its controversial 1987 policy to make standard English the only language allowed in the classroom, in effect banning the use of 'pidgin.' Charlie wrote (in Sato 1991a: 139) of the protests which followed this event: "Never before in Hawai'i's history had such a diversity of voices been raised, in a formal institutional setting, in defense of Hawai'i Creole English." Her own voice was among the loudest and clearest. The Board recanted and, after a long delay, adopted a statement which merely "encouraged" the modelling of standard English by teachers and staff members in the Department of Education. The issue is by no means dead, however.

During the same week that the policy was being debated, HCE went on trial in the form of a federal lawsuit filed by three National Weather Service employees in Honolulu against the U.S. National Weather Service, accusing them of discrimination on the basis of race and national origin. The men, who were of Japanese-American and part-Hawaiian-American background, claimed their applications had been rejected due to bias against their local accents. The NWS said they hired Caucasians with mainland accents because they "sounded better," despite the fact that these men were less experienced and had far less training than the plaintiffs. After analyzing the men's speech, Charlie gave testimony as an expert witness for the men's union to show that they in fact spoke standard Hawai'i English. (See Sato 1991b for discussion).

As far as her more academic contribution to the study of HCE is concerned, one of Charlie's key articles (Sato 1993a) addressed the topic of decreolization. Indeed, this was the subject of a $60, 000 National Science Foundation grant she

directed from 1987 to 1990 entitled, "A longitudinal study of individual decreolization." This was one of the very few longitudinal studies in our field, following
up fourteen years later on some of the informants in Bickerton & Odo's earlier
study of HCE. Charlie was also planning a book on the topic (to be called
*Language Variation and Change in Hawai'i*), which unfortunately was still in the
early stages of planning when she died. In the four or five years before her death
she was also actively engaged in the study of discourse in HCE. At the time of
her death Charlie was involved in drafting a document about language policy in
Hawai'i, inspired by developments in Australia. This followed on from the
highly successful conference she helped organize in October 1994 on Language
Rights in Hawai'i. She was also in the process of writing an invited state of the
art review of variation in second language acquisition that was to appear in the
*Annual Review of Applied Linguistics XV*.

Besides serving as Editor of the *Carrier Pidgin*, Charlie was Executive
Committee Member of the Society for Pidgin Creole Linguistics, Associate Chair
and Chair of the TESOL Research Interest Section, and a member of the
Linguistic Society of America's Committee on Ethnic Diversity in Linguistics.
She served as Visiting Professor or Lecturer at a number of universities besides
the University of Hawai'i, including the University of Pennsylvania, Concordia
University, Montreal, Temple University-Japan, Tokyo and Osaka, Universidad
Nacional Autonoma de México, the University of Western Sydney, LaTrobe
University, the University of Melbourne, and the University of Western Australia.

Between 1982 and 1994 Charlie gave more than fifty presentations on HCE,
language politics, language acquisition and related topics to academic institutions
and community organizations within Hawai'i, including the University of
Hawai'i at Mānoa, the University of Hawai'i at Hilo, the University of Hawai'i
at West O'ahu, the Honolulu Community College, Chaminade University,
Hawai'i Pacific University, Hawai'i's Department of Education, and the Hawai'i
Court Reporters. In addition, she gave more than fifty other academic presentations at TESOL conventions, and at other conferences, workshops, panels and
symposia in the US, Japan, and Europe. Her paper titles, like some of the
headings in the Carrier Pidgin while she was editor, were sometimes in HCE, for
instance "Hau fo rait in pijin: A Workshop for teachers and writers" (Hawai'i
Council of Teachers of English, Honolulu, November 1983). This was in keeping
with her lifelong belief in and advocacy on behalf of the integrity of pidgin and
creole languages.

Our field is richer for not only for Charlie's academic research and publications,
but also for her political engagement on behalf of speakers of pidgin and creole
languages. Some of us were fortunate to know her as both colleague and friend.

At the same time that she inspired us, Charlie also influenced and encouraged a generation of younger scholars in her role as teacher/mentor, particularly through her establishment of a course on pidgins and creoles at the University of Hawai'i at Mānoa.

During her illness, Charlie received hundreds of messages of support from around the world. Her memorial service on February 10, 1996 was attended by hundreds. In addition to this commemorative volume, and the one edited by Huebner and Davis (cited above), two funds have been set up with her approval and for purposes specified by her. The first will help support students doing work on any aspect — linguistic, social, educational, artistic, or political — of Hawai'i Creole English. The second will help support women members' participation in the Industrial Workers of the World [IWW]. Those wishing to do so may donate to either or both. For the former, checks should be made payable to "UH Foundation" (mentioning the Charlene Sato Memorial Fund), and sent to the University of Hawai'i Foundation, P.O. Box 11270, Honolulu, HI, 96828, USA. For the latter, checks should be made payable to "IWW" (mentioning the Charlie Sato Memorial Fund), and sent to Industrial Workers of the World, 103 West Michigan Avenue, Ypsilanti, Michigan, 48197–5438, USA.

We are grateful to Charlie's husband and academic collaborator Mike Long for the photograph of Charlie which appears at the beginning of this volume, and to Sarah Julianne Roberts for helping with proofreading and other editorial responsibilities.

*This is a revised version of an obituary for Charlene Sato which Suzanne Romaine first wrote and published in the *Carrier Pidgin* newsletter (vol. 24, no. 1, January-April 1996, pp. 1–2).

## Bibliography

1980. "Categories of transformations in second language acquisition." With Richard R. Day. *Perspectives in American English*, ed. by J. L. Dillard. The Hague: Mouton.

1982. "Ethnic styles in classroom discourse." *On TESOL '81*, ed. by M. Hines and W. Rutherford. Washington D.C.: TESOL.

1983. "Classroom foreigner talk discourse: Forms and functions of teachers' questions." With Michael H. Long. *Classroom Oriented Research in Second Language Acquisition*, ed. by H. Seliger and M. H. Long. Rowley, MA: Newbury House.

1984a. "Phonological processes in second language acquisition: Another look at interlanguage syllable structure." *Language Learning* 34(4): 43–57.

1984b. "Methodological issues in interlanguage studies: An interactionist perspective." [With Michael H. Long] *Interlanguage,* ed. by A. Davies, C. Criper, and A. P. R. Howatt. Edinburgh: Edinburgh University Press.

1985a. "Linguistic inequality in Hawai'i: the post-Creole dilemma." *Language of Inequality,* ed. by Nessa Wolfson and Joan Manes, 255–272. Berlin: Mouton.

1985b. "Task variation in interlanguage phonology." *Input in Second Language Acquisition,* ed. by S. Gass and C. Madden. Rowley, MA: Newbury House.

1986. "Conversation and interlanguage development: Rethinking the connection." *Talking to Learn: Conversation in Second Language Acquisition,* ed. by Richard Day. Rowley, MA: Newbury House.

1987a. "John E. Reinecke: His life and work." With Aiko Reinecke. *Pidgin and Creole Languages: Essays in Memory of John Reinecke,* ed. by Glenn G. Gilbert, 255–272. Honolulu: University of Hawai'i Press.

1987b. "Phonological processes in second language acquisition: Another look at interlanguage syllable structure." *Interlanguage Phonology,* ed. by G. Ioup and S. Weinberger. Rowley, MA: Newbury House. (Reprint of 1984a.)

1988. "Origins of complex syntax in interlanguage development." *Studies in Second Language Acquisition* 10: 371–395.

1989a. "Language attitudes and sociolinguistic variation in Hawai'i." *University of Hawai'i Working Papers in ESL* 8(1): 191–216.

1989b. "A nonstandard approach to standard English." *TESOL Quarterly* 23.2: 259–282.

1990. *The Syntax of Conversation in Interlanguage Development.* Tübingen: Gunter Narr.

1991a. "Language change in a creole continuum: Decreolization?" *University of Hawai'i Working Papers in ESL* 10(1):127–147.

1991b. "Sociolinguistic variation and language attitudes in Hawai'i." *English Around the World: Sociolinguistic Perspectives,* ed. by Jenny Cheshire, 647–663. Cambridge: Cambridge University Press.

1993a. "Language change in a creole continuum: Decreolization?" *Progression and Regression in Language: Sociocultural, Neuropsychological, and Linguistic Dimensions,* ed. by Kenneth Hyltenstam and Åke Viberg. Cambridge: Cambridge University Press.

1993b. *Research on narrative: A bibliography and selected annotations.* With S. Handorf and Karen A. Watson-Gegeo. Center for Second Language Research, Technical Report #10. Honolulu: Social Science Research Institute.

1993c. *Research on literacy: A selected bibliography*. With S. Handorf and Karen
    A. Watson-Gegeo. Center for Second Language Research, Technical Report
    #10. Honolulu: Social Science Research Institute.

# Writings in Hawai'ian English

## "Hawai'ian Air", "Checking the Kauai Sands after Hurricane Iniki", and "4 Eva"

Eric Chock
*Honolulu, Hawai'i*

### Hawai'ian Air

I couldn't ignore her, especially when she announced right in front of me, "I goin', I no more bags, no underwear, not'ing, I just going!"

She was a middle-aging ehu-haired wahine in tight white jeans "running away from home for da first time in seven years."

"You gotta do dat once in a while, just to keep 'em in line," the Hawai'ian lady she was talking to offered in response.

"Yeah, I jus' wen call my sista and tell her, 'Somebody can pick me up?' Where you from? You from Kaua'i?"

"I live Kapa'a."

"You know Peter dela Cruz, he use to be my brudda-in-law, but everybody hate him. He one cop."

"I don't know. I not *from* Kapa'a. I been there three years. I from Kaimuki."

"Oh, you know my sista Annie Solomon?"

The listener woman was in total, matter-of-fact sympathy. This was apparently her reality too. Men will drink with their friends, come home at all hours, and complain about what cold food you had cooked.

"My madda in Kekaha, she always telling me, 'Come back home live.' Maybe when I old. Honolulu more cheap. Kekaha, one can Spam cost two seveny-nine! Honolulu only dolla fifty-nine."

Life decided by Spam? I thought, till I saw when we landed, this big lunky
guy waiting by the lobby window. She ran to him with arms wide just like in the
movies.

"Hey Joey!" she shouted as they grabbed each other in a hug.

"Oh Sis, how you been?"

As I walked past, I could see the tears in their eyes.


## Checking the Kauai Sands After Hurricane Iniki

I see the VACANCY sign, hesitate,
and drive past the fluorescent orange
KEEP OUT — NO TRESPASSING
sprayed on the wooden road block.

The first man I see I ask
"Is the office open? I saw the VACANCY sign."
The Hawai'ian construction worker with the moustache smiles and points to the
hollow rooms:
"She took the building, but she forgot the sign. But you right. We get plenty
vacancy!"


## 4 Eva

He tot he knew what was fo'eva.
But den was pau, and we wuz at Point Panic
drinking dis whole bottle vermouth
he wen find in his madda's
underneath da sink cabinet.

Afta, wen we wuz watching da waves
smash da white bottle on top da black rocks
he wen look across da wata and tell me,
"Eh, fo'eva is how far I goin' trow
dis damn gold ring."

"Nah," I wen tell him.
"Fo'eva is how long you was trowing
up inside da bushes."

# YMCA: The Weightroom

## Darrell H.Y. Lum
*Honolulu, Hawai'i*

My fahdah used to tell me, "You can do it, you jes gotta put your mind to it."
When I told him I couldn't trim da grass by da wall cause I wasn't strong
enough fo squeeze da grass clippers, he said, "You gotta put your mind to it."
When I told him I couldn't take da garbage can out to da road cause was too
heavy, he said, "Jes put your mind to it." When I told him I couldn't catch da
ball cause he was chrowing too hard, he told me, "Can. Can. Put your mind to it."

I used to go wit him and my bruddah, Russo, to da YMCA. I nevah like go
cause most times was boring. My fahdah go play handball wit his friends and my
bruddah used to lift weights and I had to sit around watch dem cause dey said I
was too small fo do anyting.

Da handball court always stay noisy. Always get da tock, tock, tock sound
of da ball and even if get only two guys playing, sound loud cause da handball
court echo, j'like da cartoons when Elmah Fudd go to da Grand Canyon and tell,
"Helloooo … " And da ting answer back, "Hello, hello, hellooo … " You seen
da one, one time Bugs Bunny answer back instead, "Goodbye … " and he push
Elmah Fudd off da cliff.

Da weightroom stay noisy too from da sound of da weights and guys going,
"choo, choo, choo," blowing out their air jes before dey lift. Russo said dat da
more you blow out, da more air going back in and dat make you mo strong. I
donno about dat, but dey all blow out tree times before dey lift.

Had two kine guys in da weightroom: da weightlifters and da bodybuilders.
Weightlifters, dey no do too much. Mostly dey getting ready fo lift or dey
resting from lifting. And da bodybuilders, dey raddah look at demself in da
mirror, make big body and check out their muscles. Fo see if went work, eh, I tink.

I used to go down to da weightroom fo watch dem cause dat was bettah den
watching my fahdah play handball wit da old futs who always say stupid stuff
like, "Ho, your boy, big boy, eh? Like to eat, yeah? Mo bettah he come play

handball wit us." My fahdah is Kelvin Fat Chun Wat, K. F. C. Wat. Dey call him Kentucky Fried Chicken or sometimes, Ah Fat. And dey tell, "Ah Fat, your boy take aftah his fahdah, he Ah Little Fat." And everybody laugh. Or somebody go say, "Eh, here come Ah Fat and Chicken Fat!"

Da younger old futs call my fahdah Kau Goong, dat means older uncle, I tink. Or sometimes Cowboy because of his bow legs or maybe dey calling him Kauboy, like Kau Goongboy. Nah, I donno. Dey was all old Chinese guys wit Chinese names: Ah Tong, Ah Chu (Russo used to say, "Gesundheit"), Ah Yun, Ah Kong, Ah Fut (you *know* what Russo say). Russo tell me, "I ain't nevah going play handball like dose old futs."

"Even wen you one old fut?" I went ask him.

"I ain't nevah going be one old fut," he said.

"Yeah, you jes going be one stink fut," I went tell him.

Russo tink he hot stuff cause he stay in high school and he crazy about dis bodybuilding stuff. Daddy had to buy him one blender and da kine protein powder and Russo put in da powder, milk, ice cream and one raw egg, blend um up and drink um down. Sick.

Da weightlifters was da guys who only like lift da biggest ones, five hundred pounds la dat and dey wear those suits dat look like one basketball shirt connected to Speedos. Make their stomach look mo skinny and their dick mo big. Look like da big Russian guys in da Olympics wit fat stomach, fat arms, and skinny legs. To me, kinda cheat if you had one big stomach. You could rest da weight on top your stomach little while before you lift um all da way up. Weightlifters, all dey do is stand around mostly. Maybe das why dey come fat. Once in a while dey lift da bar wit da supah big chrome weights, one hundred twenty pounds each one and dey put maybe one or two on each side. Couple times I went watch dem. Dey get one big leather belt fo hold their stomach in and dey get couple other big guys on each side "spotting," my bruddah told me. Jes in case da guy no can lift um up, da spotters help um, make sure he no drop um on himself. My bruddah said one guy went die when he couldn't lift um and da ting went fall down and hit his head.

"Not even," I went tell him but I was kinda scared fo go by da bars aftah dat. Maybe das why dey wanted to get one big stomach cause might save dem yeah? J'like one car bumper.

Nevah have no Russians in da weightroom but had one guy wit one big stomach and da weightlifting suit and one big leather belt. He always fussing around wit da belt. I donno why he no leave um on, but I figgah he needed um fo hold his stomach in. Anyways he look like one of da Russians even though he was Portogee. Everybody called him Man-o. Like man-o-war, I thought. Or man-o, like instruction man-o. But Russo said his name was Man-o, like Man-you-well. Anyway, I thought he was one Russian. He look mean cause no can see his upper lip, he get one moosetash.

All da weightlifter guys chrow da ack dem, j'like on TV, Fiftieth State Wrestling, when Handsome Johnny Barend and Cowboy Bob going at it wit Ed Francis interviewing, "Mistah Francis, I'm sick of *your* stupid questions and *his* stupid cowboy songs and I'm gonna snap *his* stupid guitar over *your* little pencil neck." He talk in one rough, sore troat voice. I know supposed to be fake cause das what my fahdah said, but still little bit scary when dey talk la dat. And Russo sometimes he talk la dat night time when I stay trying fo sleep and he keep talking like Johnny Barend or Curtis "Da Bull" Iaukea, "When da Maa-noa mist come down from da mountain, it is a blessing on da land ... das when all da people gotta come togedda, pull togedda. Imua! Show um your stuff, Fooge." And Russo, he even do Fuji Fujiwara's karate punches, "Eeyah, yah!" He do da whole show almost, all da voices but he always come back to Johnny Barend, "Mistah Frances ... Mistah Frances." Softer and softer. And he even crack his knuckles and laugh until I gotta go sleep Mommy and Daddy's room. Den I hear him laughing at me. Shet, he always do dat.

Try watch da lifters wen dey start to get ready: dey walk back and fort in back of da bar and keep looking at um, giving um stink eye. J'like dey getting demself mad at da barbell cause dey stay breathing hard but dey nevah lift nutting yet. And dey put da white stuff on their hands and dey measure real careful where dey going hold da bar and dey start going "whoo, whoo, whoo." And den jes when you tink dey going lift um, dey figgah dey not ready and dey walk back and fort some more. When dey finally lift um, da weight stay so heavy their face stay straining and dey stay wobbling around wit da weight above their head. Ho da scary! But Russo said you gotta stand still fo at least one second before you can let um go. And den, dey jes drop um on da floor right in front da sign dat says, "DO NOT DROP WEIGHTS." But who going tell dem, no do dat?

When dey lifting, dey make anykine noises, "Yaaah!" and breathe chru their teet, "Sheesh, sheesh, sheesh." And da spotters stay yelling, "C'mon, c'mon! Go, go, go, go. Let's go. Push um out. Push. Hold it. Hold it!" And den everyting come quiet fo one second. And den "Craang!" dey drop um and da ting bounce couple times and da spotters jump back and you can feel da floor shake and den everybody breathe out da same time and start talking all at da same time about how was one good lift and da coach Tommy Kono showing da guy in slow motion how he went do da lift, what was good and what was junk. He telling da guy how da clean was good but da jerk had to be mo smooth. Das da name of da lift, clean and jerk. Funny, yeah? And Tommy Kono tell, "Shake um out," and da guy walk around like, "Was nutting dat," swing his arms and breathe hard. And while he wipe his sweat and start walking back and fort again, da spotters put on two more small weights and tighten da nuts on da end and wait fo him to get ready again.

Bodybuilders no do dat. Dey like their muscles look jes right. Every muscle gotta be perfeck, like Mr. Chu. He was one old guy but he was built, man. Mostly he concentrate on his stomach. He always lift little bit and den he do situps. He like to do situps. Me, I no can even do twenty in da P.E. test in school but Chu can do hundred one time. J'like one machine. Den he lift little bit more and he do some more situps. Da best part was when he brought out his wood rolling pin. Fo real! He do some situps and den he roll his stomach all ovah: da top, da sides. He stay lying down on da situp board and he jes roll his stomach like he making pie crust. I guess he tink he can make his stomach flat dat way. Roll da fat away. Chu always gotta explain to everybody dat he breaking down da fat cells but once when I was watching him, even Tommy Kono went kinda shake his head and turn around and wink at me.

And had dis uddah weird guy, Russo call him da Man/Lady cause hard to tell. I know had to be one man cause dis was da Y M C A and he smoke one pipe, but he look kinda like one lady. He was kinda fat, soft marshmellow kine fat and when you look at him, look like he get chichis not muscles kine like Tommy Kono but fat lady, flapping ovah kine and his hair was kinda long and fluffy. He no put pomade fo make um lie flat and he no mo chops either but he twist his hair in one curl in front of his ears. J'like one girl. And he put his pipe in his belt when da ting was unloaded. Gotta be one man cause whoever heard of one lady smoking one pipe? Mostly he jest sit and watch everybody. Russo said fo catch his trills but I donno what he mean by dat. Everybody jes no talk to him and walk far away from him and say mean tings. Remind me of Alfred in school so I feel little bit sorry fo him.

Man-o tell, "Dey shouldn't let persons who no lift inside hea."

Das da only time da Man/Lady went take his pipe out of his mout and tell, "Free country."

Tommy Kono went say, "Genelmen, there are young men here." Da Man/Lady went wipe da sweat from his face and walk outside take a smoke. Little while mo, we could smell da smoke coming in da weightroom, tick and sweet. Like da Man/Lady was surrounding us and we couldn't get away.

Tommy Kono stay in charge of da weight room. He coach everybody who come in da weightroom, even Russo. He was in da Olympics, you know. He get gold medals fo weightlifting against da real big Russian guys. Russo told me dat da Russian guys get bigger muscles and dey get big stomach but Tommy Kono get one stronger mind ... dat your *mind* lift da weight. I tink you still gotta have muscles though. Tommy Kono was short not even as tall as Man-o but he was big anyways. His chest look like he always stay holding his breath. Opposite of da fatso weightlifter guys. He look more like one bodybuilder den one weight-lifter. Da first time I went inside da weight room he went come by me and take off his shirt and tell me hold um fo him. Den he went stand right in front of me and make his chichis vibrate, I mean he could make his pecs, das what Russo call um really jump, man.

Everybody was laughing at me cause I was jes watching his muscles jump. I had my mout open. If he was one lady, he would make one good strip teaser. Tommy Kono went ask me if I like lift and I nevah say nutting but he went get one bar fo me. Jes one bar ... no mo weights and he went ask me, "You tink you can lift dis?" I thought, of course, no mo nutting on top, but when he went put um in my hands, was heavy ... wasn't real heavy but wasn't jes one piece of pipe. I needed two hands fo carry dat bar. Den he went show me how fo do curls. He teach me how fo grip da bar and fo keep da back straight and he told me, "Try do six repetitions," and he went stand back and watch me da same way he went watch Man-o when he was lifting 400 pounds. He was telling me, "Form, keep da form. Breathe in wit your nose ... snnnn ... breathe out wit your mout ... whooo. In ... out. Yeah, atta boy!" And I was watching myself in da mirror watching Tommy Kono behind me and den I went feel his hand on my back, showing me how fo keep um straight ... den he was right next to me in da mirror wit one bar too, no mo weights on top, and I was watching his muscles come big and hard on his arms every time he did one repetition, look like one baseball under his skin.

"You Cowboy's numbah two boy, yeah?" he went ask me.

"Huh?" I was still watching his muscle and getting tired of lifting da bar. I forgot how many I did awready.

"You Cowboy Junior's bruddah, eh?"

I went look around fo Russo. He was Cowboy Junior? I guess so, if my fahdah was Cowboy. I was looking in da mirror fo check if I had muscles yet. Wasn't like Tommy Kono's, of course, but I tink my arms was bigger.

"Huh? No, I mean yes. Almost pau? I can put da bar down now?"

"Two more. How's about two more? If you tink you tired, you stop and breathe out hard like this, 'whoo, whoo, whoo!' Give your muscles oxygen. Give your brain oxygen. Den you can go fo two more. Watch your form, no arch your back. Keep um straight."

Russo was wrong. My mind wanted to lift but my arms couldn't. I donno why my brain need oxygen. I went puff out my cheeks and blow out only ting came out, "Choo, choo, choo!" and Chu went sit up on da situp board, rolling pin still on his stomach and say in one low, spooky voice, "You calling me, Ah Fat Boy? Or you Cowboy Boy." Somebody went tell, "Or maybe Cowboy Junior Junior."

"Maybe Cowgirl," Chu went growl looking straight at da Man/Lady. Everybody in da room went laugh, "Haw, haw, haw," and I went let go da bar and da ting went clang! on da floor and I told Tommy Kono, "I no can do dis!" Da muscle in his arm went away and mines jes felt sore. Stupid! I heard Man-o growling, "No drop da weights. Eh, Choochoo Boy, you sound like one choo-choo train ... I tink I can, I tink I can." Everybody was laughing again. I went run out of dat place.

I went sit by da pool little while but I was still yet mad at Chu fo calling me Cowgirl. Aftah dat, I nevah went back to da weightroom but dry sit outside by da pool, so one time when I heard loud clapping and da loud twofingerinda-mouth whistling in da gym, I went. Was one weightlifting and bodybuilding contest. You had to have one ticket but had plenny guys standing around da door so I jes went squeeze by dem and kinda jump up and down fo see and everybody went move ovah cause I was short or maybe cause dey nevah like me jump on dem. I found one good spot right in front da stage in between da plants. Da guy collecting tickets went look at me but he nevah say nutting cause I was one kid I guess.

Tommy Kono was on stage waving at everybody. He was going be da guest lifter. When I seen Tommy Kono lift, was j'like watching him in slow motion: he went measure real careful where to put his hands, he went practice lift, jes pull at da bar until da muscles in his shoulders pop out. He nevah walk around all mad or anyting, he jes push up his glasses and look at da ceiling above our head and den, like Russo say, he went lift wit his mind.

He set his feet den his hands and he make sure every finger stay in da right place. Den he move so fast, no can tell he starting to lift and da weight no like move den it start to move slow but den he so fast he bend his knees and move under da weight as da ting stay going up and his face stay strain and his back knee stay shaking and slowly, slowly he standing up; two feet straight, da bar pressing against his chest, da bar bending. He stop rest little while.

"Huuh. Shee." And everybody stay holding their breath. And he blow out tree times, "Choo, choo, choo," j'like me. And you can see his face all straining but his eyes behind his glasses stay clear and looking straight to da back of da room, like he get x-ray vision and he can see right chru da wall and on and on chru everyting. And da weight start to move up. Everyting is moving so fast but da weight is moving slow, like it don't wanna move but Tommy Kono's mind is mo strong den da weight.

And from where I standing he look like one perfeck "X" holding da bar still and straight above his head and when da judge beep da buzzer, he look at me fo one second and I no can look at him, but I can feel him looking at me and I turn away and wait fo da weight to drop. Craaang! And everybody let out their breath, haaaa.... *Now* I know what Russo mean.

Everybody went clap real loud cause he famous, you know. Anyway he went give one speech and he said he wanted to finish da show wit a bang and he went get one hot water bottle, you know, da red rubbah kine and started fo blow um up like one balloon. Fo real! Could tell was hard fo blow cause his face was coming red and he jes smash da top against his mouth and da ting was coming bigger and bigger and everybody was holding their breath and couldn't see his face anymore was so big and den, one time, da ting went "paow!" and could smell rubbah and hot air and one small piece went fall down on da stage right in front of me. I went reach up fo grab um and Tommy Kono was bowing and went look right at me and I went pull my hand back fast but he went reach ovah and gimme da top piece he was still yet holding.

He went wink at me and gimme one head jerk, lift eyebrows kine "hi" and jiggle his pecs couple times.

I got outa dere quick and went da TV room before he or any of da uddah weightroom guys call me Cowboy Numbah Two or Cowgirl or Choochoo Train.

At da Y get plenny guys living ovah dere in da upstairs rooms. Das their house. J'like one hotel but not as nice. You always see dem in da cafeteria or in da TV room. Dey all was tough looking wit tattoos la dat and dey always get one cigrette hanging on their lip.

Everytime I go, da Man/Lady stay in da TV room, hogging um. He always sit right in front da TV and every once in a while, he take out his pipe and he pack um and smoke um and da whole room smell like his sweet, heavy smoke. Everytime when I go da TV room, he stay dere watching, so you no can change da channel. Sometimes I watch him instead. He mo interesting den da TV cause he no watch good stuff, anyways. He one man or one lady? He wasn't mean-looking or anyting, he had soft, white skin and red hair and his face had soft fuzzy hair all ovah. Not tick sticking out whiskers like when Daddy need to shave. I no tink da Man/Lady evah went shave. And j'like he always stay hot. He always sweating and fanning himself wit da *TV Guide* and everytime he wipe all ovah his face and his arms wit one old hankachief. Jes sitting dere he sweat. He no even exercise but he sweat like he jes went lift one thousand pounds. And once in a while he talk to da uddah guys in one high, kinda girly voice. He remind me of Alfred in school, da way he move slow, da way he wipe his face, da way he talk high and squeaky. What if Alfred come la dat? I tink das all he do, watch TV and smoke cause he always stay dere and hog da TV. He no say nutting to me except jes look at me chru his pipe smoke.

Dis time, nobody was dere except him sleeping so I went change da station to Chubby Roland Play-In-Your-Own-Backyard Show and even aftah I went change da station, I went watch him fo make sure he was still yet sleeping cause I nevah like him bus me: breathe in chru da nose, short, hold it, breathe out chru da mout wit one puff, "puh!" Even when I was watching him, could see da sweat come out on his uppah lip. Den one eye went pop open and he tell, "I was watching," in his high soft voice. Spooky. I guess he was talking to me cause nevah have nobody else in da room but was j'like I couldn't move. He went turn and look at me, "You Cowboy's numbah two boy?"

Chubby Roland was getting to da good part. I nevah answer. Chu came inside da TV room, his hair still yet wet from da shower. Chu almost bolohead and only get little bit hair hanging on at da back of his head so he try comb um all to da front of his head into one point. Remind me of Dracula or Da Count. He went wink at me and tell, "Choo, choo, choo" and laugh backwards, you know like he sucking air in, "Hurh, hurh, hurh." Chu nevah look so big wit his clothes on. He jes look old and spooky wit his hair like dat and his rolling pin sticking out of his Pan Am bag. Russo said dat he was one funeral parlor guy. When Russo try make me scared he tell, "Chu going get you ... he went touch ma-ke man!" I tink I saw him one time at da funeral parlor next door to da Chinese school. And when my grandfahdah, Ah Goong, went die long time ago, I donno if was him but aftah da funeral was all pau, one guy with white gloves went come and screw da coffin cover down. He went use da rachet kine screwdriver and even da music stop and everybody stay watching him screw da cover down, praack, praack, praack. He nevah even check da body fo see if Ah Goong was really dead. Had so many screws all I could tink about dat night was da sound of da rachet, praack, praack, praack and what if Ah Goong wasn't really dead and he stay inside da coffin listening to praack, praack, praack.

And den Man-o came in and he stay cracking all da bones in his body: he crack his back, his neck, two joints in each finger, his toes. He hunch his neck and his shoulders down and circle his arms in front and he crouch low like he going grab me and den he make all his muscles pop out. Shet, he look like Billy Goat Gruff. I went jump back little bit.

"Come hea, Chuckwagon," he went tell me but he really stay talking to Chu trying fo make him laugh, "Like me crack your nose? Maybe your eeyah need cracking. Maybe Jimmy gotta crack his corn … haw, huh, huh…. Huh, Chu? Maybe gotta crack your nuts," and he look straight at da Man/Lady. And da Man/Lady no care about me anymore, now he stay wiping his face wit his hankachief, sweating and wiping, sweating and wiping looking back and fort between dem two, Chu and Man-o.

I no care, I no say nutting. Chubby Roland making da three finalists line up and he hold up da picture frame and he telling, "Funny Face Number One," and da audience clap and tell, "Yea" fo da one dey like.

"Cowboy Number Two," Chubby Roland tell holding up da frame in front one kid wit one cowboy suit.

Chu and Man-o tell, "Yea." Da Man/Lady smoking big clouds of pipe smoke now. I tink he pissed cause Chu and Man-o both stay watching da Funny Face contest. Chu stay lying on da couch rolling his stomach, laughing at da TV and Man-o stay making up his own faces at da TV. And Chubby Roland he leading da kids like one choochoo train pulling his arm down like he tooting da whistle, "whoowhoooo," and I know Chu waiting to screw my coffin cover down and Man-o stay cracking his joints laughing at me and da Man/Lady stay piss off dat I went change da channel. And I donno why I no can jes get up and walk outa dere.

Den Tommy Kono went stick his head in da smoky TV room and tell me, "Eh, Cowboy Numbah … "

All da kids on Chubby Roland was going "Choo, choo, choo…." I went chrow da piece of rubbah hot water bottle at da TV. Can hardly see um get so much smoke.

"Sorry. What's your name, son?" Tommy Kono went ask me.

"Daniel." I was scared. I nevah mean to run out of da weightroom. Dey was laughing at me. And I donno why I stay here waiting wit dem: da Man/Lady, Chu, and Man-o watching da funny faces on da Play-In-Your-Own-Backyard Show. I no like stay wit dese guys. J'like I no can escape. I like you show me how fo lift. How fo make my muscles come out.

"You like my lift?" Tommy Kono went ask me.

"Yeah," I said.

"When you going come back and lift weights wit me?" He went look at Chu and Man-o still fooling around, "Choo, choo, choo … " and shake his head. "Come, I buy you one ice cream."

"Yeah, okay," I said again. I donno if he heard but I wasn't hearing da Chubby Roland choochoo train anymore. And chru da smoke, I could see his eyes, clear. I was going lift weights wit Tommy Kono. I was going put my mind to it.

# PART B

## Pidgin-Creole Genesis and Development

# Pidgins and Language Mixture

Derek Bickerton

*University of Hawai'i at Mānoa*

## 1. Introduction

In the study of pidgins, there seems to be a consensus so widely embraced that it is presupposed or assumed implicitly far oftener than it is explicitly stated. According to this consensus, pidginization is a process that occurs to particular, individual languages, and it makes perfect sense to talk of 'pidgin English', 'pidgin French' and so forth as if these were homogeneous and clearly demarcated entities. Such an attitude is implicit in the title of Hymes (1971) — 'The pidginization and creolization of languages' — or in the section heading of an article by Andersen (1980) — 'Pidginization as nativization of a second language'. That the consensus holds to this day can be seen from the comment by Bakker (1995: 27) that "A pidgin may be spoken *alongside the language from which it is lexically derived*" (emphasis added), or by Manessy (1995: 22) that "Nous entendons par pidginisation... l'ensemble des modifications que subit une langage du fait qu'elle est employée par des interlocutaires qui l'utilisent, les uns et les autres, comme langage seconde..." (emphasis added). Even the monogenetic theory of pidgin origins (Thompson 1961, Whinnom 1965) assumed that the original pidginized form of a single language, Portuguese, had given rise, via relexification, to a whole range of pidgins world-wide.

Opinions differ, of course, as to exactly what speakers do to a language in order to pidginize it. According to Aitchison (1981: 194–5) two of these processes involve "the best attempts of a people to learn a language quite unlike their own" and "unconscious attempts by native speakers of the base language to simplify it in ways that make it easier for non-native speakers to learn". Both processes were invoked in Bloomfield's (1933: 472) famous definition:

Speakers of a lower language may make so little progress in learning the
dominant speech that the masters in communicating with them resort to 'baby
talk'. This 'baby-talk' is the masters' imitation of the subjects' incorrect
speech... The subjects in turn, deprived of the correct model, can do no better
now than to acquire the simplified 'baby-talk' version of the upper language.

More recently Lefebvre and Lumsden (1989: 257) have proposed relexification as a
process applied directly to the pidgin's target ('langue du superstrat'), stating that

par relexification, nous entendons l'utilisation par des locuteurs de l'organisa-
tion du lexique de leur langue maternelle (langue du substrat) comme base
pour le reinterpretation des chaines phonetiques produites par les locuteurs
d'une autre langue (langue du superstrat).

It is clear that all of these hypothesized processes — imperfect learning,
simplification, relexification — assume a single target language and speakers
who consciously or unconsciously apply specifically linguistic processes to the
simple and straightforward task of creating a contact language.

Given the unanimity of these opinions, one is surprised at the slenderness of
their empirical support. As Aitchison (1981: 194) points out, "the formation of
most pidgins went unrecorded, and the exact process by which pidginization
occurred has been lost in the snowdrifts of time". Those processes discussed in
the previous paragraph have been arrived at, not through observation of actual
cases of pidginization, nor even through the analysis of historical texts, but rather
by extrapolation from such phenomena as 'foreigner talk' (Ferguson 1971) or
mixed languages (Muysken 1981) or by the examination of contemporary
developments presumed (rightly or wrongly) to share significant features with
pidgins, such as Gastarbeiterdeutsch (Clyne 1968; but see Bakker 1995).

## 2. The Hawaiian evidence

Over the past few years, however, research in Hawai'i (Roberts 1995a, 1995b,
1998) has unearthed a wholly unexpected, and quite unprecedented, mass of
documentation on language contact phenomena dating from Captain Cook's visit
of 1778 to the early years of the present century. This gold mine of empirical
data, consisting of well over two thousand citations ranging from single utterances to lengthy dialogues and narratives, should serve to revolutionize our understanding of pidgins, creoles and language contact phenomena in general (see also
Drechsel, this vol., for evidence of this type from Polynesia). In the present paper,
however, I shall concentrate on a single strand in the complex developments that

took place in Hawai'i in the century and a half following Cook's visit — a strand that involves the mixing of lexical items from diverse sources.

First of all, Hawai'i clearly differs from most pidgin sites in that pidgin was lexified from the 'substratum' as well as the 'superstratum'. I put these words in scare quotes simply because the Hawaiian situation does not fit neatly into the conventional straightjacket. How can we talk about a 'substratum' language — the word implies its speakers were socially and politically subordinate — when Hawai'i was a sovereign nation, and Caucasians, whether beachcombers, missionaries or traders, came only on the sufferance of that nation? A fall-back from the conventional position might want to say that, during the century after Captain Cook, two distinct pidgins co-existed: a pidgin with an English super-strate and a Hawaiian substrate, and another with a Hawaiian superstrate and an English substrate. Indeed, this position might seem to be supported by the fact that a large majority of citations from this period are lexified exclusively (or almost so) from one language or the other. We even find pairs of almost identical sentences, one English, one Hawaiian—in one case actually referring to the same person, 'Tiana', a Hawaiian leader of the 1790s:

(1)    *Take care. By and by you dead. Tiana too many men.*

(2)    *Inu, nuinui pu, make kanaka.*
       Bad plenty gun kill    person
       '[Tiana is a] bad [man who has] a lot of guns [to] kill people [with]'.[1]

However, there are certain facts that this account does not explain. First is the presence, in Pidgin Hawaiian[2] utterances during the first thirty or so years of contact, of a number of non-Hawaiian words, from Chinese Pidgin English (*kau-kau* 'food, to eat', 1791) and Portuguese (*pikinini* 'small', 1791) as well as from English (*pihi* 'fish', 1809–10) (all dates of first citation are from Roberts 1995a). While these words may all have been introduced through the medium of (some kind of contact) English, the fact that their first citations come from Pidgin Hawaiian rather than Pidgin English is indicative of the fact that the 'two pidgins' cannot in fact have been entirely separate.

Second is the frequency with which sailors and other visitors report in general terms the use of a mixed variety of pidgin. Dana (1840: 172) speaks of 'a mixed language...which could be understood by all' being spoken by Hawai-ians and Americans on the coast of California. In 1841, a writer in the *Mission-ary Herald* complained of natives 'employing a corrupted version of the Hawai-ian language and cursing and swearing in broken English'. A passenger on a small schooner heard its Hawaiian captain giving his orders 'in half English, half native' (Gilman 1845: 1). A slightly later visitor to Hawai'i habitually overheard 'detached sentences composed of Hawaiian and English nearly as unintelligible' (Bates 1854: 157). Women in Lahaina, possibly Hawaiian prostitutes, would start conversations 'in the most incomprehensible jargon of Kanaka and bad English' (Warren 1859: 245).

Some of the earliest recorded court cases contain similar evidence. A man called George Bush is reported as 'calling out in native and English' (1st Circuit Criminal #107, July 1st 1850). A native 'spoke broken English and Hawaiian so that Prisoner could understand him' (1st Circuit Criminal #1, March 21st 1854). A Chinese 'spoke partly native, partly English, and sometimes Chinese' (1st Circuit Criminal #26, February 12th 1856) In a gathering which appeared to be exclusively Chinese, 'most of them spoke some Chinese' but 'there was some native and some English. Buck spoke more English than native' (1st Circuit Criminal #87, April 8th 1856). A conversation with another Chinese suspect 'was carried on in broken English and native' (1st Circuit Criminal #12, October 6th 1856).

It is now possible to explain the apparent contradiction between the majority of verbatim citations (lexified exclusively from English or from Hawaiian) and the large number of references to the use of some kind of 'mixed' language. First, the natural tendency of anyone speaking to a Caucasian would be to use as many English words as the speaker knew; similarly, one speaking to a Hawaiian would maximize his or her use of Hawaiian words. Second, a native English speaker, in writing down pidgin utterances, would be likeliest to remember those that contained English words, and to forget, or omit non-English words from, those that had a mixed vocabulary; again, the memories of native Hawaiians would tend to work in a similar manner. These two factors between them would ensure that most verbatim citations would be monolexical (that is, have their vocabulary drawn from a single language). However, when Chinese speakers of different dialects were speaking with one another, there would be neither a speaker nor a hearer bias in favor of either language; the Chinese would simply use any words, English or Hawaiian, that they happened to know.

Thus, instead of two distinct pidgins running in parallel, we will be nearer the mark if we envisage a single pidgin continuum, with relatively pure Pidgin Hawaiian at one end, relatively pure Pidgin English at the other, and a mixed variety, used at least as frequently as the others, linking these two poles.

This situation, which characterized the first century of Hawaiian-non-Hawaiian contact, became further complicated when massive immigration into Hawai'i, from the late 1870s on, added several more ingredients to the ethnic mix. An early consequence was a rapid increase in the number of verbatim citations that mixed English and Hawaiian lexicon, to a large extent overcoming the observer biases in favor of monolexical utterances: the middle of the continuum had clearly increased in salience. Almost as often as the unmixed citation in (1)–(2) above, we find citations like (3):[3]

(3)    *Mi ko kaona polo Kukuihaele, kaukau bia, mi nuinui sahio*
    I    go town  big  K.         drink  beer I  plenty drunk
    'I went to the big town Kukuihaele to drink beer and got very drunk' (Hawaiian, 1887).

More striking still, we find utterances which in addition to Hawaiian and English words, contain words from Chinese, Japanese or Hawaiian; sometimes, as in examples (4)–(7), these words are drawn from the speaker's own language, but sometimes, as in (6) they may be drawn from the hearer's language also (Hawaiian words are in bold, those from other languages in capitals)[4]:

(4)    ***Pehea*** *you KAITAI, you **hanahana** all same lili more me*
    why       bastard      work            little    I
    ***hanamake*** *you*!                (Chinese plantation worker, 1898)
    make-dead
    'Why, you bastard, if you do that again I'll kill you.'

(5)    ***Luna*** *SAN me danburo     faia DE **mauka**   GA **pilikia**; ai*
    boss  HON I   down-below fire OBJ mountain TOP trouble
    *raiki go home **moemoe**.* (Japanese plantation worker, 1900)
    like         sleep
    'Overseer, I have burning pains in my stomach and my head aches — I'd like to go home and sleep.'

(6)    *INU SHINDA, **pake**   mejishin KOROSHITA*    (Hawaiian, 1903)
    dog die       Chinese medicine kill-do
    'My dog died, Chinese medicine killed him.'

(7)    ***Apopo***     *I go tomorrow Wailuku MANAN*'    (Portuguese, 1900)
    Tomorrow                  tomorrow
    'Tomorrow I go tomorrow Wailuku tomorrow'

While examples like these are less frequent in the total corpus than mixed English-Hawaiian utterances, they form a very high proportion of those collected from Japanese-language sources, which leads one to suspect considerable under-reporting from English and Hawaiian sources.[5]

    The abruptness and frequency of the alternations between different lexicons in (3)–(7) should assure the reader that we do not have to do with any kind of code-switching phenomenon here. Code-switching implies some degree of familiarity with at least two codes, but in these examples the speakers are

familiar with at most one, their own native language, and the alternations are not
aimed at achieving social or stylistic effects, but result from incompetence in its
most literal (and linguistic) sense.

Again, the court records provide corroborative testimony. They contain a
great deal of paralinguistic information about the (in)competence and habitual
behavior of particular individuals, such as the following:

(8)     Live in Honomu there 8 years. Keep store there…Speak enough
        Hawaiian to buy and sell…I speak a little English. I understand
        some of what is being said here but cannot carry a conversation in
        English…I can't conduct a conversation in English or Hawaiian fairly
        well (1st Circuit Criminal, #1355, May 20th 1889 — Chinese witness).

(9)     Have been on police in Kaohala several years…I speak 3 or 4
        languages, not Chinese. Can talk English, native and Portugee (3rd
        Circuit Criminal #24, May 15th 1889 — Hawaiian/Caucasian witness).

It is clear from other contemporary testimony that sentences such as (3)–(7) are
not the makeshift aberrations of some minority of marginal speakers, but
represent a powerful — perhaps the most powerful — tendency in the pidgin
continuum during at least the decades 1880–1910. A shrewd observer and
longtime resident of Hawai'i wrote:

> One cannot help thinking as he hears the street-talk of the rising generation
> that "they have been at a great feast of language, and stolen the scraps." The
> native boy is a rarity who has not several phrases in Chinese and Portuguese,
> and when it comes to single words the stock in trade of most native boys is
> not at all small. It is natural and inevitable that such should be the case. It is
> true of the Chinese, and Portuguese, and Japanese, for some of the latter
> known to the writer, who have been in the country a very brief time, have
> picked up some Portuguese words and a few native expressions, and a stray
> English word of uncertain lineage, and count themselves rich in their acquisi-
> tion. (*The Friend*, April 1886, emphasis added)

A former (and highly popular) turn-of-the-century Mayor of Honolulu, Joseph
Fern, owed at least part of his political success to his mixed-language campaigning:

> At the fish market my father would usually meet old friends — sometimes
> Mayor Joe Fern. Father would address the mayor in Portuguese and the mayor,
> though Hawaiian, would answer in broken Portuguese of his own. Mayor Fern
> would also speak phrases of Chinese, Japanese and other languages to friends
> of other national backgrounds. (Jardine 1984)

But perhaps the best description of the language-mixing process was given to the author by a person who had experienced it personally in her youth, Mrs. Rachel Kupepe of Kaua'i:

> So we use the Hawaiian and Chinese all together, in one sentence, see? And then they ask me if that's a Hawaiian word. I say no, maybe that's a Japanese word we put in, to make a sentence with a Hawaiian word. And the Chinese the same way too, in order to make a sentence for them to understand you' (Bickerton and Odo 1976).

One is reminded of example (7) above, where the speaker used words of equivalent meaning from three languages to ensure that he was understood.

Far from imperfect language learning, language simplification, relexification and all the other mechanisms hypothesized by earlier writers to account for pidginization (see 1), it seems that, in Hawai'i at least, the process may be informally characterized as a series of strategies adopted by speakers who find themselves confronted by unintelligible languages but who are driven by necessity to try to communicate with one another:

a.   try to use your own language
b.   try your interlocutor's language if you know any of it
c.   use any words you know regardless of origin and hope you hit on some you both understand.

In other words, at least the early stages of pidginization are driven solely by the desire to communicate, and, far from employing any sophisticated linguistic mechanisms for this, speakers simply string together whatever words they know or think will be understood to form utterances that are minimally structured. Indeed, one could argue that, since words in their original language always carry some degree of syntactic implication, the only way in which mixed-language utterances can be produced is by reducing their structure to a minimum.


## 3.   Other evidence

The question is therefore raised: are the patterns of linguistic behavior as documented in Hawai'i unique to that community, or do they represent universal tendencies, whose wide distribution has been obscured by the consensus that pidginization involves performing some kind of operation on a particular language? In a short introductory article such as the present one, it will not be possible to do more than briefly outline some of the evidence that supports the second of these positions.

Some of this evidence comes from 'mixed' pidgins like Russenorsk. Most pidgin surveys which mention Russenorsk imply that its vocabulary is limited to Russian and Norwegian items. According to Broch and Jahr (1984), however, the breakdown of its vocabulary is 47% Norwegian, 39% Russian, 14% other languages. This 14% is made up of items from a variety of languages: Dutch (or possibly German), English, Sami, French, Finnish, and Swedish. With the exception of the Sami vocabulary (mostly names of fish) none of these contributions can be called specialised, and most of the words constitute very basic vocabulary items for which there are certainly equivalents in both Norwegian and Russian. The above facts suggest that Russenorsk was simply the last surviving variety of an earlier Pan-Baltic pidgin, which may have been much more mixed in its lexicon than Russenorsk.

Chinook Jargon, although named after a single indigenous language, is even more radically mixed. Of the numerous dictionaries, one of the more complete is that of Gibbs (1863), which also lists the languages from which dictionary entries are derived. Of the 490 words it lists, only 200 (41%) are from Chinook. 161 (33%) are from European languages (94 French, 67 English), while the remaining 26% are divided among at least another nine Native American languages.

If we turn to West Africa, we find a literature replete with references to 'Pidgin English', 'Pidgin French' etc. However, these varieties are oftener claimed than they are cited. Without a single supporting citation, McWhorter (1994) has claimed that an English pidgin originating in Guinea was transmitted to the Slave Coast (or the Gold Coast, or both, his account is less than explicit on this point) to serve ultimately as the basis for the Surinamese creoles. Without a single supporting citation, Seuren (1995) has proposed a French pidgin based in Madagascar in order to account for some inconvenient similarities between Caribbean and Indian Ocean French creoles.

Unfortunately, the primary sources provide little support for these claims. Some of the most valuable contemporary evidence is found in the writings of Jean Barbot (1689/1732, reprinted 1992), a French commercial agent who travelled extensively in West Africa during the period 1678–1682. If there had been a well-established pidgin English or pidgin French, one would expect that Barbot, a keen and far from unsophisticated observer of language, would have noted it. But there is not a single region on the coast of West Africa, from Cape Verde to Principe, from which Barbot records a monolexical, unmixed pidgin. To the contrary, from every region he and his contemporaries report a mixture of languages being used in contacts. Some typical comments follow (all page references are to Barbot 1992 unless otherwise indicated):

Sierra Leone: "Most of the blacks around the bay speak either Portuguese or Lingua Franca...Some also understood a little English or Dutch" (p. 227).
Ivory Coast: "Some...speak a little Dutch or English. (p. 273).
Gold Coast: Some few words of Portuguese, and the Lingua Franca" (p. 549)
Whydah: "Most merchants can speak something of the Lingua Franca, or of some other European language, but more especially French" (p. 643). "The king understood a little Portuguese" (p. 653).

A slightly earlier traveller (Dapper 1668:107) describes speech on the Gold Coast as "Mostly Portuguese or Dutch, and some French too". The usual quality of the kind of speech described above is indicated by the remarks of another traveller, quoted by Jones (1985: 34): "A little English, Dutch and Portuguese, all mixed together, so that it takes some effort to understand them, and if one wants to buy something from them, one must make use of the language of the dumb, namely, making signs with one's fingers".

The picture one gets from these accounts is one of a broad base of mixed and quite primitive pidgin, with no suggestion that stable, monolexical pidgins played any role in contacts.

If pidgins in their early stages are mixed languages, and if plantation creoles typically derive from early stage pidgins, we would expect to find extensive traces of language mixture in the lexicons of the Caribbean creoles. Indeed, several of these lexicons provide further evidence of the use of mixed vocabularies in early stages of contact.

Smith (1987) drew attention to some dozen African lexical items which are found in a wide variety of English-based creoles. These words are drawn from languages extending from Wolof to Kimbundu, that is to say along the greater part of the West African coast. Smith used this evidence to suggest that all the Anglo-Creoles stemmed from an original West African pidgin English. However, a combination of statistical and historical evidence too complex to be detailed here indicates that these words formed part of the various (unrelated) pre-creole pidgins that either developed in situ or were transferred from one Caribbean island or territory to another, and that they constitute the residue of a much larger non-European vocabulary present at or near the time of creolization that has since largely disappeared.

In addition, a number of writers have commented on the mixed status of certain creole lexicons in the Caribbean. Consider the following:

Saramaccan, which according to Price (1976) has an African- derived vocabulary of up to 50%, the remainder being divided mainly between English and Portuguese.

Sranan: the items in Lichtveld (1961) divide into the following classes:

European (English/Dutch/Portuguese) 46.5%, African/ Amerindian 19.7%, compounds (all classes) 33.8%.

Guyanais, with its residue of Portuguese vocabulary, as discussed in Goodman (1985).

Berbice Dutch, with its 27% of vocabulary from a single African language, Ijaw (Smith et al., 1987).

Lesser Antillean Creole (see the careful historical analysis in Wylie 1995): this creole was immediately preceded by a baragouin or primitive pidgin drawing on Spanish, French, Carib and ultimately African lexical sources.

The last study, taken in conjunction with the situation in Surinam and the historical developments in Hawai'i described above, is particularly revealing. It suggests that many creoles, like Lesser Antillean, started out with a far more mixed lexicon than they possess today (although as Wylie points out, considerable mixture still remains even here in specialized vocabulary areas). Where contact with the main European lexifier was permanently terminated, as in Surinam, the lexicon retains a high degree of mixture to the present day; where such contact continued, as in the Lesser Antilles, items from the main lexifier tended gradually to replace items from other sources. If English as well as Hawaiian had ceased to be a significant factor in the Hawai'i of the 1890s, synchronic Hawaiian Creole could have had a vocabulary as mixed as that of Saramaccan.

## 4.   Conclusion

Most linguists see it as their mission to reduce to some form of order the superficial chaos that often appears to characterize human language. To such scholars the present paper may seem a retrograde step, replacing, as it does, a picture of systematic pidginization as a discrete process (or processes) affecting particular languages, by one of pidginization as a multilexical mess driven by a mere blind need to communicate. Unfortunately, the orderly conventional picture has little going for it beyond this desire to impose order, supported by illegitimate back-projections from synchronic states where hundreds of years of contact with a single dominant European language has all but erased prior states. The chaotic picture, alas, seems to have the support of most of the facts that are currently available, a support that grows stronger as more historical research of the caliber of Roberts (1995a) and Wylie (1995) becomes available.

# Notes

1.  Both remarks are reported by an American sea-captain, Joseph Ingraham, in his Journal of the Voyage of the brigantine 'Hope' from Boston to the North-West Coast of America, (1790–92: 58–9;70). They were allegedly uttered on two different occasions by two different Hawaiians. The first was by the man ('Opye') used by Ingraham as a translator, who had travelled to the Marquesas (and perhaps elsewhere) on foreign vessels; the second was apparently by a local member of the ali'i caste.

2.  Pidgin Hawaiian is described in Bickerton and Wilson (1987) and Roberts (1995a); a detailed grammatical description is presented in Roberts (1995b). While in the context of the present paper one might be tempted to regard Pidgin Hawaiian as merely one pole of a Hawaiian-English pidgin continuum, that pole represented the speech of a substantial portion of the population, and it did jell, over the first half of the nineteenth century, into a fairly stabilised and even partially expanded pidgin, while contact English languished in a relatively jargon-like state (Roberts, 1998). However, massive immigration from 1876 on reversed this tendency and led to the macaronic phase discussed below.

3.  (3) is an extract from a letter by John Papa, of Kukuihaele on the island of Hawai'i, to the Hawaiian newspaper *Ko Hawaii Pae Aina* in 1887, quoting the words of a local (unnamed) Hawaiian woman, which Papa may have cited in an attempt to discredit her former teacher, a Mr. Richards, also mentioned in the letter.

4.  Example (4) comes from an argument between two female workers, one Chinese, one Japanese, overheard and noted in his diary by Jack Hall, a plantation foreman who published his account in the *Honolulu Advertiser* some thirty years later; (5), from the diary of Noboru Kawada, a Japanese plantation worker, records a request for sick-leave by a female worker to her foreman or luna (whose ethnicity was not recorded); (6) was uttered by 'a blind kanaka [Hawaiian] man' in response to a query by a Japanese about what had happened to his dog, and was reported in the Japanese newspaper *Yamato Shimbun*; in (7), a government physician, E.S. Goodhue, notes the words of 'a forlorn Portuguese specimen' who came to him for medicine; . Abbreviations used in the glosses are as follows: HON Honorific, TOP topic marker, OBJ object marker.

5.  Their rarity in verbatim court-room attestations might seem to militate against this view. However, the same court records contain frequent mentions of persons speaking in 'a mixture of Chinese and English;, 'a mixture of Japanese and Hawaiian', and so on. One has to bear in mind too that most court business involving pidgin speakers was transacted through interpreters, and although alleged utterances at crime scenes were supposed to be presented in the exact words, regardless of language, that the speaker uttered, interpreters may have routinely translated into English or Hawaiian any words in those utterances drawn from the native language of the speaker, since such words would probably not have been understood by the court. Unfortunately, reports from Portuguese- and Chinese-language sources are too sparse to support the Japanese sources.

# References

Aitchison, Jean. 1981. *Language change — progress or decay*? London:Fontana.
Andersen, Roger. 1980. "Creolization as the acquisition of a second language as a first language." In Valdman and Highfield (eds.), 273–95.

Bakker, Peter. 1995. "Pidgins." In Jacques Arends, Pieter Muysken and Norval S. H. Smith (eds.), *Pidgins and Creoles: An Introduction*. Amsterdam: John Benjamins, 25–39.

Barbot, Jean. 1992. *Barbot of Guinea: The Writings of Jean Barbot on West Africa 1678–1712*. In P. E. H. Hair, A. Jones and R. Law (eds.), London: The Hakluyt Society.

Bates, G. W. 1854. *Sandwich Island Notes by a Haole*. New York: Harper Brothers.

Bickerton, Derek and William H. Wilson. 1987. "Pidgin Hawaiian." In Glenn G. Gilbert (ed.), *Pidgin and Creole Languages: Essays in Memory of John Reinecke*. Honolulu: University of Hawai'i Press, 61–76.

Bloomfield, Leonard. 1933. *Language*. New York: Holt, Rinehart & Winston.

Broch, Ingvild and Ernst Håkon Jahr. 1984. "Russenorsk: a new look at the Russo-Norwegian pidgin in Northern Norway." In P. Sture Ureland and Ian Clarkson (eds.), *Scandinavian Language Contacts*. Cambridge: Cambridge University Press, 21–64.

Clyne, Michael. 1968. "Zum pidgindeutsch der Gastarbeiter." *Zeitschrift für Mundartforschung* 35:130–39.

Dapper, O. 1668. *Africa: Being an Accurate Description of the Regions...* London: J. V. Meurs.

Dana, Richard Henry, Jr. 1840. *Two Years Before the Mast. A personal narrative*. New York: Harper Brothers.

Drechsel, Emamuel J. this vol. "Language Contact in the Early Colonial Pacific: Evidence for a Maritime Polynesian Jargon or Pidgin."

Gibbs, G. 1863. *A Dictionary of the Chinook Jargon or Trade Language of Oregon*. New York: Gramoisy Press.

Gilman, G. 1845. *Rustications on Kauai and Niihau*. MS.

Goodman, Morris. 1985. "Review of Bickerton, *Roots of Language*." *International Journal of American Linguistics* 51:109–37.

Holm, John. 1986. "Substrate diffusion." In Pieter Muysken and Norval S. H. Smith (eds.), *Substrata Versus Universals in Creole Genesis*. Amsterdam: Benjamins, 359–78.

———. 1988. *Pidgins and Creoles*. Vol. 1. Cambridge: Cambridge University Press.

Hymes, Dell (ed.). 1971. *The Pidginization and Creolization of Languages*. Cambridge: Cambridge University Press.

Jardine, J. 1984. *Detective Jardine: Crimes in Honolulu*. Honolulu: University of Hawai'i Press.

Jones, A. 1985. *Brandenburg Sources for West African History*. Stuttgart.

Lefebvre, Claire, and John Lumsden. 1989. "Les langues créoles et la théorie linguistique." *Canadian Journal of Linguistics* 34: 249–272.

Lichtveld, L. 1961. *Glossary of the Suriname Vernacular*. Paramaribo: Bureau Volklectur/ N. V. Varekamp.

Manessy, G. 1995. *Creoles, Pidgins, Variétés Vehiculaires*. Paris: CNRS Editions.

McWhorter, John 1994. "Rejoinder to Derek Bickerton." *Journal of Pidgin and Creole Languages* 9:79–93.

Muysken, Pieter 1981. "Halfway between Spanish and Quechua: the case for relexification." In Valdman and Highfield, 52–78.

Price, R. 1976. *The Guiana Maroons: A Historical and Biographical Introduction*. Baltimore: Johns Hopkins University Press.

Roberts, J. 1995a. "Pidgin Hawaiian: a sociohistorical study." *Journal of Pidgin and Creole Languages* 10:1–56.

———. 1995b. "A structural sketch of Pidgin Hawaiian." *Amsterdam Creole Studies* 12:97–126.

———, S. J. 1998. "The role of diffusion in the genesis of Hawaiian Creole." *Language* 74:1–39.

Seuren, Pieter A. M. 1995. "Notes on the history and the syntax of Mauritian Creole." *Linguistics* 33:531–577.

Smith, Norval S. H. 1987. *The Genesis of the Creole Languages of Surinam*. Unpublished Ph. D. dissertation. University of Amsterdam.

———, Ian E. Robertson and Kay Williamson. 1987. "The Ijaw element in Berbice Dutch." *Language in Society* 16:49–90.

Thompson, W. A. 1961. "A note on some possible affinities between the creole dialects of the Old World and those of the New." In R. B. LePage (ed.), *Creole Language Studies*. London: Macmillan, 107–13.

Valdman, Albert and Arthur Highfield (eds). 1981. *Theoretical Orientations in Creole Studies*. New York: Academic Press.

Warren, R. T. 1859. *Dust and Foam*. New York: Scribners.

Whinnom, Keith 1965. "The origin of the European-based pidgins and creoles." *Orbis* 14:509–527.

Wylie, J. 1995. "The origin of Lesser Antillean French Creole: some literary and lexical evidence." *Journal of Pidgin and Creole Languages* 10:77–126.

# The TMA System of Hawaiian Creole and Diffusion

Sarah Julianne Roberts
*Stanford University*

## 1. Introduction

Hawai'i Creole English (HCE), an Anglophone creole which arose by the 1930s throughout the Hawaiian Islands, bears striking similarities with other creoles around the world. Tsuzaki (1971: 332) claimed that the parallels were so close that with a few alterations one could "construct a fairly representative list of characteristics for HCE" from a creole like Jamaican.

For Tsuzaki the HCE tense-modality-aspect (TMA) system was a case in point. On the same page, he produced examples which showed "a remarkable resemblance to those reported in many other creoles by various scholars." Holm (1986) also found the parallels impressive and suggested that the Atlantic creole and HCE patterns were rooted in a shared West African substrate. The physical absence of West Africans in Hawai'i has obscured the possible role of this substrate in creolization (West Africans and their descendants populated most creole-speaking regions in the Atlantic), as substrate features could have been transmitted from the Atlantic by creole-speaking sailors.

None of the Pacific pidgins emerged in isolation and various well-documented studies (Clark 1979; Baker 1993) indicate that diffusion played a major role in their development. According to Baker (1993), many key features of the Melanesian pidgins first arose in Australia. Influence from Chinese Pidgin English and other nearby pidgins can be detected in certain Pacific varieties. Both Clark and Baker agreed that several widespread Pacific features can be traced to the Atlantic creoles. The primary issue, then, is not whether diffusion figured in the genesis of HCE but whether it was extensive enough to have shaped HCE's grammar (including its TMA system).

Some creolists believe that a language or some type of coherent linguistic system was brought into the Pacific. Holm (1992: 194) states that early 19th-century sailors "had a working knowledge of Atlantic Creole English and considered it appropriate for contact with nonwhites, including the natives of the Pacific region." Goodman (1985) posited an 18th- and 19th-century Worldwide Nautical Pidgin English (WNPE) which, originally derived from the Atlantic contact English, formed the basis of early Pidgin English in Hawai'i. Similar views were expressed by Keesing (1988) and Dillard (1995).

Others have characterized Atlantic-to-Pacific diffusion as involving the transmission of individual lexical features embedded in idiolectal foreigner-talk varieties, reflecting both conventional and improvised strategies of language reduction (Baker 1993). These features varied in their diffusion across the Pacific and spread through language contact as local pidgins arose.

The grammatical similarities between HCE and the Atlantic creoles are best explained by the Holm-Goodman model. The foreigner-talk register envisioned by Baker as the basis of the Pacific pidgins was by definition *ad hoc* and simplified. While the separate diffusion of a few grammatical items was certainly possible, the instability and impoverishment of foreigner talk would have ruled out the transmission of entire syntactic and semantic systems. Holm (1986: 265) recognized that due to later repidginization "there can be considerable loss of features in such diffusion." WNPE, or the variety of Atlantic Creole English envisioned by Holm, could easily accommodate the range of grammatical transfer needed to fix West African languages as the relevant substrate for HCE. No subsequent repidginization would need to occur and the structure of the diffused creole would remain largely intact as the structure of HCE. Baker's foreigner-talk model, on the other hand, would treat the structural systems of HCE as independent innovations. This would deny the involvement of a West African substrate in their development.

In this paper I will examine the historical development of preverbal TMA auxiliaries in HCE and its precursor, Hawai'i Pidgin English (HPE). If a shipboard creole did exist and the TMA system was imported *in toto* from the Atlantic, we should expect to find in textual data signs of an early diffusion. Court records, newspapers, personal and business correspondence, popular books, school literary annuals, and creole plays have furnished most of the data used in this study. The resultant database encompasses Hawai'i's entire modern era, which I divide into six phases: 1778–1829 (Phase I), 1830–1859 (Phase II), 1860–1899 (Phase III), 1900–1919 (Phase IV), 1920–1949 (Phase V), and 1950–present (Phase VI). These periods correspond to major divisions in my database and broadly to historical events. Phases I and II represent the early contact and whaling periods, respectively, and provide only a small quantity of texts. This study will limit itself to the latter four phases, which are better documented and represent the era which saw the rise and fall of the sugar industry and the immigration of hundreds of thousands of Chinese, Portuguese, Japanese, Koreans, and Filipinos to the Islands as labor.

Textual data would support the Holm-Goodman model if they attest a TMA system already in place by Phase III. If the HCE system did not emerge in the data until Phases IV or V, it probably evolved independent of Atlantic influence. Endogeny would also be indicated if the system was attested only within a particular segment of the population. In this case Holm would need to explain why the system was retained by these speakers but lost everywhere else. If the population in which the TMA system arose also corresponded to the native-born population, the data would support theories of creolization which link structural changes to nativization. The existence of auxiliaries unique to Hawai'i in form but shared with the Atlantic creoles in function would constitute further evidence against an exogenous origin of the system if the Atlantic forms are absent in the data.

To assess the possible role of the native-born population in the data, I have extracted from the overall database a portion of texts which are attributable by textual criteria to a focus population (FP) of native-born speakers. These texts are classified as FP if the original speakers are identified as (i) born after 1890 and (ii) either born in Hawai'i or raised there from an early age. The FP does not represent the entire native-born population (as many possible FP texts could not be classified as such due to absent contextual information) but it does consist entirely of confirmed native-born speakers. Therefore diverging patterns between FP and non-FP texts should reflect patterns in the actual native-born and foreign-born populations.

## 2.     The TMA System of HCE

Tsuzaki (1971: 332–333) was the first to describe the basilectal TMA system in detail. He identified three categories of preverbal markers in addition to negators and the epistemic modals: past tense (expressed by *been*, *went*, or *had*), future or contigent mood (*go*), and progressive aspect (*stay*). He also noted that these auxiliaries may combine, with or without the negator: "The use of up to three preposed particles in any given verbal construction is the rule (e.g. *I no eat* 'I don't eat'; *I no go eat* 'I am not going to eat'/'I will not be eating'; *I no go stay eat* 'I am not going to be eating'/'I will not be eating'). Four particles are possible, but unusual (e.g. *I no been go stay eat* 'I wasn't/hadn't been eating')."

Examples of these auxiliaries may be drawn from the "Hukilepo Joe Says"
column from the *Hawaii Tribune Herald* newspaper, which ran from 1945 to
1947.[1] The column writer used *been* for past tense, *goin* (a mesolectal variant of
*go*) for future modality, *stay* for progressive aspect, *been stay* for past progressive, and *goin stay* for future progressive:

(1)   Queek he *been* trow da lei around ma neck.
      'Quickly he threw the lei around my neck.'

(2)   Monday me I *goin* go down fo see da teecket wahine.
      'On Monday I'll go down to see the woman who sells airline tickets.'

(3)   I bet you *stay* wonda how I been get thees lump o'er my eye.
      'I bet you're wondering how I got this lump over my eye.'

(4)   Ma fadda *been stay* wait fo me on top da porch.
      'My father was waiting for me on the porch.'

(5)   I been tell you about da tourees who *goin stay* come weeset.
      'I told you about the tourists who will be coming over to visit.'

Tsuzaki (1971:333) regarded the above set of auxiliaries as belonging to "the
pan-creole type," by which he meant the abstract system shared by Sranan
(Voorhoeve 1957), Dominican Creole French and Haitian (Taylor 1956, 1961),
Saramaccan (Thompson 1961), and numerous other creoles of different lexifiers.
These creoles all possess three preverbal TMA markers which may combine but
only in the order Tense + Mood + Aspect. The semantic values of this "core TMA
system" were summarized by Bakker, Post, & van der Voort (1995:250) as follows:

> As far as tense is concerned, the reference point ... is not 'point present' as in
> the European languages like English, French and Portuguese (which distinguish
> roughly past, present and future), but the time of the event under discus-
> sion....A marker of anterior tense indicates past for state verbs and past-
> before-past, or past, for non-stative verbs....
>
> As far as mood is concerned, real events are distinguished from non-real
> events. Realis events have actually occurred or are occurring at the moment of
> speaking; irrealis events are imagined, conditional or future events. A special
> preverbal morpheme marks irrealis events, and realis events are unmarked.
>
> As far as aspect is concerned, nonpunctual events (which occur over a
> stretch of time or repeatedly) are distinguished from punctual events (which
> occur at one specific point in time and not over a long time). Nonpunctual events
> are marked with a preverbal morpheme, while punctual events are left unmarked.

Further research on the modern Hawaiian Creole system found similar semantic
restrictions: *bin/wen* indicated anterior and not absolute past as in English, *go*

was used beyond future mood to other irrealis functions such as the conditional, and *stei* expressed the habitual in addition to progressive (Bickerton 1977). The syntactic and semantic similarities between the Atlantic creole and HCE systems are evident in the following comparison of HCE, Haitian, and Sranan adapted from Masuda (1995: 29). The HCE versions (mesolectal variants in brackets) appear under (a), Haitian under (b), and Sranan under (c).

(6)  a.  Hii wak
     b.  Li mache
     c.  A waka
         'He walks.'

(7)  a.  Hii bin [wen] wak
     b.  Li te mache
     c.  A ben waka
         'He walked/had walked.'

(8)  a.  Hii go [gon] wak
     b.  L'av(a) mache
     c.  A sa waka
         'He will walk.'

(9)  a.  Hii stei wak [stei wakin]
     b.  L'ap mache
     c.  A e waka
         'He is walking.'

(10) a.  Hii bin go [wuda] wak
     b.  Li t'av(a) mache
     c.  A ben sa waka
         'He was going to walk.'

(11) a.  Hii bin stei wak [wen stei wak/wakin, waz wak/wakin]
     b.  Li t'ap mache
     c.  A ben e waka
         'He was walking.'

(12) a.  Hii go stei wak [gon stei wak/wakin]
     b.  L'av ap mache
     c.  A sa e waka
         'He will be walking.'

(13) a.  Hii bin go stei wak [waz gon wak/wakin]
     b.  Li t'av ap mache
     c.  A ben sa e waka
         'He was going to be walking.'

These comparisons are too simplistic, as they overlook a great deal of complexity in the basilectal TMA systems of these languages. There may be additional tense, modality, and aspect markers which, in combination with the other auxiliaries, affect the semantics of the overall system. Most Caribbean creoles express habitual aspect with reflexes of English *does* (an auxiliary which significantly is absent in HCE), while in HCE irrealis *go* may also occasionally mark the habitual (Holm 1988; Sato 1978). HCE and the Atlantic creoles employ separate auxiliaries for completive aspect, *pau* and *don* respectively. These may combine with the anterior and irrealis markers in the basilect (Hancock 1987; Holm 1988, 1989). Furthermore the past conditional forms *bin go* and *bin go stei* are marginal in HCE and may never have been fully established (Bickerton 1977). Nevertheless, despite these divergences and extensions to the "pan-creole" system, the similarities are still "remarkable" and "call for an explanation." (Bakker, Post & van der Voort 1995: 248).

Holm (1986: 261) also found the TMA parallels significant and regarded them as rooted in West African languages, particularly Bambara which combines auxiliaries in an almost identical fashion. He felt that "the syntactic and semantic parallels of these markers in their various combinations are striking, suggesting that the similarity of the African and creole structures are too close to have resulted from chance." He therefore proposed that the HCE features "have their origin in the diffusion of Atlantic creole features that can in turn be traced to the influence of substrate African languages" (p. 273).

The next section will assess the likelihood of this claim by examining the historical development of the TMA system in Hawai'i.


## 3.   Historical Development

Although Phases I and II were poorly documented by early writers, it is significant that none of the 153 English-lexifier utterances recorded between 1790 and 1859 contain HCE auxiliaries. The following example indicates the future with adverbial *by and by* (later *baimbai* in HPE and HCE) and perfective aspect by verbal inflection:

> (14)   Oh no, by and bye Massa get up, & he see you stolen something, &
>        he put you in Fort. (1856; Chinese merchant, Honolulu, O'ahu)[2]

However the database does contain three cases of preverbal *go* which may shed light on the genesis of the irrealis function:

(15)   I no care, every day she go sleep with that bad thing. (1838; Portuguese skilled laborer, Koloa, Kaua'i)[3]

(16)   He go stole something. (1856; Chinese merchant, Honolulu, O'ahu)[4]

(17)   I don't know, I go see. Suppose I find, I bring to you. (1856; Chinese arrested for theft, Honolulu, O'ahu)[5]

None of these cases are clearly irrealis and in context they are probably lexical: in (15) the speaker wanted to lock his wife inside the house so she would not go out and sleep with other men, in (16) the speaker was looking for a thief and had asked where he had been, and in (17) the speaker told his interrogator that he would return to his house to look for stolen watches. However adverbial *every day* in (15) indicates that the event of *go sleep* (going out and sleeping) was habitual. The lexical meaning of *go*, which expresses already given information, may be bleached without obscuring the main point about the wife's infidelity. Therefore sentences like (15) probably contributed to the reanalysis of *go* as a habitual auxiliary. Similarly, in (17), the act of going back to the speaker's house would occur in the future. If information about the act of going was recoverable from discourse in such sentences, preverbal *go* could have been reinterpreted as a future marker. So while *go* in these examples has discernible lexical meaning, it is not very far from TMA-marking functions.

The remainder of this section will explore the development of the TMA system in the latter phases. Each HCE auxiliary will be considered individually.

## 3.1   The Past/Anterior Marker *bin/wen*

### 3.1.1 *1860–1889 (Phase III)*
*Bin* was first attested in 1890. Between 1860 and 1889, unmarked verbs occurred in all 34 sentences expressing past actions and events. Examples:

(18)   Say come here, I want speak you, you no give me money last night. (1867; Hawaiian prostitute, Honolulu, O'ahu)[6]

(19)   He come here, board my house, take very good room. (1870; Chinese hotel owner, Honolulu, O'ahu)[7]

(20)   Smallpox time, he and Keo go round and scratch arm *kanaka* [Hawaiian]. (1882; Hawaiian election campaigner, Honolulu, O'ahu)[8]

### 3.1.2 *1890–1909 (Phases III-IV)*
The first instances of *bin* occurred in adult immigrant speech:

(21)    No got note, I been pay four dollars to head *luna* [boss]. (1890; Chinese plantation laborer, Kapa'a, Kaua'i)[9]

(22)    Yes, he been fight Chinaman. (1899; Japanese plantation laborer, Kahuku, O'ahu)[10]

(23)    He been stop home alone. (1899; Chinese hack driver, Honolulu, O'ahu)[11]

(24)    Big ship, you been see come? (1904; Japanese house servant, Honolulu, O'ahu)[12]

Such examples were rare in the data; *bin* occurred in only 7 of 197 (3.5%) past time sentences between 1890 and 1909 in the speech of adults. Since it was attested once in every 28 past time sentences on average, it may have existed in earlier HPE but at lower levels. Nevertheless it was a marginal feature and most past verbs were left unmarked:

(25)    Before Fraulein cry all time. (1896; Japanese house servant, Honolulu, O'ahu)[13]

(26)    What for you shoot dog? (1899; Hawaiian homesteader, Waipahu, O'ahu)[14]

(27)    I go all around Hilo town; I go ice-cream parlor Pringles. (1900; Chinese hack driver, Hilo, Hawai'i)[15]

(28)    Me *hapai* [bring], steamer come, me *hapai* camp, me charge two dollar, me pay steamer. (1904; Japanese plantation laborer, Ma'alea, Maui)[16]

The earliest cases of *bin* in the Focus Population appeared between 1900 and 1910. Although there are not enough examples to show quantitatively that *bin* was already integrated into the language of native-born children, the following qualitative remark by the later Governor of Hawai'i indicates that it in fact was:

> However pure the English, Chinese, Portuguese, or Hawaiian they [Hawai'i-born children] may speak in the school or homes, they have a complex pidgin English which is a universal language. They all meet on the "I-bin-go" method of communication. (Wallace R. Farrington, *Paradise of the Pacific,* December 1904, pp. 43–44)

A few examples of *bin* in the speech of Hawaiian children may be found in McMahon (1909: 13):

(29)    This fella bin see. (1909)

(30)    That fella think he more smarter than me, but I never 'fraid for that thing he bin tell. (1909)

### 3.1.3 *1910–1919 (Phase IV)*

Outside the FP *bin* remained a low-frequency feature throughout the following decade: only 22 cases out of 243 (9.0%). In the FP it appeared in 35 out of 59 sentences expressing past events and actions (57.4%). It was almost obligatorily included whenever a writer represented the speech of children:

(31)    Papa bin lick mama. (1910; 6–year-old girl, Palama, O'ahu)[17]

(32)    You been give all to other fella? (1912; Hawaiian girl, Kaka'ako, O'ahu)[18]

(33)    You bin say go up on roof and paint him, but I no hear you say come down. (1913; teenaged Part-Hawaiian, Kaimuki, O'ahu)[19]

(34)    I bin make pie. (1914; schoolgirl named Virginia)[20]

(35)    Maria's mother been tell lies to Venus' mother, and she been lick. (1914; Portuguese girl named Angelina, Honolulu, O'ahu)[21]

(36)    They been tease and I been swear. (1914; Chinese schoolboy named Ah Hop)[22]

(37)    The Indian he got one gun; he been shoot one cowboy. (1915; 12-year-old Portuguese boy)[23]

(38)    Gourka he been strike our father. (1916; children of Gabriel Gemsky, Papa'alea, Hawai'i)[24]

(39)    William punch my father and blood been come outside. (1916; Japanese schoolboy, Waikapu, Maui)[25]

(40)    I been go Waikiki and see many monkey. (1917; unidentified schoolboy, Mānoa, O'ahu)[26]

A chi-square analysis of the distribution of *bin* in FP and non-FP texts shows that the disparity is statistically significant ($\chi = 118.90$; $p < .0001$), indicating that it had become a stereotyped feature before 1920 (Roberts 1998). While most of the examples lack sufficient discourse context, (39) is clearly incompatible with an anterior use of *bin* and in (35) and (36) it seems to be a simple past marker. The anterior semantics of *bin* therefore probably did not yet become established.

### 3.1.4 *1920–1949 (Phase V)*

The proportion of *bin*-marked verbs did not increase in non-FP texts after 1920. Most narratives lacked any use of *bin*. Examples:

(41)    Yesterday I go Lihue Store, I buy one buggie whip, carriage kind. (1922; Japanese customer, Lihu'e, Kaua'i)[27]

(42)    Horse no good — him throw missus — she fall — too many rocks.
        (1926; Japanese woman, Haleakala, Maui)[28]

(43)    Nother day me look see one Pilipino, me long time talk, talk.
        (1932; Filipino plantation immigrant)[29]

In FP texts speakers frequently employed *bin* to indicate past tense:

(44)    I make like this, I been shake my body. (1920; 19–year-old Japanese
        girl, Wailuku, Maui)[30]

(45)    Us been go post office. (1921; attributed to schoolchildren)[31]

(46)    I make her come like you been see. (1925; 10–year-old Chinese girl,
        Honolulu, O'ahu)[32]

(47)    You still got de horse, an' you say you bin sell 'im. (1933; 15–
        year-old Japanese boy)[33]

(48)    You been eat lunch already? (1934; attributed to schoolchildren)[34]

(49)    I been broke my pencil. (1937; attributed to schoolchildren)[35]

The first instance of the variant *wen* was recorded in 1936 and it rapidly began
to displace *bin* in FP texts. Smith (1939: 186) noted that it was "a favorite
method of expressing past tense for the Koreans and is used to some extent by
all groups" of school-aged children. Examples:

(50)    I bet you wan spoil 'im already. (1936; 10–year-old Hawaiian girl)[36]

(51)    I wen' *kapu* [reserved] yum oready. (1937; neighborhood boy in
        Palama, O'ahu)[37]

(52)    Sure, you went cry. (1939; attributed to schoolchildren)[38]

(53)    She went give Setsu already, no? (1946; attributed to schoolchildren)[39]

(54)    She wen help me study and she wen tell me go talk to the prof.
        (1948; locally-born Japanese college student)[40]

## 3.2  *The Future/Irrealis Marker go/gon*

### 3.2.1  *1860–1899 (Phase III)*
Temporal adverbs such as *baimbai*, *tomorrow*, and so forth formed the usual
means of marking future events and actions. Texts for Phases III and IV contain
over 115 examples of *baimbai* which indicated either futurity or sequentially later
events in discourse. Examples:

(55)    You see, Bapa, bimeby Lole Popopo he no get many *baloka*s
        [votes]. (1882; Hawaiian election campaigner, Honolulu, O'ahu)[41]

(56)    By and by steamer come, you come get. (1890; Portuguese liquor
        seller, Hilo, Hawai'i)[42]

(57)    Bye and bye all Japanese tonight fight. (1899; Chinese plantation
        irrigator, Kahuku, O'ahu)[43]

Other unrealized or potential events and actions were indicated with epistemic
adverbs such as *maybe so* and *perhaps* or the sentence-initial tag *I think*:

(58)    Maybe so make, maybe so bimeby somebody steal his money.
        (1891; Hawaiian policeman, Honolulu, O'ahu)[44]

(59)    I think, you like give me ten dollars, you stop my cousin house.
        (1891; Hawaiian policeman, Honolulu, O'ahu)[45]

Conditional clauses were either introduced by *suppose*, as in (17), or linked by
parataxis, as in (59). The desiderative function of *like* in (59) also indicated
intended actions and events, and a further example from the same speaker
suggests an auxiliary reanalysis of preverbal *like*:

(60)    Suppose you like bribe policeman, you go jail — you sabe? (1891;
        Hawaiian policeman, Honolulu, O'ahu)[46]

The addressee was being warned in (60) of the consequences of offering bribes,
not the mere desire of offering them. In this example *like* probably marked
irrealis modality.

Textual evidence indicates that *go* was also undergoing reanalysis as an irrealis
marker. The earliest unambiguous case of irrealis *go* was recorded in 1881:

(61)    Me frightened you go die. (1881; Japanese cook, Honolulu, O'ahu)[47]

Other examples of preverbal *go* were either lexical or signified the imperative:

(62)    You go write now order Honolulu to Mr. Brown. (1890; Japanese
        immigrant, Hilo, Hawai'i)[48]

(63)    So I go speak Ah Siu he got money to pay $5.00. (1895; Chinese
        plantation laborer, Spreckelsville, Maui)[49]

(64)    Baby inside the hole, you go look, you come here. (1898; Hawaiian
        homesteader, Hilo, Hawai'i)[50]

### 3.2.2 1900–1919 (Phase IV)

Attestations of preverbal *go* increased sharply in Phase IV texts, but because of multifunctionality it is difficult to ascertain the status of irrealis-marking. This was found by Sato (1978) to be true of the HPE and HCE spoken in the 1970s. In an exhaustive analysis of recorded speech, Sato (1978: 135–136, 141) concluded that "*go* functions primarily as a marker of motion and secondarily as the tense-aspect marker of irreality," and surmised that the latter was "an extension of the motion *go*." She regarded several cases of apparent irrealis *go* as really instances of lexical *go*. The existence of further forms such as imperative *go*, habitual *go*, and emphatic *go* suggested that grammaticalization was ongoing and not limited to the irrealis.

Similar results may be obtained from the attestations from Phases III and IV. Of 75 cases of preverbal *go*, only 21 (28.0%) can be interpreted as having any future or irrealis modality. At least 25 (33.3%) are explicitly lexical with past reference, 14 (18.7%) may signal the imperative and in most cases follow the second person pronoun, and the other 15 (20.0%) are less clear and may be lexical, habitual, emphatic, or possibly something entirely different. Of the 21 irrealis candidates, 16 (76.2%) are highly ambiguous. Examples:

(65) I got not enough money, I go get some money. (1904; Chinese store owner, Keana'e, Maui)[51]

(66) I now go tell Gourka. (1916; Russian immigrant, Papa'alea, Hawai'i)[52]

The others are probably irrealis as these examples suggest:

(67) Negano want one cup milk; he go make cake. (1900; Chinese cook, Honolulu, O'ahu)[53]

(68) No can get paper tonight; tonight get married, but Monday I go get paper. (1912; Hawaiian homesteader, Honolulu, O'ahu)[54]

The high proportion of ambiguous cases of *go* supports Sato's hypothesis that the irrealis auxiliary grammaticalized locally from the lexical verb when used in future contexts.

Only 4 attestations of preverbal *go* appeared in FP texts from Phase IV, 3 of which seem to signify (with some ambiguity) future or irrealis modality:

(69) Suppose everybody like buttermilk, baimbai Kaala go get cow eh. (1908; teenaged Hawaiian boy, Honolulu, O'ahu)[55]

(70) I go fish today. (1910; 10–year-old boy, Honolulu, O'ahu)[56]

(71) I go ask my mother for new hat. (1919; teenaged Portuguese girl, Pauoa, O'ahu)[57]

In the other example *go* is either lexical or an embedded imperative marker. It is especially interesting in light of the function of *go* in HCE as a complementizer of realized predicates, a structure derived by Bickerton (1977) from embedded imperatives:

>   (72)   My mama ask me go sleep with him. (1912; 6–year-old girl, Wailuku, Maui)[58]

### 3.2.3 *1920–1949 (Phase V)*
Possible cases of irrealis or future *go* remained scarce in the non-FP group and most were highly ambiguous:

>   (73)   Me go fight Kaisy mens; then beefy too muche *gura* [good]. (1926; Chinese food vendor, Lahoka, Hawai'i)[59]

In a number of instances *go* preceded verbs of past time:

>   (74)   She go walk last night with boy — stay long time. (1924; Chinese woman, Kaliu'uwa'a, O'ahu)[60]

In FP texts preverbal *go* continued to indicate irrealis or future modality, much more frequently and less ambiguously than in the non-FP corpus:

>   (75)   I go catch mangoes. (1937; attributed to schoolchildren, glossed as: "I am going to pick mangoes")[61]
>   (76)   We go make one *puka* [hole]. (1937; 4–year-old Portuguese boy)[62]
>   (77)   I go whip you Ivanhoe. (1937; 6–year-old Portuguese/Hawaiian boy)[63]
>   (78)   I go have the same cards again. (1939; attributed to schoolchildren)[64]

There are also cases of *go* indicating habitual actions and events:

>   (79)   Oh, he go fool me every time. (1934; attributed to schoolchildren, in reply to "Why did you hit him?")[65]

However ambiguity between functions still existed. Reinecke & Tokisama (1934: 122–123) remarked that *go* was "somewhat vaguely used to show habitual or inceptive action," while Kaapu (1937: 62) distinguished between future, imperative, habitual present, and past uses of *go*. The interpretation of *go* as a past marker seems incredible, considering its status as an future auxiliary, but none of the other functions seem to fit in cases like (74). In this sentence *go* is not irrealis, nor does it express habitual aspect or the imperative. It may be lexical, but in many cases, such as *He go break the bottle*, which Coale (1938: 40) translated as "He broke the bottle," it is clearly not.

Sato (1978) recognized an emphatic function of *go* in modern HCE, and these anomalous cases probably mark its introduction in the data. Evidence in support of the emphatic analysis of *go* is furnished by Smith (1939: 184):

> [*Go*] might be considered simply as a redundancy or as an auxiliary. It is most frequently used to express future time....It seems to be used sometimes for emphasis and occurs with the present when any other tense form might be correct.

As an example, Smith (1939: 281) gave the sentence *Fred go bite my nose* and indicated "Fred did bite my nose" as a possible translation, with *go* expressing emphasis.

The origin of the emphatic use is obscure but it may lie in the irrealis. In Phase III verbs expressing unrealized events prior to the time of utterance were accompanied by *go*, cf. (61). Such events were clearly nonfactual. But if the *go*-marked action or event was later than speech time, it was prospective and may either remain irrealis (as in unfulfilled promises) or eventually become realis. The use of *go* may have varied according to the degree of commitment the speaker had in the realization of the event. Therefore in Phase IV *go* may have occurred more often in predicates which expressed actions that were certain to occur, especially if they were to be performed by the speaker as in (68). By Phase V, *go* may have been reanalyzed as an indicator of speaker certainty in the realization of events and thereafter began to occur in the past contexts observed by Kaapu, Coale, and Smith.

The increasing multifunctionality of *go* likely promoted the development and usage of unambiguous forms which solely marked futurity or irrealis. The variant *gon*, which never indicated the imperative, habitual, or emphasis in the corpus, emerged as the dominant irrealis auxiliary in FP texts:

(80)  By'm by da baby goin' wake up and my modda goin' make me carry 'im. (1936; 10–year-old Chinese girl)[66]

(81)  I no gon give you candy. (1937; 3–year-old Filipino girl)[67]

(82)  I going give Johnny one dirty black eye. (1937; 6–year-old Portuguese/Hawaiian boy)[68]

(83)  Ey, what dame you going take for the dance? (1945; 18–year-old boy at Farrington High School)[69]

(84)  Frank Seenatra no can do dat — Eef he pull hees eyebrows out, no goin' get nuttin' on hees face an' he goin' look like one *obake* [ghost]. (1948; Japanese teenaged boy)[70]

### 3.3 *The Progressive/Nonpunctual Marker stei*

### 3.3.1 *1860–1919 (Phases III-IV)*
The progressive auxiliary *stei* is unique to Hawai'i. Reinecke & Tokisama (1934: 122–123) called it "the chief glory of the Hawaiian dialect, the one endemic verbal auxiliary." As in other creoles, the progressive takes the same phonetic form as the locative copula and was probably derived from it. However no cases of locative *stei* have been found for Phase III. *Stop*, a widespread Pacific pidgin feature according to Baker (1993), was attested instead as examples (23) and (59) show. No cases are known of it as a preverbal aspect marker. The first examples of locative *stei* date to Phase IV:

(85)   Sing Ping, Charley, and Kaili and my tailor stay inside. (1904; Chinese store owner, Keana'e, Maui)[71]

(86)   No business stay this place; you go Iwilei. (1913; Chinese brothel-keeper, Honolulu, O'ahu)[72]

Progressive and habitual action was typically indicated in texts from Phases III and IV by verbal repetition and adverbs such as *all time*:

(87)   Marie, he good woman, but talk, talk all time. (1898; Portuguese lighthouse keeper, Nawiliwili, Kaua'i)[73]

(88)   He sit in dining room, and write, write, write, and say all *pau* [finished]. (1902; Japanese maid, Honolulu, O'ahu)[74]

(89)   He all time play, play piano. (1911; Chinese janitor, Honolulu, O'ahu)[75]

### 3.3.2 *1920–1949 (Phase V)*
The first known examples of *stei* in a preverbal position indicating progressive aspect were recorded in 1921:

(90)   This time he stay coming. (1921; attributed to schoolchildren)[76]

(91)   He stay playing. (1921; attributed to schoolchildren)[77]

According to Reinecke & Tokisama (1934: 122–123), there "is in *stay* something of the force of the progressive forms of the verb, and it supplements them or less often used in their place....*Stay* may also express habitual action." When *stei* indicated the progressive there was often aspectual concord on the verb with *-in*. This inflection did not occur when *stei* marked the habitual. The distribution of *stei* in Phase V was restricted to FP speakers:

(92)    He stay go. (1930; common "error" attributed to 9th grade students)[78]

(93)    Us stay sweating like hell. (1934; attributed to schoolchildren)[79]

(94)    He stay swimming. (1937; 6–year-old Portuguese boy, Honolulu, O'ahu)[80]

(95)    I stay finding for him how long but no can see him no place. (1947; schoolboy on the playground, Wailuku, Maui)[81]

(96)    He stay live Kaimuki. (1948; locally-born Japanese college student)[82]

## 3.4   Combinations of Markers

### 3.4.1  1860–1949 (Phases III-V)

All four possible combinations of *bin, go,* and *stei* (with the fixed order of tense preceding modality and modality preceding aspect) occurred in FP texts no earlier than Phase V. No cases are known to exist in non-FP texts. There was also completive *pau* which could combine with either *bin/wen* or *go/gon* but not *stei* (see § 3.5). The counterfactuals (anterior + irrealis and anterior + irrealis + nonpunctual) are problematic, so the straightforward past and future progressives (anterior + nonpunctual and irrealis + nonpunctual) will be discussed first.

As (95) shows, the past marking of progressives was optional. Because of its relatively low frequency, *bin stei* may have existed longer than its first attestation date might suggest. However it is unlikely that examples would be discovered prior to 1921, the date *stei* entered into the data. Richmond (1930: 9–10) was the first to mention "been stay" as a feature of native-born children, though it is unclear out of context whether *stei* was copular or aspect-marking. The first unambiguous examples were furnished by Ferreiro (1937: 9–10, 63), who claimed that "the words *been stay* are misused for the verbs *was* and *were*." Examples:

(97)    They been stay walk feet. (1937; attributed to schoolchildren, glossed as "They were walking")

(98)    He been stay teasing me. (1937; attributed to schoolchildren)

Coale (1938: 40) provided another example:

(99)    George been stay go play. (1938; attributed to schoolchildren, glossed as "George went to play")

The rough translation for (99) implies that the act of going (expressed by *been stay go*) was completed by the time of utterance, a restriction which Reinecke & Tokisama (1934: 122–123) noted: "When *stay* is used with *been* there is some-times a suggestion that the action is definitely concluded." This sense of completion was probably obtained when the *bin stei*-marked verb preceded a verb indicating a later event, as in (99) where the act of going would have ended before playing began.

In the Hukilepo Joe corpus, the *bin stei* combination could express either progressive or habitual action:

(100)  Dem two guys been stay watch us eat from start to feeneesh. (1946; middle-aged Hawaiian homesteader, Hilo, Hawai'i)[83]

(101)  Da reason us two newa meet was because wen me I been stay come, you been stay go. (1946; middle-aged Hawaiian homesteader, Hilo, Hawai'i)[84]

In the mesolect *waz* took the place of *bin stei* for the progressive (the *-in* concord on the verb was usually retained), and *yuwsta* was used for the habitual:

(102)  One time, you know, he was going Lihue an' he pass by, you know, and he see him come out by da mango tree. (1920; teenaged boy at Malumalu Industrial School, Koloa, Kaua'i)[85]

(103)  Ey, Peter, you wen' see my gang w'en you was coming by da road? (1937; neighborhood boy in Palama, O'ahu)[86]

(104)  Eh, Masa, who da signorita was who used to bring you ta-ma-g every morning in Leghorn? (1947; Japanese combat veteran of the 442nd Regiment, Honolulu, O'ahu)[87]

*Go stei*, or more often *gon stei*, indicated the future or irrealis progressive, as these examples demonstrate:

(105)  They going stay play the game tomorrow. (1937; attributed to schoolchildren)[88]

(106)  We going stay ahgue unteel da road gud fo nuttin. (1946; middle-aged Hawaiian homesteader, Hilo, Hawai'i)[89]

The remaining combinations *bin go* and *bin go stay*, according to (10) and (13), indicated unrealized conditions in the past such as past conditionals. Actually this use was marginal. In Phases III and IV past conditionals were often unmarked by TMA auxiliaries:

(107)  He was very much flight one Chinaman kill him if he no give pipe back. (1888; Chinese house servant, Kilauea, Kaua'i)[90]

(108)  If we stay in Manila, we make money last month. (1910; Filipino plantation laborers, Honolulu, O'ahu)[91]

As illustrated by (61), verbs expressing unrealized past actions and events were occasionally accompanied by *go*. In Phase V *bin* began to precede *go* in such cases:

(109)   This time election me hear he go *kokua* [help] some men who been
        go make this kind law. (1936; locally-born Japanese, Honolulu, O'ahu)[92]

*Go* in this example was irrealis before both *kokua* (the election had not yet
occurred) and *make* (the candidates were not yet in office); at the same time the
verb *make* was clearly past from context (the law was already in existence). The
writer's friend, who was suffering under a recently-passed tax law, was going to
vote for some candidates who would have themselves passed such a law. But
most cases of *bin/wen go* from Phase V were realis:

(110)   He been ketch da broom steek and us two been go try keel da rat.
        (1947; middle-aged Hawaiian homesteader, Hilo, Hawai'i)[93]

(111)   Ey, who wen go take off the behind license plate? The copper stop
        me, boy. (1949; Japanese college student, Honolulu, O'ahu)[94]

(112)   He da one wen go knife Mickey las' week. (1949; 18–year-old part-
        Hawaiian, Kalihi, O'ahu)[95]

Similarly Labov (1990: 29) noted that in modern HCE "*wen go* can imply a more
deliberate action ... [b]ut any difference in meaning is a subtle one, a matter of
implication rather than meaning, and there is no clear case of a *wen go* construction which could not also be *wen*."

Moreover all known attestations of *bin go stei* apart from (13a) are realis.
As noted in § 2.0, Tsuzaki (1971: 332–333) translated *I no been go stay eat* as "I
wasn't/hadn't been eating." Reinecke (1969: 214) provided the first attestation of
this combination in a story from 1933, and in context it refers to a prior event:

(113)   What for you been go stay tell that? (1933; written by a Portuguese
        girl, Honoka'a, Hawai'i)

Reinecke & Tokisama (1934: 123) supplied another example:

(114)   Us been go stay go. (1934; attributed to schoolchildren)

Although their gloss *We've gone and come back already* is unusual and probably
erroneous (the second half may have been only implicated by the sentence), it
suggests that the verb was realis and referred to a particular event in the past.

The evidence presented in § 3.2 shows that three kinds of *go* may precede
verbs with past reference: irrealis (cf. 61), habitual (cf. 79), and emphatic. *Bin go*
and *bin go stei* may therefore accompany verbs referring to events which would
have occurred, events which habitually occurred in the past, or past events which
definitely occurred. Examples 110–114 may thus attest combinations with
emphatic *go*, not the irrealis marker. The potential for ambiguity was avoided by

marking past conditionals with *waz*, the substitute for *bin stei*, in combination with *gon*, the unambiguous irrealis marker:

(115)  If you been tell me stop more quick, I no was goin' hit 'em. (1946; locally-born Japanese teenager, Kaimuki, O'ahu)[96]

### 3.4.2 *1950- (Phase VI)*
As *wen* displaced *bin* as anterior/past marker, the combination *wen stei* began to appear in the data in Phase VI:

(116)  We wen stay wait by da tree how long? (1952; 16–year-old leader of a youth gang, town near Hilo, Hawai'i)[97]

(117)  Wat da udda song you wen stay teach me last time? (1952; another 16–year-old Japanese, town near Hilo, Hawai'i)[98]

The same source furnished the first cases of *wud(a)* in past conditionals, one of which co-occurred with *go*:

(118)  If not for him, me I no would go practice the udder year. (1952; 16–year-old Japanese, town near Hilo, Hawai'i)[99]

## 3.5  *The Completive Marker* **pau**

### 3.5.1 *1860–1919 (Phases III-IV)*
In the Atlantic creoles, completive *don* is the most common extension to the core TMA system described in Bakker, Post, & van der Voort (1995) and it combines with anterior and irrealis auxiliaries. The HCE completive marker *pau* patterns similarly. However *don* itself is absent in pidgin/creole texts from Hawai'i. The Hawaiian stative verb *pau* "finished, over" is the lexical source of completive *pau* and it may have grammaticalized as an auxiliary in the late 1800s in Pidgin Hawaiian, the competing Hawaiian-lexifier pidgin (Roberts 1998).

Preverbal cases of *pau* were not common in Phases III and IV. In data for both FP and non-FP groups, 47 sentences contained *pau*. Of these 43 (91.5%) were lexical. Only 4 (8.5%) were preverbal and possibly completive:

(119)  Medicine no good; *ae* [yes] *kahuna* [priest] *pau* pray, I die. (1896; Hawaiian patient, Honolulu, Hawai'i)[100]

(120)  Kaili count too; that time I *pau* count he count. (1904; Chinese vendor, Keana'e, Maui)[101]

(121)  Me think this time you *pau huhu* [being angry with] my friend John Wise. (1915; purported Hawaiian writer, Honolulu, O'ahu)[102]

(122)   *Pau* hunt with Mister Al. (1919; middle-aged Hawaiian, Honolulu, O'ahu)[103]

### 3.5.2 *1920–1949 (Phase V)*

In addition to adverbials such as *already* and *yet*, preverbal *pau* became an increasingly common means of marking the completive in FP texts during Phase V. In a number of cases, it began to combine with *bin* and *gon*:

(123)   Me I been *pau* bury all da tripe insi ma *opu* [belly]. (1946; middle-aged Hawaiian homesteader, Hilo, Hawai'i)[104]

(124)   Lilly mo all da beeg steamas goin *pau* feex up. (1946; middle-aged Hawaiian homesteader, Hilo, Hawai'i; possible translation: "Almost all the big steamers will have been repaired by then")[105]

## 4.   Conclusion

The data presented in the previous section lend very little support to the model of diffusion advanced by Holm (1986). Of the various auxiliaries comprising the TMA system of Hawaiian Creole, only one is fairly certain to have had an exogenous origin: *bin*. It was first attested early, in Phase III, and is unlikely to have been innovated independently (McWhorter 1995). Irrealis *go* also first appeared in Phase III, but its lexical etymon is highly vulnerable to reanalysis and considerable evidence indicates that it grammaticalized locally and underwent further development in Phases IV and V. The other two auxiliaries, *stei* and *pau*, are found only in Hawai'i and cannot be traced directly to their Atlantic creole counterparts, progressive *de* or *da* and completive *don*. Neither of these, as well as present habitual *doz*, occur in the Hawai'i data. *Stei* and *pau* therefore developed locally. Baker's model can easily accommodate the transmission of *bin* but Holm's model must account for the absence of *de/da* and *don* in Hawai'i, as well as explain where *stei* and *pau* came from.

Another problem for Holm's model is the late appearance of *stei* and the marker combinations. The selection of *stei* instead of *stop* as the progressive marker points to a late innovation. The combinations reflect the existence of an integrated system but these do not occur in the data until Phase V.

Further evidence against a strong diffusionist stance is furnished by the FP sample. While early auxiliaries such as *bin*, *go*, and *pau* were shared by FP and non-FP speakers, features first attested in Phase V (*wen, stei, bin stei, gon stei, bin go, bin go stei, bin pau, gon pau*) were restricted to the FP. Even *bin*, the mostly likely exogenous feature, was far more common in the language of FP speakers. These findings suggest that the integrated system was a native-born innovation, though it built on the developments of earlier non-native speakers.

The Hawaiian Creole TMA system, influenced slightly perhaps by the diffusion of *bin*, is largely a local development. As such, it is unrelated to West African languages and the parallels noted by Tsuzaki and Holm require alternative explanations.

## Acknowledgments

An earlier version of this paper was presented at the Society for Pidgin & Creole Linguistics Annual Meeting, San Diego, California, on 5 January 1996. Research was funded in part by NSF grant SBR94–06763. John Rickford, John McWhorter, Elizabeth Traugott and several others helped improve this paper with their valuable comments, but any remaining errors are the author's sole responsibility.

## Notes

1. *Hawaii Tribune Herald*, 28 September 1946, p. 8; 17 August 1946, p. 6; 15 December 1945, p. 6; 18 January 1947, p. 6; 16 March 1946, p. 6.

2. Testimony of Assin, 1CR-15, 14 January 1856, p. 13. Court record references include the circuit number (1, O'ahu; 2, Maui; 3, western Hawai'i; 4, eastern Hawai'i; 5, Kaua'i), case type (CR, criminal), and case number, along with the date and page numbers of the testimony.

3. Letter from William Hooper to Ladd & Co., Koloa, 12 May 1838, p. 28. University of Hawai'i Archives.

4. Testimony of Assin, 1CR-15, 14 January 1856, pp. 14–15.

5. Testimony of W. C. Clarke, 1CR-87, 8 April 1856, p. 2.

6. *Nupepa Ku'oko'a*, 3 April 1867, p. 5.

7. *Pacific Commercial Advertiser*, 26 February 1870, p. 3.

8. *PCA*, 4 February 1882, p. 3.

9. Testimony of Manuel Manoiki, 5CR-1122, 17 April 1890, p. 3.

10. Testimony of Manuela Costa, 1CR-2631, 14 April 1899, p. 10.

11. *Paradise of the Pacific*, December 1899, p. 185.

12. *Oahuan*, March 1904, p. 1.

13. Helen W. McKay, *When I Was Two and Twenty* [manuscript], p. 20. Hawaii State Archives.

14. Testimony of Poipu, 1CR-2640, 11 July 1899, p. 2.

15. Testimony of Su Lam, 4CR-4, old series, 1 October 1900, pp. 86–87.

16. Testimony of Miguel Paresa, 2CR-A2546, 7 April 1904, p. 3.

17. *PCA*, 4 December 1910, p. 1.

18. *Oahuan*, December 1912, p. 12.

19. *PCA*, 31 August 1913, p. 4.

20. *Hawaii Educational Review*, February 1914, pp. 6–7.

21. *Oahuan*, March 1914, p. 11.

22. *Oahuan*, June 1914, p. 78.

23. *Oahuan*, March 1915, p. 12.

24. Testimony of Sholderbrook, 4CR-659, 20 March 1916, p. 2.

25. Testimony of Okichi, 2CR-869, 2 May 1916, p. 5.

26. *PCA*, 23 May 1917, p. 2.

27. *The Garden Island*, 5 December 1922, p. 2.

28. *POTP*, December 1926, p. 65.

29. *Voice of Labor*, 16 September 1936, p. 1.

30. Testimony of Asano Shimazu, 2CR-1022, 25 November 1920, pp. 16–17.

31. *HER*, September 1921, pp. 13–14.

32. *POTP*, March 1925, p. 23.

33. Reinecke 1969: 215.

34. Reinecke & Tokisama 1934: 122–123.

35. Ferreiro 1937: 7–8.

36. Chun 1936: 5.

37. Kwon 1937: 3.

38. Smith 1939: 282.

39. Coale 1946: 471.

40. Suyeoka 1948: 9.

41. *PCA*, 4 February 1882, p. 3.

42. Testimony of Jacinthe de Costa, 1CR-1473, 22 August 1890, p. 10.

43. Testimony of Robert Hutchins, 1CR-2631, 19 April 1899, p. 3.

44. *Ka Leo o ka Lahui*, 4 June 1891, p. 4.

45. *KLOKL*, 4 June 1891, p. 4.

46. *KLOKL*, 2 June 1891, p. 4.

47. Visger 1881: 107.

48. Testimony of J. R. Gasper, 1CR-1473, 19 August 1890, pp. 23–24.

49. Statement of Quock Yin, 2CR-A283, 3 February 1896, p. 8.

50. Deposition of Mrs. Ben Brown, 4CR-874, 8 May 1898, p. 2.

51. Testimony of Ah Lo, 2CR-A1224, 21 October 1904, pp. 26–33.

52. Testimony of Sholderbrook, 4CR-659, 20 March 1916, p. 2.

53. *Overland Monthly*, January 1900, p. 10.

54. *PCA*, 28 July 1912, p. 4.

55. Kaufman 1908: 265.

56. *Oahuan*, April 1910, p. 11.

57. *Oahuan*, June 1919, p. 32.

58. Testimony of Christina Peter, 2CR-710, 7 April 1913, p. 5.

59. *POTP*, July 1926, p. 30.

60. *POTP*, December 1924, pp. 69–70.

61. Ferreiro 1937: 63.

62. Coale & Smith 1937: 276.

63. Kaapu 1937: 80.

64. Smith 1939: 281.

65. Reinecke & Tokisama 1934: 122–123.

66. Chun 1936: 3.

67. Coale & Smith 1937: 275.

68. Kaapu 1937: 80.

69. Lum 1945: 1.

70. *Hawaiian Digest*, April 1948, p. 48.

71. Testimony of Ah Lo, 2CR-A1224, 21 October 1904, p. 27.

72. Testimony of Wong Wo, 1CR-5372, 21 January 1913, p. 5.

73. de la Vergne 1898: 106.

74. *Hawaiian Gazette*, 24 January 1902, p. 5.

75. *Oahuan*, June 1911, pp. 50–51.

76. *HER*, September 1921, pp. 9–10.

77. *HER,* September 1921, pp. 9–10.

78. Richmond 1930: 10.

79. Reinecke & Tokisama 1934: 122–123.

80. Coale & Smith 1937: 276.

81. *Hawaiian Digest*, July 1947, p. 14.

82. Suyeoka 1948: 4.

83. *HTH*, 16 November 1946, p. 6.

84. *HTH*, 13 November 1946, p. 6.

85. Dora Broadbent, *The Graveyard Ghost* [manuscript], paper read before the Kaua'i Historical Society on 26 July 1920, pp. 1–3. Kaua'i Historical Society Archives.

86. Kwon 1937: 3.

87. Toishigawa 1947: 5.

88. Ferreiro 1937: 58.

89. *HTH*, 28 June 1946, p. 8.

90. Grant 1888: 62–64.

91. *PCA*, 1 January 1910, p. 2.

92. *VOL,* 7 October 1936, p. 1.

93. *HTH,* 16 March 1947, p. 4.

94. Suyeoka 1949: 8.

95. Chun 1949: 4.

96. *POTP,* November 1946, p. 25.

97. Ikeda 1952: 5.

98. Ikeda 1952: 4.

99. Ikeda 1952: 10.

100. Richard H. Potts, "Hawaii Nei," *Harper's Weekly,* ca. September 1896. Offprint in Dukum Collection, Vol. 2, M218b, Hawai'i State Archives.

101. Testimony of Ah Lo, 2CR-A1224, 21 October 1904, p. 27–30.

102. *PCA,* 22 September 1915, p. 6.

103. *Oahuan,* June 1919, p. 30.

104. *HTH,* 30 March 1946, p. 6.

105. *HTH,* 9 March 1946, p. 6.

# References

Baker, Philip. 1993. "Australian influence on Melanesian Pidgin English," *Te Reo* 36:3–37.

Bakker, Peter, Marike Post, & Hein van der Voort. 1995. "TMA particles and auxiliaries." In Jacques Arends, Pieter Muysken, & Norval Smith (eds.), *Pidgins and Creoles: An Introduction.* Amsterdam & Philadelphia: John Benjamins, 247–58.

Bickerton, Derek. 1977. *Change and variation in Hawaiian English, vol. 2: Creole syntax.* University of Hawai'i: Social Science & Linguistics Institute.

Chun, Wai Chee. 1936. "For you a lei." *College plays,* vol. 1. Honolulu: English Department, University of Hawai'i.

Chun, Henry. 1949. "Kindness to cobras." *College plays,* vol. 5. Honolulu: English Department, University of Hawai'i.

Clark, Ross. 1979. "In search of Beach-la-Mar." *Te Reo* 22:3–64.

Coale, Willis B. 1938. Problem elements in English usage among pupils of grades one to nine in the public schools of Hawaii. Manuscript, April 1938. Hamilton Library, University of Hawai'i.

————. 1946. A sequence of learnings in English usage for grades 1 to 12 in Hawaii. In *Handbook for elementary teachers of the public schools of Hawaii (Part III: English and mathematics).* Honolulu: Territory of Hawaii Department of Public Instruction.

Coale, Willis B., and Madorah E. Smith. 1937. *Successful Practices in the Teaching of English to Bilingual Children in Hawaii.* Washington, D.C.: U.S. Government Printing Office.

Dillard, J.L. 1995. Letter to the Editor [28 July 1994], *Journal of Pidgin and Creole Linguistics* 10:219–20.

Ferreiro, John A. 1937. *Everyday English for Hawaii's Children; Activity Work Book.* Wailuku: Maui Publishing Co.

Goodman, Morris. 1985. Review of Bickerton 1981. *International Journal of American Linguistics* 51:109–37.

Grant, Minnie F. 1888. *Scenes in Hawaii; or, Life in the Sandwich Islands.* Toronto: Hart & Co.

Hancock, Ian. 1987. "A preliminary classification of the Anglophone Atlantic creoles, with syntactic data from thirty-three representative dialects." In Glenn G. Gilbert (ed.), *Pidgin and Creole Languages. Essays in Memory of John E. Reinecke.* Honolulu: University of Hawai'i Press, 264–334.

Holm, John. 1986. "Substrate diffusion." In Pieter Muysken and Norval Smith (eds.), *Substrata versus Universals in Creole Genesis.* Amsterdam & Philadelphia: John Benjamins., 259–78.

———. 1988. *Pidgins and creoles. Vol. I.* Cambridge: University Press.

———. 1989. *Pidgins and creoles. Vol. II.* Cambridge: University Press.

———. 1992. "Atlantic meets Pacific: Lexicon common to the English-based pidgins and creoles." *Language Sciences* 14:185–96.

Ikeda, Miyoshi. 1952. "Lest we forget." *College Plays,* vol. 7. Honolulu: English Department, University of Hawai'i.

Kaapu, Myrtle K. 1937. *A study of the Influence of Japanese Syntax and Idiom upon the Spoken and Written English of a Group of Ninth Grade Pupils.* M. A. thesis, University of Hawai'i.

Kaufman, Jessie. 1908. *A Jewel of the Seas.* Philadelphia: J.B. Lippincott.

Keesing, Roger. 1988. *Melanesian Pidgin and the Oceanic Substrate.* Stanford: University Press.

Kwon, Margaret C. 1937. "Mama's boy." *College Plays,* vol. 1. Honolulu: English Department, University of Hawai'i.

Labov, William. 1990. "On the adequacy of natural languages: I. The development of tense." In John Singler (ed.), *Pidgin and Creole Tense-Mood-Aspect Systems.* Amsterdam & Philadelphia: John Benjamins, 1–58.

Lum, Robert. 1945. "Conversation." In *Copies of correspondence Received by John E. Reinecke while Gathering Information for his Thesis, Language and Dialect in Hawaii.* Volume of photocopies, University of Hawaii.

Masuda, Hirokuni. 1995. *Verse Analysis and its Theoretical Contribution to the Study of the Genesis of Hawai'i Creole English.* Ph.D. dissertation, University of Hawai'i.

McMahon, Patrick. 1909. *From Fair Hawaiiland.* Honolulu: Mercantile Printing.

McWhorter, John. 1995. "Sisters under the skin: A case for genetic relationship between the Atlantic English-based creoles." *JPCL* 10:289–333.

Reinecke, John E. 1969. *Language and Dialect in Hawaii: A Sociolinguistic History to 1935.* Honolulu: University of Hawai'i Press.

Reinecke, John E. and Aiko Tokisama. 1934. "The English dialect of Hawaii." *American Speech* 9:122–31.

Richmond, Ethal B. 1930. *Oral English Errors of Ninth Grade Students in the Public Schools of Hawaii.* M. A. thesis, University of Hawai'i.

Roberts, Sarah Julianne. 1998. "The role of diffusion in the genesis of Hawaiian Creole." *Language* 74:1–39.

Sato, Charlene. 1978. *Variation in Hawaiian Pidgin and Creole English: Go + Verb Constructions.* M. A. thesis, University of Hawai'i.

Smith, Madorah E. 1939. "Some light on the problem of bilingualism as found from a study of the progress in the mastery of English among preschool children of non-American ancestry in Hawaii." *Genetic Psychology Monographs* 21:119–284.

Suyeoka, Robert. 1948. "School days." *College Plays,* vol. 4. Honolulu: English Department, University of Hawai'i.

Taylor, Douglas. 1956. "Language contacts in the West Indies." *Word* 13:399–414.

————. 1961. "New languages for old in the West Indies." *Comparative Studies in Society and History* 3:277–88.

Thompson, R. W. 1961. "A note on some possible affinities between the creole dialects of the Old World and those of the New." In Robert Le Page, (ed.), *Creole Language Studies 2.* London: MacMillan, 107–13.

Toishigawa, Bessie. 1947. "Reunion." *College plays,* vol. 2. Honolulu: English Department, University of Hawai'i.

Tsuzaki, Stanley. 1971. "Coexistent systems in language variation; the case of Hawaiian English." In Dell Hymes (ed.), *Pidginization and Creolization of Languages.* Cambridge: University Press, 327–39.

de la Vergne, George H. 1898. *Hawaiian sketches.* San Francisco: H. S. Crocker.

Visger, Jean A. 1881. *Our Honolulu Boys; a Story of Child Life in the Sandwich Islands.* London: Religious Tract Society.

Voorhoeve, Jan. 1957. "The verbal system of Sranan." *Lingua* 6:374–96.

# Language Contact in the Early Colonial Pacific

## Evidence for a Maritime Polynesian Jargon or Pidgin

Emanuel J. Drechsel

*University of Hawai'i at Mānoa*

## Introduction

Until recently, non-European contact languages have received little attention from either creolists or non-Indo-Europeanist linguists. Conventional theories of language contact have afforded no more than an incidental role to non-European languages in the development of modern pidgins and creoles, as suggested by the predominance of European-based case studies of the Caribbean and the Pacific — archetypal, even "classic" areas in the study of pidgins and creoles. Much less have creolists considered non-European contact media as possible vanguards that could have provided the initial linguistic infrastructure (including original vocabulary, a basic grammar, and a majority of speakers) for European-based pidgins and creoles, related to non-European "ancestral" forms by "relexification" and other processes of linguistic change. Many creolists have presented indigenous peoples as more or less submissive recipients of European ways of speaking, who do not play a significant role in their models of language contact or social histories. It then comes as no surprise when Muysken (1994: 104), reviewing the topics covered by the *Journal of Pidgin and Creole Languages* during its first seven years of publication, could only observe dryly: "Not a whole lot on non-European-based Pidgins and Creoles [sic], while many of the possible advances in our field will need to come from that area."

Linguistic evidence exists for contact between Hawaiians and native peoples of northwestern North America for early colonial times, but ironically not in the form of some European-based pidgin; instead, it consists of Hawaiian loanwords in Eskimo Jargon and Chinook Jargon (Drechsel and Makuakāne 1982, 1996 MS). Indications for a central role by indigenous peoples in the development of European pidgins and creoles as well as for the existence of non-European contact languages have been steadily accumulating, recently also for the Pacific. Clark (1977: 3, 5, 28, 30–8, 54; 1979: 24–40) has recognized incidental Hawaiian and other Polynesian influences in his historical surveys of South Seas Jargon, the predecessor of Beach-la-Mar or Sandalwood English. Day (1987) already argued for a Hawaiian maritime pidgin with Hawaiian as major source, and Bickerton and Wilson (1987) have sketched a pidginized Hawaiian or *'ōlelo pa'i 'ai*, literally 'pounded but undiluted taro speech' or 'hard-taro speech.' From a broadly defined comparative perspective, Keesing (1988) has also argued for a distinct Eastern Oceanic Austronesian substrate pattern in Melanesian Pidgin. Suggestions have further appeared for the existence of particular non-European pidgins in the Pacific such as Pidgin Maori in New Zealand, in use together with Pidgin English (Clark 1990), and Pidgin Fijian next to Pidgin Hindustani on Fiji (Siegel 1987). Most significantly, recent archival research, drawing on a variety of historical documents including court records, has established the existence of Pidgin Hawaiian, in use in the Hawaiian Islands after the Europeans' arrival until about the turn of the 20th century (Roberts 1995a, b).

Attestations for the wide use of Polynesian words beyond the boundaries of Polynesian languages as well as evidence for Hawaiian Pidgin and similar indigenous contact media in the Pacific have raised the question of whether some form of Hawaiian extended beyond the shores of the Hawaiian Islands as perhaps among multilingual ship crews or in contact between traders and other native peoples. Conversely, it is appropriate to ask whether early attestations of Pidgin English in the Pacific (as elsewhere) present a skewed sociolinguistic picture with an overemphasis on what English speakers interpreted and uttered rather than an actual record of what native peoples spoke in contact with Europeans or Americans. In other words, have we overestimated the extent and significance of Pidgin English not only in Hawai'i, but in the Pacific at large when, in the early colonial period, indigenous contact media still existed next to European-based ones and the lines between colonial powers and indigenous peoples were not as clearly drawn as yet?

The question of a hypercorrected interpretation of Anglophone and Anglophile historical documentation in terms of Pidgin *English* cannot be resolved by simply comparing early attestations with modern recordings. Such an approach can do no more than confirm with reasonable certainty that such a European-based variety existed in early colonial times; it still leaves us in the dark about the possibility of other, coexistent varieties, especially non-European ones. That over time native peoples indeed adopted European-based pidgins and creoles is not at issue, but only confirms the end result, the success of European-American colonialism. This observation tells us little or nothing about earlier sociolinguistic situations, and should caution against any projections from current circumstances into past ones. A different picture emerges from a careful reexamination of historical records in a broad perspective, including documentation written in languages other than English with fewer prejudices in favor of that language, pidginized or not, and by observers with greater tolerance towards native peoples (such as "transculturated" beachcombers in the Pacific) than most colonists. Even more insightful should prove accounts by Hawaiians, other Polynesians, and Asians in their own languages.

## 1.    The Philology and Ethnohistory of Language Contact in the Pacific

The following pages examine the use of Hawaiian and any other closely related Polynesian language in interlingual contexts of the greater Pacific, and focus on the period from the first contacts with Europeans through the middle of the 19th century, characterized by European and American explorations, whaling and sealing, and the trade of sandalwood and trepang (*bêche de mer* or sea slug) among other items. Considerable attention has gone to extra-Polynesian Oceania, in particular favorite venues of whalers, traders, and beachcombers such as Pohnpei and Kosrae in the Carolines, the Gilbert Islands, and Rotuma (see Keesing 1988: 15). In taking this approach, I have followed the fundamental assumptions that evidence for a Hawaiian- or Polynesian-based contact medium would be easier to identify for the period of early European-American explorations than later and outside of Polynesia than within.

Research has drawn information from a careful scanning of diverse early documents on how Europeans and their American descendants communicated with native peoples of the Pacific. My selection of sources has been fairly fortuitous beyond a reasonable expectation that they contain relevant information, and I make no claim to offering an exhaustive review. In the course, I have examined some fifty major documents of diverse kinds: accounts of explorations, government reports, travelogues, diaries, and fiction deemed to be historically quite accurate (such as the semi-autobiographical works of Richard H. Dana, Jr. and Herman Melville's). I have also skimmed through any sections whose subject matter extended beyond the Pacific or the mid-19th century. Such a broader range is justified in light of the fact that numerous Hawaiians and other Polynesians enthusiastically traveled all over the globe in the 19th century, following their own sea-faring traditions, and sometimes settled in America and Europe (see e.g. Dana 1911 [1840], Koppel 1995, and Moore 1977). In addition, I have reviewed numerous items of relevant secondary literature for leads.

My examination of relevant historical documents has not been limited to linguistic attestations (words, phrases, etc.), but has also applied to incidental sociolinguistic observations as to who spoke what, when, where, and how in a broadly conceived philological-ethnohistorical approach. Special attention has gone to:

i.     attestations of phrases and sentences with semantactic patterns distinctive from those of vernacular Polynesian languages;
ii.    references to indigenous languages serving as *lingue franche*;
iii.   comments on language contact, in particular between Polynesians and alloglossic Pacific Islanders, Asians, Europeans, or Americans;
iv.    observations on the linguistic and ethnic compositions of ship crews; and
v.     mentionings of Hawaiian and other Pacific visitors, crew members, or passengers on board European and American ships.

In the course, I have inadvertently extracted attestations of the use of European languages, including Pidgin English, if for no other than contrastive reasons.

Finding relevant information for the period of explorations through the mid-19th century has at times equaled a search for a needle in a haystack, a conclusion that is as much, if not more true for recordings of European samples. Although suggestive in many instances, the examined data are sufficient in both quality and quantity to offer an alternative perspective of how Hawaiians and other Polynesians interacted with alloglossic neighbors, European and American colonists, or other newcomers to Oceania. The available information also raises some new questions.

## 2.     Early Attestations of Language Contact in the Pacific

What follows is a review of relevant documentation, presented in a roughly chronological order. One of the early sources to provide relevant information is the Marquesan journal of Englishman Edward Robarts (1974) during the years 1797 to 1824. A beachcomber who married a native Marquesan woman, Robarts (1974: 124) observed that hearing English in the Marquesas around the century's turn was rare. When encountering a Russian ship under the command of Captain Adam Johann von Krusenstern in May 1804, Robarts (1974: 130) heard French, Dutch, Russian, German, and Swedish among its multilingual crew members. In piloting the ship to anchor and assuming the steering wheel, Robarts insisted that the captain would have to trim the sails because he was afraid of misunderstandings among the ship's officers with their insufficient knowledge of English: "They could speak but a word here and there of english, and my broken french, Dutch & Rush made a patcht up conversation" (Robarts 1974: 130, 137). Only the captain was capable of answering in "tolerable good English."

In interaction with native Marquesans, Europeans relied on translation at the time, as was the case when Robarts (1974: 46–7) made his initial encounters. His first interpreter was a native Hawaiian by the name of Sam, Tama, or — reinterpreted — Tom, who spoke a little broken English as one among few. He had served on an American ship sailing between Boston, the Juan Fernandez Islands off Chile, and China as part of the fur trade, and had reportedly jumped ship at Tahuata, attracted by the beauty of its women. The Marquesans showed great interest in Tama's ability to throw stones and spears better and farther than they could and in his story telling; but they were not particularly impressed by what Europeans had to offer (Dening in Robarts 1974: 47 [fn.4]). Some Europeans (including a missionary by the name of William Pascoe Crook of the London Missionary Society, another Englishman by the name of Walker, and Robarts' consort, a gunner) "could not get hold of the language" (Robarts 1994: 100, 113, 150). Robarts, however, recognized the need to learn Marquesan, and after almost two years acquired sufficient fluency in it to hold a conversation with his native neighbors (Robarts 1974: 68, 70, 86, 282). As evidence of his linguistic skills, he offered a vocabulary of some 1400 entries, supplemented by approximately 30 fairly complex constructions (Robarts 1974: 284–321), in need of careful evaluation by an expert on Marquesan.

Another beachcomber by the name of Jean Cabri, Cadiche, or even Joseph Kabrit, a native Frenchman, apparently spoke Marquesan better than Robarts, whose grasp of Marquesan language and culture remained limited (Dening in Robarts 1974: 5, 7, 8, 19). In one instance, Robarts confused *tomohine* 'daughter' with *tomoa*, the cry of encouragement given by women to warriors in battle (Dening in Robarts 1974: 81 [fn.18]). Nonetheless, Robarts (1974: 141–2) appears to have been sufficiently skilled to serve as unintentional interpreter when in 1805 he overheard on-board Marquesans whisper about a plot to rob the ship and he reported them to its captain. On other occasions, he conversed with a woman from Ua Pou (Marquesas Islands), Tahitians, and apparently Maori in spite of some linguistic differences that he recognized (Robarts 1974: 163, 181, 189). However, he could not understand Fijian, a language related to Proto-Polynesian, and suspected those words similar to Marquesan to have different meanings; he also rejected the claim of Bruce, an Englishman living among the Maori, to be able to converse with Fijians in broken Maori (Robarts 1974: 190–1).

Counter to Robarts, a contemporary and an American captain by the name of Edmund Fanning maintained that Crook was fluent in Marquesan, which qualified him as interpreter (Fanning 1924: 90, 99, 101). The missionary could also carry on an easy conversation with people of "the southernmost island of the Washington group" (Line Islands) with their nearly identical language; "they appeared to be greatly surprised, as well as pleased, to hear Mr. Crook speaking in their language, and were very anxious to find out where he had 'catched it,' — to make use of their own expression" (Fanning 1924: 100, 101). The captain provided no indication that this English phrase was an actual sample of what native Marquesans spoke; rather, it seems to have been a loan translation to provide some stylistic color like other renditions of their speech in English elsewhere in his book (see, e.g., Fanning 1924: 117). However, Fanning (1924: 124, 134, 137, 143) eventually gained enough confidence to write down a few samples of "broken" Marquesan as spoken on Nuku Hiva: *Otee booaugah* 'See the fat hog.' [†*ote puaka* 'catch [the] pig' (?)]; *Motakee! etee Motakee!* 'Good, see, very good/beautiful!' [†*motaki! 'ite motaki!* 'Good! see, good!']. [1] In resolving what appears to be conflicting information about Crook's linguistic skills, one would be inclined to give greater credence to Robarts' account on grounds of its greater richness, his experience as a beachcomber with more opportunities for first-hand observations, and — most importantly — his greater expertise in the language than the captain's. Yet as a trader, Robarts did not always see eye-to-eye with Crook, a missionary, and may have presented him in a negative light for no other reason than to make himself appear more attractive as interpreter. Alternatively, Robarts' and Fanning's disagreeing accounts of Crook's linguistic skills possibly point to different stages in his learning Marquesan, in which Robarts' phrase of "could not get hold of the language" perhaps refers to the learner's initial stage of confusion.

Still other sources of the period offer little else than incidental information about the sociolinguistics of encounters between Pacific Islanders and Europeans or Americans. Amasa Delano (1970 [1817]: 181–2) made a vague reference to multilingual situations on and off board in 1792:

> We had with us persons from so many [Pacific] nations and islands, that we could speak fluently more than twelve languages … We had New Guineans on board, whom we had bought of the savages, who offered them to us, and by whom we could have communication with several other islands.

In Hawaiian waters in 1801, Delano (1970 [1817]: 392–3) had with him several native Hawaiians, three of whom had sneaked on board without his knowledge.

The author offered no information on how he, his passengers, and his crew members interacted among each other.

More revealing are some observations by the French-born poet and naturalist Adelbert von Chamisso, writing in German of his travels between 1815 and 1818 and credited with having published the first extended grammatical description of Hawaiian. Chamisso (n.d.: III.163–4) described in some detail his and apparently the crew's linguistic interactions with Kadu, a native of Ratak in the Marshall Islands. Kadu had first addressed the expedition in a language that differed from Ratak, sounded strange, and was mutually unintelligible with Hawaiian (Chamisso n.d.: IV.102), but he quickly adopted the medium in use on board. Significantly, this observation and example applied not to a Polynesian native, but to a Micronesian.

> Die Sprache setzte sich aus den Dialekten Polynesiens, die Kadu redete, und wenigen europäischen Wörtern und Redensarten zusammen. … und, wie manche fremdartige Redensarten sich in unsere Schiffsprache gemischt hatten, so zählten wir auf spanisch. Da fing Kadu von selber an spanisch zu zählen, sehr richtig und mit guter Aussprache, von eins bis zehn (Chamisso n.d.: III. 163–4).

The naturalist-poet noted further:

> Es hatte sich unter uns, indem diese Sammlungen [of words in Yapese, Woleaian, and Ratakan, i.e. Micronesian languages and a Polynesian one] entstanden [waren], ein Mittel der Verständigung eingestellt, welches sich nach und nach vervollkommnete (Chamisso n.d.: IV.47).

> In unserer abgeschlossenen, wandernden Welt hatte sich aus allen Sprachen, die an Bord oder am Lande gesprochen, aus allen Anekdoten, die erzählt worden, und aus allen geselligen Vorfallenheiten eine Kantsprache ['an argot'] gebildet, welche der Nichteingeweihte schwerlich verstanden hätte (Chamisso n.d.: III.194).[2]

Chamisso (n.d.: III.163–4) provided an exemplary phrase by Kadu: *"Emo Bigar!* 'Kein Bigar!'" [†*'emo Bikar!* (with Hawaiian *'emo* meaning 'waiting, delay; to wait, to delay' and *Bikar* referring to one of the Marshall Islands)]. In addition, he listed a few Hawaiian words and common loanwords (Chamisso n.d.: IV.49), but they give no indication for any fundamental structural difference (such as, e.g., increased reduplication) in comparison with standard Hawaiian, and per se constitute insufficient evidence for demonstrating differences between a Hawaiian-based contact medium and Hawaiian proper.[3] Of greater interest is Chamisso's reference to Hawaiian as "viel kinderhafter" ['much more child-like'] than Tongan; his description would be suspect, did it not include the comparative reference to another Polynesian language:

Wir haben in derselben [i.e. Hawaiian] nur zwei Pronomina entdeckt, *Wau*
[†*wau*] für die erste Person, *Hoe* [†*'oe*] für die zweite, und nur zwei Adverbien
zur Bestimmung der Zeit der Handlung, *Mamure* [†*mamuli*] für die zukünftige,
*Mamoa* [†*mamua*] für die vergangene Zeit. Die fragende oder zweifelnde
Partikel *Paha* [†*paha*], die nachgesetzt wird, ist von häufigem Gebrauch. —
*Nue* [†*nui*] and *Nue Nue* [†*nuinui*] sehr und gross, bilden den Komparativ und
Superlativ. Etliche Partikeln bezeichnen als Präpositionen die Bezeichnungen
der Hauptwörter (Chamisso n.d.: IV.48).

This description of Hawaiian as grammatically "deficient" agrees fully with that
of Pidgin Hawaiian available in other documents. In these instances, Chamisso
evidently characterized basics of Pidgin Hawaiian rather than Hawaiian proper,
as already considered by Schütz (1994: 25–6, 47–9) and confirmed by Roberts
(1995a: 13–4). Significantly, Chamisso (n.d.: III.113–4) had learned the first
elements of "Hawaiian" not from a native Hawaiian, but from a *haole* ('foreign')
passenger of English-Portuguese ancestry on board the *Rurik*, John Elliot de
Castro, once a pearl trader on O'ahu and then a personal physician to Kamehameha. The same kind of Hawaiian-based medium presumably was also in use
on the king's ships, manned by crews consisting half of native Hawaiians and
half of Europeans and sailing as far as Canton (Chamisso n.d.: IV.182). "Viele
O-Waihier verstehen etwas Englisch, keiner aber ist der Sprache vollkommen
mächtig, selbst die nicht, die auf amerikanischen Schiffen gereist sind, wie es
sehr viele gethan [haben]" (Chamisso n.d.: IV.189).

Chamisso eventually conceded a limited knowledge of Hawaiian: "Unsere
Kenntnis der Sprache reichet nicht hin, ihre Poesie zu beurteilen" (Chamisso n.d.:
IV.190). In an appendicized correction, he also came to recognize a third-person
pronoun in Hawaiian: "Oyera" (Chamisso n.d.: IV.227), probably identified best
as equivalent to *'oia* 'he, she, it' and differing from the corresponding form *iaia*
as noted by Roberts (1995a: 7; 1995b: 117) for Pidgin Hawaiian. However
romantic at times, Chamisso's observations were more reliable than the records
by most of his contemporaries. Not only did he show greater understanding of
native Pacific traditions (such as the *hula*) than most contemporary Europeans or
Americans, which accordingly left him with little sympathy for the aspirations of
colonial powers or the missionaries in Hawai'i; but he was a protégé of Wilhelm
von Humboldt, who undoubtedly had imparted to him as much of the linguistic
knowledge as was available in the early 19th century.[4] Ultimately, Chamisso's
greater, if still limited sensitivity to Pacific traditions may explain why many of
his contemporaries with less sympathy and awareness missed recognizing linguistic
differences and, with them, the existence of a Polynesian-based contact medium.

A possible exception is Louis Isidore Duperrey (1826: 66), who noted a

Polynesian "langue vulgaire", with "vulgaire" probably best interpreted as 'common' rather than 'vulgar'. He observed in particular that

> ... une identité palpable de langage règne entre tous ces insulaires épars et semés sur le Grand-Océan, dans les limites que nous assignons aux Océaniens. Ils savent qu'un Taïtien peut être entendu aux îles Marquises, ceux-ci aux Sandwich, et un naturel de ces dernières îles à la Nouvelle-Zélande. ...
>
> Ne sait-on pas, d'ailleurs, qu'une sorte de dialecte, conservée par la classe supérieure, et consacrée aux traditions anciennes, permet aux *arikis* [†*ariki*] de se comprendre entre eux, tandis que le vulgaire en ignore les règles, que les prêtres et les chefs transmettent intactes à leurs enfants. ... les relations journalières des Européens avec ces peuples en altèrent singulièrement la langue vulgaire; et, déjà corrompue, celle-ci, dans quelques années, présentera sans doute un grand nombre des nos dénominations introduites dans les îles, où l'influence des voyageurs d'Europe est permanente. Dans toutes ces contrées, on retrouve les noms communs de *taro* [†*taro*] pain; *tané* [†*tane*], homme; *wahiné* [†*wahine*] ou *fafiné* [†*fafine* < Samoan or Tongan], femme; *motou* [†*motu*], île; *mataou* [†*matau*], hameçon; *maté* [†*mate*], mort, tuer (mort d'origine hébraïque [sic]), et tant d'autres, qu'il serait aussi fastidieux qu'inutile de rappeler ici.

Duperrey thought it superfluous to specify the differences between "la langue vulgaire" and the chiefs' 'dialect' or to provide exemplary sentences that might have clarified them. His short description thus leaves open the question of whether "la langue vulgaire" merely referred to a social dialect or, alternatively, a Polynesian-based contact medium. The latter would be indicated by his reference to ignoring the rules of speech and its "corrupted" nature, just as the French phrase of "la langue vulgaire" has applied to contact media in other French colonies (such as Mobilian Jargon of greater Louisiana).

In 1825, Hiram Paulding, an American naval officer in pursuit of mutineers of the whale ship *Globe*, cited a few words and short phrases on Nuku Hiva in the Marquesas (1970 [1831]: 34, 39, 58): "*Mattee, mattee, Typee!* 'Very bad, very bad, Taipi'" [†*mate, mate, Taipi*! 'Bad/sick, bad/sick, Taipi!'] and "*Coare ta whyhene*? 'Don't you want a wife?'" [†*koali (?) te vehine*? 'Want (?) the woman/wife?']. Another expression that figured significantly, if its number of quotations is any indication, was "motake" 'very good, very well' [†*motaki* 'good'] (Paulding 1970 [1831]: 41, 52, 53, 57, 59, 61] At first, Paulding (1970 [1831]: 34) had great difficulty understanding the people of Nuku Hiva with no one on board who knew the local language, and required interpreters in dealing with Marquesans. Among them were not only two English beachcombers who had jumped ship and could "converse in the language of the natives," but also a

Marquesan and a Tahitian who had served on whalers and had learned some "broken English" (Paulding 1970 [1831]: 47). The Englishmen apparently received a great deal of respect from the Marquesans; on the other hand, an islander by the name of John Luxon

> boasted to me of his superiority over the other Indians [i.e. natives], in speaking English. I asked John, of what advantage his speaking English was to him, to which he replied, that it enabled him to cheat his countrymen (Paulding 1970 [1831]: 70).

Yet an incident with the same John suggests that he had difficulty understanding and speaking English when the conversation turned to a native taboo, a delicate subject matter:

> One day, some one had, designedly or accidentally, thrown some bread in John's hat, which he did not perceive when he took it up, and put it on. When he felt the bread upon his head, he threw his hat off instantly, and, with a look of the utmost horror, exclaimed, "who put dat dare? Me Taboo here!" (putting his hand on his head) "To-morrow me sick, me die!" This, he repeated over a number of times, and with great earnestness of manner tried to find out who had put the bread in his hat, insisting upon it, that, on the morrow, he should sicken and die. ... I tried to find out from him what was meant by his being tabooed, but he spoke English so badly, and seemed to understand so little of the matter himself, that I was not much the wiser for his explanation (Paulding 1970 [1831]: 66).

When mutual understanding mattered, as in a hostile encounter with Marquesans, Paulding did not take any risk in relying on English, but engaged a bilingual beachcomber named William Lay, one of the *Globe*'s mutineers, to do the negotiations. After a short introduction with "a cocked pistol to his breast", Paulding (1970 [1831]: 126–7)

> ... told him then to say to the natives, that if they rose from their seats, or threw a stone, we would shoot them all; but the poor fellow, delirious with joy for the moment, knew not what he said, and, instead of obeying my command, called out in half English, and half Island language, in broken sentences, most of which was unintelligible to us.

This 'argot' undoubtedly proved also useful in interactions with the Hawaiian crew member on board and the Malay missionary, who first addressed Paulding "in the language of the Society Islands" before switching to English (Paulding 1970 [1831]: 148, 237–8).

A more intriguing source is the French naval officer and explorer, J.S.C. Dumont d'Urville (1834–35), who had first sailed the Pacific with Duperrey and then returned on his own from 1826 to 1828 and again in later years. On Tahiti, Dumont d'Urville (1834–35: I.510a, 527a, 551) took down a few sentences of what apparently was a reduced foreigner talk:

> *"Taata maïtaï, Wenoua ino."* 'les hommes bons, la terre mauvaise' [†*ta'ata maita'i, venua 'ino.* 'Men good, land bad'].
>
> *"Prancès koti taïo Turvi"* 'Français ... [cut] ami avec lequel on échange son nom ... Otouri' [name of a Tahitian?]. [†*prance koti/'oti tayo (o)turi* (?) 'French cut friend Otouri.' (with *koti* < Maori 'to cut', *'oti* < Tahitian 'to cut, to chop,' and *tayo* < Tahitian 'a very close friend')].
>
> *"Are po."* 'Il est allé dans la nuit.' [†*haere po* 'go night'].

Among the Maori, Dumont d'Urville (1834–35: II.376b) recorded another reduced phrase: *"Tekouri mate Marion."* 'Tekouri a tué Marion' (said by a Maori to scare away French visitors) [†*Tekuri mate Marion* 'Tekuri kill[ed] Marion']. A closer examination of some other samples of native speech may provide other instances of reduced Tahitian and Maori. Dumont d'Urville generously interspersed his extensive account with indigenous terms from wherever he stopped, which leave the impression that they were representative words of what the French spoke in interaction with Pacific Islanders and on board. France's James Cook had also learned some Hawaiian, apparently from a Hawaiian on board by the name of Makao who knew a little English (Dumont d'Urville 1834–35: I.426a).

As surgeon on the British whaling vessel *Recovery*, Francis T. Bishop (1954 [1835]) cited single Polynesian words in his narrative of sailings in the Pacific during the years of 1832 to 1835, and provided short vocabularies of Hawaiian and Marquesan (Bishop 1954 [1835] MS: II.38, 57–8). Unfortunately, he neglected to offer any supplementary information on their use in terms of either syntactic or non-linguistic information. The only exceptions are two verb phrases that possibly provide evidence of features distinct from standard Marquesan (Bishop 1954 [1835] MS: II.58): "Anna Kie-ki, to eat" [†*hana kekai* 'to do food' (in contrast to *kekai* 'to eat')] and "Anna-pah, don't do it" [†*hana pa* 'do not' (with †*pa* < French *pas* [pa]?)].

A primary literary source of the period is Richard Henry Dana, Jr. (1911), who described his experiences as a sailor in 1835 and 1836. With American or English officers and two or three experienced sailors "before the mast to do the work upon the rigging," many vessels engaged in the Pacific hide and tallow trade, and had crews of Hawaiians, known as Kanakas [< Hawaiian *kanaka* 'human being, man, person'] and appreciated as experienced boatsmen in rough surf and excellent swimmers (Dana 1911 [1840]: 68–75). Hawaiians also were active in the rigging, showed no fear in tackling sharks or rattlesnakes, helped cure hides, and served as messengers swimming after a by-passing vessel; they

adapted easily to new conditions other than cold climates, and formed a community
of their own in San Diego (Dana 1911 [1840]: 103, 177, 179, 195, 207, 217–18).

The literary sailor compared the sociolinguistic situation on board to Babel,
and found several languages spoken on ships of Hawaiian, Italian, and Mexican
origin with their mixed crews of Americans, English, Spaniards, French, and
Indians in addition to Hawaiians — with "all talking at once" and with the
Hawaiians apparently conversing continuously (Dana 1911 [1840]: 103, 166,
186–7). On board, English did not figure as a major medium with the Hawaiians,
only one of whom spoke a little of it (Dana 1911 [1840]: 75, 80, 102). On shore
in California, yet another language prevailed in interlingual interactions:

> The Spanish was the common ground upon which we all [the crews of several
> vessels] met; for every one knew more or less of that. We had now, out of
> forty or fifty, representatives from almost every nation under the sun, — two
> Englishmen, three Yankees, two Scotchmen, two Welshmen, one Irishman,
> three Frenchmen (two of whom were Normans, and the third from Gascony),
> one Dutchman, one Austrian, two or three Spaniards (from old Spain), half a
> dozen Spanish-Americans, and half-breeds, two native Indians from Chili and
> the Island of Chiloe, one negro, one mulatto, about twenty Italians, from all
> parts of Italy, as many more Sandwich-Islanders, one Tahitian, and one
> Kanaka from the Marquesas Islands (Dana 1911 [1840]: 198–9).

A little English was in use among the Hawaiians of the San Diego community
(Dana 1911 [1840]: 180). Whereas one Hawaiian by the name of Tom Davis
reportedly was quite fluent in English, another, older member of the community,
Mr. Bingham, "spoke very little English, — almost none, and could neither read
nor write." Nonetheless, Dana (1911 [1840]: 181–2) had him respond to a large
extent in Pidgin English when teased about being a cannibal:

> "*Aole!*" [†*'a'ole*] (No) "Me no eatee Cap'nee Cook! Me pickaninny — small
> so high — no more! My fader see Cap'nee Cook! Me — no! ... New Zealand
> Kanaka eatee white man; Sandwich Island Kanaka, — no. Sandwich Island
> Kanaka *ua like pu na haole,* — all 'e same a' you! [†*ua like pū nā haole* 'Also
> like the white people'].
> ... I once heard old Mr. Bingham say, with the highest indignation, to a
> Yankee trader who was trying to persuade him to keep his money to himself
> [rather than to share it with his fellow Hawaiians], "No! we no all 'e same a'
> you! — Suppose one got money, all got money. You, — suppose one got
> money — lock him up in chest. — No good!" — "Kanaka all 'e same a' one!"

Unless one is to question Dana's observations about Bingham's linguistic skills,
this example suggests that it was not an accurate rendition of what the old man
said; instead, Dana apparently used Pidgin English as no more than a literary tool

to represent the Hawaiian's speech in transliteration.

Significantly, the quote in Hawaiian with the perfective *ua* and the plural definite article *nā* constitutes standard Hawaiian rather than some reduced form, as do his other samples (see Dana 1911 [1840]: 150, 175, 184, 207, 309, 334; T. Haunani Makuakāne-Drechsel, personal communication).[5] The only evidence that Dana offered of any form of linguistic compromise was "Kail ho!" [†*kel ho*] for 'Sail ho!' (Dana 1911 [1840]: 334). Unlike other Europeans, Dana had apparently learned or begun learning standard Hawaiian.[6] This finding is not surprising in light of the fact that he showed much sympathy towards the Hawaiians and associated with them on board and in San Diego over several months; Dana became a close friend or *"aikane"* [†*aikāne*] of a Hawaiian by the name of Hope, whom he assisted in illness when others refused help (Dana 1911 [1840]: 102, 179–85, 308–11, 347).

A few, rather limited impressions by a native of the period come from a Rarotongan by the name of Ta'unga, one among many Polynesian missionaries engaged in the early 1840s to do frontline evangelizing among Pacific Islanders before European or American proselytizers would take over. Most of his linguistic observations have revealed few details or little substance. Ta'unga had learned other Polynesian languages (including Tahitian and Samoan) as well as a few languages of New Caledonia and neighboring islands (Ta'unga 1968: xvii, 8, 31, 41, 43, 44, 60, 62, 71, 82, 116, 146). Yet he knew little or no English (Ta'unga 1968: xvii, 146), which seems indicative for the sociolinguistic situation of the southern Pacific at the time. This fact renders suspect a contrary observation by him: "The people of this island [Rotuma, north of Fiji] have an extensive knowledge of the English language" (Ta'unga 1968: 20). In making this suggestion, Ta'unga could hardly have relied on his own experience, but probably drew on somebody else's claim, which then raises questions of interpretation. Similarly revealing is his observation that the Rotumans would not listen to Samoan missionaries (Ta'unga 1968: 20), with whom he had no difficulty interacting in their own language.

A better, if romanticized, source for a Polynesian-based medium is Herman Melville's semifictional, autobiographical novel *Typee* (1959 [1846]), relating his experiences on Nuku Hiva (Marquesas) in 1842. Not only did he garnish his writing throughout with common words of Polynesian origin: *nuee* 'much', *whinhenies* 'young girls', *motarkee* 'good', *kanaka* 'South Sea Islander', *ki-ki* 'eat', *moee* 'sleep, sit down', *mukee* 'killed', and *taboo*; but he also integrated numerous examples of short phrases that he could recall from his interactions with Marquesans (1959 [1846]: 23, 99, 102, 107, 128, 137, 145, 149, 150, 188, 189, 197, 304, 350, 357, 358, 359, 380):

"puarkee nuee" 'big hog' [†*puaka nui*]
"Happar ... Motarkee" [†*Hapa motaki* '[The] Hapa (spelling?; name of a community hostile to the Taipi]) [are] good'].
"Typee motarkee" [†*Taipi motaki* '[The] Taipi [are] good'].
"Nukuheva motarkee?" [†*Nukuhiva motaki*? '[Is] Nuku Hiva good?'].
"Ki-ki, muee muee, ah! moee moee motarkee" 'Eat plenty, ah! sleep very good.' [†*kaikai*[7] *nuinui* (?), *a! muimui motaki* (with "m" in "muee muee" as an apparent misspelling of [n])].
"Tommo, Toby, ki ki!" [†*Tomo, Tobi, kaikai* 'Tomo [and] Toby, eat'].
"Awha! awha! Toby mukee mooe!" 'Alas! alas! Toby is killed.' [†*avi! avi! Tobi make mui* 'Toby [is] dead asleep' (?)].
"Happar keekeeno nuee ... nuee, nuee, ki ki kanaka! — ah! owle motarkee!" 'Terrible fellows those Happars! — devour an amazing quantity of men! — ah, shocking bad.' [†*Hapa kikino nui* ... '[The] Hapa [are] very miserable Those most miserable Hapa.' [†*nui, nui kaikai kanaka*! 'Very many [of them?] eat people.' — †*a, 'a'o'e/'a'ole motaki*! 'Alas, not good!']
"Ah! Typee motarkee! — nuee, nuee mioree — nuee, nuee, wai — nuee, nuee poee-poee — nuee, nuee kokoo — ah! nuee, nuee, kiki — ah! nuee, nuee, nuee!" 'Ah, Typee! Isn't it a fine place though! — no danger of starving here, I tell you! — plenty of bread-fruit — plenty of water — plenty of pudding — ah! plenty of everything! — ah! heaps, heaps, heaps!' [†*a, Taipi motaki*! 'Alas, Taipi [is] good'. — †*nuinui* (...?) 'Very much/many ...'— †*nuinui, vai* — 'Very much water' — †*nuinui poipoi* 'Very much poi' — †*nuinui kaukau* (?) 'Very much food.' — †*a, nuinui kaikai* 'Very much to eat.' — †*a, nui, nui, nui*! 'Plenty, plenty, plenty!].
"Mehevi hanna pippee nuee Happar." [†*Mehevi hana* ... *nui Hapa*. 'Mehevi does/makes ... (?)'].
"Happar poo arva!" 'The cowards had fled' [†*Hapa poho'e*! '[The] Hapa flee'].
"Marnoo pemi!" [†*Marno pimai*[8] 'Marno comes'].
"pehee pemi" 'fish come' [†*pihi pimai*].
"Arware poo awa, Tommo?" 'Where are you going, Tommo?' [†*ihea* (?) *poho'e, Tomo*? 'Where [do] you flee/go, Tomo?' — "Wai" 'water'[†*vai* 'water'].
"Toby pemi ena" 'Toby has arrived here.' [†*Tobi pimai ina* 'Tobi come here'].
"Toby owlee pemi." 'Toby had not arrived.' [†*Tobi a'o'e pimai* 'Tobi not arrive'].
"Motarkee nuee" [†*motaki nui* 'very good'].

In addition, Melville (1959 [1846]: 204–5, 351) cited two examples of "broken English," of which one included a longer exchange, but both still relied substantially on native vocabulary, including *kaikai, kanaka, make, muimui, puaka, tapu*, and *wahine*. The speaker had reportedly learned Pidgin English when kidnapped as a boy by the captain of a trading vessel and living with him in Sydney for three years. Melville even cited him as referring to it as "Pueearka Kanaka" [†*puaka kanaka* 'Islanders' pig language'], probably in analogy to Pig Latin. The indigenous language, however, remained to Melville (1959 [1846]: 183, 235) "an indescribable jargon of words, that it almost put me in bodily pain to listen to him" [his companion] and "almost entirely destitute of terms to express the delightful ideas conveyed by our endless catalogue of civilised crimes." Ultimately, he never learned the language fully (Melville 1959 [1846]: 98, 116, 200).

Melville's sequel novel, *Omoo*, drew on his subsequent experiences on Tahiti and neighboring islands, and similarly included numerous phrases and longer utterances in reduced Tahitian (Melville 1908 [1847]: 180, 201, 249, 263, 265, 267, 269, 283, 284, 285, 287, 290, 293, 322):

> "Oee tootai owree! ... itai maitai!" 'you are a good-for-nothing huzzy, no better than you should be.' [†*'oe tutae* (?) ... *'ita maita'i*! 'You [are] feces (?) ... not/no good'].
> "Ita! ita! — oee matttee — mattee nuee." 'no, no; you too sick.' [†*'ita, 'ita — 'oe mate — mate nui.* 'No, no! — You [are] sick — very sick'].
> "hanree perrar!" 'be off with himself.' [†... (?)]
> "ah, eda maitai" 'this one will do' [†*a, tei maita'i* 'Alas, this [is] good'].
> "Keekee maitai ... nuee nuee hanna hanna portarto" 'Zeke ... makes plenty of potatoes.' [†*Keke maita'i ... nuinui hanahana potato.* 'Zeke [is] good ... much/many makes potato'].
> "Yar onor boyoee" [†...].
> "Peehee Lee Lees" 'small fish' [†*pihi li'ili'i*]
> "Ah, karhowree sabbee lee-lee, ena arva tee maitai!" 'what a blockhead of a white man! this is the real stuff!' [†*a, haole* (?; < Hawaiian?) *sawe li'ili'i, ena 'ava* (?) *ti maita'i* 'Alas, [the] white man [?] knows little; that kava drink [is] good!'].
> "Ah, karhowree, ena hannahanna arva tee! 'This, you see, is the way it's done.' [†*a, haole* (?), *ena hanahana 'ava ti!* 'Alas, white man, that makes kava drink'].
> "Tootai Owrees" 'contemners of the missionaries' [†*tūtae 'a'ole* (?) 'No[t] shit' (?)].
> "Aramai! aramai, karhowree!" 'Come in! come in, strangers!' [†*haere mai! haere mai, haole*!].
> "Ah! mickonaree tata matai!" 'What a pious young man!' [†*a, mikanere ta'ata maita'i*! (< Hawaiian) 'Alas, [a] missionary [and a] good man!'].
> "Pomaree! Pomaree! armai kow kow." [†*Pomare! Pomare, haere mai kaukau* 'Pomari, Pomari, come in and eat!'].

As in his first novel, Melville (1908 [1847]: 118) included "jabbering broken English" in his second book, and offered an example: "Ah nuee nuee olee manee! olee manee!" 'Alas! they are very, very old! very old!' [†*a, nuinui ole mani* (?)'! 'Alas, very old man!']. The speaker, a Tahitian woman called

Arfretee, apparently believed that she spoke "very respectable English" (Melville 1908 [1847]: 289–90). Similarly, Maori sailors on board spoke "the South Seaman's slogan" as their best English (Melville 1908 [1847]: 73). If the examples of Pidgin English offered by Melville (1908 [1847]: 102, 103, 122, 123, 124, 176–7, 181, 201, 214, 220, 289, 305) are any indication, its vocabulary still consisted of a substantial number of native terms, attested in *hana*, *ita*, *kanaka*, *mate*, *maita'i*, *muimui*, *nui*, *pimai*, *tapu*, and *taro* among others.

As compared to the indigenous foreigner talk, these samples of Melville's Pidgin take a greater proportion of English in *Omoo* than in *Typee*. Does this observation then permit the conclusion that in the early 1840s, Pidgin English was more common and widespread in Tahiti than in the Marquesas — overlooking the fact that the Society Islands as well as the Marquesas were under French influence? Or did Melville — like Dana apparently — solely take the literary liberty of embellishing his writing with Pidgin English, because he had not kept a journal (Melville 1908 [1847]: x) and had to rely on his recollections instead?

In 1842, Andrew Cheyne (1971: 98), an Australian trader doing business on Lifu north of New Caledonia, recorded another telling incidence:

> On the night of the 2nd of September The above chief names Zoulah [Zeula] remained on board the schooner at his own request, and at bed time I gave him a mat to sleep on in my Cabin. Before turning in, I locked the cabin door and took the Key to bed with me. After laying in bed about an hour I saw Zoulah get up and try to open the door, but finding it locked, he again lay down, he appeared to be very uneasy and wanted to go on shore apparently. Having a suspicion that something was wrong I did not go to sleep, but lay watching him for about two Hours. Every now and then he would get up and try the door and again lay down, at last he called me, saying, 'Aliki, Aliki, Pago nuba meculada — Congazu meculada, Panasādu Sapi Hāe Troame, Towa da Hāe nuba. Chelleda, Chelleda.'. which was 'Chief Chief do not you go to sleep. No good sleep — By & By plenty War Canoes are coming here to fight your ship, Get up, Get up.' I asked him how many canoes were coming and at what time, he said, 'Thabumb Whyanu da Hāe — Asāhea Trumman. — Troame Bong Ahu — Nacung Gweeath da Dohu — Mesheentie da Hae nuba' — which is 'Twenty War Canoes full of Men — they are coming to night, and are commanded by the chief Gweeaths Son. They will Kill your ship'. [sic]

What renders this attestation relevant is *aliki* 'chief' and apparently other Polynesian influences. Jean Guiart (in Cheyne 1971: 98 [fn.16]) has interpreted it as follows:

> This is an interesting transcription of local words. The sentences are a jumble of Lifuan and Uvean words. Most of the words are Dehu (from Lifu), some Iai

(from Uvea), and some Uea (from Uvea, a Polynesian language). This is understandable, as Zeula lived part of his life in Uvea, and in his excited state possibly mixed the two languages or used some kind of lingua franca in the process of being built. They mean roughly what Cheyne translates, except that eight not 'twenty' war canoes are spoken of in the second sentence.

Zeula's response deserves closer examination. Cheyne (1971: 175–9) also provided a list of Ponapean words, which J.L. Fischer has interpreted as part of the local foreigner talk or a kind of Ponapean pidgin, but shows no immediately obvious Polynesian influences. At no point did Cheyne, however, make references to any form of English spoken on the islands of the southwestern Pacific that he visited. Wherever he dropped anchor, he depended on his own linguistic skills or local interpreters, as was the case on Uvea and Ponape (Cheyne 1971: 108, 110, 120, 157, 159).

English came to assume a greater role in the Pacific only in the decades to follow. Albert Hastings Markham (1970 [1873]: 131, 187, 224), a Royal Navy commander in pursuit of 'blackbirders', mentioned a few sociolinguistic incidentals that suggest increased use of English in the 1870s: a Polynesian by the name of Tumo, who used 'yes', 'no', 'good morning', and '*no savez*' in communication with Englishmen; an instance of Pidgin English interspersed with †*kaikai* in the New Hebrides; and a reference to a chief on Aniwa (southern New Hebrides) speaking a few words of English. Yet perhaps more revealing of a major language shift in the making was the following incident during the second half of the 19th century:

> One of our officers, who had been some time on the Australian Station, wishing to display his knowledge of divers tongues to his shipmates, tried the salutations in the Maori, Fiji, and Samoan languages, on one of the natives alongside, who to his astonishment, and perhaps discomfiture, answered in very fair English, "Good morning, sir."

Still, such predominantly English-based interactions could well have been limited to contact between indigenous peoples on the one hand and English-speaking explorers and colonists on the other, just as an English-based pidgin did not come to predominate in Hawai'i until the 1890s (Roberts 1995a: 43–5; 1995b: 97–103).

### 3.   Synopsis of Findings and Implications

Early documents of the Pacific do not offer much information on the area's sociolinguistics — a conclusion that applies to the use of European just as indigenous languages. The information collected so far, however, has proved surprisingly consistent across diverse kinds of historical documentation as well as across its recorders' different languages and nationalities. There are inconsistencies in the data, but these do not support the accepted Anglophile-Anglophone model of language contact in the early colonial Pacific when examined in their broader sociohistorical contexts.

The evidence at hand presents strong indications for make-shift or foreigner-talk versions of the indigenous languages of the Hawaiian Islands, the Marquesas, Tahiti, New Zealand, and other parts of Polynesia — in use not only among alloglossic peoples of Oceania, but also between Europeans and Americans on the one hand and Polynesians and other Pacific Islanders on the other, during the first half of the 19th century and probably later. Examples provided by Fanning, Chamisso, Paulding, Dumont d'Urville, and Melville document reduced forms of Hawaiian, Marquesan, Tahitian, Maori, and possibly other Polynesian languages, with the following features:

i.    reduced tenses with only past and future particles (Chamisso);
ii.   limited number of personal pronouns, including the first and second person plus an unmarked third person (Chamisso);
iii.  rare use of articles (Paulding) or their complete omission;
iii.  postnominal position of adjectives and zero copula;
iv.   initial position of the negative, a pattern that also applies to Chamisso's phrase †'emo Bikar, but apparently does not in one of Melville's examples "Tootai Owrees" 'contemners of the missionaries' or †tūtae 'a'ole [?] 'No[t] shit' [?];
v.    predominance of single- or two-argument sentences with no attestations of subordinate clauses collected thus far; and
vi.   basic SVO word order (in contrast to VSO of Hawaiian and other Polynesian languages);

A common vocabulary also existed, exhibiting phonological variations characteristic of Polynesian languages (such as ' ~ k and k ~ t): †ali'i ~ †ariki 'chief', 'a'ole ~ †'a'o'e 'no', 'not,' NEG, †hana 'to do, to make', †haole 'white person/ people', †'ite 'to see', †kaikai ~ †kekai 'to eat', 'food' ~ †kaukau (etymologically not related; < Chinese Pidgin English chowchow), †kanaka 'Pacific Islander', †kapu ~ †tapu 'taboo', †make ~ †mate 'dead, sick; to die, to kill', †maika'i ~ †motaki 'good' (etymologically not related), †moku ~ †motu 'island, ship', †mui 'to sleep', †nui ~ †nuinui 'big, much, very', †pihi 'fish' (< English), †pimai 'to come', †puaka ~ †pua'a 'pig', and †wahine ~ †fafine 'woman, wife'. Many of these very same Polynesian words entered Pacific Pidgin English, and provide a cue, although hardly any solid evidence, for the significance of Polynesian-based foreigner talks.

The available evidence agrees surprisingly well with what Roberts (1995a: 6–9; 1995b: 111–9) has already described for Pidgin Hawaiian used locally. The data are also fully consistent with what Ross Clark (1990: 100–3) has outlined for the grammar of Pākehā Maori ('European Maori'): substantially reduced use or omission of particles; subject-first word order and even SVO (in contrast to Maori's verb-initial sentence pattern); absent markings for tense, aspect or mood in verbs; and increased reduplication. The similarities in grammar and the common vocabulary of Polynesian foreigner talks suggest not so much separate linguistic entities as rather a single Polynesian-based contact medium in use across much of the central Pacific. The attested phonological and lexical variations would not have significantly hampered the mutual intelligibility of its varieties for speakers of closely related Eastern Polynesian languages or new-comers with exposure to one or the other. This fact probably made such a Polynesian contact medium all the more useful and attractive as a lingua franca for early European and American explorers, whalers, traders, beachcombers, and colonists.

The data are convincing enough to suggest that, at least through the mid-19th century, Europeans and Americans made regular and concerted efforts to use the natives' language(s), even if most never learned more than rudimentaries; if the arrivals did not do so, they willy-nilly required interpreters, who probably employed the native contact medium unless they had acquired a vernacular like some missionaries. The currently examined evidence however is insufficient to determine whether this Polynesian-based maritime medium was only a jargon with a quite variable grammar, reflecting substrate patterns of its speakers' first languages, or a pidgin with distinctive set rules of its own (see e.g. Mühlhäusler 1986: 134–76).

The present findings raise some questions about the nature and existence of Pidgin English in the early colonial Pacific. All suggestions for the regular use of some form of English in the Pacific during this period draw on secondary, often questionable information (Ta'unga), or rely on what appear to be no more than literary renditions or transliterations of native speech into its nearest equivalent, i.e. Pidgin English (Dana and Melville). If English served as an interlingual medium at the time, it was not the exclusive or even primary one; but it was only one among several others — indigenous Pacific, Asian, and other European languages (as attested by Robarts, Chamisso, Paulding, Dana, and Cheyne).

This scenario differs from the widely accepted model of language contact in the early colonial Pacific as outlined by Clark (1977, 1979) in his major surveys of Pacific pidgins and creoles, in which he has proposed the use of an area-wide Pidgin English by the beginning of the 19th century and its acceptance on practically every island by the 1830s. For evidence of an early English-based South Seas Jargon, Clark has relied to a great extent on renditions by Dana and

Melville, which however are suspect as to their historical accuracy. He noted, but then apparently dismissed as irrelevant, several contrary indicators for that period: the virtual absence of references to natives using English; the multilingual composition of ship crews; the Europeans' willingness to adapt to new linguistic conditions; the use of indigenous contact media in place of European languages; and the continuous need for interpreters competent in vernaculars (Clark 1979: 26–30, 33–4). At the same time, Clark (1979: 23–4; 1977: 31) has shown little concern about stereotyping or other misrepresentations in the Pidgin English of non-fictional documentation, and has accepted its reliability solely on grounds of its scientific nature, while largely ignoring attestations of non-English speech (pidginized or not) in literary writings. At one point, he recognized Melville's samples to agree quite closely with other writers' only to dismiss them as evidence of "Melville's tendency to mix up Hawaiian, Tahitian and Marquesan words in his jargon" (Clark 1979: 60 [fn.27]). Such lexical mixing seems to be evident in the second example of Dumont d'Urville's recordings, and indeed would not have been the least surprising in light of interlingual contacts among multilingual crews, including Pacific Islanders and native beachcombers (see Chappell 1994). What Clark (1979: 24) has observed for Pidgin English applies even more so to the attestation of its non-European counterparts in early historical sources of the Pacific: "There is also, particularly in longer texts, a tendency to drift into standard English, either from the same lack of competence, or because long stretches of real pidgin would be too hard for the reader to understand." One only needs to read "Pidgin English" in place of "standard English."

The author of another major survey of pidgins in the early colonial Pacific, Keesing (1988: 13–34), showed little more concern about problems of interpretation due to transliteration or hypercorrection, although he acknowledged such explicitly (Keesing 1988: 32, 41) and was otherwise sympathetic to the idea of native influences in Pacific pidgins as evident in his arguments for an Oceanic substrate in Melanesian Pidgin. While accepting the idea of pidginized Polynesian languages and, with it, the need for systematic philological and historical-sociolinguistic research, more recent studies (see Clark 1990 and Siegel 1987: 33–46) have yet to answer the methodological and theoretical questions raised by a broader perspective and a critical reexamination of Pidgin English attestations.

By currently available indications, literary writers' recordings of indigenous speech such as Chamisso's, Dana's, and Melville's were historically more accurate than contemporary renditions of Pidgin English (including their own) — for a very simple reason: Europeans and Americans generally had neither the knowledge nor the need to hypercorrect the speech of Pacific or other indigenous peoples to some real or imagined indigenous standard. Conceivably, a novelist could have made up the native speech of non-European people by drawing on linguistic resources available at the time; such an endeavor would however have been much more difficult than to "put Pidgin English into their mouth." Not only would it have required considerable linguistic sophistication on part of the author to maintain consistency with already existing records; but there was little linguistic information available on Pacific languages in the early 19th century, and what was available was hard to come by. These conditions did not apply to Pidgin English, used widely in historical documents, literary sources, and other writings of the period. Attestations of Pidgin English also were continuously subject to stereotyping and cleansing of foreign elements for a mix of stylistic color and easy intelligibility. The circumstances of Pidgin English recordings in fact recall an observation by a contemporary American writer, William Gilmore Simms (1856: 391), about Catawba, a Native American language of the piedmont Carolinas related to Proto-Siouan, or a contact medium based on it: "We have endeavoured to put into the [American] Indian English, as more suitable to the subject, and more accessible to the reader, that dialogue which was spoken in the most musical Catawba." In this case, a difference in quality is evident not so much in the nature of source (historical records versus literary writings) as rather in the kind of attested language (non-European versus European; see Drechsel 1997: 2.3 for an extended analogous discussion of so-called American Indian Pidgin English in relation to American contact media).

    Doubts about Clark's model of language contact in the early colonial Pacific further require some caution about his notions of "macaronic alternation, at word, phrase or sentence level, between jargon English and (sometimes pidginized) vernacular languages" (Clark 1979: 33), for which he again drew on Dana and Melville among other sources. At this point, it is not clear whether there existed as much *grammatical* variation as Clark's quote suggests, notwithstanding attested alternations in phonology and vocabulary. The currently available evidence for Hawaiian or other Polynesian languages in make-shift forms reveals surprisingly little variation at the phrase or sentence level, when one considers the consistent use of SVO. This finding lends support to Keesing's suggestion for considerable structural stability in place of a highly variable jargon (Keesing 1988: 13, 24). Considering that SVO is the predominant word order of Oceanic languages and appears also as surface variations of VSO languages (see Keesing 1988: 77–88), it is by no means evident that this word order originated from English, as Clark (1977: 30; 1979: 26) has suggested; rather, it likely resulted from a wider compromise without necessarily reflecting the influence of English as exclusive or even principal source, when one keeps in mind the great variety of European and non-European languages of the participants in contact.

## 4. Future Research

Although yielding only a limited amount of evidence, the present research on a maritime Polynesian jargon or pidgin has been most encouraging in that the linguistic data gathered so far have been consistent "internally" (i.e. with other, independent linguistic attestations) as well as with findings on Pidgin Hawaiian (Roberts 1995a, b) and recent sociohistorical research recognizing a greater role by native peoples of the Pacific (such as the study on native beachcombing by David Chappell [1994]). Notwithstanding the obstacles of limited historical attestations, the current project is well worth pursuing further. The prime goal remains to unearth additional historical documentation, including linguistic and sociohistorical information. Only a widened data base, ideally including accounts by observers of Pacific and Asian origin, can promise a fuller reconstruction of the proposed Polynesian pidgin.

Among one of the major issues to be resolved is the question of whether SVO possibly reflects a *projection* of the native-language grammars of European or American authors. A positive answer does not appear likely in light of consistent evidence of Pidgin Hawaiian or Keesing's arguments; but it would seem premature to dismiss this consideration, as reliable as these documents have proved otherwise. Other topics that deserve closer attention are:

i.    the extent and nature of variation in the proposed maritime Polynesian jargon or pidgin;
ii.   its geographic range and sociolinguistic distribution;
iii.  the history of diffusion of Hawaiian loanwords into Chinook Jargon, Eskimo Jargon, English, and other languages;
iv.   the jargon's or pidgin's relationship and change to Pidgin English and other European languages; and
v.    its origin.

The currently assembled evidence is too meager to suggest a pre-European origin; but increased and better data may potentially require consideration of such a hypothesis. The proposal for a pre-European origin of the maritime Polynesian jargon or pidgin becomes attractive in the light of confirmed long-distance voyaging by Polynesians in the central and south Pacific, including regular contacts with Micronesians and Melanesians (see Finney 1994: Ch. 8).

## Acknowledgments

This paper has developed from my final report to Derek Bickerton as part of his National Science Foundation Project "Language Contact in Hawai'i and the Pacific, 1778–1930, with Particular Reference to Hawaiian" (NSF Grant No. SBR-94–06763), and is a preliminay assessment of historical evidence for a maritime Hawaiian/Polynesian jargon or pidgin. I would like to thank Ms. Eleanor Au, former Director of the Pacific Collection at Hamilton Library of the University of Hawai'i at Mānoa for her kind assistance. I further acknowledge Derek Bickerton, Anthony P. Grant, my wife Teresa Makuakāne-Drechsel, Sarah Julianne Roberts, and Suzanne Romaine for valuable suggestions. I only wish Charlie Sato with her wit, intelligence, and expertise were here to give her thoughtful critique as well.

## Notes

1. The dagger [†] in the examples here identifies *reconstitutions*, which differ from reconstructions established by the comparative-historical method and marked with an asterisk. The first are based on early written records, whereas the second usually draw on modern linguistic recordings. This distinction serves as a useful reminder of the nature of early linguistic documentation, which was frequently incomplete or distorted. For comparative evidence, the present reconstitutions draw on Pukui and Elbert (1987) for Hawaiian, Ngata (1993) for Maori, Dordillon (1931–2) for Marquesan, Milner (1966) for Samoan, Andrews and Andrews (1944) for Tahitian, and Churchward (1959) for Tongan. When approriate, comparative data and reconstitutions will include the glottal stop (') and vowel length, indicated by the macron, although it is reasonable to suppose that they were not always phonemic in the foreigner talk or make-shift versions of Hawaiian or other Polynesian languages (Bickerton and Wilson 1987: 73[fn.5]).

2. Elsewhere Chamisso (n.d.:IV.26) observed that, in contrast to the great linguistic diversity of California Indians, "Die Insulaner der Südsee, weit von einander geschieden and zerstreut über fast ein Drittel des heissen Gurtes der Erde, reden eine Sprache." One might read this statement by itself as an oversimplified observation about the similarity of Polynesian languages, but we should perhaps interpret it as another reference to a common Polynesian-based medium in the light of Chamisso's extended, comparatively detailed sociolinguistic observations of Pacific islands elsewhere (Chamisso n.d.:IV.117–147).

3. Chamisso (n.d:IV.49) included the following reduplications (with reconstitutions added in brackets): "*Moku-moku* Krieg [†*mokomoko* 'rough, hand-to-hand fighting of any kind']. *Moku* Insel und europäisches Schiff [†*moku* 'island', 'ship']. *Make-make* lieben, mögen [†*makemake* 'to want', 'to like']. *Make* oder *Mate* töten, schlagen [†*make*/†*mate* 'to die', 'to kill' 'to beat']. *Mire-mire* schauen, sehen [†*milimili* 'to examine with interest or curiosity and admiration']. *Moe-moe* und *moe* schlafen [†*moe* and †*moemoe* 'to sleep']. *Nome-nome* sprechen, sagen [†*nomenome* 'to move the lips silently, as though speaking to oneself']. *Hane-hane* sprechen [†*hanihani* 'to hint', 'to suggest']. *Para-para* zeichnen [†*palapala* 'document/writing of any kind, printing on paper or tapa', 'to write', 'send a written message']. *Mi-mi* [Latin] mingere [†*mimi* 'to urinate']. *Wite-wite* schnell, rasch [†*wikiwiki* 'fast', 'speedy']. *Rike-rike* gleichwie, ebenso [†*likelike* '(a)like' 'similar', 'resembling', 'equal', 'same']".
   On the same page Chamisso listed the following loanwords, their sources, and their corresponding native words: "*Kau-Kau* [†*kaukau* 'to eat'], chinesisch *Tschau-tschau* für *Païni* essen

[†pā'ina 'to eat dinner']. *Pane-pane* [†*panipani* 'coition'], chinesisch für *Aïni*, *Coïtus* [†*aina* 'sexual intercourse'], welches fremde Wort noch euphemisch zu sein scheint, da bei der allgemeinen Entblödung züchtigere Matronen das andre doch vermeiden. *Pihi*, englisch Fish [†*pihi* 'fish'], für *Haïna* Fisch [†*i'a* 'fish'(?); †*haina* 'offering'(?)]. *Neipa* englisch Knife, Messer [†*naipa* 'knife']. — *Pike-nene*, spanisch pequeño [†*pikinini* 'small'], für *Käea* klein [†..]."

4. Chamisso (n.d.:IV.227) explicitly acknowledged Humboldt in his corrections regarding Polynesian languages. However, it is not obvious whether Humboldt's research on Kavi of Java sensitized Chamisso to the possibility of mixed languages, a topic in which he apparently became interested late in his life, or whether there perhaps existed a reverse relationship of influence with Chamisso's observations on the Pacific alerting his mentor.

5. Clark (1979: 60[fn.25]) has suggested that one of Dana's samples, "maikai hana hana nui", was pidginized, but Makuakāne-Drechsel considers it acceptable, if not exactly the best Hawaiian.

6. In one situation, Dana (1911[1840]:311) "could not understand half of them [Hawaiians];" but this instance was apparently due to several speaking at one time, expressing their gratitude to him for his generous help, rather than a lack of knowledge of Hawaiian.

7. Clark (1979: 31) has suggested Maori as the origin of *kai* 'to eat' and its reduplicated form, but he gives no explanation for his claim other than the word's early attestation among the Maori. It actually occurs in several Polynesian languages, and need not have had a single source.

8. Roberts (1995a: 8; 1995b: 112) considers *pi mai* 'to come' as Pidgin Hawaiian in contrast to either standard Hawaiian *hele mai* or *mai* or pidginized Marquesan.

# References

Andrews, Edmund, and Irene D. Andrews. 1944. *A Comparative Dictionary of the Tahitian Language*. Tahitian-English with an English-Tahitian Finding List. Chicago: Chicago Academy of Sciences.

Bickerton, Derek, and William H. Wilson. 1987. "Pidgin Hawaiian." In Gilbert (ed.), 61–76.

Bishop, Francis T. 1954 [1835] MS. *Narrative of a Voyage in the North and South Pacific Oceans, With Recollections of the Society, Sandwich and Other Islands Visited During the Years 1832–1835*. Typescript of manuscript. 3 vols. Hawaiian/Pacific Collection, Hamilton Library, University of Hawai'i at Mānoa.

Chamisso, Adelbert von (n.d.) *Adelbert von Chamissos sämtliche Werke in vier Bänden*. Mit Bildnis, einer Biographie und Charakeristik Chamissos von Adolf Bartels. Leipzig: Max Hesses Verlag.

Chappell, David A. 1994. "Secret Sharers: Indigenous Beachcombers in the Pacific Islands." *Pacific Studies* 17:1–22.

Cheyne, Andrew. 1971. *The Trading Voyages of Andrew Cheyne 1841–1842*. Edited by Dorothy Shineberg. Honolulu: University of Hawai'i Press.

Churchward, C. Maxwell. 1959. *Tongan Dictionary*. Tongan-English and English-Tongan. London: Oxford University Press.

Clark, Ross. 1977. "In Search of Beach-la-Mar: Historical Relations Among Pacific Pidgins and Creoles." *Working Papers in Anthropology, Archaeology, Linguistics, Maori Studies* Vol. 48. Department of Anthropology, University of Auckland.

———. 1979. "In Search of Beach-la-Mar: Towards a History of Pacific Pidgin English." *Te Reo* 22:3–64.

———. 1990. "Pidgin English and Pidgin Maori in New Zealand." In Allan Bell and Janet Holms (eds.), *New Zealand Ways of Speaking English*. Clevedon, England: Multilingual Matters.

Dana, Jr., Richard Henry. 1911 [1840]. *Two Years Before the Mast. A Personal Narrative.* Boston: Houghton Mifflin Co.

Day, Richard R. 1987. "Early Pidginization in Hawaii." In Gilbert (ed.), 163–76.

Delano, Amasa. 1970 [1817]. *Narrative of Voyages and Travels in the Northern and Southern Hemispheres, Comprising Three Voyages Round the World; Together with a Voyage of Survey and Discovery, in the Pacific Ocean and Oriental Islands.* Reprint. New York: Praeger Publishers.

Dordillon, René Ildefonse. 1931–32. *Grammaire et dictionnaire de la langue des îles Marquises.* (Travaux et mémoires de l'institut d'éthnologie 17–18.) Paris: Institut d'éthnologie.

Drechsel, Emanuel J. 1997. *Mobilian Jargon: Linguistic and Sociohistorical Aspects of an Americna Indian Pidgin.* Oxford: Oxford University Press.

———. forthcoming. "Indigenous Pidgins of North America in the Their Sociohistorical Context." *Proceedings of the 22nd Annual Meeting of the Berkeley Linguistics Society.* Berkeley: Berkeley Linguistics Society.

——— and T. Haunani Makuakāne. 1982. "Hawaiian Loanwords in Two Native American Pidgins." *International Journal of American Linguistics* 48:460–67.

——— and T. Haunani Makuakāne. 1996. "The Sociolinguistic History of Hawaiian Loan Words in Northwestern North America." Presented at the Hawai'i/Pacific and Pacific Northwest Joint Regional Conference of the Association for Asian American Studies, "Configuring Pacific Diasporas: Indigenous and Immigrant Communities." Honolulu, 25–26 March 1996.

Dumont d'Urville, J. S. C. 1834–35. *Voyage pittoresque autour du monde.* Resumé général des voyages de decouvertes. Paris: L. Tenré and Henri Dupuy.

Dupperey, L[ouis] I[sidore]. 1826. *Voyage autour du monde, exécuté par ordre du roi sur la corvette de sa majesté, la coquille, pendant les années 1822, 1823, 1824 et 1825 ...* Volume 1, Part 1. Paris: Arthus Bertrand, Libraire-Éditeur.

Fanning, Edmund. 1924. *Voyages and Discoveries in the South Seas 1792–1832.* Salem, MA: Marine Research Society.

Finney, Ben. 1994. *Voyage of Rediscovery. A Cultural Odyssey Through Polynesia.* Berkeley: University of California Press.

Gilbert Glenn G., (ed.). 1987. *Pidgin and Creole Languages.* Essays in Memory of John E. Reinecke. Honolulu: University of Hawai'i Press.

Keesing, Roger M. 1988. *Melanesian Pidgin and the Oceanic Substrate*. Stanford: Stanford University Press.

Koppel, Tom. 1995. *Kanaka*. The Untold Story of Hawaiian Pioneers in British Columbia and the Pacific Northwest. Vancouver: Whitecap Books.

Markham, Albert Hastings. 1970 [1873]. *The Cruise of the "Rosario" Amongst the New Hebrides and Santa Cruz Islands, Exposing the Recent Atrocities Connected With the Kidnapping of Natives in the South Seas*. Folkestone, England: Dawsons of Pall Mall.

Melville, Herman. 1959 [1846]. *Typee*. A Real Romance of the South Sea. With an introduction by C. Merton Babcock. New York: Harper & Brothers.

———. 1908 [1847]. *Omoo*. Edited by Ernest Rhys. London: J. M. Dent & Sons.

Milner, G. B. 1966. *Samoan Dictionary*. Samoan-English, English-Samoan. Aotearoa: Polynesian Press.

Moore, Anneliese. 1977. "Harry Maitey: from Polynesia to Prussia." *Hawaiian Journal of History* 11:125–61.

Mühlhäusler, Peter. 1986. *Pidgin and Creole Linguistics*. Oxford: Blackwell.

Muysken, Pieter. 1994. "The First Seven Years, Fat or Lean?" *Journal of Pidgin and Creole Languages* 9:103–7.

Ngata, H. M. 1993. *English-Maori Dictionary*. Wellington: Learning Media.

Paulding, Hiram. 1970 [1831]. *Journal of a Cruise of the United States Schooner Dolphin Among the Islands of the Pacific Ocean and a Visit to the Mulgrave Islands, in Pursuit of the Mutineers of the Whale Ship Globe with a Map*. Reprint with a new introduction by A. Grove Day. Honolulu: University of Hawai'i Press.

Pukui, Mary Kawena, and Samuel H. Elbert. 1987. *Hawaiian Dictionary*. Hawaiian-English, English-Hawaiian. Revised and enlarged edition. Honolulu: University of Hawai'i Press.

Robarts, Edward. 1974. *The Marquesan Journal of Edward Robarts 1797–1824*. Edited by Greg Dening. (Pacific History Series No. 6.) Canberra: Australian National University Press.

Roberts, J. 1995a. "Pidgin Hawaiian: A Sociohistorical Study." *Journal of Pidgin and Creole Languages* 10:1–56.

———. 1995b. "A Structural Sketch of Pidgin Hawaiian." *Amsterdam Creole Studies* 12:97–126.

Schütz, Albert J. 1994. *The Voices of Eden*. A History of Hawaiian Language Studies. Honolulu: University of Hawai'i Press.

Siegel, Jeff. 1987. *Language Contact in a Plantation Environment*. A Sociolinguistic History of Fiji. Cambridge: Cambridge University Press.

Simms, W. Gilmore. 1856. *The Wigwam and the Cabin*. Revised Edition. New York: W. J. Widdleton.

Ta'unga. 1968. *The Works of Ta'unga*. Records of a Polynesian Traveller in the South Seas, 1833–1896. Translated and edited by R. G. and Marjorie Crocrombe, with annotations by Jean Guiart, Niel Gunson, and Dorothy Shineberg. Canberra: Australian National University Press.

# Copula Patterns in
# Atlantic and Non-Atlantic Creoles

John Holm et al.

*University of Coimbra*

This study is part of a continuing report of a research project on comparative creole syntax lasting from 1992 to 1998. Contributors, all then at the City University of New York unless otherwise indicated, include: Lilian Adamson (U. Amsterdam) [Sranan CE*], Dwijen Bhattacharjya [Nagamese*, or creolized Assamese], Daniel Chapuis [Dominican* and Seychellois CF], Michel DeGraff (M.I.T.) [Haitian CF*], Christa de Kleine [Negerhollands CD], Nicholas Faraclas (U. Papua New Guinea) [Tok Pisin P/CE*), Kate Green [Palenquero CS], Gerardo Lorenzino [Angolar CP*], Heliana Mello [Cape Verdean CP], Abigail Michel [Papiamentu CS*], Jonathan Owens (U. Bayreuth) and Cornelia Khamis (U. Hamburg) [Nubi Creole Arabic*], Peter Patrick (U. of Essex) [Jamaican CE*], Salvatore Santoro [Zamboangueño CS], Ronald Simon [Guyanese, Gullah CE], Miki Suzuki [Guiné-Bissau CP] and Sorie Yillah [Krio CE*]. Most are native speakers of the Creole they are describing and/or its superstrate; data for languages with an asterisk (*) are from the authors' native intuitions or fieldwork, unless the source of a particular sentence is otherwise identified. Holm has coordinated their work and put together this report, incorporating their syntactic analyses.

This article is a reassessment of creole copula patterns in light of an expanded data base that includes not only Atlantic creoles (based on English, French, Dutch, Spanish and Portuguese) but also five non-Atlantic creoles (Tok Pisin, Nagamese, Nubi, Seychellois and Zamboangueño). Our study focuses on the relationship between the form of the copula and the following syntactic environment: Before nouns (Section 1.0), before locatives (2.0), and before adjectives or adjectival verbs (3.0). There is also a brief survey of highlighters (4.0), after which we discuss our findings and draw some conclusions about their relevance to various theories regarding the genesis of Creole languages (5.0).

Our findings can be summarized in Table 1 below, which present the varying forms of the copula as determined by the following syntactic environment. The following general pattern can be seen in Table 1. Among the Atlantic creoles, with few exceptions, an expressed copula is required before NPs; a copula of a different form occurs before locative expressions, but this can often be deleted. No copula usually occurs before adjectives; a highlighter of the same form as the equative copula often occurs before fronted constituents. The general Atlantic pattern is not found in the non-Atlantic creoles.

Our findings will be discussed in more detail in the conclusion, but it can be noted here that the prevalence of this pattern in the Atlantic creoles and its absence in the non-Atlantic creoles suggests that the Niger-Congo languages, which form the substrate of the Atlantic creoles and often share the same copula pattern, are the most likely source of this pattern, which is not found in the Western European languages that form the Atlantic creoles' superstrates.

The term copula has come to be used in creole studies for a number of words that either link subjects and predicates or serve to emphasize the following word. This extension of the Latin term (used only for the copula before NPs) began with Labov (1969), who used the term to cover any word (or zero) corresponding to a form of English *be*. Using quantitative methods, Labov discovered that African American Vernacular English [AAVE] has a definite pattern for "deleting the copula" (i.e. using zero) depending on the following syntactic environment: a low rate of deletion before nouns, a higher one elsewhere, and so on. Bickerton (1973a, b) showed that a similar pattern prevailed in Guyanese CE, and Holm (1976, 1984) demonstrated that this copula pattern could be found in not only African American but also African languages, arguing that the Atlantic creole pattern reflected a substrate pattern. Variationists found this convincing evidence for AAVE's creole origins (Labov 1982: 198, Rickford 1998), leading to further research in this area. Important studies were done on copulas in Sranan (Favery et al. 1976; Arends 1986), Guyanese CE (Edwards 1980), Belizean CE (Escure 1983), and other varieties including AAVE (Baugh 1980) and across lexical boundaries (Taylor 1977: 184–90). More recent studies have focused on copulas in Negerhollands CD (Sabino 1986), Samaná English (Poplack and Sankoff 1987), Liberian CE (Singler 1991), Barbadian CE (Rickford and Blake 1990), and again Guyanese (Winford 1990) and Belizean (Migge 1994), as well as across lexical boundaries (McWhorter 1997). So far the only non-Atlantic (or semi-Atlantic) creoles for which a detailed study of the copula has been done are Mauritian CF (Baker and Syea 1991) and Hawaiian CE (Day 1972). Of interest too is Ho and Platt's (1993) study of the copula in Singapore English, which is sometimes classified as a "creoloid" (ibid,. p. 1).

Table 1: *Forms of Creole copulas in various environments*

|  | __NP | __Loc | __Adj | Highlighter |
|---|---|---|---|---|
| **Atlantic Creoles** | | | | |
| JC CE | a/iz | de/Ø | Ø | a/iz |
| GC CE | a | de | Ø | a |
| GU CE | ɩz | də | Ø | — |
| KR CE | na | de | Ø | na |
| SR CE | na | de | Ø | (d)a |
| NH CD | (n)a | bi(n) | mi | (n)a |
| HA CF | sé/Ø | Ø | Ø | se |
| DM CF | sé | Ø | Ø | sé |
| PL CS | é/hwe | (a)ta | ta/hwe | — |
| PP CS/P | ta | ta | ta | ta |
| CV CP | e | sta | e/sta | — |
| GB CP | i/sedu | sta | Ø/sta/sedu | — |
| AN CP | tha | tha | tha/Ø | — |
| **Non-Atlantic Creoles** | | | | |
| SY CF | Ø | Ø | Ø | — |
| NG CAs | ase/Ø | ase | ase/Ø | — |
| TP P/CE | Ø | stap | Ø | em |
| NB CA | Ø | fi/Ø | Ø | — |
| ZM CS | Ø | t-alya | Ø | — |

The languages selected for the present study reflect our purpose: to determine to what degree the prevailing pattern of copulas is found not only in Atlantic creoles of all lexical bases, but also in non-Atlantic varieties, and what light this might cast on the question of whether the pattern is to be attributed principally to substrate languages, universals, or other influencing factors.

## 1.   Copulas before nouns

### 1.1   *Atlantic creoles*

An expressed (i.e. non-zero) form of the copula is required before an NP in all of the Atlantic creoles except Haitian, in which the two vary. This is also the case in a number of Niger-Congo languages like Yoruba:

(1)      mo  ṣe  káfiíntǎ  rí
         1SG  COP  carpenter  once
         'I was once a carpenter.'                    (Rowlands 1969: 152)

In the English-based creoles and Negerhollands CD, the oldest form of the
equative copula before NPs was apparently *na* (judging from the conservative
nature of the creoles in which this form is found); *na* was denasalized to *da* and
later reduced to *a*. In the English-based creoles of the Caribbean proper, basilectal *a* became mesolectal *iz*.

(2)   JC   ebry day *da* fishing day, but ebry day no fe catch fish.
           'Every day is a fishing day, but you won't catch fish every
           day.'          (Rampini 1873, cited in Cassidy and Le Page 1980)

(3)   JC   di saiyans man *a* mi kozin.                    (Patrick ms.)
           'The scientist is my cousin.'

(4)   GC   bot if yu  *o*   wan kyaptin an  yu  get nak,
           but if 2SG COP DET captain and 2SG get knocked,
           di   hool   said out
           DET whole side out
           'But if you're a captain and you get knocked, the whole side is
           out.'                                       (Rickford 1987: 134)

(5)   GU   an yu *z* mi murǝ...
           'And you are my mother...'                   (Turner 1949: 270)

(6)   KR   olu *na* di dɔkta wo   i   si.
           Olu COP the doctor whom 3SG saw
           'Olu was the doctor whom she saw.'            (Yillah ms.)

(7)   SR   a   man di  e    waka drape *na* en      papa.
           DET man who ASP walk there COP 3SG.POSS father
           'The man who is walking over there is her father.'
                                                       (Adamson ms.)

Sranan also uses the copula *de* before NPs, and Favery et al. (1976: 89) point out
a semantic distinction between it and *na*. Considering the two equivalents of 'I
am a boatman,' "Mi *na* botoman" expresses general qualifications or capability,
while "Mi *de* botoman" expresses a current occupation. This seems parallel to
the distinction made in Yoruba by using two different copulas before NPs: "*jẹ́*
is used when we are thinking of natural, in-born, permanent characteristics, while
*ṣe* is used of what is accidental, acquired or temporary" (Rowlands 1969: 152).

In Negerhollands Creole Dutch there are four different copulas instead of the single one found in Dutch: *we:s*, *mi*, *(n)a*, and *bi(n)*. Despite some variation, there is a clear preference for *(n)a* as the equative copula before NPs unless a preverbal marker occurs, in which case the copula is always *we:s* regardless of the following syntactic environment, according to Stolz (1986: 152–155) and Sabino (1986).

(8)    NH    am *a* e:n difman.
       'He is a thief'          (de Kleine ms., citing Stolz 1986: 153)

Unlike all other Atlantic creoles examined in this study, Haitian CF does not always require an expressed (i.e. non-zero) form of the copula before an NP; both a zero form (9) and an expressed form (11) are possible:

(9)    HA    Bouki Ø doktè
             Bouki Ø doctor
             'Bouki is a doctor.'                    (DeGraff ms.)

Note, however, that if the predicate is fronted, the "exposed" copula must be expressed:

(10)    HA    Se yon doktè  Bouki *ye*.
              HL DET doctor Bouki pro-P
              'What Bouki is is a doctor.'          (ibid.)

(11)    HA    Aristide *se* prezidan Ayiti.
              Aristide ?  president Haiti
              'Aristide is the president of Haiti'   (ibid.)

DeGraff (1992a) demonstrates that this use of *se* is categorical only when the predicate is determined. He doubts the existence of a copula in Haitian and considers *ye* in (10) a "pro-predicate", i.e. a morpheme that stands in for a displaced predicate (DeGraff ms.). But then what is *se* in (11)? If its function is to "equate" the subject and the predicate NP, then why is it not needed in (9), or indeed in the following sentences? Can the complementizer *ki* (12), the negator *pa* (13), and the anterior marker *te* (14) take on a similar equative function?

(12)    HA    Kimoun *ki* prezidan ayiti?
              who COMP president Haiti
              'Who is the president of Haiti?'

(13)    HA    Aristide *pa* prezidan ayiti.
              Aristide NEG president Haiti
              'Aristide is not the president of Haiti.'

(14) HA     Aristide *te* prezidan Ayiti.
            Aristide ANT president Haiti
            'Aristide was the president of Haiti.'

DeGraff (1992a, b, c) proposes that *se* in (11) is a resumptive pronominal like
its superstrate etymon *c'est*, not an equative copula.

Dominican CF can also have *se* before predicate nouns. In the closely
related varieties of Lesser Antillean CF spoken on Guadeloupe and Martinique,
this *se* is considered a copula by Bernabé (1983: 1322).

(15)    DM kókóti *sé* yon dòktè.
        Kokoti COP DET doctor
        'Kokoti is a doctor.'                                  (Chapuis ms.)

In Palenquero CS, the equative copula *hwe* (cf. S *fue* 'was ') alternates with
*é* (cf. S *es*, P *é* 'is'):

(16)    PL   papa  mi  *hwe* pekaró.
             father my  COP  fisherman
             'My father is a fisherman.'                  (Lewis 1970: 124)

(17)    PL   yo  *é*    prieto sí.
             1SG COP black yes
             'I'm [certainly] black.'        (Friedemann and Patiño 1983: 130)

Papiamentu CS/P is the only Atlantic creole in which the form of the copula
does not depend on the following syntactic environment; it is *ta* (cf. S, P *está*
'is') in all cases:

(18)    PP   robert  *ta*   mener di skol.
             Robert COP master of school
             'Robert is a schoolteacher.'                      (Michel ms.)

In Cape Verdean CP the equative copula is *e* (<P *é* 'is'):

(19)    CV  bo  *e*  galinha.
            you be chicken
            'You are a chicken.'                         (Macedo 1979: 179)

Guiné-Bissau CP has three equative copulas, *i*, *sedu* and *era*. The first, *i*, is
homophonous with the third person singular pronoun and functions much like a
subject referencing pronoun (see SY *i* below). It cannot take verbal markers:

(20)    GB  abó  *i*    nha amigu.
        you COP my friend
        You are my friend.'              (Suzuki ms., citing Peck 1988: 134)

Unlike *i*, the GB copula *sedu* can take verbal markers. In addition, "this form is also used with auxiliaries or when the copula is stressed or in sentence-final or exposed position" (Peck 1988: 133–4):

(21)    GB  abó na    *sedu* nha amigu.
        you PROG COP my friend
        'You will be my friend.'                                       (ibid.)

The copula *era* is an anterior form (cf. P *era* 'was') but it can redundantly take the anterior marker *-ba* and retain its anterior meaning (Peck 1988: 136):

(22)    GB  i    *era(-ba)*  bon  kuridur.
        3SG was(-ANT) good runner
        'He was a good runner.'                            (Peck 1988: 137)

In Angolar CP, the copula used before an NP is *tha* (present tense); its past form is *ta*.

(23)    AN  angu *tha*      ua txiba.
        angu be-PRES a  banana
        'The "angu" is a banana.'                          (Lorenzino ms.)

(24)    AN  ola ma kuma    *ta*       mina pikina.
        when   comadre be-PAST girl   little
        'When "comadre" was a little girl...'              (Lorenzino ms.)

## 1.2  *Non-Atlantic creoles*

While nearly all the Atlantic creoles examined above require an expressed equative copula (except Haitian and Dominican CF), nearly all the non-Atlantic creoles below can have a zero copula with a predicate NP.

In Seychellois CF, predicates can be marked with the subject referencing pronoun *i*, which Corne (1977: 35–40) calls the "reprise." Similar subject-referencing pronouns (also coincidentally *i*) are found in GB (in which it is considered an equative copula according to Peck 1988: 134), and in TP (in which it is not considered a copula according to Faraclas ms.). The copular status of SRP *i* in Seychellois CF is unclear; it may in fact function more like Haitian *se* as in (11) above, which DeGraff considers a resumptive pronominal rather than a copula:

(25)   SY  lerua *i*   ê   bô   dimun.
       king 3SG DET good person
       'The king is a good person.'                   (Corne 1977: 62)

Note, however, that if the predicate is fronted, the "exposed" copula must be
expressed, as in Haitian:

(26)   SY  ki   Zâ   ti   *ete*?
       what John ANT COP
       'What was John'? (ibid. 63)

In Nagamese, the creolized Assamese of northeastern India, the equative copula
*ase* can be deleted (note that when expressed, it follows rather than precedes the
predicate NP in this SOV language):

(27)   NG  tay mur baba  *ase*. OR Tay mur baba Ø
       he  my  father is
       'He is my father.'                              (Bhattacharjya ms.)

In Tok Pisin P/CE, there is no overtly marked equative copula:

(28)   TP  em  Ø meri.
       3SG   woman
       'She is a woman.'                               (Faraclas ms.)

Nubi, the creolized Arabic of Uganda and Kenya, also has no equative copula;
in the present tense, subjects and nominal predicates are simply juxtaposed:

(29)   NB  uwo Ø malimu.
       3SG   teacher
       'S/he is a teacher.'                            (Khamis and Owens ms.)

In Zamboangueño CS, which has verb-first word order, a copula might be expected
in the verbal position at the beginning of a sentence, but in fact none occurs:

(30)   ZM  Ø soltéro  el  anák disúyo.
       Ø bachelor the son  of his
       'His son is a bachelor.'                        (Forman 1972: 161)

Thus in the creoles examined here, there is a marked difference between the
Atlantic varieties (all having an expressed equative copula) and the non-Atlantic
varieties (all of which can or do have a zero copula). Both Haitian and Nagamese can have either expressed or zero equative copulas, but this similarity
seems coincidental given the dissimilarity of their use of copulas in other
syntactic environments.

## 2.   Copulas before locatives

### 2.1   *Atlantic creoles*

Most of the Atlantic creoles have an expressed copula before expressions of place that differs in form from the copula before NPs. This locative copula is often optional. Yoruba is similar to these creoles and a number of Niger-Congo languages in that it has an expressed locative copula. This is *wà*, which differs in form from the Yoruba equative copulas *jé* and *ṣe*, as in (1) and (5) above:

(31)   YÌ   ó *wà* nínú ápóti.
        3SG LOC in box
        'It is in the box.'                                    (Rowlands 1969: 154)

In the English-based creoles, the locative copula takes the form *de*, which is homophonous with the word for 'there' (which may have been reanalyzed as a locative copula):

(32)   JC   house never *deh* nearby.
        'There were no houses nearby.'
                                    (Patrick ms., citing Sistren 1986: 46)

However, the locative copula is variable in some environments, and may be absent.

In Guyanese CE the locative copula is *de*; Winford (1993) notes that *de* is much more verbal than equative *a* and can be preceded by a variety of auxiliaries and preverbal markers (unlike JC *de*):

(33)   GC  Mieri don *de* a skuul.
        Mary COMP LOC at school
        'Mary is already at school.' (Simon ms., citing Rickford 1987)

In Gullah CE, spoken on the South Carolina and Georgia Sea Islands, the form of the copula before locatives is *dɛ*:

(34)   GU  tri   ə hi fren   bʊn *dɛ* de.
        three of his friend ANT LOC there
        'Three of his friends were there.'
                                    (Simon ms., citing Hancock 1987: 282)

In Krio CE, spoken in Sierra Leone, the form of the copula before locatives is *de*:

(35)    KR i  *de*  na Salon.
        he LOC in  Sierra Leone
        'He is in Sierra Leone.'                    (Yillah ms.)

In Sranan, the copula *de* is optional before a locative expression:

(36)    SR a    ben  (*de*) na ini a    kamra.
        3SG PAST COP LOC in DET room
        'S/he was in the room.'                     (Adamson ms.)

In Negerhollands CD the form of the copula that typically precedes an expression of place is *bi(n)*:

(37)    NH wama ju  *bi*  hi?
        why   you LOC here
        'Why are you here?'                         (Stolz 1986: 153)

In Haitian there is no locative copula (38), although a fronted predicate is replaced by *ye* (39), which DeGraff (ms.) considers a pro-predicate rather than a copula, as in (10) above.

(38)    HA Bouki Ø anba  tab  la.
        Bouki Ø under table the
        'Bouki is under the table.'                 (DeGraff ms.)

(39)    HA se anba tab  la Bouki *ye*,  li  pa  nan amwa  an.
        HL under table the Bouki pro-P 3SG NEG in  armoire the
        'Bouki is under the table, not in the armoire.'      (ibid.)

In Dominican CF there is no copula before a locative predicate:

(40)    DM kókóti Ø anba tab  sala.
        Kokoti Ø under table DEM
        'Kokoti is under this table.'               (Chapuis ms.)

In Palenquero CS the locative copula is *ta* (cf. S, P *está*), which alternates in the present tense with *a-ta*:

(41)    PL numano manwé *a-ta*    ayá  pa monte.
        brother Manuel TMA COP there in fields
        'Manuel's brother is there is the fields.'
                            (Friedemann and Patiño 1983: 130)

Papiamentu CS/P uses *ta* in all syntactic environments, including the position before locative expressions:

(42)  PP  Wancho *ta*  na Kòrsòw
John  COP in Curaçao
'John is in Curaçao.'  (Michel ms.)

In the CP of both Cape Verde and Guiné-Bissau, the locative copula is *sta* (<P *estar* 'to be' [e.g. in a location]):

(43)  CV  el debe  *sta* na sementera.
he should be  in field
(Macedo 1979: 201, cited in Mello ms.)

(44)  GB  i  *sta*  na kasa.
he COP in  house
'He's at home.'  (Peck 1988: 36, cited in Suzuki ms)

In Angolar CP the locative copula is the same as the equative copula, i.e. *tha* (present tense) and *ta* (past tense).

(45)  AN  kikie *tha*  thɔn.
fish  be-PRES ground
'The fish are on the ground.'  (Lorenzino ms.)

## 2.2 *Non-Atlantic creoles*

Locative copulas in the non-Atlantic creoles examined in this study are unlike those of the Atlantic creoles (2.1). While the latter generally have an expressed locative copula which differs in form from the equative copula (and which can be deleted in the English-based creoles), there is no such general pattern in the non-Atlantic creoles.

In Seychellois CF, the pattern before locative predicates is the same as that before predicate NPs: unless there is fronting, only the subject-referencing pronoun *i* occurs:

(46)  SY  mo let  deman i  dâ pos  mô boper.
1SG letter request SRP in  pocket 1SG father-in-law
'My letter asking for her hand is in my father-in-law-to-be's pocket.'  (Corne 1977: 63, cited in Chapuis ms.)

In Nagamese, the copula *ase* (also used with NPs) is obligatory before expressions of place:

(47)  NG  moti yate *ase*.
Moti here COP
'Moti is here.'  (Bhattacharjya ms.)

In Tok Pisin, the copula *stap* can be used with a locative or an existential meaning. In some cases, *stap* can take a locational object:

> (48)   TP   ol   *stap* (long) haus.
>         they COP (LOC) house
>         'They are at home.'                                    (Faraclas ms.)

In Nubi, locative predicates (like nominal predicates) require no verb or copula in the present:

> (49)   NB   uwo Ø gidam ina.
>         3SG Ø front 1PL
>         'S/he is in front of us.'                       (Khamis and Owens ms.)

However, locative adverbials and prepositional phrases can also follow the existential copula *fí* (which is stressed, unlike the preposition *fi* 'at'):

> (50)   NB   umwon *fí*    fi be.
>         3PL     exist at home
>         'They are at home.'                                          (ibid.)

In Zamboagueño CS, the locational/existential predicator *t-alya* (cf. S *está allá* 'is there') is used with locative predicates. Note that in (51) this copula occurs in the initial position of the verb (right after a time adverbial), followed by the subject and then the locative complement.

> (51)   ZM   ese díya, *t-alyá* tamén el   muhér na kása.
>         that day COP PART DET girl   in house
>         'That day the girl was there at the house.'
>                                     (Forman 1972: 35, cited in Santoro ms.)

## 3.   Copulas before adjectives or adjectival verbs

### 3.1 *Atlantic creoles*

In many of the Atlantic creoles, adjectives behave like verbs, i.e. they take preverbal markers rather than a copula, and they undergo the kind of predicate clefting that only verbs can undergo (4.0). This is also the case in substrate Niger-Congo languages like Yoruba:

> (52)   Y   ó   Ø léwà.
>         3SG Ø beautiful
>         'She is beautiful.'                                 (Rowlands 1969: 12)

(53)   JC   mi   Ø mad
             1SG Ø mad
             'I am mad'                                    (Alleyne 1980: 98)

(54)   GC   ting Ø baad!
             'Things are bad.'       (Rickford 1987: 235, cited in Simon ms.)

(55)   GU   [i    Ø min   tɪd    dat]
             3SG Ø mean to do that
                                        (Turner 1949: 216, cited in Simon, ms.)

(56)   KR   olu Ø big
             'Olu is big.'                                 (Yillah ms.)

(57)   SR   a    wroko Ø bun.
             DET work   Ø good
             'The work was good.'                    (Voorhoeve 1962: 73)

However, in varieties of Sranan that Winford (1992) considers less conservative, the copula *de* can also be found before adjectives, apparently under the influence of Dutch.

In Negerhollands, unlike most other Atlantic creoles, it is common to find an expressed form of the copula (i.e. not the zero form) before an adjective. The predominant form that occurs in this construction is *mi*:

(58)   NH   mi *mi* kwa:t
             'I am angry.'           (Stolz 1986: 153, cited in de Kleine ms.)

Like most other Atlantic creoles, Haitian has no copula before adjectives:

(59)   HA   bouki  Ø malad
             Bouki Ø sick
             'Bouki is sick.'                              (DeGraff ms.)

Although Haitian adjectives behave like verbs in most other respects as well (i.e. they take preverbal markers and undergo the kind of fronting restricted to verbs), DeGraff (ms.) considers them a distinct syntactic category. Both adjectives and verbs can enter into parallel serial constructions to indicate comparison:

(60)   HA   boukinèt *bèl*       *pase*   mari
             Boukinèt be-beautiful exceed Mari
             'Boukinèt is more beautiful than Mari.'       (DeGraff ms.)

(61)   HA   boukinèt *mache pase*    mari
             Boukinèt walk   exceed Mari
             'Boukinèt walks more than Mari.'              (ibid.)

However, only adjectives can be preceded by *pi* (cf. F *plus* 'more'):

(62)   HA boukinèt *pi*    bèl      pase   mari
        Boukinèt more beautiful exceed Mari
        'Boukinèt is more beautiful than Mari.'                    (ibid.)

Holm analyzes (62) as likely to reflect later influence from French and (60) as the original comparative construction in an earlier stage of the language when adjectives were indistinguishable from verbs.

In Dominican CF, there is no copula before predicate adjectives:

(63)   DM kókóti  Ø malad
        Kokoti Ø sick
        'Kokoti is sick.'                                         (Chapuis ms.)

In Palenquero CS, two different copulas are used before adjectives (which are clearly not verbs) to indicate a distinction in permanence. The copula *hwe* (cf. S *fue* 'was' from *ser* 'to be [permanently]') is used for permanent conditions (as in 64), while *ta* (cf. S *estar* 'to be [temporarily]') is for more temporary situations (as in 65). In addition, on rare occasions, there is no copula (as in 66):

(64)   PL   e   kamisa *hwe* gande
            the shirt   COP big
            'The shirt is big.'        (Lewis 1970: 125 cited in Green ms.)

(65)   PL   akí   suto *ta*   ma    frehko
            here we   COP more cool
            'Here we are cooler.'                                 (ibid.)

(66)   PL   machete sí     Ø bueno nu.
            machete your Ø good   NEG
            'Your machete is no good.'
                        (Friedemann and Patiño 1983: 130, cited in Green ms.)

In Papiamentu CS/P, the same copula, *ta*, is used in all syntactic environments for either permanent conditions (67) or temporary states (68):

(67)   PP   Maria *ta* bunita (cf. S *Maria es bonita*)
            'Mary is beautiful'                                   (Michel ms.)

(68)   PP   Maria *ta* kansá (cf. S *Maria está cansada*)
            'Mary is tired'                                       (ibid.)

In Cape Verdean CP, either *e* or *sta* may precede an adjective, the choice depending on the permanence or temporariness of the quality, as in Palenquero CS. This distinction is also found in the use of the Portuguese copulas *ser* and *estar*:

(69)   CV   el *e* bonito                    (Silva 1985: 149, cited in Mello ms.)
       'He is handsome' (i.e. all the time)

(70)   CV   el *sta* bonito                                              (ibid.)
       'He is handsome.' (i.e. at this moment)

Only one example was found in which the copula was omitted:

(71)   CV   n Ø kontenti ku   bo
            I Ø happy   with you
            'I am happy with you.'
                                         (Almada 1961: 154. cited in Mello ms.)

In Guiné-Bissau CP, according to Peck (1988: 217), adjective predicates are not generally preceded by copulas:

(72)   a.   GB   nya pirkitu Ø karu
                 my parrot  Ø expensive
                 'My parrot is expensive.'
                                         (Kihm 1994: 34, cited in Suzuki ms.)

However, Kihm (1994: 35) points out that these adjectives, which generally behave like verbs, are limited to those which refer to "basic qualities" (e.g. 'big,' 'happy,' colors, and so on). Other adjectives referring to "more complex qualifications" (e.g. *demokrátiku, produtivu*) behave more like adjectives in that they may be preceded by copulas but not by preverbal markers:

(72)   b.   GB   kil  tera    (*sedu*) demokrátiku
                 that country COP    democratic
                 'That country is democratic.'
                                         (Kihm 1994: 35, cited in Suzuki ms.)

Furthermore, Kihm (1994: 91–2) also points out that adjectives denoting mental or physiological states (e.g. *dwenti* 'ill' or *kontenti* 'happy') are often preceded by the locative copula *sta*. He explains that *sta* in *N sta dwenti* 'I'm ill,' for example, is less punctual than *N dwenti*.

In Angolar CP, *tha* (the present-tense copula used before NPs and locatives, which has *ta* as its past form) is also used before adjectives. However, it can also be absent in this environment. The frequency and nature of this absence have not been determined.

(73)   AN   mɛngai-ɛ    Ø bwaru
            woman-DEM Ø kind
            'This woman is kind.'                              (Lorenzino ms.)

## 3.2  *Non-Atlantic creoles*

While adjectives generally take no copula in the Atlantic creoles since they behave like verbs (3.1), there is no such general pattern in the non-Atlantic creoles examined here.

In Seychellois CF, only the subject-referencing pronoun i occurs before adjectival predicates "when a state is generally true" (Corne 1977: 62):

> (74)    SY   lerua i    bet
>         king  SRP stupid
>         'The king is stupid.'    (Corne 1977: 62, cited by Chapuis ms.)

In Nagamese, the use of the copula *ase* (required before locatives but optional with nominal predicates) was optional with adjectives until recently; today, however, the omission of *ase* with adjectives is considered obsolete.

> (75)    NG   suali bal   *ase* OR suali bal   Ø
>         girl  good  COP OR girl   good Ø
>         'The girl is good.'                  (Bhattacharjya ms.)

In Tok Pisin, as in most of its substrate languages, adjectives do indeed usually function as verbs and therefore are not normally preceded by copulas, as in (76) below. Nominalized or pronominalized adjectival verbs may also be found in zero equative copular constructions, as in (28) above. The existential copula *stap* can also be used with certain adverbs such as *gut* and *orait*, both 'well', to convey adjectival meanings, as in (77) below:

> (76)    TP   mi   Ø hamamas
>         1SG  Ø happy
>         'I am content/well.'                 (Faraclas ms.)
>
> (77)    TP   mi   *stap* gut
>         1SG  COP well
>         'I am content/well.'                         (ibid.)

In Nubi, adjective predicates, like noun predicates, take no copula:

> (78)    NB   umwon Ø tajir
>         3PL   Ø rich
>         'They are rich.'                     (Khamis and Owens ms.)

Zamboangueño CS has verb-first word order, so a copula might be expected in the initial position of the verb, but in fact none occurs:

(79)  ZM  Ø dágan el  salagán
      Ø old   the strainer
      'The strainer is old.' (Forman 1972: 161, cited in Santoro ms.)

## 4. Highlighters

Many creoles have a particle that highlights or emphasizes the following word to make it the focus of discourse. Because this highlighter is homophonous with the equative copula in a number of Atlantic creoles (cf. JC, KR, SR, NH *(n)a*, HA and DM *se*, PP *ta*), it is often included in creole copula studies. Yoruba, like a number of other Niger-Congo languages that formed the Atlantic creoles' substrate, has a similar highlighter that emphasizes the word it follows,which is brought to the front of the sentence as in (80) below. Here a verb is fronted and followed by the highlighter *ni* for emphasis. The verb is prefixed by its initial consonant plus *í*, then recopied in its original position. For example, "Nwǫ́n *pa* á" 'They killed it' becomes:

(80)  Y  pí- *pa  ni* nwǫ́n *pa* á.
      PREF-kill HL 3PL  kill 3SG
      'They really *killed* it.'                  (Rowlands 1969: 189)

There is a similar kind of predicate clefting with copying — for verbs as well as adjectives — in many of the Atlantic creoles, as in this JC example:

(81)  JC  *a*  swel it   swel, luk  da.
      HL swell 3SG swell look there
      '[See how] it swelled, look there.'          (Patrick ms.)

Valdman (1978: 262) considers the fact that creole adjectives can undergo predicate clefting as evidence that they are related to verbs: "Par leur comportement dans les constructions emphatiques les adjectifs s'apparentent aux verbes." When other syntactic categories besides verbs and adjectives are fronted (for instance, noun phrases), they are not recopied in their original position.

However, this predicate clefting structure was not found in certain Altantic creoles (Gullah CE, Palenquero CS, Cape Verdean CP, Angolar CP) nor in non-Atlantic varieties (Seychellois CF, Nagamese, Nubi or Zamboangueño CS).

A number of the creoles examined in this study also use highlighters before question words and in certain other constructions; because of space constraints, we are unable to give examples of these structures here.

## 5. Conclusions

A summary of our findings can be found in Table 1 above. There we made the following general observations: Among the Atlantic creoles, with few exceptions, an expressed copula is required before NPs; a copula of a different form occurs before locative expressions, but this can often be deleted; no copula usually occurs before adjectives; a highlighter of the same form as the equative copula often occurs before fronted constituents.

The principal exceptions to this general pattern are Papiamentu and Angolar (which have a uniformly expressed copula) and Haitian and Dominican CF (which can have a zero form throughout, except for the highlighter). Two Atlantic creoles which have expressed copulas before adjectives, Palenquero and Cape Verdean, preserve their superstrates' distinction between permanent and temporary states.

This general Atlantic pattern is not found in the non-Atlantic creoles. Nubi can have zero copulas throughout and Nagamese can have expressed copulas throughout, and neither has a highlighter comparable to the kind generally found in the Atlantic creoles. Tok Pisin has the system of copulas most resembling the general pattern of the Atlantic creoles, but it has no expressed copula before predicate NPs. Zamboangueño, which also has an Austronesian substrate, has a similar pattern of copulas but no highlighter. Seychellois CF has no pre-predicate copulas at all if i is considered a pronoun rather than a copula.

Regarding the related issue of whether adjectives are verbs, a good case can be made for this from the lack of pre-adjectival copulas in many Atlantic creoles. However, as indicated by further data which we were unable to include in this article because of lack of space, the occurrence of preverbal markers before adjectives is not convincing proof of their verbal status, since preverbal markers can often occur directly before other syntactic categories and therefore cannot be said to specify verbs. The most convincing evidence for the verbal status of adjectives is their ability to undergo predicate clefting with recopying. However, continuing superstrate influence has often pulled creole adjectival verbs in the direction of European adjectives (e.g. the pre-adjectival copula in Papiamentu, the comparative suffix -a in Jamaican, the comparative with pi in Haitian), so that in many cases it is more useful to regard adjectives and verbs as distinct syntactic categories.

Having acknowledged the importance of superstrate influence, we must also recognize the pervasive structural influence of the substrate throughout the copula system of both the Atlantic creoles and the non-Atlantic creoles for which we have comparable substrate data. This by no means excludes the possibility of influence of the kind of universals suggested by Ferguson (1971) and others, or the creole-internal innovation suggested by McWhorter (1997). However, the latter's claim that the substrate copula pattern was "lost in transmission" to the creoles is clearly not supported by our data.

## Acknowledgments

We would like to express our gratitude to the editors of this volume for their advice on improving this article, but we accept sole responsibility for any shortcomings that may remain. Holm would also like to to express his particular thanks to Professor Sato and Mrs. John E. Reinecke for all their help in arranging an earlier visit to the University of Hawaii. This paper is an abbreviated version of a paper entitled "A reassessment of creole copula patterns", which we presented at the January, 1995 meeting of the Society for Pidgin and Creole Linguistics in New Orleans. We later expanded the data base and adopted the present title for the paper we presented at the conference on "Creole Cultures in Latin America and the Caribbean" at the University of Delaware in April, 1995.

## Abbreviations

Abbreviations include the following: A = Arabic; AAVE = African American Vernacular English; AN = Angolar CP; ANT = anterior marker; ART = article; As = Assamese; ASP = aspect marker; BVP = Brazilian Vernacular Portuguese; C = Creole; CD = Creole Dutch; CE = Creole English; CF = Creole French; COMP = completive marker or complementizer; COP = copula; CP = Creole Portuguese; CS = Creole Spanish; CV = Cape Verdean CP; D = Dutch; DM = Dominican Creole French; E = English; EMPH = emphasis marker; F = French; FUT = future marker; GB = Guiné-Bissau CP; GC = Guyanese CE; GU = Gullah; HA = Haitian CF; HAB = habitual aspect marker; HL = highlighter; IRR = irrealis marker; JC = Jamaican CE; KR = Krio CE; LOC = locative; NB = Nubi CA; NEG = negator; NG = Nagamese CAs; NH = Negerhollands CD; NP = noun phrase; P = Portuguese; PL = Palenquero; POSS = possessive; PP = Papiamentu; PRES = present tense; pro-P = pro-predicate; PROG =progressive aspect marker; REL = relative; S = Spanish; SOV = subject-object-verb; SR = Sranan CE; SRP = subject referencing pronoun; ST = Sãotomense CP; SVO = subject-verb-object; SY = Seychellois CF; TP = Tok Pisin P/CE; TR = transitive suffix; Y = Yoruba; ZM = Zamboangueño CS; 1SG = first person singular pronoun or possessive, 2PL = second person plural, 3PL = third person plural, and so on.

## References

Adamson, Lilian. ms. "Sranan." In J. Holm. ed.

Alleyne, Mervyn. 1980. *Comparative Afro-American*. Ann Arbor: Karoma Press.

Alleyne, Mervyn. 1987. "Predicate structures in Saramaccan." In Mervyn Alleyne (ed.), *Studies in Saramaccan Language Structure*. Jamaica: University of the West Indies, and Amsterdam: University of Amsterdam, 71–88.

Almada, Maria Dulce. 1961. *Cabo Verde: Contribuição para o estudo do dialeto falado no seu arquipélago*. Lisbon: Junta de Investigação do Ultramar.

Arends, Jacques. 1986. "Genesis and development of the equative copula in Sranan." In Pieter Muysken and Norval Smith (eds.), *Substrata versus Universals in Creole Genesis*. Amsterdam and Philadelphia: John Benjamins, 103–127.

Bailey, Beryl L. 1966. *Jamaican Creole Syntax: A Transformational Approach*. Cambridge: Cambridge University Press.

Baker, Philip and Anand Syea. 1991. "On the copula in Mauritian Creole, past and present." In Francis Byrne and Thom Huebner (eds.), *Development and Structures of Creole Languages: Essays in Honor of Derek Bickerton*. Amsterdam and Philadelphia: John Benjamins, 159–178.

Baugh, John. 1980. "A re-examination of the Black English copula." In Labov (ed.), 1980:83–106.

Bernabé, Jean. 1983. *Fondal-Natal: Grammaire Basilectale Approchée des Créoles Guadeloupéen et Martiniquais*. Paris: L'Harmattan.

Bickerton, Derek. 1973a. "The structure of polylectal grammars." In Roger W. Shuy (ed.), *Report of the 23rd Annual Round Table Meeting on Linguistics and Language Studies*. Washington DC: Georgetown University Press, 17–42.

Bickerton, Derek. 1973b. "On the nature of a creole continuum." *Language* 49:640–669.

Bickerton, Derek. 1975. *Dynamics of a Creole System*. Cambridge: Cambridge University Press.

Bhattacharjya, Dwijen. ms. "Nagamese." In J. Holm (ed.).

Boretzky, Norbert. 1983. *Kreolsprachen, Substrate und Sprachwandel*. Wiesbaden: Harrassowitz.

Bruyn, Adrienne. 1995. "Relative clauses in early Sranan." In Jacques Arends (ed.), *The Early Stages of Creolisation*. Amsterdam and Philadelphia: John Benjamins, 149–202.

Cassidy, F. G. 1964. "Toward the recovery of early English African Pidgin. In *Symposium on Multilingualism (Brazzaville)*. London: Conseil Scientifique pour Afrique; Commission de Coopération Technique en Afrique, publication 87, pp. 267–277.

Cassidy, F. G. and R. B. Le Page. 1980. *Dictionary of Jamaican English*. Cambridge: Cambridge University Press, 2nd ed.

Chapuis, Daniel. ms. "Dominican and Seychellois Creole French. In J. Holm (ed.).

Corne, Chris. 1977. *Seychelles Creole Grammar: Elements for Indian Ocean proto-creole reconstruction*. Tübingen: Gunter Narr.

Day, Richard R. 1972. *Patterns of Variation in Copula and Tense in the Hawaiian Post-Creole Continuum*. Ph. D. dissertation, Department of Linguistics, University of Hawaii, Reprinted in 1973 as *Working Papers in Linguistics* 5.2, Department of Linguistics, University of Hawaii.

DeGraff, Michel. 1992a. "The syntax of predication in Haitian." In Proceedings of the 22nd Annual Meeting of the North Eastern Linguistics Society. University of Massachusetts, Amherst: GLSA.

DeGraff, Michel. 1992b. "Predication in Haitian: Se vs. French C'est." To appear in *Selected Papers from the 22nd Annual Linguistic Symposium on Romance Languages.* Amsterdam: Benjamins.

DeGraff, Michel. 1992c. *Creole Grammars and the Acquisition of Syntax: the Case of Haitian.* Ph. D. dissertation, University of Pennsylvania.

DeGraff, Michel. ms. "Haitian." In J. Holm (ed.).

de Kleine, Christa. ms. "Negerhollands." In J. Holm (ed.).

Edwards, Walter F. 1980. "Varieties of English in Guyana: Some comparisons with BEV." *Linguistics* 18: 289–309.

Edwards, Walter F. and Donald Winford, eds. *Verb Phrase Patterns in Black English and Creoles.* Detroit: Wayne State University Press.

Escure, Geneviève. 1983. "The Belizean copula: A case of semantic shift." In Lawrence D. Carrington (ed.), *Studies in Caribbean Language.* St. Augustine: U. of the West Indies, pp. 190–202.

Faraclas, Nicholas. ms. "Tok Pisin." In J. Holm (ed.).

Favery, Margot; Brenda Johns, and Fay Wouk. 1976. "The historical development of locative and existential copula constructions in Afro-Creole languages." In Sanford B.Steever, Carl A. Walker and Salikoko Mufwene, eds. *Papers from the Parasession on Diachronic Syntax.* Chicago: Chicago Linguistic Society, pp. 88–95.

Ferguson, Charles A. 1971. "Absence of copula and the notion of simplicity: a study of normal speech, baby talk, foreigner talk, and pidgins." In Dell Hymes (ed.), *Pidginization and Creolization of Languages.* Cambridge University Press, 141–150.

Forman, M. 1972. *Zamboangueño with grammatical analysis.* Ph. D. dissertation, Cornell University.

Friedemann, Nina S. de and Carlos Patiño Rosselli. 1983. *Lengua y Sociedad en el Palenque de San Basilio.* Bogotá: Instituto Caro y Cuervo

Green, Kate. ms. "Palenquero." In J. Holm (ed.).

Hancock, Ian. 1987. "A preliminary classification of the Anglophone Atlantic Creoles." In G. Gilbert (ed.), *Pidgin andCreole Languages: Essays in Memory of John E. Reinecke.* Honolulu: University Press of Hawaii, 264–354.

Ho, Mian-Lian, and John T. Platt. *Dynamics of a Contact Continuum: Singaporean English.* Clarendon Press: Oxford.

Holm, John. 1976. "Variability of the copula in Black English and its creole kin." First version of a paper presented to the Society for Caribbean Linguistics, Guyana; published in 1984 with an afterword in *American Speech* 59(4): 291–309.

Holm, John. 1988–89. *Pidgins and Creoles.* Cambridge: Cambridge University Press, 2 vols.

Holm, John, ed. ms. *Comparative Creole Syntax.* Department of Linguistics, City University of New York.

Khamis, Cornelia and Jonathan Owens. ms. "Nubi." In J. Holm (ed.).

Kihm, Alain. 1994. *Kriyol syntax: the Portuguese-based creole language of Guinea-Bissau.* Amsterdam: John Benjamins.

Labov, William. 1969. "Contraction, deletion, and inherent variability of the English copula." *Language* 45: 715–762.

Labov, William. 1982. "Objectivity and commitment in linguistic science: The case of the Black English trial in Ann Arbor." *Language in Society* 11: 165–201.

Labov, William, ed. 1980. *Locating Language in Time and Space*. New York: Academic Press.

Lewis, Anthony. 1970. *A Descriptive Analysis of the Palenquero Dialect*. M. A. thesis, University of the West Indies at Mona, Jamaica.

Lorenzino, Gerardo. ms. "Angolar." In J. Holm (ed.).

Macedo, Donaldo P. 1979. *A linguistic approach to the Capeverdean language*. D.Ed. dissertation, Boston University. Ann Arbor: University Microfilms.

McWhorter, John. 1997. "Lost in transmission: A case for the independent emergence of the Atlantic creole copula." In Arthur Spears and Donald Winford (eds.), *The Structure and Status of Pidgins and Creoles*. Amsterdam: John Benjamins, 241–61.

Mello, Heliana. ms. "Cape Verdean." In J. Holm (ed.).

Michel, Abigail. ms. "Papiamentu." In J. Holm (ed.).

Migge, Bettina. 1994. "The emergence of creole copulas: evidence from Belize Creole." Paper presented at the annual meeting of the Society for Caribbean Linguistics, Georgetown, Guyana.

Patrick, Peter. ms. "Jamaican." In J. Holm (ed.).

Peck, Stephen M., Jr. 1988. *Tense, aspect and Mood in Guinea-Casamance Portuguese Creole*. Ph. D. dissertation, University of California, Los Angeles.

Poplack, Shana and David Sankoff. 1987. "The Philadelphia story in the Spanish Caribbean." *American Speech* 62(4): 291–314.

Rickford, John R. 1987. *Dimensions of a Creole Continuum*. Stanford: Stanford University Press.

Rickford, John. 1998. "The creole origins of African American Vernacular English: Evidence from Copula absence." In Salikoko S. Mufwene, John R. Rickford, Guy Bailey and John Baugh (eds.), *African American English*. London: Routledge, 154–200.

Rickford, John and Renee Blake. 1990. "Copula contraction and absence in Barbadian English, Samaná English and Vernacular Black English." In K. Hall et al. (eds.), *Proceedings of the 16th Annual Meeting of the Berkeley Linguistics Society*. Berkeley: Berkeley Linguistics Society, pp. 257–268.

Rowlands, E. C. 1969. *Teach Yourself Yoruba*. London: The English Universities Press.

Sabino, Robin. 1986. "An examination of the copula in Negerhollands." Paper presented to the Society for Caribbean Linguistics, Trinidad.

Santoro, Salvatore. ms. "Zamboangueño Creole Spanish." In J.Holm (ed.).

Sebba, Mark. 1986. "Adjectives and copulas in Sranan Tongo." *Journal of Pidgin and Creole Linguistics* 1:1, 109–121.

Seuren, Pieter A. M. 1981. "Tense and aspect in Sranan." *Linguistics* 19, 1043–1076.

Seuren, Pieter. 1986. "Adjectives as Adjectives in Sranan: A reply to Sebba." *Journal of Pidgin and Creole Linguistics* 1:1, 123–134.

Silva, Izione. 1985. *Variation and change in the verbal system of Capeverdean Crioulo.* Ph. D. dissertation, Georgetown University. Ann Arbor: University Microfilms.

Simon, Ronald. ms. "Guyanese and Gullah Creole English." In J. Holm (ed.).

Singler, John V. 1991. "Copula variation in Liberian Settler English and American Black English." In Walter Edwards and Don Winford (eds.), 1991:129–164.

Sistren, with Honor Ford Smith, ed. 1986. *Lionheart Gal: Life Stories of Jamaican Women.* London: The Women's Press.

Stolz, Thomas. 1986. *Gibt es das kreolische Sprachwandelmodell? Vergleichende Grammatik des Negerholländischen.* Frankfurt: Peter Lang. Europäische Hochschulschriften 21 (46).

Suzuki, Miki. ms. "Guiné-Bissau Creole Portuguese." In J. Holm (ed.).

Taylor, Douglas. 1951. "Structural outline of Caribbean Creole." *Word* 7:43–59.

Taylor, Douglas. 1977. *Languages of the West Indies.* Baltimore: Johns Hopkins University Press.

Turner, Lorenzo D. 1949. *Africanisms in the Gullah Dialect.* Ann Arbor: University of Michigan Press (1969 reprint).

Valdman, Albert. 1978. *Le Créole: Structure, Statut et Origine.* Paris: Klincksieck.

Voorhoeve, Jan. 1957. "The verbal system in Sranan." *Lingua* 6:374–396.

Voorhoeve, Jan. 1962. *Sranan Syntax.* Amsterdam: North Holland.

Winford, Donald. 1990. "Copula variability, accountability, and the concept of 'poly-lectal' grammars." *Journal of Pidgin and Creole Linguistics* 5(2): 223–252.

Winford, Donald. 1992. "Attributive predication in Sranan and New World creoles." Paper presented at the annual meeting of the Society for Caribbean Linguistics, Barbados.

Winford, Donald. 1993. *Predication in Caribbean English Creole.* Amsterdam and Philadelphia: John Benjamins.

Yillah, Sorie. ms. "Krio." In J. Holm (ed.).

# Skeletons in the Closet

## Anomalies in the Behavior of the Saramaccan Copula

John McWhorter

*University of California, Berkeley*

## 1.  Introduction

In McWhorter (1996a) I argue that despite the demonstrability of substrate influence in some areas of Atlantic creole grammar, the traditional application of the transfer hypothesis to copular items is, while superficially plausible, in fact invalid upon examination, and points the way to more constrained versions of the transfer hypothesis in creolistics. In this paper, I will supplement that argument with a demonstration from a single creole, Saramaccan of Suriname, South America, in order to more fully demonstrate that the transfer hypothesis founders upon the synchronic, diachronic, comparative, and demographic evidence pertinent to a particular, relatively well-studied context. Specifically, I will here demonstrate that the Saramaccan copula *dé*, which is traditionally analyzed as a locative verb calqued upon West African equivalents, in fact developed independently of the West African equivalents, which themselves had no appreciable impact upon the development of Saramaccan grammar.

## 2.  The Traditional Case for the Locative Copula as Substrate Calque

Dennis & Scott (1975) were the first to suggest that the distribution and behavior of copular morphemes in these languages demonstrated strong influence from their substrate languages. However, Baugh (1979) and Holm (1976, 1984, 1988: 175–82) developed the argument and were the first to bring it to wide attention. Taylor (1977: 184–90) made a similar argument, and Alleyne (1980: 165–6) went on to lend support, with Boretzky (1983) later concurring.

The preliminary spur for this argument is that traditional descriptions of Atlantic English-based creoles (henceforth AECs), including Saramaccan (henceforth SM), describe a division of labor between the copula *da* (*na* or *a*) for equative sentences and *dɛ* for locative. For example, Rountree (1992) presents for SM a division of labor between *da* and *dɛ:*

> (1)     Sambíli **da**  wómi.
>         Sambili COP man
>         'Sambili is a man.'                                                              (9)
>
> (2)     Mi **dé**  akí.
>         I   COP here
>         'I am here.'                                                              (ibid. 8)

A similar subdivision is documented by Bailey (1966) for Jamaican Creole English, Escure (1983) for Belizean Creole English, Bickerton (1975) and Rickford (1987) for Guyanese Creole English, Todd (1973) for Krio, Seuren (1981) for Sranan, among many others.

The substratist derivation, then, proceeds from the fact that West African languages important in the Atlantic-based English Creole substrate typically also use a variety of copulas according to syntactic and semantic context. For example, Ewe uses one copula, *nye*, in the equative context:

> (3)     Ló        é-**nye** tɔmelã.
>         crocodile he-is aquatic animal
>         'The crocodile is an animal that lives in the water.'
>
>                                                               (Westermann 1930: 91)

while there is another, *lè*, used in locative sentences:

> (4)     É-**lè**    xɔ    me.
>         he-COP house in
>         'He is in the house.'                                  (Westermann 1930: 91)

The situation is similar in all of the important substrate languages, including the following:[1]

Table 1: *Copulas in the Atlantic Creole Substrate*

|          | Wolof | Mandinka | Akan | Yoruba | Ewe | Gã   | Igbo | Kikongo |
|----------|-------|----------|------|--------|-----|------|------|---------|
| Equative | *la*  | *mu*     | *yɛ* | *jé*   | *nye* | *dzhi* | *bù* | *i*     |
| Locative | *nekk* | *be*    | *wɔ* | *wà*   | *lè* | *yɛ* | *dì* | *-ina*  |

However, diachronic syntactic analysis, in combination with the tenets of language contact, suggest that the above correspondences are actually merely coincidental, as I have shown in McWhorter (1996a). The substratist case is weakened even further when viewed in the light of Saramaccan [SM] specifically.

## 3.  The Copula in Modern SM

In order to make clear the grounds for my claims, it will first be necessary to provide a more extended description of the copular domain in SM than has hitherto appeared in the literature. All uncredited sentences were tested on five informants by the author, unless otherwise noted.

I will operate under a definition of the copula which is somewhat constrained in comparison to that utilized in many other creole studies. A copula is here defined, along the lines of Lyons (1968: 322–3, 388–9), as an overt connecting link between a subject and a verbless predicate. The copula under this definition is traditionally described as appearing in two sentence types, the equative and the locative/existential.

Equative sentences are subdivided into two subtypes. Identificational sentences connote an equation between the subject and the predicate, as in *George is my father.* In class sentences, the subject is a subset of the set denoted by the predicate, as in *George is a dog,* or *a fork is something you eat with.* In locative sentences, the predicate denotes location in time or space, as in *George is in the garden.*

### 3.1 *Equative Sentences*

While European languages do not overtly mark the difference described above between identificational and class sentences within the equative realm, my research shows that this distinction is indeed encoded in SM. With identificational sentences, *da* is used:

(5)    Mi **da** i    tatá.
       I   COP your father
       'I am your father.'

(6)    Adám **da**  dí  fósu líbisɛmbɛ.
       Adam COP the first human-being
       'Adam is the first person.'

(7)    Noo dí nɛ́n,  hɛn **da**  sukúma.
       then the name it   COP foam
       'Foam was his name.'

However, in class equative sentences, it is not only grammatical but also customary to use *dé* rather than *da*. Note:[2]

(8)    Dágu **dé** wan mbéti ku  fó  fútu.
        dog  is a    animal with four paw
        'A dog is an animal with four paws.'

(9)    A **dé**  wan gaán dágu.
        it COP a   big  dog
        'It is a big dog.'

(10)   Méliki **dé** wan soní dí  miíi ta-bebé.
        milk  is a    thing REL child HAB-drink
        'Milk is something that a child drinks.'

(11)   ... bigá   dí wómi **dé** témbɛma.
        because the man  COP carpenter
        ... because he was a carpenter. (Glock 1972: 58)[3]

Furthermore, in identificational sentences, *da* is only grammatical in present tense sentences upon which no constituent movement has applied. In a non-present identificational sentence, *da* is replaced categorically by *dé*. Thus typical AEC constructions like the Guyanese *Jan bin-a wan dakta* "John was a doctor" are foreign to SM:

(12)   Dí fósu líbisɛmbɛ     bi-**dé**   Adám. (*... bi-**da** Adam.)
        the first human-being ANT-COP Adam
        'The first person was Adam.'

(13)   Mi tatá  o-**dé**   dí kabiténi.
        my father FUT-COP the captain
        'My father is going to be the captain.'

Nor can *da* appear sentence-finally, in which case *dé* replaces it as well. Note this pair:

(14)   Mi sábi  ámbɛ **da**  i.
        I   know who  COP you
        'I know who you are.'

(15)   Mi sábi  ámbɛ i   **dé**.
        I   know who  you are
        'I know who you are.'

### 3.2 *Locative and Other Sentences*

As in related creoles, *dé* is used as the copula in locative sentences:

(16)   Dí wómi **dé** a    wósu.
       the man  COP LOC house
       'The man is at home.'

(17)   Dí wómi **dé** a    páu déndu.
       the man  COP LOC tree inside
       'The man is in the tree.'

(18)   Anasí **dé** a    wan kɔndé.
       Anasi COP LOC a    village
       Anasi was in a village.

It is also used in existential sentences:

(19)   A bi-**dé**  hángi   tén.
       it ANT-be hungry time
       'There was a famine.'         (collected from informant V, 12/5/92)

(20)   Sɛmbé seéi an   **dé** u  bebé wáta.
       person EMPH NEG be for drink water
       'No one could drink the water.'     (Rountree & Glock 1976a: 177)

However, this hardly exhausts the wide range of uses of *dé*, and it is clear that
the characterization of *dé* in SM as "locative" would be too narrow. Most of the
contexts in which *dé* is used are not even metaphorical extensions of locativity,
as the existential usage is. In SM, *dé* is best characterized simply as a verb "to
be", rather than "to be at". Note its use in expressions of general condition:

(21)   A sa-**dé** an   kaí dé  wánte.
       it FUT-be NEG fall there immediately
       'It could be that it won't drop right away.'
                                          (Rountree & Glock 1976a: 185)

We also see that *dé* translates best simply as "to be" in sentences in which it is
used to indicate "to conduct oneself [in a certain way]":

(22)   Ma je i   **dé** bumbúu miíi...
       but if you be good    child
       'But if you are a good child...'     (Rountree & Glock 1977: 188)

Under a characterization as simply a verb "to be", various other uses of *dé* are unsurpris-
ing. For example, *dé* is used to indicate manner, often with adverbial ideophones:

domains, *de* always shared the equative domain with equative *de*. However, much additional evidence has shown that *da* in SM, Sranan, and related creoles was absent at the emergence of the language and only arose later via the reanalysis of a demonstrative subject pronoun (McWhorter 1996a, 1996b). This licenses a stronger hypothesis that in fact, *dé* originally had the field to itself. The historical development can be represented as in Table 3.

Table 3: *The reorganization of the Saramaccan copula domain over time*

|  | Proto-Sranan/ Early Saramaccan: | | | Modern Saramaccan: | | |
|---|---|---|---|---|---|---|
|  | Present | Non-present | S-final | Present | Non-present | S-final |
| identity | *dé* | *dé* | *dé* | ***da*** | *dé* | *dé* |
| class | *dé* | *dé* | *dé* | *dé* | *dé* | *dé* |
| locative | *dé* | *dé* | *dé* | *dé* | *dé* | *dé* |

To base this assumption solely upon the historical documents would be danger-ous, given the caveats against reading too much into sources of such uneven representativeness (Rickford 1986). However, considerations of economy support reconstructing *dé* as having originally applied across the board. It is much more likely that a once-categorical copula (*dé*) was gradually encroached upon by a new item, than that *dé* emerged adhering to an odd lack of application to one narrow area, the identificational. However, even if *dé* indeed shared the iden-tificational domain with *da* originally, we are still confronted with a very poor candidate for a calque upon a West African verb of location.

## 5.    The Substratist Hypothesis and SM *dé*

Thus we have seen that in modern SM, *dé*, while traditionally described as "locative", in fact has a distribution and behavior quite distinct from any substrate copula, and that furthermore, this can be assumed to have been even more the case in the late 1600s, when in both SM and Sranan, *dé* was a general copula meaning "to be" rather than a "locative" copula meaning "to be at".

The significance of this lies in the fact that the late 1600s were a period during which these languages were undergoing just the kind of heavy influence from West African substrate languages which is thought to have licensed transfer. Price (1976) observes that the importation of slaves was particularly heavy in Suriname, partly to replace the unusually large numbers of slaves who regularly perished because of the brutal conditions (the chance of premature death was nearly 50%) and partly because of the enormity of the task of wresting plantations out of jungle terrain. Thus, the ratio of slaves to whites was often as high as 65 to 1 (that is, with Blacks constituting 98% of the local population). These appalling conditions were responsible for the fact that native-born "creole" speakers never numbered more than about 10% of the slave population. The death rate, combined with the high volume of escapees, had the effect that at any given time until 1750, over half of the slave population had been in Suriname for less than ten years, and until 1710, 95% of the slaves were African-born. On top of this, until 1735, 70% of the imported Africans were male (Price 1976: 4); thus, a low birth rate would have further hindered the development of a significant creole element in the country.

If SM *dé* is a West African calque, then, we are at a loss to explain why its behavior departed so sharply from such sources at just the time when impact from West African languages would have been heaviest. This is especially significant given the popularity in current creolist writings of the gradual creolization hypothesis, which allows substrate influence to have exerted itself through slave importations over an extended period (e.g. Arends 1989). If strictly locative West African copulas such as the Ewe *lè* had any appreciable influence upon Proto-Sranan *de*, then whence the early Sranan token *suma de masra fu yu* ((27) above), if we accept that this was what the transcriber actually heard?

It is with such discrepancies in mind that we seek other sources for *dé*. As noted in McWhorter (1997), there are other reasons for suspecting as much. For example, despite the fact that English "there" and *dé* share locative semantics, they do not share constituency, and a deictic adverb would be a highly implausible choice by originators of a contact language as an equivalent to a verb of location. Note the metaphorical leap which such a recruitment would entail:

| | Subject | Copula | Predicate |
|---|---|---|---|
| Ewe | *Kofi* | *is* | *in the tree* |
| SM | *Kofi* | *there (??)* | *in the tree* |
| Ewe | *You* | *are* | *a good boy* |
| SM | *You* | *there (??)* | *a good boy* |

Participants in the Stanford NSF project BNS-8913104, and Devitt (1990), have examined Swahili, Nama, Hausa, Russian, Arabic, Chinese, Hawaiian, Yagaria, Jacaltec, Irish, West Greenlandic Eskimo, Melanesian Pidgin English, Hungarian, Vietnamese, Tagalog, Finnish, Bengali, Hindi, Nahuatl, Twi, Ewe, Gã, Yoruba, Igbo, Haitian Creole, African-American Vernacular English, Spanish, Portuguese, Mangarayi, Turkish, Alyawarra, Kiowa, Tamil, Zuni, Hebrew, Tigre, Kui, Kilba,

Greek, Quechua, Shuswap, Lakhota, and Karok, and found no copulas derived from adverbs; this author has encountered no others in years of study of the copula worldwide.

For such reasons, I propose that it is more responsible to derive *dé* not from direct calquing during the development of a contact language, but via gradual internal change, specifically, grammaticalization. The form *dé* is most plausibly reconstructed as the product of the grammaticalization of what began as an expressive deictic marker generated at the level of discourse.

In modern SM, the deictic adverb *dé* is often optionally inserted into sentences in order to lend deictic emphasis. In this usage, *dé* is not integral to the grammaticality of the utterance; the usage is expressive in nature. Note:

(37)   Nóiti fa    mi **dé** a    Winikíi **dé**,  nóiti mi jéi  táa...
       never since I   COP LOC Winikii there  never I   hear talk
       'Never since I've been at Winikii there have I heard that...'
                                                        (Glock 1986: 51)

(38)   Dí Gaamá dí   Kófi gó lúku **dé**   **dé** ku   suwáki **dé**.
       the chief  REL Kofi go see   there COP with sickness there
       'The chief who Kofi went to look at is sick.'      (Byrne 1990: 673)

(39)   Dí bɛ wáta **dé**   wɛ  hɛn da buúu.
       the red water there well it   is blood
       'The red water is blood.'            (Rountree & Glock 1977: 186)

It is from this expressive usage of the adverbial *dé* that the copula in SM is most plausibly derived. Presumably, at first, there would have been no expression of the locative copula just as there was none of the equative, in line with the tendency for pidgins to lack copulas:

(40)   Dí wómi Ø   a    wósu.
       the man   COP LOC house.
       'The man is at home.'

However, it would plausibly have been a common expressive strategy to insert a deictic *dé* between subject and predicate, similar to today's usage:

(41)   Dí wómi Ø **dé**   a    wósu.
       the man       there LOC house
       'The man is there at home.'

Modern colloquial English retains a possible model for this usage, in utterances such as *He's there in the garden*, or *She gets cranky when she's there at Tony's*.

When the "expressive" *dé* occurred in this position, it would have undergone

various proceses documentable cross-linguistically. First, it would have undergone gradual semantic, and thus functional, bleaching, along the lines of the
general process of grammaticalization described by Sweetser (1988), a process
which expressive elements are particularly susceptible to (witness the evolution
of *awful* from describing true cosmic *frisson* to describing a burnt meat loaf). At
this point, *dé* was ripe for reanalysis as, specifically, a copular item. This would
have arisen from a general tendency for items of low phonetic substance and
bleached semantics to reanalyze as copulas when occurring between subject and
predicate (McWhorter 1992b, 1996a; Frajzyngier 1986). The result would have
been a new locative copula where previously there had been zero copula and a
expressive adverb:

(42)    Dí wómi **dé** a    wósu.
        the man   COP LOC house
        'The man is at home.'

In support of this pathway, Berbice Dutch provides another instance in which an
apparently expressive *there* is used heavily enough in locative predications to
become syntacticized (virtually, in this case). In Berbice Dutch, the locative
copula is *jen*:

(43)    O sukwa lu    was **jen** dí "canister" ben.
        he want   look what COP the box        inside
        'He wanted to look at what was inside the box.'

However, it is usually followed by *da* "there", a dummy complement:

(44)    No, o  **jenda** mete dí  man ka.
        no she COP   with the man NEG
        'No, she isn't with her husband.'

(45)    Dunggru A. wa  **jenda** hiri.
        at-night A. ANT COP   here
        'At night A. was here.'                    (Kouwenberg 1994: 120–4)

Note, however, that no West African locative copula was involved in the process
of generating the Surinamese *dé*, which took place quite independently of
transfer. Might we argue that the West African items nevertheless were important
"influences"? It is unclear why, when we recall that *dé* immediately went on to
spread into the equative domain (a process paralleled by, for example, the
evolution of Proto-Indo-European *sta-* "to stand" into the equative *estar* of
Spanish: *yo estoy el hombre que llamó* "I am the man he called"). West Africans
appear to have created an across-the-board copula in the contact language

grammar despite the equative-locative division of labor in their native grammars. Nevertheless, to some readers, the simple presence of the equative/locative split both in West Africa and the Caribbean may give this argument an air of forcing the data into a preset thesis. In that light, perhaps it will be useful to show that the equative/locative division of labor is by no means a West African-Caribbean peculiarity, nor even a typologically marked feature. On the contrary, the equative/locative split is nothing short of common cross-linguistically, as shown via a few typologically disparate languages:

Table 4: *Languages other than West African with separate equative and locative copulas*

|            | Equative | Locative | Source                                   |
|------------|----------|----------|------------------------------------------|
| Irish      | *is*     | *tá*     | (Stenson 1981)                           |
| Vietnamese | *là*     | *o*      | (Thompson 1965)                          |
| Nama       | *'a*     | *hàa*    | (Hagman 1977)                            |
| Hawaiian   | *he*     | *aia*    | (Hawkins 1982 and Linda Uyechi, p.c.)    |
| Chinese    | *shi*    | *zai*    | (Hashimoto 1969)                         |
| CiBemba    | *ni*     | *lì*     | (Sadler 1964)                            |

Thus the equative-locative split can as easily have been an independent development as a transfer.

Furthermore, pidgins and creoles worldwide have often developed locative copulas independently of any influence from either superstrate or substrate. For example, Russenorsk had a specifically locative copula despite the absence of a locative copula in Russian (a zero-copula language) or Norwegian (with a categorically expressed copula not sensitive to the equative/locative distinction): *Kor ju ligga ned?* where you lie on "Where were you?" (Broch & Jahr 1984: 47).

Conversely, the substrate becomes even less promising as a source for locative copulas when we see that the French-based Atlantic creoles have no true locative copula despite also having had substrates which had them uniformly, as in the Haitian: *Mo Ø te nã bulõžeri* "I was in the bakery" (Phillips 1982: 250).

Finally, to take a more general perspective, it might seem that since transfer can readily be demonstrated in various areas of creole grammar, then this implies that we can plausibly extend such an analysis to cases where the data itself allow various interpretations. However, copulas constitute an area of structure predictably unlikely to transfer into a creole. Namely, as discussed in detail in McWhorter (1997a), copulas are items of little or no semantic content, and abstract syntactic function. In pidginization, we would expect such items not to be transferred from source languages into the emerging grammar, given that pidgins are strictly functional vehcles of exigent communication. Even as speakers expand a pidgin using resources from their native languages, copulas tend not to be transferred, as a result of this low semantic content. In fact, the transfer of such elements of grammar into a new reduced language is perhaps outright impossible, given that cross-lingustically, copulas are always products of the grammaticalization of erstwhile lexical items, usually demonstrative nouns (i.e. *that*) or full verbs of location (i.e. *sit*). The development of grammaticalized items requires usage and time, of which pidgins and creoles, of course, have had little. Complementizers fall into this class as well.

Thus to summarize:

1.  West African locative copulas have strictly locative semantics. SM *dé* is in actuality simply a verb "to be", occurring in equative contexts as well as locative, and also obligatory in all contexts sentence-finally.
2.  This feature had developed by the 1670s at the very latest, at which time influence from West African substrate languages would be expected to have been at its highest.
3.  West African locative copulas are verbal constituents. SM *dé* is derived from an adverb, an unlikely recruitment as a calque on a verb, especially given the lack of documentation at this writing of any other cases of adverbially-derived copulas anywhere in the world but the AECs.
4.  The equative/locative division of labor between copulas is not unique to West Africa and the Caribbean; on the contrary it is quite common cross-linguistically.
5.  Pidgins and creoles often develop locative copulas with no superstrate or substrate models; they also often fail to develop them in the face of substrate models.

The above indicate that there is no justification, scientifically, for deriving *dé* in any of the AECs from a West African source, despite the accidental similarities which make such an analysis synchronically tempting.

## 6.   A Revision

Having pointed out the problems which the traditional substratist copula account leaves, I will conclude by offering a constructive revision of that analysis, couching it within a currently promising genesis framework and even indicating where substrate influence may have had some significant effect.

I have elsewhere argued (McWhorter 1997b) that the AECs, Saramaccan included, ultimately had their origins in a contact language which arose on the coast of present-day Ghana in the 1630s; the case is licensed by a combination of comparative, diachronic and sociohistorical evidence which make these creoles all but impossible to derive from Caribbean plantations. These ideas build upon those earlier proposed by Hancock (1969, 1986, 1987), Cassidy (1980) and Smith (1987) in particular.

Along these lines, I specifically propose that *dé* did not develop in Surinam, but most likely within an English-based pidgin emerging between African castle slaves and English tradesmen, soldiers, and sailors at the Cormantin slave fort on the Gold Coast in the 1630s and 1640s, a context in which the West African languages most strongly represented were most likely Twi and Igbo. In this context, two remaining questions have possible answers.

First, we have seen that *dé* evolved from an erstwhile deictic adverb but quickly spread into the equative domain. This occurrence allows us to incorporate Alleyne's suggestion (1980: 163–4) that *dé* is a direct borrowing from the Twi *de*. In McWhorter (1996c) I discuss the problems with this derivation accounting for the creole *dé* having arisen in the plantation context. One is that the Twi were usually minority presences, even if consistently present (Le Page & DeCamp 1960: 74–5). Another is that Twi *de* is a highly specialized copula of naming, meaning "to be called", and in no sense locative (Ellis & Boadi 1969: 30). However, in the slave fort context, Twi *de* would have been much more plausible as a model for an emerging contact language copula. First, Twis would not have been a mere minority representation here, since the first English trade settlements in West Africa were on the coast of present-day Ghana, a Twi-speaking area. The disproportional Twi component shared by all AECs is evidence that they all stem from a language which formed not on plantations, where Twis were usually a minority presence, but in a context where they were a dominant force — slave forts on the Ghanaian coast would have been just such a place, where Twis were a significant component of the castle slave crews (Huber 1997). Second, while it would have been unlikely for plantation slaves of various ethnicities to calque a locative copula upon a copula of naming such as Twi's *de* on the other hand, the spread of a locative *de* in a slave fort English pidgin into the equative context could easily have been influenced by the equative *de* in Twi, fortuitously of the same phonetic shape, given the reinforcement that the dominant numbers of the Twi there would have lent.

Second, I have noted the extreme anomaly of the development of an adverb into a locative copula. My sketching of a process via which it would have done so does not belie the fundamental unexpectedness of such an occurrence, which makes the search for some outside influence attractive (although not strictly necessary). There is a possible model in Igbo *dì*. Again, this source is implausible in the Caribbean plantation context, given that the Igbo were a minority representation of little especial cultural impact on Caribbean plantations, notoriously resistant to incorporation within the plantation way of life (LePage & DeCamp 1960: 79; Postma 1990: 107–8). However, evidence suggests that they could have been significant presences in the slave fort context: the Dutch often used Igbos as castle slaves (Postma 1990: 60, 72, 112), and as prime suppliers to the English, may have sold them for the same use. The Igbo presence at English trade settlements seems particularly likely given the otherwise inexplicable impact of Igbo, down to the grammatical level, on basilectal AECs, pronoun *unu* being an example (see McWhorter 1997b for details). If so, then the development of *de* into a copula may have been connected in some fashion to Igbo *dì*, although I maintain that cross-linguistic evidence shows that it could have happened independently as well.

From Ghana, this pidgin would have been transported first to St. Kitts or Barbados, and then to Surinam in 1651, where it developed into Sranan and SM. In the meantime, transported from Surinam as well as Barbados, the language spread to Jamaica and other Caribbean plantation systems, taking various forms according to local sociolinguistic conditions (as per Hancock 1987, 1993). Outside of Surinam, it would seem that equative *da* spread more vigorously, such that in other AECs, *de* is ungrammatical in the equative domain, thus leading to the neat equative-locative division of labor on view in such creoles today. Most plausibly, after the migration of some Barbadian settlers to Surinam in 1651, an equative-locative division jelled in Barbados and was subsequently diffused to Jamaica, Guyana, South Carolina (as per Cassidy 1980), while *dɛ* developed otherwise in Surinam.

However, this does not license us to suppose that everywhere but in Surinam, the substratist argument remains valid. This would beg the simple question as to why transfer did not occur in the Surinamese creoles, supposedly the creoles most heavily influenced by West African languages of all AECs. This must in turn be viewed in light of the fact that as we have seen, pidgins and creoles quite often develop copulas quite independently of their source languages (e.g. Haitian, Russenorsk). Since West Africa clearly had little if any influence on copulas in Surinam, it is much more economical to suppose that the equative/locative split in AEC copulas outside of Surinam reflects the same universal tendencies in language change which have produced the same configuration all over the world.

## Acknowledgments

The research reported in this chapter was originally done for an NSF-supported project (BNS-8913104) entitled, "Copula Contraction and Absence in Vernacular Black English and Other Varieties," directed by John R. Rickford (Dept. of Linguistics, Stanford University). The support of the National Science Foundation is hereby gratefully acknowledged. See McWhorter (1997a) for a broader and more detailed treatment of the transfer question in relation to the Saramaccan copula.

## Notes

1.  Sources for substrate language data unless otherwise noted: Wolof: Fal, Santos & Doneux 1990; Mandinka: Gamble 1987; Akan: Christaller 1875; Gbe: Westermann 1930; Igbo: Welmers & Welmers 1968; Yoruba: Ogunbowale 1970; Kikongo: Seidel & Struyf 1910.

    The languages are those most widely spoken in the areas from which documentation shows that the English brought most slaves during the crucial period when the creoles were forming (LePage & DeCamp 1960; Curtin 1969; Postma 1990), and which are documented to have had the strongest lexical (Mittelsdorf 1978; Hancock 1971; Cassidy 1983; Smith 1987), grammatical (Alleyne 1980; Boretsky 1983; Holm 1988; McWhorter 1992a), and cultural imprint (Turner 1949; Price 1983; Alleyne 1993).

2.  The equative usage of *dé* in Saramaccan was unrecorded as of the conference presentation of this paper in January 1994; Bakker, Smith & Veenstra (1995) have mentioned it subsequently.

3.  *Da* is by no means ungrammatical in such contexts; however, in texts, *dé* occurs in the context more often, and informants spontaneously give *de* more often than *da*.

4.  In these documents, *da* and *dé* appear to co-exist in free variation in this context. The non-native competence of the transcribers leads us to be leery of overburdening this evidence with quantificational computations; most important is that both the documents and the modern language display a relatively equal alternation between the two copulas in class equatives.

5.  Smith (1987:99) quite plausibly derives *suma* from *someone*, which might lead some to assert that the transcriber indeed heard *somebody* in a zero-copula sentence (as the 1765 correction represents). However, the derivation of *suma* from *somebody* has always been tenuous, and in fact the presence of *som-man* in Krio (and Cameroonian) suggests that this is the actual derivation. Note, for one, that the phonological derivation is much smoother.

## References

Alleyne, Mervyn C. 1980. *Comparative Afro-American*. Ann Arbor, MI: Karoma.

————. 1993. "Continuity versus creativity in Afro-American language and culture." In Salikoko S. Mufwene, (ed.), *Africanisms in Afro-American Language Varieties*. Athens, GA: University Of Georgia Press, 167–181

Arends, Jacques. 1989. *Syntactic Developments in Sranan*. University of Nijmegen dissertation.

Bailey, Beryl Loftman. 1966. *Jamaican Creole Syntax: A Transformational Approach*. London: Cambridge University Press.

Bakker, Peter, Norval Smith and Tonjes Veenstra. 1994. "Saramaccan." In Jacques Arends, Pieter Muysken and Norval Smith (eds.), *Pidgins and Creoles: An Introduction*. Amsterdam and Philadelphia: John Benjamins, 165–78

Baugh, John. 1979. *Linguistic Style-Shifting in Black English*. University of Pennsylvania Dissertation.

Bickerton, Derek. 1975. *Dynamics of a Creole System*. Cambridge: Cambridge University Press.

Boretsky, Norbert. 1983. *Kreolsprachen, Substrate und Sprachwandel*. Wiesbaden: Harrassowitz.

Broch, Ingvild and Ernst Håkon Jahr. 1984. "Russenorsk: a new look at the Russo-Norwegian pidgin in Northern Norway." In P. Sture Ureland and Iain Clarkson (eds.). *Scandinavian Language Contacts*. Cambridge: Cambridge University Press, 21–65.

Byrne, Frank. 1990. "Pre-clausal forces in Saramaccan." *Linguistics* 28:661–88.

Cassidy, Frederic G. 1980. "The place of Gullah." *American Speech* 55:3–16.

———. 1983. "Sources of the African element in Gullah." In Lawrence Carrington, in collaboration with Dennis Craig and Ramon Todd Dandaré (eds.), *Studies in Caribbean Language*. St. Augustine, Trinidad: Society for Caribbean Linguistics, 75–81.

Christaller, Rev. J. G. 1875. *A Grammar of the Asante and Fante Languages called Tshi*. (Republished in 1964 by Gregg Press, Ridgewood, NJ.)

Curtin, Phillip D. 1969. *The Atlantic Slave Trade: A Census*. Madison: University of Wisconsin Press.

Dennis, Jamie and Jerrie Scott. 1975. "Creole formation and reorganization: evidence of diachronic change in synchronic variation." Paper presented at the International Conference on Pidgins and Creoles, University of Hawaii, Honolulu, Hawaii.

Devitt, Dan. 1991. "Beingness and nothingness: zero allomorphy in copula constructions." MS, Department of Linguistics, State University of New York, Buffalo.

Ellis, Jeffrey and Lawrence Boadi. 1969. " 'To be' in Twi." In J. W. M. Verhaar (ed.), *The Verb "Be" and its Synonyms: Philosophical and Grammatical Studies*, Vol. IV. Dordrecht: Reidel, 1–71.

Escure, Genevieve. 1983. "The Belizean copula: a case of semantactic shift." In Lawrence Carrington, in collaboration with Dennis Craig and Ramon Todd Dandaré (eds.), *Studies in Caribbean Language*. St. Augustine, Trinidad: Society for Caribbean Linguistics, 190–202.

Fal, Arame, Rosine Santos, and Jean Léonce Doneux. 1990. *Dictionnaire Wolof-Français*. Paris: Éditions Karthala.

Frajzyngier, Zygmunt. 1986. "From preposition to copula." In Vassiliki Nikiforidou, Maary Van Clay, Mary Niepokuj and Deborah Feder (eds.), *Proceedings of the Meeting of the Berkeley Linguistics Society*, 371–86.

Gamble, David P. 1987. *Elementary Mandinka*. San Francisco: Gambian Studies No. 20.

Glock, Naomi. 1972. "Clause and sentence in Saramaccan." *Journal of African Languages* 11:45–61.

Glock, Naomi. 1986. "The use of reported speech in Saramaccan discourse." In George Huttar and Kenneth Gregerson (eds.), *Pragmatics in Non-Western Perspective*. Dallas and Arlington, Texas: Summer Insititute of Linguistics and University of Texas at Arlington, 35–61

Goodman, Morris F. 1987. "The Portuguese element in the American creoles." In Glenn Gilbert (ed.), *Pidgin and Creole Languages: Essays in memory of John E. Reinecke*. Honolulu: University of Hawaii Press, 361–405.

Hagman, Roy S. 1977. *Nama Hottentot Grammar*. Bloomington: Indiana University Publications.

Hancock, Ian F. 1969. "A provisional comparison of the English-based Atlantic creoles." *African Language Review* 8:7–72.

———. 1971. *A Study of the Sources and Development of the Lexicon of Sierra Leone Krio*. School of Oriental and African Studies, University of London dissertation.

———. 1986. "The domestic hypothesis, diffusion, and componentiality: an account of Atlantic Anglophone creole origins." In Pieter Muysken and Norval Smith (eds.), *Substrata Versus Universals in Creole Genesis*. Amsterdam: Benjamins, 71–102.

———. 1987. "A preliminary classification of the Anglophone Atlantic creoles with syntactic data from thirty-three representative dialects." In Glenn G. Gilbert (ed.), *Pidgin and Creole Languages: Essays in memory of John E. Reinecke*. Honolulu: University of Hawaii Press, 264–333.

———. 1993. "Creole language provenance and the African component." In Salikoko S. Mufwene (eds.), *Africanisms in Afro-American Language Varieties*. Athens, GA: University of Georgia Press, 182–191.

Hashimoto, Anne Yue. 1969. "The verb 'to be' in Modern Chinese." In John W. M. Verhaar (eds.), *The Verb "Be" and its Synonyms: Philosophical and Grammatical Studies*. New York: Humanities Press, 72–111.

Hawkins, Emily. 1982. *A Pedagogical Grammar of Hawaiian: Recurrent Problems*. Honolulu: University Press of Hawaii.

Herskovits, Melville J. and Frances S. Herskovits. 1936. *Suriname Folk-Lore*. (Columbia University Contributions to Anthropology 37.) New York: Columbia University Press.

Holm, John. 1976. "Copula variability on the Afro-American continuum." In George Cave (compiler), *Conference Preprints: First Annual Meeting of the Society for Caribbean Linguistics*. Turkeyen: University of Guyana.

———. 1984. "Variability of the copula in Black English and its creole kin." *American Speech* 59:291–309.

———. 1988. *Pidgins and Creoles*. Vol. I. Cambridge: Cambridge University Press.

Huber, Magnus. 1997. "Atlantic English creoles and the Lower Guinea coast: Afrogenesis reconsidered." In Magnus Huber and Mikael Parkvall (eds.), *Spreading the*

*Word: Papers on the Issue of Diffusion of Atlantic Creoles.* London: University of Westminster Press.

Kouwenberg, Silvia. 1994. *A Grammar of Berbice Dutch Creole.* Berlin: Mouton de Gruyter.

Kozelka, Paul R. 1980. *Ewe (for Togo) — Grammar Handbook.* Brattleboro, VT: The Experiment in Modern Living.

LePage, R. B. and David De Camp. 1960. *Jamaican Creole.* London: MacMillan.

Lyons, John. 1968. *Introduction to Theoretical Linguistics.* Cambridge: Cambridge University Press.

McWhorter, John H. 1992a. "Substratal influences on Saramaccan serial verbs." *Journal of Pidgin and Creole Languages* 7:1–53.

———. 1992b. "Ni and the copula scenario in Swahili: a diachronic approach." *Diachronica* 9:15–46.

———. 1994. "Rejoinder to Bickerton's reply to McWhorter 1992a." *Journal of Pidgin and Creole Languages* 9:79–93.

———. 1995. "Sisters under the skin: a case for genetic relationship between the Atlantic English-Based creoles." *Journal of Pidgin and Creole Languages* 10:289–333.

———. 1996a. "Looking into the void: zero copula in the creole mesolect." *American Speech* 70:339–60.

———. 1997d. "Lost in transmission: a case for the independent emergence of the Atlantic creole copula." In Arthur Spears and Donald Winford (eds.), *The Structure and Status of Pidgins and Creoles.* Amsterdam and Philadelphia: John Benjamins, 241–61.

———. 1997a. *Toward a New Model of Creole Genesis.* New York: Peter Lang.

———. 1997b. "It happened at Cormantin: Locating the origin of the Atlantic English-based Creoles." *Journal of Pidgin and Creole Languages* 12:59–102.

Mittelsdorf, Sibylle. 1978. *African Retentions in Jamaican Creole: A Reassessment.* Evanston, IL: Northwestern University dissertation.

Ogunbowale, P. O. 1970. *The Essentials of the Yoruba Language.* London: University of London Press.

Phillips, Judith Wingerd. 1982. *A Partial Grammar of the Haitian Creole Verb System.* SUNY Buffalo Dissertation.

Postma, Johannes. 1990. *The Dutch in the Atlantic Slave Trade: 1600–1815.* Cambridge: Cambridge University Press.

Price, Richard. 1976. *The Guiana Maroons: A Historical and Bibliographical Introduction.* Baltimore: The Johns Hopkins University Press.

———. 1983. *First Time: The Historical Vision of an Afro-American People.* Baltimore: Johns Hopkins University Press.

Randt, Andreas Christoph. 1781. *Oto va Oure fri Gado bi Meki Ko Sombre.* Bambey. (Housed in the Utrecht Rijksarchief).

Rickford, John R. 1986. "Short note." [On the significance and use of early pidgin-creole texts]. *Journal of Pidgin and Creole Languages* 1:159–63.

———. 1987. *Dimensions of a Creole Continuum.* Stanford: Stanford University Press.

Rountree, S. Catherine. 1992. *Saramaccan Grammar Sketch*. Paramaribo: Summer Institute of Linguistics.

———— and Naomi Glock. 1976a. *Lesi Buku a Saamaka Tongo*, Deel I. Paramaribo: Summer Institute of Linguistics.

————. 1977. *Saramaccan for Beginners*. Paramaribo: Summer Institute of Linguistics.

Sadler, Wesley. 1964. *Untangled CiBemba*. Kitwe, N. Rhodesia: The united Church of Central Africa in Rhodesia.

Schumann, C. L. 1783. *Neger-Englisches Wörterbuch*. MS. Paramaribo: Moravian Archives.

Seidel, A., & I. Struyf. 1910. *La langue Congolaise*. Paris: Jules Groos.

Seuren, Pieter A. M. 1981. Tense and aspect in Sranan. *Linguistics* 19:1043–1076.

Smith, Norval S. 1987. *The Genesis of the Creole Languages of Surinam*. University of Amsterdam PhD Dissertation.

Stenson, Nancy. 1981. *Studies in Irish Syntax*. Tübingen: Günter Narr.

Sweetser, Eve 1988. "Grammaticalization and Semantic Bleaching." In Shelley Axmaker, Annie Jaisser, and Helen Singmaster (eds.), *Berkeley Linguistics Society, Proceedings of the Fourteenth Annual Meeting*, 389–405.

Taylor, Douglas. 1977. *Languages of the West Indies*. Baltimore: Johns Hopkins University Press.

Thompson, Laurence C. 1965. *A Vietnamese Grammar*. Seattle: University of Washington Press.

Todd, Loreto. 1973. " 'To be or not to be' — what would Hamlet have said in Cameroon Pidgin? An analysis of Cameroon Pidgin's 'be'-verb." *Archivum Linguisticum* 4:1–15.

Turner, Lorenzo D. 1949. *Africanisms in the Gullah Dialect*. Ann Arbor: University of Michigan Press.

Warburton, Irene, Kpotufe, Prosper and Roland Glover. 1968. *Ewe: Basic Course*. Bloomington, IN: African Studies Program, University of Indiana.

Weitz, Br. 1805. *Die Apostelgeschichte in der Saramakka Negersprache*. (Housed in the Utrecht Rijksarcief.)

Welmers, Beatrice F., and William E. Welmers. 1968. *Igbo: a Learner's Dictionary*. Los Angeles: African Studies Center.

Westermann, Diedrich. 1930. *A Study of the Ewe Language*. London: Oxford University Press.

# Variation in the Jamaican Creole Copula and its Relation to the Genesis of AAVE

## New Data and Analysis

### John R. Rickford
*Stanford University*

## 1. Introduction

As Hazen (1998: 1) observes, "Copula absence has been the hallmark sociolinguistic variable of the past thirty years." It has certainly been pivotal in the study of African American Vernacular English [AAVE] — both as a demonstration of the regularity and complexity of synchronic sociolinguistic variation in this variety (beginning with Labov et al 1968 and Labov 1969), and as a counter in diachronic arguments about the origins of AAVE and its ongoing development (see Rickford 1998). In controversies about the creole origins of AAVE, in particular, analyses of copula absence have played a central role. But while quantitative sociolinguistic studies of the AAVE copula abound, comparable studies of the copula in English-based creoles of the Caribbean and elsewhere — critical for evaluating whether copula absence follows similar patterns in AAVE and the creoles — are much rarer.

   One creole data set which has been especially influential in discussions of the genesis of AAVE are the texts of Emmanuel 'Baba' Rowe, the Jamaican in his seventies whose stories were published by De Camp (1960). Those texts and their 300-odd copula tokens have been at the center of discussions of Caribbean/American copula connections over the past two decades — see Holm (1976, 1984), Baugh (1979, 1980), Labov (1982), Poplack and Sankoff (1987), Rickford and Blake (1990) and Rickford (1996). Useful though the Baba Rowe data set is — and having gone through each of its copula tokens for the reanalysis in Rickford (1996) I certainly do appreciate its value — it is important to see if other Jamaican Creole [JC] speakers exhibit similar patterns of copula variability.

The JC copula data I'll discuss in this paper are the fruits of fieldwork I conducted in Jamaica in 1991 in an attempt to go beyond the Baba Rowe texts.[1] They derive from an interview I did with Jack and Gertrude Harris — pseudonyms for two retired Jamaicans in their seventies (comparable in age to Baba Rowe) who live off the land in the rural and relatively isolated northeastern village of Woodside, near the town of Highgate in the parish of St. Mary, between Ocho Rios and Kingston (see map 1). This interview yielded nearly four hundred tokens of the copula and auxiliary forms which are usually discussed together as the 'copula,' broadly conceived. In the rest of this paper I'll discuss the procedures I followed in analyzing these tokens, and the results and implications of my analysis.

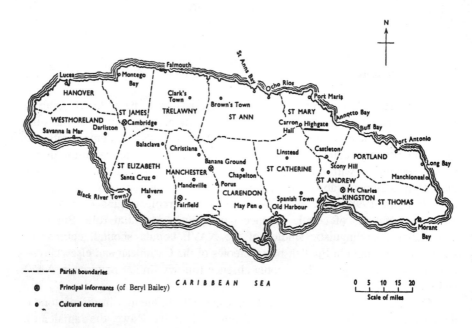

Map 1: *Jamaica (Adapted from Bailey 1966)*

## 2.  Don't count cases

In any variation study it is vital to begin by setting aside categories of the grammar in which all of the variants do not occur or in which the conditioning is categorical or nearly so (causing one variant to occur always or never), since tokens from such categories might skew our analysis of constraints on the main body of variation (see Blake 1997a). It is also important to set aside occurrences of the variable which are acoustically unclear, or whose analysis is indeterminate. Table 1 shows the "Don't Count" [DC] types which I was forced to set aside in doing this study. They are substantially the same as those recognized in my (1996) study of Baba Rowe's JC texts, and account for about a fourth of all the copula tokens produced by Jack and Gertrude Harris. The "Don't Count" types in Table 1 — about a fourth of all copula tokens in my JC data set — fall into this category.

Topping the list are highlighting or cleft structures [HI] like *a tell me a tell yu* and *iz God du dat fi dem* (see Table 1 for glosses and more examples) which Bailey (1966: 85ff.) described as the "inverted structure type." These topicalizing structures occur almost categorically with a full form of the copula (*a* or *iz*). The cases of no overt subject [NS] as in *pus a push an [NS] a draa back* also show nearly categorical copula presence (specifically *a*), even where Standard English would require a gerundial form of the verb with no copula, as in *Bruda guot de pan Rockstore a wach i*. In this latter sentence, the continuative *a wach i* is the JC equivalent of the SE gerundial "watching him."[2]

Existential sentences [ES] like *der iz tuu young fela* categorically block copula absence in JC, as noted also for AAVE by Blake (1997a: 65). However, as Bailey (1971: 344) pointed out, the relevant existential form is sometimes not *iz* or *ar* or any inflected form of *be*, but *hav*, as in *de hav tuu up puos ruod. Gat* is yet another alternative. The eleven "clause-final" [CF] cases exemplified in Table 1 work as they do in Standard English and AAVE (see Labov 1969; Holm 1984; Blake 1997a: 61) — blocking either contraction or deletion. Note however, that there are once again creole alternatives to conjugated or inflected *be*: *tan* (*a so mi tan*) and *stie* (*mek mi sii how it stie*).

In a sense, the non-finites [NF] could have been glossed over, because while they are definitely treated as "Don't Count" cases in all prior research on the AAVE or Caribbean English Creole copula, they are almost never mentioned (Labov 1968 is one exception). But note their occasional realization as zero rather than *be* before adjectives in JC: e.g. *dat mos [Ø] big*,[3] and also their occasional realization by tensed forms, as in *wi hav tu bin livin in fier*. Finally, Table 1 includes two other DC categories, unclear [UN] or indeterminate

Table 1: *"Don't Count" Types in 1991 JC Data: Examples and Frequencies*

| "Don't Count" type | Examples | Frequency |
|---|---|---|
| Highlighter/ cleft (HI) | *a tel mi a tel yu* "Telling you—that's what I'm doing" (J 2–296); *iz Gad du dat fi dem* "It is God that did that for them" (G 3–203'); *a chrii broda i gat* "He has THREE brothers" (G 3–252) | 43 |
| No overt subject (NS) | *pus a push an [NS] a draa bak* "Puss was pushing and drawing back" (J 3–407); *mii sidoun siemwie [NS] a sii di man* "I sat down in the same way, seeing the man" (J 2–314') | 20 |
| Existential sentence (ES) | *der iz tuu yong fela* "there are two young fellows" [J 2–197]; *der waz no karn* "there was no corn" [G 3–434]; *de hav tuu op puos ruod* "They have two up Post Road." [G 2–362] | 10 |
| Clause final (CF) | *ov kuors it iz* "Of course it is!" [J 2500]; *a so mii tan* "That's how I am" [2–304]; *ton aaf di lait, L, mek mi sii hou it stie* "Turn off the light, L, let me see what it's like" [G 3–507'] | 11 |
| Non-Finites (NF) | *mosii fat; dat [liedii] mos Ø big* "She must be fat; that lady must be big" [J 2–357, 358]; *wi hav tu bin livin in fier* "We have to be living in fear" [J 2–232]; *it wil bii hel* "It will be hell" [G 3–427] | 18 |
| Unclear cases (UN) | *di gon a ishuu* "The gun is an issue" or "The gun is being issued" [J 2–268; ambiguous between Noun/Verb readings] | 2 |
| Other (OT) | *ai had woz tu se* "I had to say" [J 2–427]; *if yu fa taak su, dem Ø veks wid yu* "If you talked like that, they would be angry with you" [G 2–440] | 4 |
| | TOTAL, ALL DC TYPES | 108 |

[J=Jack Harris; G=Gertrude Harris; #'s in parentheses = tape and counter # of example]

examples like *di gon a ishuu* and other structures [OT] like *ai had woz tu se* (more stereotypically associated with Trinidadian Creole English), where the *had* functions as a modal of obligation and *woz* supplies the tense.

Table 2 shows the relative frequency with which the main copula variants occurred in the DC subcategories, allowing researchers to gauge what the effects of including

Table 2: *"Don't Count" Types in 1991 JC Data: Copula & Auxiliary Variants*

| "Don't Count" type | Ø | a | de | be | hav | stan/stie | Frequency |
|---|---|---|---|---|---|---|---|
| Highlighter/cleft (HI) | 2 | 24 | | 17 | | | 43 |
| No overt subject (NS) | 3 | 17 | | | | | 20 |
| Existential sentence (ES) | | | | 7 | 3 | | 10 |
| Clause final (CF) | | | | 2 | | 9 | 11 |
| Non-Finites (NF) | 4 | | 1 | 13 | | | 18 |
| Unclear cases (UN) | | 2 | | | | | 2 |
| Other (OT) | 2 | | | 1 | | 1 | 4 |
| TOTAL, ALL DC types | 11 | 43 | 1 | 40 | 3 | 10 | 108 |

one or more of these "Don't Count" categories in the main analysis might be.

It should be emphasized before moving on to the quantitative analysis of the "Count" tokens that the "Don't Count" cases, although specially treated and set aside because they show less variability, are nevertheless an integral part of the description of the copula and auxiliary in Jamaica.

## 3.   Copula Variability in the "Count" Cases

We come now to the "Count" tokens of the copula in Jack and Gertude Harris' corpus, exemplified in Table 3, and quantified by following environment in Table 4. Unlike the case in AAVE, "Count" tokens of the copula include past tense (*waz, wor*) and first person singular present tense (*am, 'm*) tokens, where zero is a real possibility, as it is elsewhere in the Caribbean (see Rickford and Blake 1990).[4] We will discuss the results for each of the following environments in turn.

Although Bailey (1966: 32) identified *a* as the creole equating copula with a **nominal** predicate, as in *mi a big uman*, only three cases in the corpus (6%) involved nominal *a*. However, the principal alternative to *a* is not zero, but inflected or conjugated *be*, as in *wen shiiz a bieb* and *mi dadi woz a hefti trang man*. To some extent Bailey (1966) was aware of this, for she lists *iz* alongside *da* as a morpheme variant of equative *a* (page 139). The frequency of zero copula in Jack and Gertrude Harris's corpus (4%) is much lower than in the Baba Rowe corpus (22% in Holm 1984, 28% in Rickford 1996),[5] and in most studies of AAVE (where percentages in the twenties and thirties are most common). But it is comparable to the very low percentages and/or feature weights for nominal copula absence reported for Barbados (.08 in Rickford and Blake 1990, .07 in Rickford 1992) and Trinidad (1% in Winford 1992), and

Table 3: *"Count" Copulas in 1991 JC Data: Examples of Variants by Following Grammatical Environment*

| Environment | Examples |
|---|---|
| __NP | *wen im dai 1930, mi a likl bwai* "When he died in 1930, I was a little boy" [J 2–479]; *wen shiz a beeb* "When she was a baby"[G3–231] |
| __Loc | *it de di nart kuos . . . it Ø at—at nart kuos* "It is at the north coast" [J 3–319–2(0]; *E. woz hier* "E. was here" [G3–142] |
| __Adj | *im Ø taal* "He is tall" [J2–199]; *tinggz waz raiyal chiip* "things were very cheap" [J2–519]; *a Ø glad* "I am glad" [G3–051] |
| __V(ed) | *mi daata E. Ø ded an gaan* "My daughter E is dead and gone" [J3–368]; *no chrash Ø kot* "No trash was cut" [J2–346]; *wi Ø neva fraikn* "we were never frightened (afraid)"[G3–130]; *a duon nuo if di piipl dem did fraikn* "I don't know if those people were frightened (afraid)" [G3–156]; *ai waz barn in seent iilizobet* "I was born in St. Elizabeth" [G2–379] |
| __V+in | *in wat wie dem Ø livin* "how they are living" [J2–451]; *die ar livin a bruutalitii laif* "they are living a life of brutality" [J2–444]; *wat unu Ø seyin* "What you-all are saying" [G3–091] |
| __V (continuative) | *piipl a kil wan anado* "People are killing each other" [J2–281]; *shi a waak, yu nuo* "She was walking, you know" [G3:149] |
| __gwain (tu) V | *dem Ø gwain chrai fi let go* "they are going to try to let go" [J2–243]; *yu Ø gwain go in di juu* "You are going to go in the dew" [G3–067] |
| __go V6 | *shi a go kyari mii* "she is going to carry me" [J2–125]; *laika dem a go ded* "as though they are going to die" [G3–308] |

[J=Jack Harris; G=Gertrude Harris; #'s in parentheses = tape and counter # of example]

dramatizes the contrast between the copula-demanding nominal environments and the copula-eschewing adjectival and verbal environments.

For **locative** complements, Bailey (p. 33) specified the creole locating verb *de*, and this occurs in our corpus about a third of the time (31%). However, zero occurs almost as often (28%) — the *de* and Ø variants following on the heels of each other at one point in Jack's transcript (*it de di nart kuos ... it Ø at — at nart kuos* — see Table 3) — and inflected *be* (as in *E. woz hier*) occurs slightly more often than either of these variants (38%). One observation which occurred to me while doing the analysis was that the presence of a locative preposition in the

Table 4: *"Count" Copula Tokens in 1991 JC Data: Relative Frequency of Variants By Following Grammatical Environment (n=286)*

| Variant | __NP<br>n=48 | __Loc<br>n=32 | __Adj<br>n=57 | __V(ed)<br>n=20 | __V+in<br>n=43 | V(cont.)<br>n=68 | __gwain V<br>n=14 | __go V<br>n=4 |
|---|---|---|---|---|---|---|---|---|
| Ø | 4% | 28% | 60% | 80% | 58% | | 93% | |
| a/bina | 6% | | 5% | | 2% | 99% | | 100% |
| de | | 31% | | | | 1% | | |
| be | 90% | 38% | 30% | 10% | 37% | | 7% | |
| bin/did | | 3% | 10% | 5% | 2% | | | |

[*be* includes conjugated/inflected forms, present and past: *aml'm, iz/'z, arl'r, waz, wor*]

complement seemed to favor Ø over *de*. However, as I discovered later, Bailey (1966) had anticipated me, providing (pp. 82–83) for the optional deletion of *de* when a locative preposition follows. The extent to which this is a regular constraint (i.e. whether locative complements with prepositions favor zero more than locative complements like "home" or "here" without prepositions) is worth investigating more generally, with bigger corpora and in other varieties besides JC.

With respect to **adjectives**, Bailey (1966: 146) had noted that "The creole adjective, like the verb, predicates without use of a copula," as in *im Ø taal* and *a Ø glad*. This was one of her nine "principal differences between Jamaican Creole and English Syntax." But Bailey herself (pp. 42–43) identified several respects in which Jamaican adjectives were distinguished from verbs, including the fact that they co-occur with intensifiers like *so*. And although Jack and Gertrude's data certainly do show the "High Adj" pattern of copula absence which Holm (1984), Poplack and Sankoff (1987) and others treated as the trade mark of creole copula distributions, it is notable that adjectives occur with inflected *be* as in *tingz woz raiyal chiip* 31% of the time in the new JC corpus. The fact that adjectival copula absence is markedly higher than locative copula absence both in Jack and Gertrudes's 1991 corpus (60% vs. 28%) and in Baba Rowe's 1960 corpus (81% vs. 18%) suggests that the distinction might be quite robust in Jamaica. But it should not be taken as a universal creole pattern, since Trinidadian data (Winford 1992) and at least one set of Barbadian data (Rickford and Blake 1990) show us the reverse relationship, and there is lots of evidence (see Rickford et al 1991; Rickford 1996: 190) that the relative ordering of adjectival and locative is variable and tenuous at best, for reasons that we do not yet fully understand, although the tenacity of creole *de* appears to play a role.

I won't say much about the **stative** __V(ED) predicates, as in *no chrash Ø kot* or *ai waz barn*, which come next in Tables 3 and 4. Bailey (1966: 81) called the passivized subtypes adjectivized verbs, and since they pattern conceptually and quantitatively with the adjectives, most researchers include them with adjectives in copula analyses. I do the same in this paper, collapsing them with the __Adj category in Table 6.

The next two categories in Tables 3 and 4, __V+IN and __V (**continuative**), are, as I argued in Rickford and Blake (1990) and Rickford (1996), critical to distinguish, as are the final two categories, __GWAIN (TO) V [=GOING TO V) and __GO V. The continuative verb stem and the *go*+Verb futures occur categorically with continuative *a* or *bina* (see Table 4), as in *piipl a kil wan anado* and *shii a go kyari mii*, while the V+in and *gwain* V futures virtually never do.[6] The sole exception is a single instance of "Brudda Anansi *a* fishin," and the exception is more apparent than real, since *fishin* is arguably the verb stem.[7] Failure to separate __V+*in* from __V(continuative); and __*gwain*V from progressive __goV is a shortcoming of Holm's (1984) analysis of DeCamp's Baba Rowe data set, and the principal reason why a following __Verb(+*in*) and __*gonna* (=__*gwain*) seem to lead to reduced frequencies of copula absence, as in Figure 1. Table 5 and Figure 2 show what happened when the __V+*in* and __*gwain*V categories in De Camp's Baba Rowe data were appro-priately reanalyzed in Rickford (1996):[8] the Jamaican pattern of copula absence by following grammatical environment turned out to be much more similar to that of AAVE, lending further weight to the hypothesis that AAVE may have been derived from or influenced by a creole typologically similar to JC.

Table 5: *Copula Variants by Following Grammatical Environment in JC Texts of Decamp (1960), as Reanalyzed in Rickford 1996 (n = 236)*

| Variant | __NP n=68 | __Loc n=40 | __Adj n=82 | __V+in n=21 | __Gwain V n=25 |
|---------|-----------|------------|------------|-------------|----------------|
| Ø | 28% [18%][4] | 18% | 79% | 86% | 100% |
| a | 18% | | 1% | | |
| de | | 65% | | 5% | |
| be | 54% | 18% | 18% | 9% | |

[Note: __Adj includes __V(ed); __V+in excludes __V(cont); __Gwain V excludes __go V]

Figure 3 adds in the 1991 data from Jack and Gertrude Harris, using the relative frequencies shown in Table 6.[9] Although copula absence with __Verb+*in* shows a slight decline from the level set by __Adjective (from 65% to 58%), the overall pattern is decidedly similar to that of the Jamaican 1960 data and the NYC and

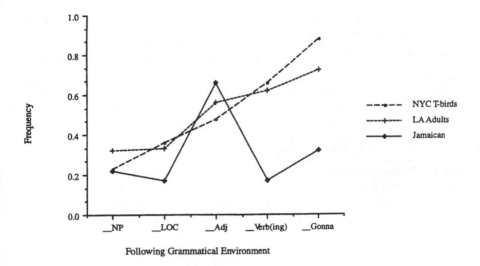

Figure 1: *Copula Absence in 3 African American Dialects, with JC Data from Texts in Decamp (1960) as Originally Analyzed by Holm (1984)*

Table 6: *Copula Variants in 1991 JC Data by Following Grammatical Environment, Using Categories as in Table 5 (n=239)*

| Variant | __NP<br>n=48 | __Loc<br>n=32 | __Adj<br>n=77 | __V+in<br>n=68 | __Gwain V<br>n=14 |
|---------|------|------|------|------|------|
| Ø | 4% | 28% | 65% | 58% | 93% |
| a | 6% | | 1% | 2% | |
| de | | 31% | | | |
| be | 90% | 38% | 25% | 37% | 7% |
| ben/did | | 3% | 9% | 2% | |

[Note: __Adj includes __V(ed); __V+in excludes __V(cont); __Gwain V excludes __go V]

LA data, further reinforcing the validity of the creole hypothesis, especially in the light of comparable quantitative data from Trinidad (Winford 1992) and Barbados (Rickford and Blake 1990; Blake 1997b).[10]

## 4.    Other Constraints

In an attempt to explore the full range of constraints on copula absence in JC, I coded the 1991 data for a variety of other factors besides following grammatical

Table 7: *Constraints on Copula Absence (ø Variant) in 1991 JC Data, as Analyzed by Variable Rule (Varbrul) Program*

| Input: .59 | Following Grammatical environment | | Tense | | Person of Subject (not selected*) | |
|---|---|---|---|---|---|---|
| | _Gwain V | .83 | Present | .70 | 3rd sing. | .54 |
| | _Adj | .52 | Past | .30 | 2nd & plural | .50 |
| | _V+in | .45 | | | 1st sing. | .46 |
| | _Loc | .19 | | | | |
| | [_NP | .00] | | | | |

[Note: *Person of subject was not selected as significant by the regression (step-up/step-down) routine of the Variable rule program. Other factors coded in data but not analyzed for this particular variable rule run are: Preceding and Following phonological environment, Speaker (Jack vs. Gertrude) and Subject type (pronoun vs noun phrase).]

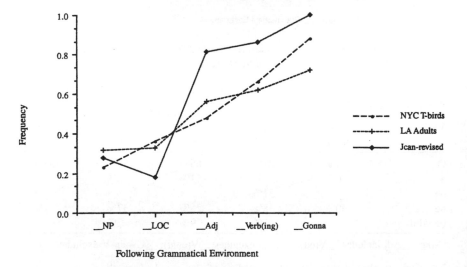

Figure 2: *Copula Absence in 3 African American Dialects, with JC Data from Texts in Decamp (1960) as Reanalyzed by Rickford (1996)*

environment and did two variable rule (VARBRUL) runs. In the first analysis, not reprinted here, Jack Harris was shown to favor zero over inflected *be* much more than his wife Gertrude, who tended to talk "up" more than he did; the difference between pronominal and Noun Phrase subjects also appeared to be insignificant. In the second variable rule analysis, the results of which are shown

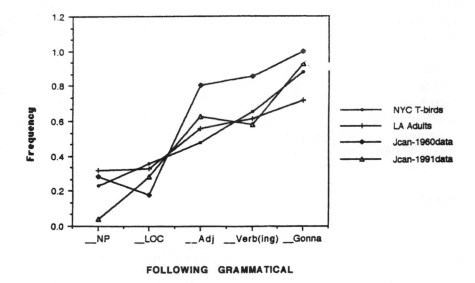

Figure 3: *Copula Absence in 4 African American Dialects, Including 1991 JC Data From Table 6*

in Table 7, following grammatical environment was selected as the most significant constraint on copula absence, but tense was also selected (present tense contexts more favorable to zero than past, somewhat as in AAVE). However, the person of the subject — whether the form to be deleted or inserted is *is*, *are* or *am* — was not found to be significant. Coded, but still to be analyzed, is the effect of the preceding and following phonological environment. Partly because of the presence of creole copula/auxiliaries like *de*, *a* and *bin/did* in the data, phonological conditioning is likely to be irrelevant, and in any case different from the way it is in AAVE.

## 5. Summary and conclusion

New data from the Jamaican Creole continuum, from interviews with Jack and Gertrude Harris conducted in 1991, analyzed with the categories and counting procedures established in Rickford (1996), essentially replicate the patterning of copula absence by following grammatical environment which was found in DeCamp's (1960) JC data set from Baba Rowe, with __Gwain/Gonna V most favorable, __Adj fairly high, and __NP and __Loc least favorable. The parallelism between the zero copula patterning in these JC data sets and in AAVE argues in favor of creole influences in the history of this latter dialect. The fact that zero is also favored in present over past copula contexts also makes JC parallel to the other mesolectal Caribbean creole English varieties which have been analyzed to date. Although quantitative (including variable rule) analyses of copula variability in the Caribbean are much rarer than similar analyses of AAVE, their number is growing, and virtually every such analysis reinforces the sense that there is a typological and possible historical/genetic relationship (see Rickford (1997) between them.

## Notes

1. This is a revised version of a paper originally presented at the American Anthropological Association meeting in Chicago in 1991. My fieldwork in Jamaica (also in 1991) was facilitated by Dr. Velma Pollard (School of Education, University of the West Indies, Mona, Jamaica), her sister Erna Brodber (writer and sociologist, also in Jamaica), and the latter's research assistant, Jennifer Thomas. It is a pleasure to thank them — along with Angela Rickford and Hilary Jones, who helped with the preparation of this paper — while absolving them of responsibility for the data or their analysis.

2. Compare on this point Rickford (1987: 175), referring to Guyanese Creole English: "In the case of line 772 (*wii dee in de — a JRINGK*, with the complement capitalized), deletion of the underlying subject of the second clause, by identity with the subject of the first clause, is obligatory (**wii dee in de WII A JRINGK* is ungrammatical). And though the line contains an aspect (*not* tense) marker, this is merely the basilectal equivalent of the continuative "-ing" complementizer that English has in comparable constructions ..."

3. As noted in Rickford (1987: 89), the absence of non-finite *be* before adjectives (which are more verb-like in the creoles than in AAVE) is attested both diachronically and synchronically in Guyanese Creole, and it may be one reason why *be* does not emerge as an independent habitual marker (after the deletion of habitual *does* in *does (be)* structures) in the Caribbean varieties while this is a possible historical derivation in AAVE and Gullah (see Rickford 1980).

4. Note that "copula absence" and "zero copula" in the case of JC and similar creole data refer not only to the absence of inflected forms of be, but also to the absence of creole copula variants like *de, a, bin* and *bina*

5. Although the percentage of zero with nominal predicates in Baba Rowe's corpus is reported as 28% in Table 3 and Figures 1 and 2 of Rickford (1996) — reprinted below as Tables 5 and Figures 1 and 2 — I noted there (p.364) that almost half of the zero copula tokens involve *niem*, as in *an mi Ø niem andro*, which could either be nominal ("And my name is Andrew") or as verbal, as an instance of the special naming verb recognized by Bailey 1966 ("And I am named Andrew"). As I concluded (ibid.), "If ... they were removed from the NP pool (as I now think they should be), the relative frequency of zero copula before __NP would drop from 28% (19/68) to 18% (11/60), a figure even lower than Holm's [22%]."

6. The *a* + Verb construction — *piipl a kil* — is after all, the basilectal equivalent of mesolectal

Ø/be Verb+in — *piipl Ø/ar kilin* for rendering continuatives or progressives, and the basilectal progressive future is just a special case of this *a*+Verb construction — *shii a go kyari mii* = *shii Ø/iz gowin tu/gwain kyari mii*. Note that non-progressive futures, e.g. *mi go tel dem* "I will tell them" are excluded from the data count or analysis since they don't vary directly with copula/auxiliary forms.

7.  Compare "to courten," and "to fishen" for the English verbs "court" and "fish" respectively, and the progressive form *fishenin*, in Guyanese Creole at least.

8.  Table 5 corrects a small error in Table 6 of Rickford 1996, where the relative frequency of be in the __Ving column is listed as 2% instead of 9% (the correct figure).

9.  Note that Table 6.16 in Rickford (1998) lists the relative frequency of zero copula for __Adj in the 1991 JC data set as 59% instead of 65%, the correct figure depicted in Table 6.

10. Blake (1997b: 133, 146) analyzes her Barbadian present tense and past tense copula variants separately, with the following results for copula absence (provided as VARBRUL probabilities or feature weights):
    Present tense: __NP .16, __Adj .67, __Loc .75, __V+ing .76, __Gonna 1.00
    Past tense: __NP .26, __Adj .65, __Loc .41, __V+ing .64, __Gonna .86
    Note that while __Loc is more favorable to copula absence than __Adj in the present tense, as in previous analyses of zero copula in Barbadian (Rickford and Blake 1990; Rickford 1992) and Trinidadian (Winford 1992), __Adj is more favorable than __Loc in the past tense, as in all JC data sets analyzed to date.

# References

Bailey, Beryl. 1966. *Jamaican Creole Syntax: A Transformational Approach*. Cambridge: Cambridge University Press.

Baugh, John. 1979. *Linguistic style shifting in Black English*. Ph. D. dissertation, Department of Linguistics, University of Pennsylvania.

———. 1980. "A re-examination of the Black English copula." In William Labov (ed.), *Locating Language in Time and Space*. New York: Academic Press, 83–106.

Blake, Renee. 1997a. "Defining the envelope of linguistic variation: The case of 'Don't Count' forms in the copula analysis of African American Vernacular English." *Language Variation and Change* 9.1:57–80.

———. 1997b. *"All o'we is one": Race, Class and Language in a Barbados Community*. Ph. D. dissertation, Department of Linguistics, Stanford University.

DeCamp, David. 1960. "Four Jamaican Creole texts with introduction, phonemic transcriptions and glosses." In Robert B. Le Page and David DeCamp (eds.), *Jamaican Creole (= Creole Language Studies 1)*. London: Macmillan, 128–179.

Hazen, Kirk. 1998. "Shining both sides of the coin: Linguistic and sociolinguistic aspects of copula absence in a Southern tri-ethnic community." Ms., submitted to XXXX. [Email Hazen to ask where it's been submitted.]

Holm, John. 1976. "Copula variability on the Afro-American continuum." In George Cave (ed.), *Conference Preprints,* First annual meeting of the Society for Caribbean

Linguistics, Turkeyen, Guyana. Linguistics Section, Department of English, University of Guyana, 301–309.

———. 1984. "Variability of the copula in Black English and its creole kin." *American Speech* 59(4):291–309.

Labov, William. 1969. "Contraction, deletion, and inherent variability of the English copula." *Language* 45:715–62.

———. 1982. "Objectivity and commitment in linguistic science: The case of the Black English trial in Ann Arbor." *Language in Society* 11.2:165–201.

Labov, William, Paul Cohen, Clarence Robins, and John Lewis. 1968. *A Study of the Non-Standard English of Negro and Puerto Rican Speakers in New York City*, vol. 1. Philadelphia: US Regional Survey.

Poplack, Shana, and David Sankoff. 1987. "The Philadelphia story in the Spanish Caribbean." *American Speech* 62:291–314.

Rickford, John R. 1980. How Does DOZ Disappear?" In R. Day (ed.), *Issues in English Creoles: Papers from the 1975 Hawaii Conference*. Heidelberg: Julius Groos, 77–96.

———. 1987. *Dimensions of a Creole Continuum: History, Texts, and Linguistic Analysis of Guyanese Creole*. Stanford: Stanford University Press.

———. 1992. "The Creole Residue in Barbados." In Joan Hall, Nick Doane, and Dick Ringler (eds.), *Old English and New: Studies in Language and Linguistics in Honor of Frederic G. Cassidy*. New York and London: Garland, 183–201.

———. 1996. "Copula Variability in Jamaican Creole and African American Vernacular English: A Reanalysis of DeCamp's Texts." In Gregory R. Guy, John G. Baugh, Deborah Schiffrin and Crawford Feagin (eds.), *Towards a Social Science of Language: A Festschrift for William Labov*. Philadelphia and Amsterdam: John Benjamins, 357–372.

———. 1997. "Prior creolization of AAVE? Sociohistorical and textual evidence from the 17th and 18th centuries." *Journal of Sociolinguistics* 1.3:315–336.

———. 1998. "The creole origins of African American Vernacular English: Evidence from Copula absence." In Salikoko S. Mufwene, John R. Rickford, Guy Bailey and John Baugh (eds.), *African American English*. London: Routledge, 154–200.

Rickford, John R., and Renee A. Blake. 1990. "Copula contraction and absence in Barbadian English, Samana English and Vernacular Black English." *BLS* 16 (Proceedings of the Sixteenth Annual Meeting of the Berkeley Linguistics Society), 257–268.

Rickford, John R. 1991. "Rappin on the Copula Coffin: Theoretical and Methodological Issues in the Analysis of Copula Variation in African American Vernacular English." *Language Variation and Change* 3.1:103–132.

Winford, Donald. 1992. "Another look at the copula in Black English and Caribbean Creoles." *American Speech* 67.1:21–60.

# Accountability in Descriptions of Creoles

## Salikoko S. Mufwene
### University of Chicago

## 1. Introduction

This paper is largely inspired by Labov's (1972: 72) "principle of accountability," which exhorts linguists to "report values for every case where the variable element occurs in the relevant environments as we have defined them." This statement follows those in which he explains what counts as a "linguistic variable:"

> The correct analysis of the linguistic variable is the most important step in sociolinguistic investigation. We want to isolate the largest homogeneous class in which all subclasses vary in the same way. If we fail to do this, and throw together invariant subclasses, high-frequency, and low-frequency subclasses, our views of sociolinguistic structures will be blurred. The regular pattern of the variable may be submerged by a large number of irregular cases — or even elements varying in a reverse direction. Once we have established this linguistic definition of the variable, we are in a position to follow the important *principle of accountability* (...)

Labov seems concerned here mostly with *justifying* why items that alternate with each other, for instance, the full copula, the contracted copula, and absence of the copula before nonverbal predicative elements, should be lumped together as one "variable." He is joined in this concern by Rickford (1986: 41), who characterizes the principle of accountability as a requirement to "report[...] the number of occurrences of a feature out of the total number of cases in which it could have occurred."

In this essay, I focus on the justification aspect of the principle of accountability, perhaps in ways that hard-core variationists will find diverging from Labov's but which I nonetheless consider relevant to creole linguistics. I discuss some common assumptions about creoles and how they have negatively influenced some hypotheses about these new vernaculars. I also propose ways in which the situation may be redressed. Chief on my mind are the questions of whether creoles form a structurally defined type of languages and whether they need be investigated in ways that are seemingly unique to them. These questions lead to another: what can creolistics contribute methodologically to general linguistics, after we creolists have learned from creoles things that seem to have escaped linguists' attention in studies of non-creole languages? The essay is organized in two main parts in which I raise some diachronic issues and highlight some treacherous areas in our synchronic structural analyses.

## 2.    Some Unjustified Diachronic Assumptions

The significance of the contribution of creolistics to variation analysis is incontrovertible. A large proportion of research in this field has been in the quantitative paradigm, especially "sociolinguistic" studies of New World English creoles since the mid-1970s.[1] These works have helped refine variationist research techniques. It is noteworthy that an important part of Section 2 of Rickford (1986), to which I return below, is devoted to the principle of accountability, reflecting the central role that variationist working assumptions have played in the development of creolistics during the same period of time. Quantitative techniques have highlighted variation within diverse creoles on some specific variables, often showing which variant appears to be dominant. Schneider (1989) makes very good use of this approach in determining whether aspects of the grammatical system of African-America Vernacular English (AAVE) are more English- or creole-like, arguing against the putative development of this language variety by decreolization (see below).

On the other hand, variation has been invoked in several cases to argue for what has been identified as "decreolization," i.e., change of creoles from their basilectal features to those of their acrolects, a process that Mufwene (1994a) prefers to identify as "debasilectalization." In the specific case of the Anglophone Caribbean speech communities, the continuum which variation produces was characterized by DeCamp (1971) as "post-creole" and treated as symptomatic of decreolization. In the same vein, variation in AAVE has been used to bolster Stewart's (1967, 1968) hypothesis that this vernacular developed from an erstwhile, Gullah-like creole putatively once widely spoken in North America among descendants of Africans — the thesis disputed by Schneider (1989, cited above) and Poplack and Tagliamonte (e.g., 1988, 1991, 1993, 1994). I find it especially useful in this context to invoke an extension of the principle of accountability to encompass *social and historical justification*.

As much as we have learned about speech continua since DeCamp's (1971) seminal work, the correlation of the mesolect with decreolization has left a lot to be desired. Several questions arise from this position. I will begin with the easiest part: the characterization of speech continua in the Anglophone Caribbean as "*post*-creole." I will then touch on a number of related questions that further support my thesis.

I subscribe to the position that creoles are not defined by their structural features, which they share with several other non-creole languages and in relation to which they differ among themselves (Mufwene 1986a; Singler 1990).[2] As argued in Mufwene (1997a), the sociohistorical factors that identify them as peculiar are political, confined to a particular period in the colonization of the New World and Indian Ocean. They are not the kinds of structural and ethnographic factors (which I have also identified as ecological) that influence structural outcomes of language change in contact settings, in variable ways.

The term *creole*, as applied to several new vernaculars that developed particularly in former European settlement colonies of the New World and the Indian Ocean, is justified mostly by the social history of the territories (Arveiller 1963; Valkhoff 1966; Stephens 1983; Chaudenson 1992). It has been used by non-linguists exclusively for varieties spoken primarily by descendants of non-Europeans rather than for those spoken chiefly by descendants of Europeans. The reason is not because these vernaculars called "creoles" were the only ones that developed out of contact-induced restructuring of their European lexifiers nor because they developed by any diachronic process peculiar to them (Mufwene 1996a, 1996b). Rather, those lay persons who identified them as "creoles" — more restrictively than in the earlier application of the term to people (Mufwene 1997b) — apparently sought to disfranchise them, more or less like children out of wedlock, from the other new vernaculars spoken by descendants of Europeans, which they considered the legitimate or natural offspring of the lexifiers.[3] In fact, the vernaculars spoken by descendants of Europeans in the former colonies have typically been presented as continuations of their metropolitan counterparts, as much as restructuring may be shown to have been involved in their developments (Trudgill 1986) by selection principles similar to those invoked by Mufwene (1996a) for creoles. Thus, Algeo (1988) could claim that British English as a national variety started the same time that American English began, because before that time (at least between 1707 and 1776), there was only English common to all its speakers.[4]

Given the above circumstances, one would expect any vernacular identified as "creole" (because of the ethnic identity of those who appropriated the lexifier!) to follow the principle *once a creole, always a creole*, regardless of whatever changes it may have undergone. The principle applies for the same reasons that standard English remains a Germanic language variety despite influence from French, and Romanian remains a Romance language, despite influence from other Balkan languages. Several creolists seem to have perceived this problem in DeCamp's decreolization hypothesis. Today rarely does anybody refer to continua in creole-speaking communities as "*post*-creole."

Still, it has often been suggested that Barbados may not have a true creole, because it allegedly does not have a basilect comparable to what is found in Jamaica and Guyana (e.g., Alleyne 1980). However, Fields (1995) and Rickford & Handler (1994) have provided evidence of basilectal Bajan in the 19th century, and Rickford (1992) presents evidence that basilectal features are still used in Barbados today. Even if basilectal Bajan had disappeared and today's Bajan were only mesolectal, such a state of affairs would not be convincing justification for claiming that it is no longer a creole. However, it would be quite informative to figure out what ecological factors would have brought about the putative erosion of the basilect.

Reliance on specific structural features among linguists in identifying contact-based varieties spoken by descendants of non-Europeans as different languages has led some of us to identify varieties such as AAVE and Réunionnais as "semi-creoles." Unfortunately these structural considerations may have little to do with the sociohistorical reasons why Jamaican and Guyanese creole continua, for example, have been called "creoles." As a matter of fact, Jamaicans and Guyanese who claim that they speak *Patois*[5] — the term more commonly used by lay people in the Anglophone Caribbean instead of *Creole*–are not necessarily basilectal speakers. This is not to say that for at least such speakers, if not all natives of such communities, creoleness has nothing to do with structural features. Rather, the features identified by such speakers as creole do not necessarily accord with the stereotype used by linguists to identify a variety as creole or basilectal.

Another problem with DeCamp's (1971) thesis lies in the fact that, by correlating creole continua with decreolization, he and most of his followers made a strong diachronic claim that they did not bother justifying with *diachronic evidence*.[6] In most publications on the subject, from DeCamp (1971) through Bickerton (1973) to Winford (1992), little conclusive diachronic evidence has been adduced.[7] Yet, no comparable correlations of variation and change, without diachronic evidence, have likewise been shown in non-creole communities!

The above argument is undoubtedly a weak one, because we cannot always wait for a precedent before proposing a particular hypothesis. However, solid evidence is typically expected with such unprecedented explanations of facts. In the particular case of the decreolization hypothesis, the kind of historical and synchronic evidence needed was not adduced, just as it has never been shown in what way(s) and to what extent "creole continua" are unique and specifically "creole." This shortcoming is germane to the "basilect" vs. "mesolect" vs. "acrolect" distinction itself, to which I return below. It has likewise never been shown how or to what extent these notions are specifically creole and how they can justifiably be used to support DeCamp's seminal conjecture.

To be sure, DeCamp (1971) invokes some ethnographic considerations, including mass education, socioeconomic mobility, and access to the mass media. However, these plausible factors become evidence only when they are situated in valid histories of the regions and matched against adequate hypotheses of creole genesis. Sato (1993) shows that speakers' sentiments against external pressure may actually counter the alleged effect of the DeCamp factors and inject more life into the local creole. In any case, as today's findings reveal, Alleyne (1971) was apparently right in arguing that creoles of the New World had no pidgin antecedents. The more we re-examine the sociohistorical ecologies of the developments of creole vernaculars, the more it appears that no pidgins could possibly have developed during the initial, homestead stages of the histories of their communities. During the homestead phase, the African laborers were typically the minority and lived side by side with the European indentured laborers, with whom they probably had more than limited interactions in the workplace (Mufwene 1996a). The small demographics of these initial, intimate communities do not suggest the development of pidgins, unless we change the meaning of this term to 'interlanguage' or 'any second-language variety'.[8]

In colonial history, racial segregation was generally not institutionalized until the colonies moved, within 20 to 50 years of their foundation, into the plantation phase, during which the non-European laborers were generally the majority and were perceived as threats to the Europeans. (Segregation was subsequently adopted as a principle even in colonies where the Africans never became the majority, but apparently it would not become institutionalized until the late 19th century, with the enactment of the Jim Crow laws in 1877, after the abolition of slavery and the Civil War.) The plantation phase was also marked by rapid population replacements, due to the high mortality rates which occurred while the servile labor population kept growing. This state of affairs led the local colonial vernaculars to be continually restructured until basilectal varieties emerged as consolidated sociolects (Mufwene 1996a) within the non-European communities, marking them as more conspicuously different.[9]

Note that the rapid population replacements which contributed to the gradual restructuring of the lexifier were staggered and the newcomers still learned the local vernaculars from the preceding creole and seasoned slaves whom they found in place. None of the contexts of this *normal* language transmission favored the development of pidgins as varieties for limited communicative functions; nor did they favor complete disappearance among non-Europeans and their descendants in the New World and the Indian Ocean of earlier language varieties that were closer to those spoken by the European colonists. The large presence of children among slaves imported to the New World in the eighteenth century (Lovejoy 1989) probably acted also as a stabilizing factor in slowing down the restructuring process (Mufwene 1996a), as the varieties acquired by this age group may be considered closer approximations of the local vernaculars targeted by the newcomers.[10]

Baker (1990), Bickerton (1988), Chaudenson (1979, 1989, 1992), and Mufwene (1992a) agree that, consistent with the history of settlements in the colonies, creoles seem to have developed in the direction of basilectalization, becoming structurally more and more different from their lexifiers. The perpetuation of institutionalized segregation in the United States from the late 19th century, with Jim Crow laws, to the 1960s simply suggests that if anything close to the putative process of decreolization took place,[11] it would have been more recent than the abolition of slavery (per DeCamp's 1971 conjecture).

From a diachronic perspective, the whole decreolization hypothesis was flawed because it is not consistent with the social history of the regions and because its proponents generally adduced no diachronic linguistic facts, having capitalized on synchronic variation as symptomatic of change in progress. There have been a few exceptions, such as Rickford (1987), which, although quite informative in several important ways, may not be interpreted to support debasilectalization conclusively (Mufwene 1989), as much as it may be interpreted to support the position of quantitative decreolization and indeed of normal language change in Guyanese Creole. However, we have no sense of what the proportions of basilectal vs. mesolectal speakers were around even a century ago.[12] Guyanese Creole still has a basilect comparable to what emerges from the texts in Lalla and D'Costa (1990). The latter also argue that it is implausible to hypothesize that Jamaican Creole may have decreolized during the past two centuries (p. 98). Likewise, Mille (1990) and Mufwene (1991a, 1994a) argue against the possible decreolization of Gullah since the second half of the nineteenth century.

Overall, contrary to arguments by advocates of decreolization qua debasilectalization, interethnic interactions in North America have not been particularly conducive to the merger of speech varieties of descendants of Europeans and non-Europeans. For instance, the development of vacation resorts on the coast of South Carolina and Georgia has not produced the requisite kinds of racial and/or socio-economic class integration that may bring about decreolization. Vacationers and the African-American populations "indigenous" to the coastal islands and marshlands of these states do not socialize together.[13] The new, more affluent, and typically White residents in these coastal settings live in different neighborhoods from the majority of African-Americans who have lived there for several generations since the plantation days. Linguistic features simply do not spread like cold germs, on minimal contact! (See Mufwene 1997c on why Gullah has survived despite the influx of outsiders from the hinterlands to the South Carolina and Georgia Sea Islands.)

I maintain that the hypothesis that AAVE developed by decreolization has been advanced in disregard of history and without support from other aspects of African-American culture. The existence of the Gullah-like ancestor of AAVE putatively once spoken among all, or most of, African Americans even outside the rice fields of coastal South Carolina and Georgia (and perhaps also on the coastal marshes of the Chesapeake colonies) has never been established. The evidence for this creole ancestor has often been identified in Jamaica, in part because Beryl Bailey (1965) compared features of AAVE with those of Jamaican Creole and showed some "typological" similarities (p. 172).[14] To be sure, she conjectures that the North American vernacular has "its origins as it undoubtedly does in some Proto-Creole grammatical structure" (p. 172). However, nowhere has this Proto-Creole, if it need be posited at all, been situated conclusively in the Caribbean. I maintain that although Rickford (1997, 1998) is correct in arguing that the Caribbean restructured varieties brought to North America by Caribbean slaves must have contributed to the development of AAVE, this does not mean that AAVE was based primarily on those varieties or any antecedent creole. Rather, consistent with the gradual development hypothesis to which I subscribe and which I find consistent with the divergence hypothesis, the elements from Caribbean varieties became part of the ongoing competition-and-selection process that characterized the development of AAVE, as of other new contact varieties that were developing during the same period. Again, differing ecologies yielded varying outputs, as Rickford (1997, p.c. February 1998) correctly observes, a point also made in Mufwene (1996a).

History shows that Virginia, where the roots of AAVE are to be sought, was colonized forty-eight years earlier (1607) than Jamaica (1655). Part of its slave population, like the latter's, was imported from Barbados, which was an important slave distribution point for British American colonies in the seventeenth century, although Barbados was colonized only in 1627, eight years after

Virginia had acquired its first African laborers in 1619. Part of the slave population may have also come from St. Kitts, which was having a difficult start and experienced emigrations of European colonists and their slaves. The Founder Principle and ethnographic-ecological considerations suggest a partly-independent development for the Virginia black vernacular, despite these importations of slaves from the Caribbean during a time (17th century) when, in the first place, the relevant creoles may not have formed yet in those territories (Corcoran & Mufwene 1998).

Unlike Jamaica, Virginia launched into tobacco cultivation, in a socio-economic ecology in which the African slaves were not much desired, and these never exceeded 38% of the total colonial population by the end of the eighteenth century in the Chesapeake area (Perkins 1988: 98–99). They were no more than 15% at the end of the 17th century. In Jamaica, whose economy was based on sugar cane cultivation, the African population was then 10 times that of the European population. It was already three times the size of the European population in 1690! There is no reason to suspect parallel linguistic developments for both colonies, as sugar cane plantations were generally more densely populated than tobacco plantations.

I conjecture that Barbados, from which a large proportion of the slaves were imported during the 17th century, may not yet have developed a basilectal sociolect of the same demographic significance as in Jamaica during this first century of slavery. Around 1690, there were 50,000 Africans against 18,000 Europeans, at a ratio of less than 3 to 1 sixty-three years after its founding (Williams 1985: 31). However, we have no evidence that those slaves all came from large plantations, on which basilectal sociolects may have started to develop, given the rapid population replacement on all plantation colonies (due to high mortality rate) and the more extensive restructuring that the social process would have triggered. Barbados is also known to have been a slave entrepot, on which slaves were kept only for a while before being exported to other colonies. Several of the slaves may thus have not spoken the local colonial vernaculars, at least not fluently and were therefore like those coming directly from Africa, before being transported to North America. This reduced the significance of Caribbean varieties' influence on the development of Gullah and AAVE. Also, depending on where the Caribbean slaves wound up in North America, they certainly made adjustments to what was developing locally while contributing to the pool of features to which the competition-and-selection process that restructured the lexifier applied.

Undoubtedly, since the metropolitan English varieties exported to the colonies and the African languages were similar in terms of pools of features (though certainly not identical demographically in terms of careers of features), one cannot rule out the possibility that with or without Caribbean input, Gullah and AAVE may have still have developed structures typologically related to the Caribbean varieties. Although the presence of Caribbean slaves, whose varieties had not developed earlier than the North American ones, was certainly instrumental in determining the gradual restructuring of colonial English into Gullah and AAVE, it need not have been the most critical factor. After all, we still must explain where the so-called "creole" features were selected from and we must explain why several structural features of AAVE are so similar to those of White nonstandard vernaculars that developed in other colonial settings in which the presence of Africans was marginal. All these considerations seem to argue against insisting excessively on the putative creole origins of AAVE.

All things being equal, the colonial English lexifier was bound to be restructured more extensively in Jamaica than in Virginia. The closest matches to Jamaica were coastal South Carolina and Georgia, where Gullah's ancestor developed, at least fifty years later than AAVE's ancestor in Virginia.[15] Note that it is primarily from the latter colony, not the former, that the founder slave populations in North American hinterland colonies, which thrived later on cotton cultivation, were brought. Thus, there seems to be no motivation whatsoever for assuming that AAVE may have developed from an antecedent Gullah-like variety.

The South Carolina and Georgia hinterlands themselves were more typical of other southeastern colonies in their developments. Their slaves were not necessarily imported from the coastal areas, although they originated from the same places in Africa and the Caribbean. The Coastal areas and the hinterlands developed around the same time, but on different economic schemes: small farms and fur trade as the dominant industry in both during the first thirty years or so of colonization, then the coast launched into rice and indigo cultivation, as well as naval stores, typically on the same plantations, hence the large labor force on them. However, the hinterlands continued on the same scheme as earlier until they launched into the cotton plantations later on.

Thus the ecologies varied enough to produce different vernaculars among descendants of Africans, as among descendants of Europeans. Coastal Whites who grew up on the plantations have spoken English vernaculars closer to those spoken by (White) Bahamians and Caribbeans than to American Southern White English. The sociohistorical scenario presented here is consistent with Winford's (1993, 1997a) new position that creole speakers imported from the Caribbean to North America shifted to some ancestor of AAVE, contrary to Winford's (1992) earlier claim that AAVE developed by decreolization. This is not to say that all Caribbean slaves shifted successfully, as evidenced by the Tituba case (discussed in Cassidy 1986 and Rickford 1997), whatever the proportion of such speakers may have been. Neither does my position deny the contribution that such speakers must have made to the pool of competing features in the ongoing restructuring of colonial English (as a set-theory union of competing vernaculars) that would produce today's Gullah and AAVE. As the restructuring was gradual, the contribution of Caribbean slaves was no more important than that of slaves brought directly from Africa, the majority after the early 18th century, as much as the English model from which features were being selected and re-articulated into the new systems were largely predetermined by the earlier varieties. The Founder Principle proposed in Mufwene (1996a) does not preclude influence from populations that arrived after the founding of the colonies. Actually, it assumes that they contributed to the basilectalization process, inasmuch as more and more non-native speakers served as models to newcomers. In any case, the present position disputes arguments that a Caribbean creole-like or Gullah-like variety was once spoken throughout the American Southeast and debasilectalization has produced today's AAVE.

Also significant in the above scenario is my earlier observation that segregation was not instituted at the same time in all colonial settings. The enactment of the Jim Crow laws in 1877, fostering separate rights and social lives between Blacks and Whites, attests to the fact that most of the descendants of Africans and at least the poor Whites who descended largely from the former indentured labor and other small farmers (all in the majority!) had had about 200 years of closely related socioeconomic histories, which must have borne on the development of their vernaculars. To date, these Black and White varieties are considered similar on many features, consistent with the fact, well reported by Rickford (1997, 1998) and Bailey & Maynor (1989) that up to the end of the 19th century close to 90% of African Americans lived in the Southeast, the cradle of AAVE. It is also consistent with the divergence hypothesis — despite questions about how divergence is proceeding — to the extent that the separation of communities, which continued in the northern cities with the ghetto system, fostered the development of erstwhile related vernaculars in different directions. However, their long shared past accounts for the continuing similarities of their features.

The institution of racial segregation was well established in the United States till the 1960s, a century after the abolition of slavery, with which the decreolization hypothesis has been associated. Even if, contrary to history, most of the cotton plantations' founder populations had come from coastal South Carolina and Georgia, and AAVE had indeed developed through some adaptation of a Gullah-like variety to the new socio-economic ecology, one would have to assume that African Americans have always wanted to be like Americans of European descent in order to hypothesize that AAVE developed by decreolization, with the creole moving closer and closer to educated speech, associated primarily with the White norm. This explanation, based undoubtedly on the ability of educated African Americans to code-switch (like other Americans from stigmatized regional and/or socio-economic backgrounds), has simply ignored the fact that social segregation fostered the development of diverse American cultures. Code-switching does not entail abandoning one's native variety. Although there are several individuals who do the latter, there are many, many more who do not and revert to their native varieties in the right ethnographic settings.

It is worth noting that in many ways African Americans have developed their own religious styles, their own music trends, their own cooking traditions, and kept their own identities, without wanting to be confused with Americans of European descent or other ethnic groups. One should wonder why they would have wanted to speak like (educated) European Americans, with whom the variety identified in the literature as "standard" or "mainstream" American English has been associated. It is just as though linguists misunderstood the Civil Rights movements' quest for equality in the mid-1960s with a pseudo-quest for identity! Against these historical and cultural backgrounds, it is surprising that Poplack and Tagliamonte would have such a hard time convincing their peers that AAVE could not have developed by decreolization. None of the hypotheses that AAVE developed by debasilectalization seems to be historically and culturally accountable, and, as I agree with Rickford (1998), nor is any hypothesis which claims that AAVE is a straight preservation of some British or colonial English dialect in the way hypothesized by Krapp (1924) or Kurath (1928).

However, the latter position is different from the more plausible arguments that features of AAVE have been selected from features available in colonial English and reorganized in a system of its own which shows similarities in different respects with other new vernaculars which developed concurrently with it, including Gullah, Caribbean creoles, and also other nonstandard vernaculars in North America. The conclusions of Bailey and Thomas (1998) articulate this family-resemblance condition well on the basis of phonological considerations. The ecology-based competition-and-selection approach proposed in Mufwene (1996a) seeks precisely to explain why every new vernacular wound up different in a way but shares so many features (though not always the same and in different proportions) with others. I must, however, reiterate that I do not deny that language varieties brought from the Caribbean, creole or noncreole, have contributed to the restructuring of English in North America into today's Gullah and AAVE. The challenge for us is to figure out how, since, after all, English and African linguistic inputs to the Caribbean and North America were similar, subject to demographic ecological variation in terms of proportion of speakers who carried the relevant features that competed with each other (Mufwene 1996a). Eventually even creoles' features can be traced back to their colonial lexifiers.

The main point of the above arguments is that the decreolization hypothesis is a diachronic claim that must be supported with diachronic evidence. In the absence of such evidence, it would help to correlate the hypothesis with other diachronically-grounded cultural phenomena. Creolists have typically not provided such evidence. Colonial history and the few earlier texts investigated in the literature suggest just a development contrary to decreolization, viz., a basilectalization process that is consistent with the divergence hypothesis (e.g., Labov & Harris 1986; Labov 1987; Bailey & Maynor 1987, 1989; Bailey & Thomas 1998), or simple preservation of basilectal varieties which may have been in place since the late 18th century (Lalla & D'Costa 1990; Mille 1990; Mufwene 1991a, 1994).

Reliable observations on the speech of African slaves in North America do nor appear until the early 18th century (Brasch 1981). Deviant speech is typically associated with slaves who have not been long in the colony and "good English" is associated with those born here. Textual, literary evidence does not emerge until the late 18th century and there is reason to assume that it is stereotypical. In any case, because negative attitudes to Blacks were already established since the mid-17th century, one may surmise that if (descendants of) the Africans spoke differently (barring normal cases of interlanguage), they would have been so represented in the literature. Also, as noted by Brasch, the earliest writers who suggested that (descendants of) the Africans spoke differently and claimed that they had influenced (descendants of) the Europeans with whom they interacted on a regular basis were European visitors to North America. There may be a number of reasons for this, one of which is the obvious similarities that started early on between the speech ways of (descendants of) Africans and Europeans, where segregation was not instituted early.

It is perhaps not by accident that the earlier attestations of African-American speech in the literature are creole-like. Earlier manifestations of basilectal sociolects in the Caribbean, where large plantations started earlier, may have been stereotypically extended to North America by such European writers. Overall, however, colonial speech, even among Africans, must have been more variable than the creole origins hypothesis has suggested, despite several accurate sociohistorical observations in Rickford (1997, 1998). What I see suggested by history is the consolidation of basilectal sociolects after the mid-18th century, triggered by the rapid growth of the population by importation more than by birth and its rapid replacement (due to a high mortality rate), which favors restructuring away from the lexifier (Mufwene 1996a).

## 3. Treacherous Areas in Structural Analyses

Above I extended the principle of accountability to diachronic issues, invoking extra-linguistic considerations bearing on diachronic claims. I should perhaps not have extrapolated the principle before showing how useful it is indeed in synchronic structural analyses. Variationists have often chastised theoretical linguists for idealizing language. I myself will plead guilty to this charge, as I sometimes have not lived up to my own observation that basilects are constructs posited for the convenience of our analyses; they have not been identified as such in any data base other than literary texts (Mufwene 1987). Ignoring Rickford's (1990) observation that in creole communities the mesolect, rather than the basilect, is actually the norm, it has been too easy to give only lip service to variation and still promote the concept of a *basilectal underlying creole structure*.

I will focus here on Mufwene (1986b), in which I present Gullah's number delimitation system as having an underlying **individuated/nonindividuated** system similar to that found in numeral classifying languages. The main exception is that, as in English, numeral classifiers are not required for most nouns when they are simply **individuated** or used with a numeral quantifier or with a demonstrative, as in *hi wɔn ə dʌk/dɪs dʌk/wʌn dʌk* 'he wants a/this/one duck'. Otherwise, as in numeral classifying languages, a **nonindividuated** noun, as in *hi don laik dʌk* may be used as much for **generic** reference, 'he/she does not like ducks', as for **mass** reference, 'he/she does not like duck (meat)'. Like demonstratives and numeral quantifiers, the **plural** marker *dem* delimits only **individuated** nouns. Thus nouns bearing the English suffix {Z} as the **plural** marker were assumed to have borrowed the marker from English and to belong in mesolectal speech.

There is no doubt that the proposed analysis accounts adequately for part of the Gullah data. In light of what I say below, it is also quite possible that some Gullah data behave in the way hypothesized by Rickford (1986, 1990), especially that the **plural** suffix {Z} may be the normal marker of **plural** for some speakers or some words and that it may be considered variably absent or deleted where it is not attested in **plural** contexts. Some data may even be interpreted ambiguously; but I will not go into those details here, so that I may focus on the question of accountability qua justification in the way I discuss diachronic problems above.

Part of the mistake with my own analysis lies in assuming that a true creole system was necessarily monolithic, in the sense of 'systemically homogeneous' (Mufwene 1992b). This is germane to the then common mistaken assumption that creoles, sometimes equated with basilects, are characterized by structures that made them totally different from their lexifiers.

The above assumption was perhaps a partial consequence of the few subsystems of creoles that had been investigated, especially nominal number, the time reference system, and some syntactic constructions such as predicate serialization, subordination with *se* or with the complementizer *fə/fi/fʊ* and predicate clefting. It also reflects the lexifier's corpora that were used for comparison with the creoles' data, viz., the standard varieties rather than the nonstandard varieties spoken by the indentured laborers, to which the African slave laborers were exposed. The same basic methodology was responsible for Stewart's (1965) distinction between the basilect, mesolect, and acrolect, which came to be associated later on with the decreolization hypothesis.

I assumed gratuitously that Gullah's nominal number system would consist exclusively of the monolithic model summarized above; any English-like subsystem should be attributed to importation, consistent with the conception of the mesolect as a by-product of the societal coexistence of the basilect and acrolect. Yet, it has never been explained why the restructuring of the lexifier would of necessity have yielded a totally different system in the ensuing creole vernacular nor why this system would have to be monolithic in the first place, i.e., would not allow heterogeneity in systemic constraints nor rules that overlap in their functions. As argued in Mufwene (1992b), a grammatical system need not be monolithic, not even in the more rigidly codified standard varieties. Thus, since the time when it was identified as a separate variety, Gullah may have allowed generic reference both through **nonindividuated** delimitation and through the English **indefinite plural** as part of its system. This non-monolithic view is what is now advocated by Labov (1998) as "co-existent systems."

The colonial socio-economic historical details invoked in Part 1 are not consistent with assuming that creoles developed from antecedent pidgins, that these changed uniformly into basilects, which in turn would debasilectalize under the influence of the acrolect. Not only were the social ecologies not favorable to the development of pidgins (which does not rule out the development of transitional individual interlanguages) but also history suggests that the new vernaculars developed gradually in the direction of basilectalization. Barring a few individuals who hardly developed enough competence in the local vernacular, slaves of the homestead phases of the colonies must have spoken closer approximations of the colonial varieties spoken by the European indentured laborers with whom the non-Europeans typically interacted. With the development of larger plantations, the rapid increase of the African labor population on them, the rapid population replacement caused by high mortality rates, and the institutionalization of segregation, the local English vernacular underwent more and more restructuring, with the process yielding different outputs depending on specifics of the local ethnolinguistic and demographic ecologies.

Let me emphasize that there is no reason for assuming that all people of non-European descent participated uniformly in the above basilectalization process. Alleyne (1980), for example, was right in claiming that variation in the creole vernaculars obtained from their beginnings. Winford (1997b) is quite explicit about why a continuum would have obtained early in the development of Guyanese Creole, owing in part to the diverse origins of the slave labor. Although he focuses especially on the other Caribbean islands from which they were imported and on whether they wound up in the rural areas or in an urban environment, let me add as additional factors the specific kind of communities from which they came (small farm vs. large plantation), their status (as house or field slave), and whether or not they wound up in the same kind of community they had been brought from. One may invoke a host of other relevant factors. There is thus no more reason to associate the mesolect phenomenon with the societal coexistence of the basilect and acrolect rather than with the variable, non-monolithic way the lexifier was gradually being restructured by different speakers. We must remember that variation exists in every language and speech community, even though what obtains in creole communities may have been made more conspicuous by their development out of contacts not only of speakers, the normal case everywhere (Hagège 1993), but also of languages. What we must do first is try to understand how structural variation, with which most variationists have been concerned since the 1960s, develops in monolingual communities, an issue which need not be addressed here.

To those who, like me, hold that what makes a vernacular a creole is not its structural features but its social history and how it came to be disfranchised (see below), the above considerations suggest caution when we discuss creoles' systems. Because creole vernaculars did not basilectalize uniformly nor become different systems from their lexifiers in all respects, we really cannot justify a priori what parts of their data must be covered by our analyses and what may be overlooked. This is difficult especially because the mesolect appears to be the norm everywhere (Rickford 1990) and because the basilect/mesolect distinction does not seem to matter to speakers of these vernaculars as much as they do to creolists. After all, creole speakers often think they speak varieties of the relevant lexifiers (Mühlhäusler 1985, Mufwene 1988), albeit different and stigmatized ones, as is well connoted by names such as *patois* (used by community members in the same negative sense as in French).

An adequate analysis of the creole vernaculars is therefore one that, at least initially, takes into account all the alternatives for the same grammatical function, independently of whether or not they may all be lumped together as one "variable" in the variationist sense of the word (see Labov 1972: 72, quoted above). In the case of **plural**-marking in Gullah, both the English-like and non-English-like subsystems are equally significant. More meticulous research should reveal whether or not they form a monolithic system (with a clear division of labor among the variants), whether or not they are supported by a unified body of principles, and whether or not a traditional variationist analysis applies to the whole domain or to only some subdomain of the data. This helps us put in a healthy perspective the exchange between Mufwene (1986) and Rickford (1986, 1990), as I see both analyses shedding light on the data but neither of them presenting the full picture. My projected basilectal model was definitely unrealistic if attributed to the whole vernacular's continuum, because it is an idealization that just helps the linguist gauge toward what pole of the continuum a speaker gravitates.

Another example comes to mind here: complement clauses in Gullah. Both some clauses introduced by *fə* and some introduced by *sɛ* allow alternatives with a null complementizer, but this would not constitute enough evidence for *fə, sɛ* and the null complementizer to all count as one variable. While *ʌ tɛl ʌm (fə) kʌm* 'I told him/her to come', *ʌ trai (fə) go* 'I tried to go', and *ʌ hiɛ (sɛ) fei kʌm* 'I heard that Faye has come' are all well-formed, the following alternatives are not: *\*ʌ trai sɛ go* or *\*ʌ hiɛ fə fei kʌm*. That is, a null complementizer may not be replaced randomly by any lexical complementizer. As complementizers, *sɛ* and *fə* have different functions but overlap in their alternations with a null form in environments in which their functions are still different. One could in fact argue that Gullah has more than one null complementizer.

On the other hand, while discussing as separate syntactic strategies subordinate clauses introduced by *fə* and *sɛ*, relevant clauses that are introduced by the null complementizer may not be ignored. There is no proven grammatical principle that precludes separate grammatical strategies from sharing a variant in the way that in American English the phonemes /t/ and /d/ share the allophone [D] in unstressed intervocalic position. Labov's (1972: 72) statement of the principle of accountability may thus be extended to require more justification, other than "isolat[ing] the largest homogeneous class in which all subclasses vary in the same way," before one may identify what items form a variable. In the particular examples cited here, two overlapping variables may be posited, as suggested by the data.

In the same vein, I feel justified in my study of the infinitive in Gullah (Mufwene 1991b) to have considered not only tokens introduced by *fə* and the null complementizer, but also those introduced by *tə/də* (< *to* in English). Although the distribution of the latter is not identical with that of *fə* (e.g., *wɔn fə/\*tə* *hi pɛi mi mi mʌni* 'I want him/her to pay me my money'), I saw no justification for characterizing one as more creole/Gullah than the other. Both fit in the system although they do not have identical distributions even if treated as free variants.

To begin with, I had no reason for assuming a priori that if Gullah had an infinitive this would be associated only with one complementizer. Just in case it had an infinitive and was associated with two or more complementizers, I could not determine a priori that the complementizers would have identical syntactic distributions, not any more than I would be justified in assuming that in English *wh*-forms and the complementizer *that* have identical distributions because they both introduce relative clauses (Mufwene 1992b). Neither did I have any ground for hypothesizing that the *tə/də* alternatives were imported from a different system and had not been in Gullah's communal system from the beginning. Mufwene and Dijkhoff (1989) were mistaken in overlooking the functional overlap of *fə* and *tə/də* in arguing against the finite/non-finite distinction in Gullah, although their basic position remains valid. Methodologically, there may be some problems in identifying a priori only some constructions that are structurally different from the lexifier as creole and disregarding the other alternatives. It would be like mistakenly focusing only on structural differences and ignoring similarities in typological studies of languages around the world.

To the extent that forms and constructions similar to those of the lexifier are considered mesolectal, one must note that the notions of 'basilect' and 'mesolect' themselves have often been used in ways that are problematic, for instance, when, as noted above, some creolists characterize some vernaculars, such as Bajan, Trinidadian, and AAVE, as mesolectal, claiming that they have no basilect. It is just as though some uniform basilect must have developed everywhere a creole or any new vernacular spoken by descendants of Africans emerged, especially in the New World. The social histories of New World and Indian Ocean colonies suggest no such absolute conception of 'basilect', because the social and contact history of each colony was different — a point well made by Rickford (1997) as in Mufwene (1996a) — and these ecological differences account for structural differences among these creoles' systems (Mufwene 1996a). Therefore each creole vernacular would have its own basilect determined by the most extreme extent to which its lexifier — which need not have been identical from one colony to another[16] — was restructured. That is, the extent of structural differences between a creole and its acrolect (i.e., the local standard variety of the lexifier) varies from one polity to another. Understandably, Gullah's basilect is different from Guyanese Creole's basilect, and both are different from Jamaican Creole's basilect, although they all have similar structures. Despite similarities in the initial inputs for the restructuring of their similar lexifiers, differences in the ecologies of their developments account for why and how their systems, including their basilects, vary. Consequently, no creole could possibly be more mesolectal or "intermediate" (Winford 1992) than any other, although the basilect of one may well correspond to another's mesolect. The notions 'basilect', 'mesolect', and 'acrolect' are community-relative. This position is not in conflict with saying that one creole is more restructured than another, because creoleness is not determined by specific structural features and no creole is more creole than another.

This kind of metalanguistic matter is evidently tied in to the question of whether a creole ever developed in Barbados. Until Fields (1995) and Rickford & Handler (1994), it was generally assumed that no creole developed in Barbados, because some creolists such as Alleyne (1980) have claimed that today this island has no basilect comparable to those found in Jamaica or Guyana. It turns out, according to the above studies, that such a variety was spoken in Barbados in the nineteenth century and, as Rickford (1992) points out, a basilectal variety is still spoken there. Thus it is history and reliable observation of current ethnographic facts, but not just some equivocal synchronic comparison with vernaculars spoken elsewhere, that will justify speaking of some varieties as mesolectal.

As in many cases, creolists may be happy not to have been totally consistent with some of their working assumptions. Otherwise, we would also have claimed creoles' grammatical systems incorrectly to consist only of the features that distinguish them from their lexifiers', in the same way that dictionaries of creoles have typically represented, inadequately, mostly entries that distinguish them from those of their lexifiers' (e.g., Cassidy & Le Page 1981). The result would have been incomplete systems permitting their speakers to communicate (if at all) no more than with the incomplete vocabularies represented in such dictionaries and the grammatical subsystems that make them different. If I may add another point of dissent here, this lexicographic practice itself suggests correctly that creoles may be considered dialects (albeit stigmatized ones) of their lexifiers, consistent with the sentiments of several native speakers. The fact that, for instance, the demonstrative *dis* and *dat* are accepted as part of Gullah, despite the fact that they are used as in its English lexifier, is evidence that the restructuring which produced creoles need not have produced systems that at some time were totally different from the lexifiers'.

Interestingly, the clearer the picture that develops of the colonial lexifiers that were gradually restructured into AAVE and its creole kin, the harder it is to isolate individual features as particularly creole in nature, although their integration into novel systems (with naturally some concurrent extensions or other modifications of their distributions and functions) are what produced creoles under the non-negligible influence of substrate languages as part of the linguistic ecologies of those settings. This etymological observation is true of **habitual** markers *dəz/doz*, of demonstratives *disya* 'this' and *dem ya* 'these', of serial verb constructions (which could have been extended from *go/come* + V-kind of constructions with the concurrent loss of inflections), of **perfect** *dʌn/dɔn* + Past Participle or Preterit in AAVE but with the verb stem in creoles), of **progressive/durative** constructions with *a* + V (with the *-in* suffix in AAVE), of relativizers with *wɛ* and of many other features.

The practice of identifying only some structural features as creole in nature leads me to address one problem with our inclination to identify creole vernaculars as separate languages from their lexifiers. We know well in linguistics that mutual intelligibility is not a reliable gauge for determining whether two vernaculars are dialects of the same language or separate languages. We have not shown whether the contact-induced restructuring which produced creoles was different in kind from what produced the vernaculars spoken by descendants of Europeans outside Europe. We cannot deny the fact that the latter varieties are contact-induced ones too, even if we could prove, contrary to history (Mufwene 1996a, 1996b), that speakers of the lexifiers were in contact (only) among themselves.

Besides, we have not demonstrated that restructuring induced by the contact of dialects of the same language is different in kind from that induced by the contact of different languages. Although the first focuses on extra-European English dialects and the second on creoles, Trudgill (1986) and Mufwene (1996a) agree in showing similarities in how these new varieties have selected their features through similar competition-and-selection processes, subject to similar ecology-sensitive markedness constraints, out of the pools of options available to speakers. Virtually the same factors have determined which options were less marked and gained selective advantage over other alternatives. When the factors were in conflict, more than one alternative was selected into the new varieties, producing non-monolithic systems.

We must also bear two facts in mind: 1) restructuring is less extensive when contact is among typologically related language varieties (Mufwene 1986a; Thomason & Kaufman 1988), and 2) it still occurs even when contact is among dialects of the same language or languages that are closely related genetically (Silverstein 1972; Thomason 1983; Mufwene 1994b, 1996a; Siegel 1985; Trudgill 1986). These observations are evidence that what matters to restructuring qua system reorganization is not so much whether or not dialects of the same language are in contact but whether or not typological kinship preempts competition of features, hence selection of (more) advantageous ones (Mufwene 1996a). We have no reason for insisting that creoles are separate languages, especially since

we have no yardstick for measuring when two language varieties are two
separate languages and not dialects of each other. We have depended on what
native speakers think, except of course in dealing with creoles. Besides, for the
purposes of our system analyses, synchronic and diachronic alike, we have not
established the relevance of the language/dialect distinction, because there are no
particular techniques that we apply to languages only but not to dialects, and vice
versa. We creolists simply must admit that we have operated on assumptions that
are not socially accountable in the above respect. We have done no better than the
people who disfranchised the new colonial vernaculars developed by non-Europeans
in naming them "creoles" and making them look like children out of wedlock.


## 4.    Conclusions

Above, I have interpreted Labov's (1972) principle of accountability as a
requirement for linguists to *justify* details of their analyses. I submit that the
principle must be satisfied not only by justifying one's analysis with structural
considerations but also by supporting diachronic hypotheses either with historical
facts or with evidence from other cultural phenomena to which the hypothesis
may be related. Considerations of the relevant sociohistorical ecology seems
absolutely imperative in regard to diachronic claims.

    Assuming that accountability bears on more than variation analysis and the
quantitative aspects of linguistic descriptions, I took the liberty of surveying a
range of aspects of creolistics that have wanted sound justification. Hypotheses
about creoles which present these vernaculars as different from other linguistic
systems call for rigorous empirical and sometimes multi-disciplinary justification,
just as such new interpretations of facts should, if they are adequate, invite us to
re-examine our conventional assumptions about non-creole systems, which we
thought we already understood, and about Language in general. This approach is
consistent with that dialogue which remains open-ended between theory and facts
and should help us accomplish what is expected of studies of particular language
varieties: understanding Language more adequately.

    I could go on citing several examples of inadequate analyses based on
unjustified assumptions in creolistics, some of them underlying general linguistics
itself. However, space and time constraints preclude this longer critique. Suffice
it to say that in many ways, creolistics should help reshape general linguistics,
for instance in asking why continua are typically not assumed of other speech
communities, why the latters' varieties are not ranked as basilectal vs. mesolectal
vs. acrolectal, why we expect linguistic systems to be monolithic and therefore

treat creole vernaculars as diverging from the norm, why variationist techniques are not as often applied to non-stigmatized varieties such as standard French or English as to creoles and AAVE, or why field techniques applied to the study of nonstandard vernaculars are not applied to data collected about their "standard" counterparts. Consequently, we may ask ourselves what, if anything, makes creoles unique and what contribution we (can) make to the general, bottom-line endeavor to understand Language.

Even though I have addressed subsets of these questions in part of my previous work, I am very grateful that, by inviting me to participate in her *Panel on Research Methods in Pidgin and Creole Studies* in 1993, Charlene Sato gave me an opportunity to integrate them and to show our practices in a mirror which, I hope, is not too distorting. Undoubtedly several of our traditional working assumptions and research methods can be improved in a number of ways, even if not necessarily in the ways I advocate. Creoles should not be treated in more special ways than they need be, unless creolists persist in shying away from inviting general linguists to re-examine some assumptions about Language in general.

Charlene Sato also worked to reinfranchise Hawaiian Creole in the Hawaiian ethnographic ecology. May the modest contribution of this essay be considered a suitable tribute to her efforts.

## Acknowledgments

A preliminary draft of this essay was presented at the Panel on Research Methods in Pidgin and Creole Studies, at the Society for Pidgin and Creole Linguistics meeting in Los Angeles in January 1993. Charlene Sato invited and persuaded me to participate in the Panel despite my reluctance. I explained that, not being a variationist and having had no fiield methods class in my academic training, I probably would not contribute much on the subject matter. Charlene had faith in the less orthodox thinking I could contribute to the Panel. Although I still believe that my contribution remains modest and perhaps marginal, I am very grateful that her trust and persuasion led me to think over issues that I consider legitimate if we expect the field of creole studies to contribute to general linguistics in more or less the same extent or ways that it has contributed methodologically to variation analysis and sociolinguistics. I am also deeply indebted to Sali Tagliamonte and to John Rickford for useful comments on, respectively, the first and the final drafts of this essay, I remain solely responsible for all its remaining shortcomings.

## Notes

1. I use *sociolinguistic* in quotation marks because it is not evident that all variationist studies are necessarily sociolinguistic; several of them exhibit no particular correlation of structural features with sociological variables such as gender, social class, age group, level of education, and

construction jobs "that do not entail extensive interaction with speakers outside their social group."

14.  Labov (1998: 148) characterizes this in terms of "family resemblance," which highlights the fact that despite the undeniable contribution of the varieties spoken by African slaves of the 17th and 18th- century Caribbean to the development of varieties spoken by African American today, there are also differences. Both similarities and differences matter in discussing the relationship between AAVE, Gullah, and Caribbean varieties, and the relationship need not be that of filiation, as I argue below.

15.  As Rickford (1997) argues, something similar may have developed on the coastal marshes of the Chesapeake colonies but this has hardly been studied to date. The likelihood of such developments in the hinterlands is, however, rather remote, based on sociohistorical conditions. (see Winford 19997a:320).

16.  Works such as Trudgill (1986) explain why, as they show how more or less the same dialects of English brought in contact with each other among (descendants of) Europeans in different colonies produced different varieties, such as Australian and North American English vernaculars. In the USA, thanks to the work of historians such as Bailyn (1986) and Fischer (1989), we can understand why and how differences in settlement patterns (such as between New England, the Chesapeake area, the Appalachian mountains, and the Southeast) produced different regional dialects.

# References

Algeo, John. 1988. The year British English began. *SECOL Review* 12.176–185.

Algeo, John. 1991. Language. In *The Reader's companion to American history*, ed. by Eric Foner and John A. Garraty, 637–640. Boston: Houghton Mifflin.

Alleyne, Mervyn C. 1971. Acculturation and the cultural matrix of creolization. In *Pidginization and creolization of languages*, ed. by Dell Hymes, 169–86. Cambridge: Cambridge University Press.

Alleyne, Mervyn C. 1980. *Comparative Afro-American: An historical-comparative study of English-based Afro-American dialects of the New World*. Ann Arbor: Karoma.

Arveiller, R. 1963. *Contribution à l'étude des termes de voyage en français (1505–1722)*. Paris: D'Artrey.

Bailey, Beryl L. 1965. Toward a new perspective in Negro English dialectology. *American Speech* 40.171–7.

Bailey, Guy. 1987. Contribution to *Are Black and White vernaculars diverging? Papers from the NWAVE XIV Panel discussion*, ed. by Ralph Fasold and Ron Butters, 32–40. *American Speech* 62.1.

Bailey, Guy & Natalie Maynor. 1987. Decreolization? *Language in Society* 16.449–473.

Bailey, Guy & Natalie Maynor. 1989. The divergence controversy. *American Speech* 64.12–39.

Bailey, Guy & Erik Thomas. 1998. Some aspects of African-American vernacular phonology. In *African-American English*, ed. by Salikoko S. Mufwene, John R. Rickford, Guy Bailey, and John Baugh, 85–109. London: Routledge.

Bailyn, Bernard. 1986. *The peopling of British North America: An introduction*. New York: Random House.

Baker, Philip. 1990. Off target? Column, *Journal of Pidgin and Creole Languages* 5.107–119.

Bickerton, Derek. 1973. On the nature of a creole continuum. *Language* 49.640–669.

Bickerton, Derek. 1988. Creole languages and the bioprogram. *Linguistics: The Cambridge survey*. Volume II. *Linguistic theory: Extensions and implications*, ed. by Frederick J. Newmeyer, 268–84. Cambridge: Cambridge University Press.

Bloomfield, Leonard. 1933. *Language*. New York: Holt, Rinehart, & Winston.

Brasch, Walter. 1981. *Black English and the mass media*. Lanham, MD: University of America Press.

Calvet, Louis-Jean. 1999. *Mei you tiao cha jiu: pour une écologie des langues du monde*. Paris: Plon.

Campbell-Kibler, Kathryn. 1998. *History in the making of language: A critique of the literature on the development of African-American English*. MA thesis, Department of Linguistics, University of Chicago.

Cassidy, Frederick G. 1986. Barbadian Creole: Possibility and probability. *American Speech* 61.195–205.

Cassidy, Frederic G. & R.B. Le Page. 1980. *Dictionary of Jamaican English*. Second edition. Cambridge: Cambridge University Press.

Chaudenson, Robert. 1979. *Les créoles français*. Paris: Fernand Nathan.

Chaudenson, Robert. 1989. *Créoles et enseignement du français*. Paris: L'Harmattan.

Chaudenson, Robert. 1992. *Des îles, des hommes, des langues: essais sur la créolisation linguistique et culturelle*. Paris: L'Harmattan.

Corcoran, Christine & Salikoko S. Mufwene. 1998. Sam Matthews' Kittitian: What is it evidence of? In *St. Kitts and the Atlantic creoles: The texts of Samuel Augustus Matthews in perspective*, ed. by Philip Baker & Adrienne Bruyn. London: The University of Westminster Press.

DeCamp, David. 1971. Toward a generative analysis of a post-creole speech continuum. In *Pidginization and creolization of languages*, ed. by Dell Hymes, 349–70. Cambridge: Cambridge University Press.

Dubois, Sylvie & Megan Melançon. 1997. Cajun is dead, long live Cajun: Shifting from a linguistic to a cultural community. *Journal of Sociolinguistics* 1.63–93

Fields, Linda. 1995. Early Bajan: Creole or non-creole? In *The early stages of creolization*, ed. by Jacques Arends, 89–111. Amsterdam: John Benjamins.

Fischer, David Hackett. 1989. *Albion's seed: Four British folkways in America*. New York and Oxford: Oxford University Press.

Hagège, Claude. 1993. *The language builder: An essay on the human signature in linguistic morphogenesis*. Amsterdam & Philadelphia: John Benjamins.

Krapp, George Philip. 1924. The English of the Negro. *The American Mercury* 2.190–5.

Kripke, Saul.1972. Naming and necessity. In *Semantics of natural language*, ed. by D. Davidson & G. Harman, 253–335. Dordrecht: D. Reidel.

Kurath, Hans. 1928. The origin of dialectal differences in spoken American English. *Modern Philology* 25.385–395.

Labov, William. 1972. *Sociolinguistic patterns*. Philadelphia: University of Pennsylvania Press.

Labov, William. 1987. Contribution to *Are Black and White vernaculars diverging? Papers from the NWAVE XIV Panel discussion*, ed. by Ralph Fasold and Ron Butters, 5–12. *American Speech* 62.1.

Labov, William. 1998. Co-existent systems in African-American vernacular English. In *African-American English: Structure, history, and use*, ed. by Salikoko S. Mufwene, John R. Rickford, Guy Bailey, and John Baugh, 110–153. London: Routledge.

Labov, William & Wendell A. Harris. 1986. De facto segregation of Black and White vernaculars. In *Diversity and diachrony*, ed. by David Sankoff, 1–24. Amsterdam: John Benjamins.

Lalla, Barbara & Jean D'Costa. 1990. *Language in exile: Three hundred years of Jamaican Creole*. Tuscaloosa: University of Alabama Press.

Lavandera, Beatriz. 1978. Where does the sociolinguistic variable stop? *Language in Society* 7:171–182.

Lovejoy, Paul. 1989. The impact of the Atlantic slave trade on Africa: A review of the literature. *Journal of African History* 30.365–394.

Mille, Katherine. 1990. *A historical analysis of tense-mood-aspect in Gullah Creole: A case of stable variation*. Ph. D. dissertation, University of South Carolina at Columbia.

Mufwene, Salikoko S. 1986a. Les langues créoles peuvent-elles être définies sans allusion à leur histoire? *Etudes Créoles* 9.135–150.

Mufwene, Salikoko S. 1986b. Number delimitation in Gullah. *American Speech* 61.33–60.

Mufwene, Salikoko S. 1987. Review article on *Language variety in the South: Perspectives in black and white*, ed. by Michael Montgomery & Guy Bailey. *Journal of Pidgin and Creole Languages* 2.93–110.

Mufwene, Salikoko S. 1988. Why study pidgins and creoles? Column. *Journal of Pidgin and Creole Languages* 3.265–276.

Mufwene, Salikoko S. 1989. Some explanations that strike me as incomplete. Column. *Journal of Pidgin and Creole Languages* 4.117–128.

Mufwene, Salikoko S. 1991a. Is Gullah decreolizing? A comparison of a speech sample of the 1930s with a sample of the 1980s. In *The emergence of Black English: Text and commentary*, ed. by Guy Bailey, Natalie Maynor, and Patricia Cukor-Avila, 213–230. Amsterdam: John Benjamins.

Mufwene, Salikoko S. 1991b. On the infinitive in Gullah. In *Verb phrase patterns in Black English and creole*, ed. by Walter Edwards and Donald Winford, 209–222. Detroit: Wayne State University Press.

Mufwene, Salikoko S. 1991c. Review of *Language in exile: Three hundred years of Jamaican Creole* by Barbara Lalla and Jean D'Costa. *SECOL Review* 15.200–205.

Mufwene, Salikoko S. 1992a. Africanisms in Gullah: A re-examination of the issues. In *Old English and new: Studies in language and linguistics in honor of Frederic G.*

*Cassidy*, ed. By Joan H. Hall, Dick Doane, & Dick Ringler, 156–182. New York: Garland.

Mufwene, Salikoko S. 1992b. Why grammars are not monolithic. In *The joy of grammar: A festschrift in honor of James D. McCawley*, ed. by Diane Brentari, Gary N. Larson, and Lynn A. MacLeod, 225–250. Amsterdam: John Benjamins.

Mufwene, Salikoko S. 1994a. On decreolization: The case of Gullah. In *Language and the social construction of identity in creole situations*, ed. by Marcyliena Morgan. Los Angeles: Center for Afro-American Studies, UCLA.

Mufwene, Salikoko S. 1994b. Restructuring, feature selection, and markedness: From Kimanyanga to Kituba. In *Proceedings of the Twentieth Annual Meeting of the Berkeley Linguistic Society: Special session on historical issues in African linguistics*, ed. by Kevin E. Moore, David A. Peterson, & Comfort Wentum, 67–90. Berkeley: BLS.

Mufwene, Salikoko S. 1996a. The Founder Principle in creole genesis. *Diachronica* 13.

Mufwene, Salikoko S. 1996b. Development of American Englishes: Some questions from a creole genesis perspective. In *Varieties of English Around the World: Focus on the USA*, ed. by Edgar Schneider. Amsterdam & Philadelphia: John Benjamins.

Mufwene, Salikoko S. 1997a. The legitimate and illegitimate offspring of English. In *World Englishes 2000*, ed. by Larry E. Smith and Michael L. Forman, 182–203. College of Languages, Linguistics, and Literature, University of Hawai'i and the East-West Center.

Mufwene, Salikoko S. 1997b. Jargons, pidgins, creoles, and koinés: What are they? In *Structure and status of pidgins and creoles*, ed. by Arthur Spears & Donald Winford, 35–70. Amsterdam: John Benjamins.

Mufwene, Salikoko S. 1997c. The ecology of Gullah's survival. *American Speech* 72.69–83.

Mufwene, Salikoko S. & Marta B. Dijkhoff. 1989. On the so-called "infinitive" in Atlantic creoles. *Lingua 77.297–330.*

Mühlhäusler, Peter. 1985. The number of pidgin Englishes in the Pacific. *Papers in Pidgin and Creole Linguistics* 1. *Pacific Linguistics* A-72.25–51.

Nichols, Patricia C. 1984. Networks and hierarchies: Language and social stratification. In *Language and Power*, ed. by Cheris Kramarae, Muriel Schulz, and William O'Barr, 23–42. Beverly Hills: Sage Publications.

Perkins, Edwin J. 1988. *The Economy of Colonial America*. Second edition. New York: Columbia University Press.

Poplack, Shana & Sali Tagliamonte. 1991. African American English in the diaspora: Evidence from old-line Nova Scotians. *Language Variation and Change* 3.301–339.

Poplack, Shana & Sali Tagliamonte. 1994. -*S* or nothing: Marking the plural in the African American diaspora. *American Speech* 69.227–259.

Rickford, John R. 1983. What happens in decreolization. In *Pidginization and creolization as language acquisition*, ed. by Roger Andersen, 298–319. Rowley: Newbury House.

Rickford, John R. 1985. Ethnicity as a sociolinguistic boundary. *American Speech* 60.2:99–125.

Rickford, John R. 1986. Some principles for the study of black and white speech in the South. In *Language varieties in the South: Perspectives in black and white*, ed. by Michael Montgomery and Guy Bailey, 38–62. University: University of Alabama Press.

Rickford, John R. 1987. *Dimensions of a creole continuum: History, texts, and linguistic analysis of Guyanese creole*. Stanford: Stanford University Press.

Rickford, John R. 1990. Number delimitation in Gullah: A response to Mufwene. *American Speech* 65.148–163.

Rickford, John R. 1992. The creole residue in Barbados. In *Old English and new: Studies in language and linguistics in honor of Frederic G. Cassidy*, ed. By Joan H. Hall, Dick Doane, & Dick Ringler, 183–201. New York: Garland.

Rickford, John R. 1997. Prior creolization of AAVE? Sociohistorical and textual evidence from the 17th and 18th centuries. *Journal of Sociolinguistics* 1.315–336.

Rickford, John R. 1998. The creole origins of African-American vernacular English. In *African-American English*, ed. by Salikoko S. Mufwene, John R. Rickford, Guy Bailey, and John Baugh, 154–200. London: Routledge.

Rickford, John R. & Jerome S. Handler. 1994. Textual evidence of the nature of early Barbadian speech. *Journal of Pidgin and Creole Languages* 9.221–255.

Sato, Charlene. 1993. Language change in a creole continuum: Decreolization? In *Progression and regression in language: Sociocultural, neuropsychological, and linguistic perspectives*, ed. by Kenneth Hyltenstam & Ake Viberg, 122–143. Cambridge: Cambridge University Press.

Schneider, Edgar W. 1989. *American Earlier Black English: Morphological and syntactic variables*. Tuscaloosa: University of Alabama Press.

Schuchardt, Hugo. 1914. *Die Sprache der Saramakkaneger in Surinam*. Amsterdam: Johannes Muller. Translated as "The language of the Saramaccans" in *The ethnography of variation: Selected writings on pidgins and creoles [by Hugo Schuchardt]*, 73–108, by T. L. Markey. Ann Arbor: Karoma.

Siegel, Jeff. 1985. Koines and koineization. *Language in Society* 14.357–78.

Silverstein, Michael. 1972. Chinook Jargon: Language contact and the problem of multi-level generative systems. *Language* 48.378–406, 496–625.

Singler, John. 1990. On the use of sociohistorical criteria in the comparison of creoles. *Linguistics* 28.645–659.

Stephens, Thomas M. 1983. Creole, créole, criollo, crioulo: The shadings of a term. *SECOL Review* 7.28–39.

Stewart, William. 1965. Urban Negro speech: Sociolinguistic factors affecting English teaching. In *Social dialects and language learning: Proceedings of the Bloomington, Indiana, Conference 1964*, ed. by Roger Shuy, 10–19. Champaign, IL.: National Council of Teachers of English.

Stewart, William. 1967. Sociolinguistic factors in the history of American Negro dialects. *Florida Foreign Language Reporter* 5.11, 22, 24, 26, 30.

Stewart, William. 1968. Continuity and change in American Negro dialects. *Florida Foreign Language Reporter* 6. 3–4, 14–16, 18.

Tagliamonte, Sali & Shana Poplack. 1988. Tense and aspect in Samaná English. *Language in Society* 17.513–533.

Tagliamonte, Sali & Shana Poplack. 1993. The zero-marked verb: Testing the creole hypothesis. *Journal of Pidgin and Creole Languages* 8.171–206.

Tate, Thad W. 1965. *The Negro in eighteenth-century Williamsburg*. Williamsburg, VA: The Colonial Williamsburg Foundation.

Thomason, Sarah G. 1983. Chinook Jargon in areal and historical context. *Language* 59.820–70.

Thomason, Sarah G. & Terrence Kaufman. 1988. *Language contact, creolization, and genetic linguistics*. Berkeley: University of California Press.

Trudgill, Peter. 1986. *Dialects in contact*. Oxford: Blackwell.

Valkhoff, Marius F. 1966. *Studies in Portuguese and creole — With special reference to South Africa*. Johannesburg: Witwatersrand University Press.

Williams, Jeffrey P. 1985. Preliminaries to the Study of the Dialects of White West Indian English. *Nieuwe West-Indische Gids* 59.27–44.

Winford, Donald. 1992. Another look at the copula in Black English and Caribbean creoles. *American Speech* 67.21–60.

Winford, Donald. 1993. Back to the past: The BEV/Creole connection revisited. *Language Variation and Change* 4.311–357.

Winford, Donald. 1997a. On the origins of African-American vernacular English — A creolist perspective. Part 1: The sociohistorical background. *Diachronica* 14.305–344.

Winford, Donald. 1997b. Re-examining Caribbean English creole continua. *World Englishes* 16.233–279.

# On the Possibility of Afrogenesis in the Case of French Creoles

Mikael Parkvall

*Stockholms Universitet*

## 1. Background

Since the demise of the monogenetic idea as it was expressed in the 1960s and 1970s (Taylor 1961, 1963; Thompson 1961; Stewart 1962; Whinnom 1965; Pottier 1966; Voorhoeve 1972; Granda 1976; and Allsopp 1976), it has commonly been assumed that most creoles emerged in the communities where they are now spoken. Because of the problems with imagining the New World creoles as relexifications of a Portuguese pidgin, it was believed safer to posit a genesis *in situ*.

However, some creolists have begun to reconsider the possibility of Afrogenesis within each lexical group. This view, usually referred to as *diffusionist*, has meant a revival of Afrogenetic claims in the past ten years. Hancock (1969), Stewart (1971) and Alleyne (1971: 179–80) were the first to suggest an African pidgin English (as opposed to one of Portuguese lexicon) as the ancestor of New World English creoles (ECs), and they were followed by Hancock (1986, 1987), Carter (1987), Smith (1987) and McWhorter (1995, 1997). This far, however, diffusionist claims have all centered around ECs, and no one has made an attempt at elaborating the possibility of French creoles (FCs) having emerged in and spread from Africa without a preceding Portuguese pidgin.[1]

In Parkvall (1994, 1995a, 1995b), I proposed that the creolization of French in Louisiana, Mauritius, and to some extent Haiti, received an input of restructured French from Africa. In the case of Lesser Antillean, such an input is simply incompatible with the historical and demographic facts, and as I see it, these varieties can only be traced back to St. Kitts (Jennings 1995a; Parkvall 1995a, 1995c).[2] An Antillean FC may have had some influence on Louisianan and Mauritian, perhaps through stimulus diffusion, but although the striking uniformity of FCs in the Americas and in the Indian Ocean (excluding Réunion) makes such a scenario tempting indeed, again, history and demographics are not entirely compatible with it. I would therefore like to forward the possibility that FCs are the outcomes of two separate pidginizations, one on St. Kitts and one in Senegal.[3]

Among features shared by modern or obsolete varieties of Louisiana and Mauritius but not by any Ant dialects are affrication (i.e. /t, d/ → [ts, dz]/_i), negation *napa*, depalatalization of postalveolar fricatives, possession indicated by a morpheme derived from *il y en a*, a word for 'to give' derived from *donner*, reflexive constructions with derivates of *même*, absolute possessive with *pu(r)*, various reflexes of *après* used for aspect marking, preposed demonstratives and possessive adjectives, identity between emphatic possessive adjective and possessive pronoun, *gete* for 'to look' and an obligatory distinction between subject and oblique forms of 1SG. Conspicuously absent, on the other hand, are consonant-initial indefinite articles, postvocalic allomorphs of 3SG, fluctuation between word-final [ʒ] and [j], preposed pluralizers older than 150 years, aspect marker *ka* and benefactive serializations. Mauritian and Louisianan can also, as opposed to other FCs, introduce a predicative NP without the use of an overt equative copula. Haiti and (French) Guianese include features from both the above categories, possibly due to a mixing in an early stage of Senegalese and Kittitian proto-pidgins.

The rest of this paper will concentrate on the sociohistorical circumstances under which I postulate that a French pidgin emerged in Senegal. For further discussion of the linguistic facts, I refer the reader to Parkvall (1995a, in press), and McWhorter (1997).

## 2.    Previous views of FC interrelatedness

The fact that Louisianan and Mauritian (and in some cases Haitian) share traits that are normally not found in Lesser Antillean, and vice versa, has been hinted at before by a few writers, notably Faine (1939), Goodman (1964), Hull (1979a, 1979b), Baker & Corne (1982) and Hall (1992), but most have not tried to explain the similarities in terms of history or demographics. Although Hall is a historian rather than a linguist, she is, to my knowledge, the only one who has explicitly proposed a common origin for Louisianan and Mauritian not shared by other FCs. She claims (1992: 191–2) that this common ancestor is a Senegalese pidgin French (PF).

Goodman (1992: 355–7) mentions in passing a scenario not completely unlike the one presented here. He considers St. Kitts the focal point of creole dispersion in the Caribbean, and sees Mauritian as having possibly evolved from a Senegalese Pidgin. This would, however, not have arisen locally (i.e. in Senegal), but would have been implanted from the Caribbean, perhaps through stimulus diffusion via France where Whites would have acquired it as an African's speech stereotype. Goodman thus sees Mauritian and Louisianan as genetically related to the Lesser Antillean varieties, which I doubt. Some degree of stimulus diffusion from the Antilles to Senegal and to Louisiana and the Indian Ocean is quite possible, but its impact is likely to have been fairly limited.

However, no author attempts to explain in much detail where, when or how West African pidgin French (PF) would have evolved, and the only fairly detailed Afrogenetic scenario concerning FCs known to me is the one given by Hull (1979a, 1979b), who claims that the common ancestor of all FCs emerged — as a deliberate calque of a Portuguese-based pidgin — in the town of Whydah in Benin.

## 2.1 *Problems with Hull's scenario*

Hull is fairly representative of creolists who have postulated an African source for FC languages. I think this view has two serious faults: First of all it takes for granted that the hypothesized African pidgin emerged in Whydah, since it is a quite common misconception that this was the only permanent French establishment in sub-Saharan Africa, and secondly, it tries to trace the origins of all Atlantic and Indo-Oceanic FCs to this early Afro-French speech.

Postulating, as Hull does, the emergence and spread of a PF from Whydah encounters several difficulties. First of all, it is doubtful that many Africans in the area ever knew much French. It even seems that at least in the late 18th century, Fon served as a lingua franca in the area, for the French traveler Labarthe (1803: 111) says with reference to the French slaves in Whydah that "...*les nègres ignorent notre langue, tandis qu'ils savent celle des Dahomets*".[4] Even if there ever were a need to learn a European language in the area, this would not necessarily have been French, since there were also a Portuguese and an English establishment in the very same town, not to mention the numerous English, Portuguese, Dutch, Danish, Swedish, Brandenburgian and even Courlandic slave factories and trading posts elsewhere in the same region. Among these nations, France was a late-comer on the coast, and never had any post other than the one in Whydah for any longer period of time, whereas in 1709, there were several other forts in the area, at least 13 British, 9 Dutch, 1 Danish and 1 Brandenburgian (Donnan [ed.] 1931: 71).[5] Even in Whydah itself, the European competitors were more active than the French. Contemporary observer Du Casse reported in 1688 (Jones 1985: 164) that in a normal year, the English exported 14,000–15,000 slaves from Whydah, but the French only 600–700. For reasons still obscure — perhaps due to lack of financial means — France was never very devoted to its slave trade in Africa. Despite the desperate need for slaves in the French colonies, France seems to have been more interested in trying to keep other nations from developing their trade. The French factory in Whydah was established in 1671, and given a couple of years for a pidgin to evolve, such a language cannot possibly have influenced speech in the Caribbean until the second half of the 1670s at the very earliest. By then, slaves had been present in the French West Indies for almost half a century, had formed the majority in both Guadeloupe and Martinique for more than ten years, and locally-born slaves already constituted an important part of the servile population. In the latter island, slaves accounted for more than two thirds of the total population.

Furthermore, France entered the transatlantic slave trade as such later than its competitors, and for quite some time, about fifty years or so (Chauleau 1966: 103; Curtin 1969: 121; Klein 1986: 52; Thornton 1992: 155), most French slaves in the West Indies, either bought or stolen, were brought across the ocean on board foreign ships (which had loaded them in ports controlled by other nations than France).

Of course, the fact that there was only one French fort in Lower Guinea does of course not *a priori* eliminate the possibility of pidginization there. Language restructuring can occur within one single small settlement, as is proven by the existence of for instance Unserdeutsch in Papua New Guinea. Whydah was, however, very frequently visited by slave ships, and captives spent less time there than in the Senegalese ports. As opposed to these, Whydah did not have any interior posts attached to it where slaves were collected and kept before being brought to the coast. This may, as we shall see, make a crucial difference.

Hull (1979a: 209) was aware of the problem posed by the late establishment of Whydah, and claimed therefore that the larger numbers of PF-speaking slaves imported from Whydah to the Antilles would have made a previous domestic pidgin disappear. So far as I can see, there is no reason to assume that slaves already present in the Caribbean would give up their local tongue, a probably quite well developed and perhaps rapidly nativizing pidgin, in favor of a doubtlessly much more rudimentary speech form spoken by newcomers whose numbers gradually rose, but who definitely did not outrival an already established culture merely by quantitative superiority. Besides, beginning in the early 1680s, it took another twenty years for slave populations to double in both Guadeloupe and Martinique. Let us not forget that there are few, if any, cases in world history where the language of an immigrant population has been adopted by the inhabitants of the host country, unless the former has been socioeconomically superior or numerically dominant, neither of which was the case here, hardly even if every single slave exported from Whydah to the Caribbean spoke the pidgin postulated by Hull.

So, if we are to consider one single speech variety as the ancestor of all or some of the FCs, we must search elsewhere, at least so far as the Lesser Antillean varieties are concerned. As I have claimed before, I consider them to be descendants of a now extinct Kittitian FC. Louisiana and Mauritius, on the other hand, received little or no Lesser Antillean input in their respective formative periods, but instead quite a number of forced immigrants from Senegambia. We must thus consider two starting points for FC languages.

### 3.    General knowledge of French among natives in Senegambia

Alas, mentions of language use in the French posts in Senegal are extremely scarce, especially in the period before 1750. It is equally difficult to determine how widespread knowledge of (possibly restructured) French, or any other European language for that matter, may have been among Africans in general at this time. All that we have are scattered references to the language skills of isolated individuals or groups of individuals, and even these are scarce. We do know however, that the French (Cultru 1910: 36, Lajaille 1802: 84–5), just like the Portuguese (Ancelle 1887: 20) and the British (Hancock 1986; Holm 1989: 427), sometimes sent Africans to Europe to make them learn the language and to strengthen the ties between Europeans and local populations. In Senegambia (Lajaille 1802: 84), as well as in Sierra Leone (Fyfe 1962: 30) and on the Gold Coast (Mettas 1984: 259, 262), it happened now and then that local rulers asked that their sons be taken to France for this purpose. According to Cultru (1913: xvi) this was fairly common in Senegambia even in the late 16th century. In fact, the first known report of French being spoken in Senegal, that of the English traders Richard Reynolds and Thomas Dassel from the 1550s, mentions precisely this practice. They wrote that:

> The French have traded thither [Rufisque] about thirty years from Dieppe in Newhaven [=Le Havre]. Commonly with four or five ships every year ... [we have] several of the Negroes going to France and returning again, to the great increase of their mutual friendship. (Kerr 1812: 342–50)

Their fellow countryman George Fenner, an English trader, complained a little later, in 1566, that he and other foreign traders had to speak French in order to make themselves understood when dealing with the natives of Cape Verde (Delafosse 1931: 7). In 1595, the Portuguese traveler d'Almeida noted that many

Africans knew French (Harris 1992: 115), and a couple of years later, another Portuguese, Alvares reported that the people around Cape Verde spoke French "like natives" (Thornton 1992: 215). Referring to the same period, the Dutchman Pieter de Marees (1605) said that the Blacks living around Cape Verde "trade with all foreign nations, and hence speak Spanish [sic], English, French and Dutch," and added that they spoke mostly French. His countryman van den Broecke said in 1606 that the local inhabitants knew French, English and Dutch (Thornton 1992: 216), and Cultru (1910: 40, 1913:xxii) claims that "almost all" of the inhabitants of Rufisque spoke "un français assez intelligible" in the 1630s.[6] Alexis de Saint-Lô, when setting up a mission there in 1635, found that "la population de Rufisque parle une sorte de jargon français assez intelligible et qu'elle profère en notre langue des grossièretés et des jurons" (Delafosse 1931: 11).[7] The next testimony is that of a certain Dubois, who in 1669 reported that the natives of Cape Verde spoke "a little Dieppois, because the Dieppe folk often sail in this neighborhood" (Dubois 1897: 10). His observations are supported by John Barbot (1732: 47), according to whom "The inhabitants of Rufisque even today employ a number of French or Norman French words."

When de la Courbe arrived in Saint Louis (see map 1) sixteen years later, he wrote that natives who came to see him in the fort spoke a "français corrompu" (Courbe 1913: 43).[8] He also visited the chief Jean Bart, who lived in the area, and who spoke "très bien le français" (ibid: 53),[9] as well as francophones in Bintam and Albréda, both in present-day Gambia (ibid: 198, Cultru 1910: 111). Also in Gambia, Demanet (1767: 125) noted that the inhabitants of the kingdom of Bar often were Christians, and that many of them spoke French. From the inland, Saugnier (1792: 218) and Lamiral (Sprengel & Ehermann 1803: 106) reported in the mid-1780s that the king of Galam spoke French after having lived in St. Louis.

About 30 km from St. Louis, Corréard (Savigny & Corréard 1818: 300) met an African who had learned French in town. As there were no schools for Africans, he could not possibly have been *taught* French, and this fact suggests that although many Frenchmen learnt Wolof (Adanson 1795: 24, Amanda Sackur, p.c.), French was actually spoken in the homes and in the streets of St. Louis.

## 4.    The French establishments in Senegal

The French presence in 17th and 18th century Senegal was primarily confined to the two towns of St. Louis and Gorée, both of which were located on very small, inhospitable islands close to the Atlantic coast. The former was founded by *la*

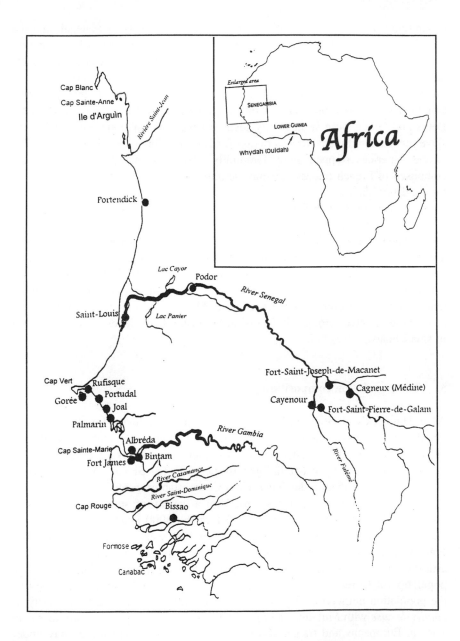

Map 1: *Senegambian Coast, with inset showing location in Africa*

*Compagnie des Indes* in 1659 close to the mouth of the River Senegal, and the latter was conquered from the Dutch in 1677. The economy of Gorée was entirely dependent on the slave trade, whereas St. Louis also exported considerable amounts of gum and other commodities. No agricultural activities were pursued, and, concentrated on trade as these enclaves were, the French preferred to buy the necessary provisions from neighboring African kingdoms. Both St. Louis and Gorée were strategically located keypoints for trade with all French slave markets, and many vessels bound for Lower Guinea, the Mascarenes, India or the Americas stopped there. Gradually, a racially mixed society emerged, composed of French traders, artisans, seafarers and soldiers, free blacks, mulattoes and fort slaves.

18th century French Senegal consisted not only of Gorée and St. Louis, but also of a number of lesser posts, administratively attached to either Gorée or St. Louis. The purpose of these dependencies was partly to deliver slaves for export, and partly to supply provisions and export products to the two towns. Many of the lesser posts had only a handful of French employees. Galam, which has a central role in this scenario of FC genesis, was more important, but still no more than about 80 Frenchmen ever lived there. Most of the exports from the lesser posts were directed through St. Louis and Gorée, where slaves were transported in small boats.

## 5.    The population composition

As in Hancock's (1986: 80) scenario of EC genesis in Sierra Leone, five basic population groups can be distinguished in the French settlements in eighteenth century Senegal: (1) Europeans; (2) Mulattoes; (3) Blacks working for the Europeans or Mulattoes; (4) Indigenous peoples; (5) Slaves. About the same categories are identified in the Dutch Gold Coast establishments by Postma (1990).

My very approximate guess, based on a variety of sources (see Parkvall 1995a for details) is that perhaps only 5% of the 3000 inhabitants of St. Louis were slaves waiting to be exported. A further 10% were Europeans, about 40% Free Blacks and Coloreds and almost 50% *captifs de case*, i.e. house slaves, artisans and other servile workes. There is less information available on the population of Gorée in the early 18th century, but a rough estimate may be that the population numbering slightly more than a thousand included a majority of *captifs de case* with Mulattoes and Free Blacks each making up slightly less than a tenth. Europeans and transit slaves, whose numbers varied more, may under normal circumstances each have hovered in the vicinity of 10–15%.

## 5.1  *Europeans*

The French at the trading posts were of three basic categories: Administrators and clericals, troops and workers. Most of the employees were recruited among marginal elements, who had fled personal or financial problems in Dieppe, Bordeaux and Marseilles, and lack of success was sometimes ascribed to their alleged intellectual and moral weakness. Corruption, alcoholism and immoral conduct were everyday sources of complaints from Company officials, and the climate and the idleness further degenerated these miserable beings, according to contemporary observers (Machat 1906: 102).[10]

As far as the geographical origins are concerned, Bretons constituted the major group. Out of 621 French sailors and workers in Senegal whose origins are mentioned in Lacroix (1986: 1–2), two thirds (67%) were from Brittany, while the rest came from the usual areas of colonial emigration along the French Atlantic coast. The Breton dominance is probably best explained by the fact that the Company's headquarters was in Lorient, a town founded by the king for the purpose of conducting trade with overseas countries. Almost all of the Company's slaving expeditions departed from Lorient (Stein 1979: 21), and most of the private slaving enterprises were based in Nantes, another Breton city.

The contracts of indenture were rather similar to those signed by workers going to the Caribbean, and so were the signers. The engagés in Senegal were with very few exceptions employed on three-year contracts (Lacroix 1986: 2), and extremely few women were indentured, much fewer than in the West Indies; almost all the *engagés* were single men, 30 years of age or younger (ibid: 3).

## 5.2  *Métis (Mulattoes)*

Race mixing was absolutely necessary in Senegal for two reasons: Firstly, almost three fourths of the early batches of European settlers died within a year or less after their arrival. In the early 18th century, about a third succumbed annually, and since locally born children were more likely to survive, intermarriage was a question of survival for Europeans as a group in Africa. In the English establishments in Lower Guinea between 1683 and 1737, 60% of all Europeans died within eight months following arrival (Curtin 1990: 80, Postma 1990: 66). Secondly, the Company forbade their employees to bring their families with them, and although intermarriage with native women was officially not tolerated either, it was usually accepted for practical purposes, and it did occur to a great extent.

Many Goréens, especially those of mixed ancestry, looked upon themselves as Frenchmen (Knight 1977: 52–53), even though a great many Mulattoes were actually not of French descent, but rather a legacy from the Portuguese (Machat 1906: 88). Some intermarriage also occurred later between Goréens and Portuguese mulattoes of mainland villages (Knight 1977: 48). Regrettably, there is no evidence as to what language the *Métis* used among themselves, but since they often regarded themselves as Frenchmen (Knight 1977: 52–53), it would not seem unlikely if adoption of French linguistic habits was a feature of such an identification, at least as far as this was possible.

Couto (1993: 383) discusses the possible linguistic outcomes of mixed marriages in the Portuguese establishments on the Guinea coast (child learns Portuguese, child learns mother's African language, child learns Creole) and comes to the conclusion that a Portuguese creole emerged quickly and was nativized by the first generation of Mulattoes, since the creole — unlike the other languages — would have had the advantage of being understood by all ethnic groups in the community. Couto does not seem to have reflected upon an obvious third possibility, namely that the child chooses to learn *both* Portuguese (or in our case, French) *and* one or several African languages. That alternative is no less likely than the ones mentioned by Couto, and must be considered as well. Whereas the Portuguese discussed by Couto were independent traders living in or in close proximity to native villages, the French presence in Senegal was mostly confined to the towns of St. Louis and Gorée, where native Africans' access, exposure and motivation to learn the European language may have differed from that in the Portuguese establishments.

## 5.3  *Free Blacks and Colored in Company service*

The French posts had all the artisans and other skilled labor it needed, but to reduce costs, Africans were employed, and if necessary trained, as interpreters, pilots and so on. Hancock (1986: 82) refers to all these people as grumettes, but in French colonies, these were just one of at least four groups of indigenous Blacks employed by the Company. First, there were the *maîtres de langue*, whose main task was to act as interpreters. Then, we have the *maîtres des barques*, who were usually mulattoes. Their job was to handle the large numbers of small craft used to transport persons and small objects to and from the mainland and between St. Louis and ships at anchor in the roadstead, and now and then to lead expeditions inland. A small group of free Blacks also performed various household duties, although most of the black *servants* and *workers* were slaves who were not permanently working on these tasks. Finally, the *laptots* or *gourmets*, sometimes also called *mousses*, were usually free, though sometimes enslaved. This last group of Blacks was not permanently employed by the

Company, but their services were bought when needed to handle shipping to and from the interior, either via the Senegal or the Gambia. Laptots also gathered goods and, not least important, transported slaves from minor posts along the coast to Gorée and St. Louis. According to Delcourt (1952: 129), Bambaras, the usual favorites of the French, were preferred, but Fulbes were also common, and Yolofs and members of other ethnic groups sometimes occurred in this role as well.[11] Ly (1955: 277), however, claims that all laptots in St. Louis were from Waalo, and thus Wolof-speaking, and Curtin (1975: 114) believes the majority of laptots on Gorée were Wolof-speaking Lebus or Portuguese Creole-speaking mulattoes. Most laptots dwelt in St. Louis or Gorée, but a minority was based on the mainland, sometimes as far away as in Sierra Leone (Colvin 1981: 212).

### 5.4 Tribal populations

Most black St. Louisians were Yolofs, but there were sizable minorities of Tukuloors, Bambaras, Fulbes, and Soninkes. In this multiethnic setting, one of the main concerns of the French was to maintain the power balance between the Yolofs, the Tukuloors, and the other groups around St. Louis. This divide-and-rule tactic was an efficient way of kindling the tribal discord that was essential to keep the slave trade going.

Adanson (1795: 23) notes that all Free Negroes in St. Louis came from Waalo, the Wolof-speaking kingdom that surrounded the town. According to Camara (1968: 39), though, the few non-Muslim Blacks in the town were from Kayor. In any case, they too would have been Wolof-speaking.

### 5.5 Slaves

Slaves in Gorée and St. Louis were of two rather different kinds; the *captifs de traite* were slaves brought from the interior or from lesser posts along the coast and kept in *captiveries* in the towns awaiting shipment to the plantation colonies. The *captifs de case*, on the other hand, were usually born into bondage, albeit occasionally chosen among the *captifs de traite* (Flutre 1961: 286).

The little demographic information I have seldom distinguishes these two groups, but it is probable that *captifs de traite*, whose numbers must have been subject to considerable fluctuation, are usually not included at all. Visits by slave ships thrice yearly and an annual export of 500–1000 would yield an average of slightly less than 100–150 transit slaves in town at any given moment.

Usually, slaves were bought from native peoples in the area, and most peoples delivered prisoners of war to the Europeans at one time or the other.

Rarely, members of the own nation were sold for various reasons,[12] and only occasionally, the French themselves raided hostile villages and delivered the inhabitants as slaves to St. Louis (see e.g. Sprengel & Ehermann 1803: 85).

Initially, most slaves exported from St. Louis were Yolofs, but subsequently more and more Mandes (mostly Bambaras and Malinkes) were sold (ibid: 59). In course of time, the Bambaras became so dominant that the very word *Bambara* completely lost its ethnic connotations and came to be used for any slave exported from St. Louis, regardless of origins (Curtin 1969: 184). The Bambaras were indeed the most-sought slaves in most French colonies. They were thought to be less likely to revolt than the Yolofs, and were generally considered hardworking, loyal, efficient and hardy, though somewhat unintelligent (Mettas 1975: 41, Hall 1992: 41, 42, Cultru 1910: 266). They were not yet converted to Islam, which was also seen as an advantage. Most house slaves in St. Louis, as well as in the lesser posts of Arguin and Galam, were Bambaras, and they were even so well trusted that a local defense force consisting of Bambaras was set up (Delcourt 1952: 130–131).

"Moors" (a term referring to all Arab-speaking peoples north of the Senegal) were not usually bought by the Company, but when demand exceeded supply, as was often the case, authorities could not afford making ethnic distinctions (Wadström 1791: 19), and large numbers of "Moors" were delivered from St. Louis to e.g. French Guiana after the signing in 1777 of a contract regulating exports to Guinea.

On Gorée, the first slaves owned by the French were 62 captives that the Dutch left behind when surrendering the island (Labat 1728, vol. 2:113). These slaves, who may have spoken a pidginized variety of either Portuguese or Dutch, may have influenced a possible PF on the island. The only other slaves on Gorée mentioned by Labat (1730, vol. 2:49) were Bambaras, and they no doubt dominated among the house slaves there. However, since deliveries from the Bissao post and from various places along the coast strip between Cape Verde and Bissao, as well as from the interior, arrived quite regularly, there must have been speakers of languages such as Papel, Diola, Mandinka, Biafada, Balanta, Manjaku and Bijago present, as well as people from the ethnolinguistic groups living in the immediate hinterland, i.e. around Cape Verde, most of whom would have been speakers of Wolof and Sereer.

Cultru (1910: 272) states that most slaves shipped from Gorée were Yolofs and Sereers, though Mandes are likely to have made up a large proportion of the exports here as in St. Louis, as are speakers of Bak languages such as Manjaku, Papel and Balanta. Curtin (1969, 1975: 187) estimates that between half and two thirds of all slaves exported from Senegambia were originally from the inland beyond the navigable rivers (which implies that they were Mande-speakers). Of these, one third — a figure that appears underestimated to me — would have been shipped from St. Louis, via Galam, while the others, many of whom were exported by the British, would have come through the Gambia. Numbers given in Hall (1992: 289) and Curtin (1975: 188) suggest that of Senegalese slaves exported by the French in the first half of the 18th century, about 60% were Mande-speakers, the remaining 40% being equally divided between speakers of Wolof and other Atlantic languages. Yolofs seem to have made up a larger proportion in the early years, with Mande peoples gradually increasing and becoming dominant (Biondi 1987: 59).

## 6.    Exposure to French

Whatever the linguistic diversity among slaves in the colonies, the slave entre-pôts were by definition less heterogeneous, and if there were ever need for a lingua franca, the major local language, in our case Wolof, may have been more accessible than (pidgin) French (cf. Goodman 1987: 364). It is therefore unlikely that a PF would have become the main medium of expression of Africans before leaving Senegal. But, although the motivation to actively learn it remains doubtful, it is not unlikely that slaves were exposed to considerable amounts of French or French approximations or PF while still in Africa, and that, once in the plantation colonies, they made use of what they had acquired.

### 6.1   *For how long?*

Baker (Baker & Corne 1982: 244) says that it is possible that captives spent several weeks or even months in the depots before the slave trade had been fully developed — which it had when Louisianan and Mauritian began to form — thereby suggesting that slaves involved in the formation of at least these varieties on average spent less time than a couple of months, at the very most, in French captivity before leaving for the colonies. "It seems unlikely, " Baker adds, "that most West Africans bound for the Indian Ocean spent anywhere near as much time in a depot as on board a ship" (ibid: 245).

What Baker, and most others who have commented on this, have failed to take into account, is that most slaves were actually not delivered directly to St. Louis or Gorée, at least not to the former town. St. Louis received the bulk of its slaves from the Fort Saint-Joseph in Galam (Machat 1906: 81, 83), some 1500 km upstream the Senegal. The most interesting thing about this is that the captives in Galam were transferred to St. Louis only once a year (Cultru 1910: 272, Delcourt 1952: 91–92, Curtin 1975: 169), because following the dry season, the Senegal did not permit any navigation; only three months a year could the trip to Galam be undertaken (Barry 1992: 269, Levtzion 1975: 216). The implication, obviously, is that *"Slaves bought ... just after the boats left had to be held for at least* [my emphasis] *nine months"* (Curtin 1975: 169). Assuming that deliveries to Galam from peoples in the area did not depend on weather conditions, but rather politics, the average time spent in Galam before being shipped to St. Louis must have been almost six months. In fact, however, interethnic strife (and thereby slave deliveries) was partly conditioned by climatological factors, since agricultural preoccupations determined how much time could possibly be spent on warfare without jeopardizing the food supply (Amanda Sackur, p.c.). In general, most of the fighting took place in the dry season, in other words when the French flotilla had just left for St. Louis. The average waiting time in Galam may thus have been even longer than six months.

The trip from Galam to St. Louis, made every summer, also took quite some time. The size of the convoys increased continuously throughout the 18th century, but in the 1750s, it typically consisted of 2–4 officers and 25 laptots from St. Louis. The crews were probably mostly French in the early days, but were gradually Africanized over time (Curtin 1975: 114). Lajaille (1802: 24) says that although it took almost three months for the 40–ship-convoy to go up the river to Galam, the descent usually required only two weeks.

Evidence in Mettas (1978 and 1984),[13] indicates that Senegal was visited by 101 French slavers carrying off an estimated 31,300 slaves between 1710 and 1750. If one out of every two ships called at more than one port, which seems to be the case, this makes about 150 visits in 41 years, or slightly more than 14 weeks between each export possibility. The average captive would thus have spent almost two months in St. Louis or Gorée before embarking on a slaver.

The voyage from West Africa to the eastern Caribbean or to Mauritius took about three and four months respectively (Stein 1988: 30, Baker & Corne 1982: 177). It has often been pointed out that most French slaves, perhaps as many as three fourths (Curtin 1969: 121, Chauleau 1966: 103, Klein 1986: 52, Thornton 1992: 155), were taken away on board foreign ships. This is true so far as the early colonies are concerned, but when Mauritius and Louisiana were colonized, French ships actually did provide most of the slaves imported. In the 18th century, until after the outbreak of the Seven Years' war, French shipping did largely meet the needs of the planters, and it was only in the 17th century and again after 1760 that the French had to rely on foreign trade (Stein 1979: 26).

So, upon arrival in America or Mauritius, a slave coming from St. Louis could have been exposed to French for about a year (approximately 0–12 months in Galam, two weeks on the Senegal, 0–4 months in St. Louis and 1–6 months at sea, thus with a theoretical variation between one and a half months and two years, and an average somewhere around 12 months). As we shall see, the amount of French heard need not necessarily have been less than that heard on the plantation.

## 6.2  *How many?*

Since slaves were shipped from Galam only once a year, the number of slaves present there at any given time would vary greatly. According to Lajaille (1802: 48), annual exports were usually around 3,000 when the trade had become organized, but dropped to 1500 as competition from the British at Fort James became more serious in the 1760s. Machat (1906: 83–84) claims that 1,000–1,200, and occasionally as many as 1,500 slaves a year passed through Galam in the mid-18th century, but deliveries fell to 400–500 as British activity increased. The captain of the Saint-Louis, a Company-owned ship that visited Senegal in 1729–30, says in a letter to a Company representative in Lorient, that about 600–800 Blacks came from Galam to St. Louis annually (Mettas 1984: 582).

There were usually about 40 Frenchmen in Galam and the same number of Company-employed non-whites (Delcourt 1952: 114–117, 403), including some mulattoes, who may have been native speakers of French, thus about 50 probable francophones. Assuming a storage capacity of about 800 would give us a mean of 400 slaves present in Galam at any given moment, thereby yielding an average ratio of about 8:1, not very different from the proportions found in many colonies, for example Haiti in the same period.

As claimed above, native French speakers made up about 10–20% of the coastal town populations in the early 18th century, depending on the extent to which people of mixed race had $L_1$ competence in French.

The ships usually carried about 300 slaves (from 50 to almost 600; Cultru 1910: 269, Klein 1986: 145, Mettas 1978, 1984) and had a crew of about 40 (usually ranging from 30 to 70; Stein 1988: 25, Mettas 1978, 1984), thus roughly giving an average slave-to-white ratio of about 6–8:1, again, a figure no higher than on the plantations.

Therefore, the linguistic conditions of the middle passage need not have differed significantly from those in the West African forts, except perhaps that slaves were slightly more mixed on the ship (but still less than in the plantation colonies), since it sometimes stopped in one or two more ports before leaving for America or the Indian Ocean.

## 6.3   Under what circumstances?

Slaves are usually thought to have been chained or locked up in dungeons for most of their time in the African ports. In fact, practices varied greatly depending on the sex and the ethnicity of the slaves. Women and children were usually not chained at all, neither in the port nor aboard the ship (Cultru 1910: 266). In the case of Mandes (except Soninkes), the men were not chained either, and in town they were often used for various kinds of work while awaiting shipment (ibid: 267), this presumably giving them opportunities to learn French if motivated. Yolofs, Soninkes and Fulbes were treated with greater caution, and were usually kept in chains (Saugnier 1792: 334). However, Faidherbe (1889: 21–2) claims that all slaves, regardless of nationality, were chained together in pairs.[14] In his account, slaves were also locked up for the night, but brought to work by an interpreter every morning. The fact that an interpreter was present indicates of course that slaves generally could not communicate with their foremen (unfortunately, we don't know from what ethnic group these were recruited), but the mere fact that they were brought out to work nevertheless gives the slaves better opportunities to hear French or PF spoken than does the traditional scenario where slaves sat locked in most of the time awaiting departure.

Even on board the ships, contacts between whites and slaves were not really as rare as one may imagine. Besides being fed soup twice daily and given water three times a day, slaves were taken onto deck, one at a time, to be examined by the surgeon. They were encouraged to wash themselves and their loincloths frequently, and their hair was cut once in a while. When not busy taking care of their personal hygiene, the slaves were forced to clean the ship itself, which was done every day. The toilets were also cleaned several times daily. When not working, eating or sleeping, the captives were, according to Stein (1979: 101–3) strongly encouraged to sing and dance, which, besides keeping them in a reasonably good mood, gave them some well needed exercise. Unfortunately, I have no information about the amount and nature of the oral interaction associated with these activities.

We still know far too little about conditions in posts like Galam to determine to what extent slaves actually were exposed to some French-related form of speech, and what this may have been like. The relative lack of ethnic diversity also has to be considered, although diversity is not an inevitable prerequisite of language learning and/or restructuring. In Galam, the vast majority of incoming slaves were Mande-speakers, and, at least in St. Louis, the wardens often were too. As stated above, about 60% of all slaves exported from Senegal by the French were Mandes, about 20% Yolofs and the remaining 20% speakers of

other Atlantic languages. Though the town of St. Louis as such was predominantly Yolof, the Mandes were numerically superior in the depots, and they were
in many ways favored by the French. While many of them may have understood
some Wolof, the social difference between a Mande warden employed by the
French and a Yolof captive might have called for a language other than Wolof.
Although I don't have any documentation of the ethnicity of the non-European
fort personnel in Galam, the most important post from the creolist's point of
view, we do know that the British and the Dutch drew slaves for use in their
forts not from the immediate vicinity, but from more distant areas in order to
minimize their solidarity with the surrounding peoples (Magnus Huber, John
McWhorter, p.c.). Although this claim is, of course, highly speculative, it may
well be that the French for this reason used Mandes on the coast, but Atlantic-
speakers in Galam, thereby increasing the likelihood of PF usage in warden-
captive interactions. Even if this were not the case, we now know that the
concept of what Whinnom (1956) termed tertiary hybridization is not a *sine qua
non* for language restructuring to take place, and there are numerous cases where
pidginization processes have involved only two linguistic groups (e.g. Tay Boi
Vietnamese PF, Russenorsk, and Chinese pidgin English).

## 7.   Senegalese slaves in the French plantation colonies

So, if some Senegalese slaves had a rudimentary command of some French-
related speech form upon arrival in the colonies, would they have been able to
impose this language on their fellows in misfortune? As noted above, I do not
think this could have happened in the Lesser Antilles, but in the later colonies of
Louisiana and Mauritius, and to a lesser extent in Haiti, where Senegalese made
up an important proportion of the servile population in the early stages, this
would in fact have been possible, given appropriate sociolinguistic conditions.
Note that I do not propose that pidgin speakers would have arrived in any
considerable numbers; most of the slaves who were transported from Senegal
probably did not know the slightest smattering of French.

      First, it must be remembered that slave-owning was very unevenly distribut-
ed, and in some colonies, the Company was often one of the major slave-owners,
or sometimes the major one. As language restructuring on large estates is more
likely to have had an effect on the final outcome of creolization, this has a few
interesting implications. The Company sometimes had (possibly because it had
more intimate relations with the suppliers in Africa) different preferences, and
most certainly a greater possibility of choosing among incoming slaves than

ordinary planters did. In the case of Mauritius, for instance, where the Company was the largest single slave owner, and alone possessed a fifth of all slaves in the early 1730s, it clearly favored West Africans (Baker & Corne 1982: 171, 180), possibly suggesting that these played a more important role in creolization than might otherwise be assumed. The trading companies of other nations, for instance, the Dutch West Indian Company (Hornby 1980: 91), sometimes had similar biases. Furthermore, the Company could have special connections with other Company representatives overseas, which sometimes resulted in inter-colonial population movements. When P. F. B. David, who had spent 18 years in Senegal, was appointed governor of Mauritius in 1746, he took with him a number of his own slaves. These, given their great access to French, are perhaps more likely to have spoken or at least understood some variety of French than any other slaves from Senegal. Another group of potential French or PF speakers is the Bambara boatsmen who had earlier handled the shipping on the river Senegal, but who, because of their skills, were taken to Mauritius to perform the same tasks in the harbor of Port-Louis (Baker, p.c.). There are also examples where long-term members (white, black or colored) of the French settlements in Senegal either moved voluntarily or were deported to Louisiana (Hall 1992: 128, Usner 1992: 238). A few obviously also moved in the opposite direction, and Lacroix (1986) mentions the presence of a colored Louisianan sailor in Senegal.

Usually, the numbers of slaves coming from various ethnolinguistic groups are used to prove the linguistic influence of one African tongue or the other in creole formation. We know, however, that familiar sociolinguistic factors, not unlike those operating in our own societies, were indeed present in the 17th century Caribbean as well. There is little reason to doubt that certain individuals must have had a more significant impact on language restructuring than others, although we don't know exactly who, how or why. Perhaps the most obvious factor would be timing. If the first immigrants attempted to create a Medium for Interethnic Communication (using Baker's 1990 terminology), and succeeded in doing so, their vernacular would have constituted the target for later arrivals, along the lines of what is usually referred to as the *Founder Principle* (Mufwene 1996).

Equally obviously, language use was connected to social status, here as in all other communities, although the possibilities of promotion might seem limited, to say the least, in a slave society. Documentation on this point is extremely scarce, but to the extent that there were any material benefits (such as getting one's own plot of vegetables) or non-material ones (like being transferred to less strenuous occupations than cane cutting) that could be obtained by a *bossal* (newly arrived) slave, it would have been rather surprising if language learning were *not* used to obtain these privileges. This, however, does not necessarily imply that the lexifier was the target language.

In the particular scenario suggested here (as in more traditional Afrogenetic accounts), the question arises why other slaves on a plantation would have imitated the few who were possibly able to speak a hypothetical West African pidgin. However, we must not forget that the pidgin in question would probably have been somewhat unstable, and it is by no means evident that other slaves, once they had decided to try to learn at least the vocabulary of the superstrate (for such a decision must after all have been made at some point) were able to distinguish French and Pidgin as two discrete linguistic systems. If not, and if the learning of either was required to ensure interethnic communication, the pidgin in which, say, a tenth of all slaves may have had some competence, however minimal, would probably have been sociolinguistically and typologically more accessible than the French spoken by masters and supervisors.[15]

Knowing a speech form that allowed communication with both the masters and fellow slaves of other ethnolinguistic backgrounds may in itself have entailed a certain status. Furthermore, in the more heterogeneous settings, it is by no means evident that every individual was able to communicate with more than a tenth of his workmates; the small group of pidgin speakers may even in some cases have constituted the largest group having a common language, and most certainly one that had greater possibilities than others to make useful contacts with people, both black and white, outside their own ethnolinguistic group.

The possibility of isolated individuals or small groups of speakers influencing language practices in the early phases of creolization can neither be proven nor dismissed, but it does deserve further discussion. Evidently, lexical items can in some cases be traced back to identifiable individuals,[16] and even though the possibility has been explicitly denied by some scholars (e.g. Bickerton), I do think that a relatively small group of people, given favorable conditions, can also have an influence upon the grammar of the emerging language that exceeds their numerical importance.

Fortunately, the above argumentation does not rely exclusively on speculation. Recent research on Pacific pidgins, which are more recent, and whose early stages are thus better documented, provides some compelling data on this point. At the beginning of the 20th century, 400 Hiri Motu policemen were detached to the inlands of Papua New Guinea. With a distribution of about two policemen in each village, the linguistic outcome three quarters of a century later was 150,000 Hiri Motu speakers (Dutton 1985: 3, 72). Furthermore, Keesing (1988: 35–9) shows that the Melanesian English Pidgin was introduced to large numbers of plantation laborers by groups of foremen who were numerically far inferior.[17]

The settlement histories of Mauritius and Louisiana are documented in considerable detail in Baker & Corne (1982) and Hall (1992) respectively. Both show a Senegalese dominance in the earliest periods of settlement. Typologically speaking, Haitian and French Guianese in many respects occupy positions intermediate between Lesser Antillean on the one hand and Mauritius and Louisiana on the other. These colonies were also founded after the first settlement of the Lesser Antilles (1625) but before colonization of Louisiana and Mauritius (early 18th century), and at about the same time as the first permanent French establishment in Senegal (1659). Their mixed nature may well be due to these colonies having received pidgin-speakers from both Senegal and St. Kitts. In the case of Haiti, Lesser Antilleans, including some slaveholders, were the first settlers (Cornevin 1982: 23, Crouse 1940: 82, Exquemelin 1684:25, Hornot 1776: 490), and in the single year of 1695, the entire French population of St. Croix was resettled in Haiti, leading to a 15% increase of the number of slaves there (calculated from Larsen 1928: 12).

Senegambian imports to Haiti were not very significant in terms of numbers, but were strategically located in time and space. When large-scale imports to the Port-au-Prince area begun in the early 1730s, Senegambians constituted the largest group of arrivals, and continued to do so for another decade (calculated from Mettas 1978, 1984).

In French Guiana, the bulk of the servile work force in the late 17th and early 18th centuries was imported from Lower Guinea (Jennings 1995b), but in 1777, the *Compagnie de la Guyane* obtained exclusive rights to export slaves from Senegambia for a fifteen-year period (Tardieu 1847: 84). The contract signed in August 1777 stipulated that all its exports be directed to French Guiana (Stein 1979: 39). After the signing of this contract, Senegambians became the dominant group among newly imported slaves, and quite likely among the African-born population as a whole. Between 1785 and 1792, all eleven slavers delivering slaves to French Guiana came from Senegal. Of course, French Guiana FC already existed by this time, but the language nevertheless exhibits traits that could well be due to Senegambian influence.

The figures concerning slave exports from Senegal may appear low (annual averages were often below 1,000 in the earliest part of the relevant period), but it must be borne in mind that in the formative period, slave populations of the relevant plantation colonies were still quite small. In Haiti, it did not surpass 5,000 until about 1700. In Louisiana, it never did at all until after the Spanish takeover, and in 1735, there were still only 1,450 slaves on Mauritius. This was at the end of the period studied by Baker & Corne (1982) and after 15 years of French colonization.

## 8. Conclusion

While it is still too early to make any firm claim regarding the possibility of Afrogenesis in the case of FCs, the possibility has in my view been overlooked by too many creolists. Creole languages of French lexicon spoken in the Americas and in the Indian Ocean present numerous interesting similarities, some of which might be explained through a common progenitor. I believe that slaves coming from Senegal had been exposed to quite a lot of French before arriving in the colonies. If motivated, they would have been no less able to learn some of it than a plantation slave would have been. Given the appropriate circumstances, once in the Caribbean or in the Indian Ocean, they might well have exerted a considerable linguistic influence on their fellow slaves.

### Acknowledgments

I am grateful to Gunnel Källgren, Chris Corne, Philip Baker and John McWhorter for their views on an earlier draft of this paper. The usual disclaimers apply.

### Notes

1. Some of those who once advocated a monogenetic scenario (e.g. Goodman 1964) have admitted that what was brought over the Atlantic might have been a French rather than a Portuguese pidgin. No one, however, tried to correlate their proposal with historical and demographical facts.

2. I suspect that this is true for French Guiana too, but I can unfortunately not support such a statement with any evidence.

3. This label is used here as a cover term for the American FCs and the so-called *Isle de France* creoles. Reunionese, Tayo, etc. are excluded from the discussion.

4. "The Negroes ignore our language, whereas they know that of the Dahomeans."

5. Still, this list is obviously incomplete. Among others it does not include the Portuguese fort (*São João d'Ajuda*) in Whydah, which was held by the Portuguese until 1961.

6. "A fairly intelligble French."

7. "The population of Rufisque speak a fairly intelligible kind of French and that they pronounce in our language offenses and swearwords."

8. "A distorted French."

9. "French very well."

10. The British, the Dutch and the Portuguese encountered similar problems in their African trading posts (e.g. Postma 1990: 13; Do Couto 1993: 387–8).

11. Yolof refers to a speaker of the Wolof language.

12. According to Curtin (1990: 122), indigenous rulers now and then sold political prisoners to European slave traders. Besides yielding an economical profit, this was a convenient way of getting rid of internal opposition.

13. I have extrapolated his data by calculating the number of slaves, wherever missing, from the tonnage of the ships.

14. While Cultru wrote about St. Louis, Faidherbe referred to Gorée; perhaps practices differed?

15. The role of the indentured servants, likely to be the main transmitters of the superstrate in the early days, was very limited in the formation of the later creoles, which are the only ones for which a possible Franco-Senegalese input is assumed to have had any decisive impact.

16. An excellent example being [mɔːgə] 'thin' in Pitcairnese, the presence of which can be attributed to one single immigrant from St. Kitts (Baker & Corne 1982: 257).

17. I am very grateful to John McWhorter for bringing the works of Dutton and Keesing to my attention.

## References

Adanson, Michel. 1795. *Resa till Senegal*. Uppsala: J. F. Edmans Kungliga Academiska Boktryckeri.

Alleyne, Mervyn. 1971. "Acculturation and the Cultural Matrix of Creolization." In Dell Hymes (ed.), *Pidginization and Creolization of Languages*. Cambridge: Cambridge University Press, 169–186.

Allsopp, Richard. 1976. "The case for Afrogenesis." In George Cave (compiler), *Conference Preprints: First Annual Meeting of the Society for Caribbean Linguistics*. Turkeyen: University of Guyana.

Ancelle, J. 1887. *Les Explorations au Sénégal et dans les Contrées Voisines Depuis l'Antiquité Jusqu'à Nos Jours*. Paris: Maisonneuve et Leclerc.

Baker, Philip. 1990. "Off Target?" *Journal of Pidgin and Creole Languages* 5(1):107–119.

Baker, Philip (ed.). 1995. *From Contact to Creole and Beyond*. London: University of Westminster Press.

Baker, Philip & Chris Corne. 1982. *Isle de France Creoles: Affinities and Origins*. Ann Arbor: Karoma Publishers.

Barbot, John. 1732. "A description of the coasts of North and South Guinea." In Messrs. Churchill (eds.), *A Collection of Voyages*. London: Thomas Osborne.

Barry, Boucabar. 1992. "Senegambia from the sixteenth to the eighteenth century: evolution of the Wolof, Sereer and 'Tukuloor'." In Ogot (ed.), 262–299.

Bickerton, Derek. 1977. "Pidginization and creolization: Language acquisition and language universals." In Albert Valdman (ed.), *Pidgin and Creole Linguistics*. Bloomington and London: Indiana University Press.

Biondi, Jean-Pierre. 1987. *Saint-Louis-du-Sénégal: Mémoires d'un Métissage*. Paris: Denoël.

Camara, Camille. 1968. *Saint-Louis-du-Sénégal: Évolution d'une Ville en Milieu Africain*. Dakar: Université de Dakar/Institut Fondamental d'Afrique Noire.

Carter, Hazel. 1987. "Suprasegmentals in Guyanese: Some African Comparisons." In Gilbert (ed.), 213–263.

Chauleau, Liliane. 1966. *La Société à la Martinique au* xv *ᵉ siècle (1635–1713)*. Caen.

Colvin, Lucie Gallistel. 1981. *Historical Dictionary of Senegal*. Metuchen & London: The Scarecrow Press.

Cornevin, Robert. 1982. *Haïti*. Paris: Presses Universitaires de France.

Courbe, Michel Jajolet de la. 1913. *Premier Voyage du Sieur de la Courbe Fait à la Coste d'Afrique en 1685*. Paris: Édouard Champion/Émile Larose.

Couto, Hildo Honório do. 1993. "The Genesis of Portuguese Creole in Africa." In Francis Byrne & John Holm (eds.), *Atlantic Meets Pacific: A Global View of Pidginization and Creolization*. Amsterdam & Philadelphia: John Benjamins, 381–389.

Crouse, Nellis. 1940. *French Pioneers in the West Indies 1625–1664*. New York: Columbia University Press.

Cultru, Prosper. 1910. *Histoire du Sénégal du* xve *Siècle à 1870*. Paris: Émile Larose.

Cultru, Prosper. 1913. "Introduction." In Jajolet de la Courbe.

Curtin, Philip. 1969. *The Atlantic Slave Trade: A Census*. Madison: University of Wisconsin Press.

Curtin, Philip. 1975. *Economic Change in Precolonial Africa. Senegambia in the Era of the Slave Trade*. Madison: University of Wisconsin Press.

Curtin, Philip. 1990. *The Rise and Fall of the Plantation Complex. Essays in Atlantic History*. Cambridge: Cambridge University Press.

Delafosse, Maurice. 1931. "Afrique Occidentale française." In Gabriel Hanotaux & Alfred Martineau (eds.): *Histoire des Colonies Fançaises et de l'expansion de la France dans le monde, tomé* v. Paris: Société de l'Histoire/Librairie Plon, 1–356.

Delcourt, André. 1952. *La France et les établissements Français au Sénégal entre 1713 et 1763*. Dakar: Institut Français d'Afrique Noire.

Demanet. 1767. *Nouvelle Histoire de l'Afrique Françoise, Tomé 1*. Paris: Libraire Duchesne/Libraire Lacombe.

Donnan, Elizabeth (ed.). 1931. *Documents illustrative of the History of the Slave Trade to America. Vol. 2: The Eighteenth Century*. Washington, D.C.: Carnegie Institution.

Dubois, S. 1897. *The Voyages Made by Sieur D.B. to the Islands of Madagascar & Bourbon or Mascarenne in the Years 1669–70–71 & 72. Edited and translated by P. Oliver*. London. David Nutt.

Dutton, Tom. 1985. *Police Motu: Iena Sivarai*. Port Moresby: University of Papua New Guinea Press.

Exquemelin, Alexandre-Olivier. 1684 [1986]: *Boucaniers et Flibustiers des Antilles. Les Colons-Marins du* xv *ᵉ Siècle*. [Fort-de-France: Éditions Desormeaux].

Faidherbe, Louis Léon César. 1889. *Le Sénégal. La France dans l'Afrique Occidentale*. Paris: Hachette.

Faine, Jules. 1939. *Le Créole dans l'Univers. Études Comparatives des Parlers Français-Créoles 1: Le Mauricien.* Port-au-Prince: Imprimerie de l'État.

Flutre, Louis-Fernand. 1958. "De quelques termes usités aux XVII$^e$ et XVIII$^e$ siècles sur les côtes de l'Afrique Occidentale et qui ont passé dans les récits des voyageurs français du temps." *Etymologica: Festschrift Walther von Wartburg.* Tübingen: Niemeyer Verlag, 209–238.

Flutre, Louis-Fernand. 1961. "De quelques termes de la langue commerciale utilisée sur les Côtes de l'Afrique Occidentale aux XVII$^e$ et XVIII$^e$ siècles, d'après les récits des voyageurs du temps." *Revue de Lnguistique Romane 25,* 274–289.

Fyfe, Christopher. 1962. *A History of Sierra Leone.* London: Oxford University Press.

Gilbert, Glenn, ed. 1987. *Pidgin and Creole Languages: Essays in Memory of John E. Reinecke.* Honolulu: University of Hawaii Press.

Goodman, Morris. 1964. *A Comparative study of Creole French Dalects.* The Hague: Mouton.

Goodman, Morris. 1987. "The Portuguese Element in American Creoles." In Gilbert (ed.), 361–405.

Goodman, Morris. 1992. "Review of Holm (1989)." *Journal of Pidgin and Creole Languages 7 (2):* 352–361.

Granda, German de. 1976. "A socio-historical approach to the problem of Portugues Creole in West Africa." International Journal of the Sociology of Language 7:11–22.

Hall, Gwendolyn Midlo. 1992. *Africans in Colonial Louisiana. The Development of Afro-Creole Culture in the 18th Century.* Baton Rouge & London: Louisiana State University Press.

Hancock, Ian. 1969. "A Provisional Comparison of the English-based Atlantic Creoles." *African Language Review,* 7–72.

Hancock, Ian. 1986. "The Domestic Hypothesis, Diffusion and Complementiality. An Account of Atlantic Anglophone Creole Origins." In Pieter Muysken & Norval Smith (eds.): *Substrata Versus Universals in Creole Genesis.* Amsterdam & Philadelphia: John Benjamins, 71–102.

Hancock, Ian. 1987. "A Preliminary Classification of the Anglophone Atlantic Creoles, with Syntactic Data from Thirty-Three Representative Dialects." In Gilbert (ed.), 264–333.

Hanotaux, Gabriel, and Alfred Martineau (eds.). 1929–1931. *Histoire des Colonies Françaises et de l'Expansion de la France dans le Monde.* Paris: Société de l'Histoire/Librarire Plon.

Harris, J. E. 1992. "The African Diaspora in the Old and New Worlds." In Ogot (ed.), 113–136.

Holm, John A. 1989. *Pidgins and Creoles, vol. 2: Reference Survey.* Cambridge: Cambridge University Press.

Hornby, Ove. 1980. *Kolonierne i Vestindien.* Copenhagen.

Hornot, A. 1776. *Anecdotes Américaines, ou Histoire Abrégée des Principaux Evénements Arrivés dans le Nouveau Monde depuis sa Découverte jusqu'à l'Epoque Présente*. Paris: Librairie Vincent.

Hull, Alexander. 1979a. "On the Origin and Chronology of the French-based Creoles." In Ian Hancock, Edgar Polome, Morris Goodman & Bernd Heine (eds.): *Readings in Creole Studies*. Ghent: Story-Scientia, 201–215.

Hull, Alexander. 1979b. "Amérique du nord: vue d'ensemble. Affinités entre les variétés du français." In Albert Valdman & Robert Chaudenson (eds.): *Le Fançais hors de France*. Paris: Édouard Champion, 165–180.

Inikori, Joseph E., and Stanley L. Engerman (eds.). 1992. *The Atlantic Slave Trade. Effects on Economics, Societies and Peoples in Africa, the Americas, and Europe*. Durham and London: Duke University Press.

Jennings, William. 1995a. "Saint-Christophe: Site of the first French Creole." In Baker (ed.), 63–80.

Jennings, William. 1995b. *The First Generations of Voyages and Travels Arranged in Systematic Order*, vol. 7. Edinburgh: George Ramsay and Company.

Jones, Adam. 1985. *Brandenburg Sources for West African History 1680–1700*. Wiesbaden: Franz Steiner Verlag.

Keesing, Roger. 1988. *Melanesian Pidgin and the Oceanic Substrate*. Stanford: Stanford University Press.

Kerr, Robert. 1812. *General History and Collection of Voyages and Travels Arranged in Systematic Order*, vol. 7. Edinburgh: George Ramsay and Company.

Kiple, Kenneth F., and Brian T. Higgins. 1992. "Mortality caused by dehydration during the middle passage." In Inikori and Engerman (eds.), 321–337.

Klein, Herbert. 1986. *African Slavery in Latin America and the Caribbean*. New York: Oxford University Press.

Knight, Marie-Hélène. 1977. "Gorée au XVIIIᵉ siècle: L'appropriation du sol." *Revue Française d'Histoire d'Outre-Mer 64 (324)*: 33–54.

Knight-Baylac, Marie-Hélène. 1970. "La vie à Gorée de 1677 à 1789." *Revue Française d'Histoire d'Outre-Mer 57 (209)*: 377–420.

Labarthe, P. 1803. *Voyage à la Côte de Guinée...* Paris: Chez l'auteur/Librairie Debray/Bossage, Masson et Besson.

Labat, Jean-Baptiste. 1728. *Nouvelle Relation de l'Afrique Occidentale...* Paris: Guillaume Cavelier.

Lacroix, Jean-Bernard. 1986. *Les Français au Sénégal au Temps de la Compagnie des Indes de 1719 à 1758*. Vincennes: Service Historique de la Marine.

Lajaille, G. 1802. "Reise nach Senegal." In M. C. Sprengel (ed.): *Bibliothek der Neuesten und Wichtigsten Reisebeschreibungen... vol. 7* Weimar: Verlage des Landes-Industrie-Comptoirs.

Larsen, Kay. 1928. *Dansk Vestindien 1666–1917*. Copenhagen: C. A. Reitzels Forlag.

LePage, Robert B. (ed.). 1961. *Creole Language Studies 2: Proceedings of the Conference on Creole Language Studies held at the University College of the West Indies, March 28–April 4, 1959* London: Macmillan.

Levtzion, Nehemia. 1975. "Africans and European in the trade of Senegambia." In Richard Gray (ed.), *The Cambridge History of Africa, vol. 4: From c. 1600 to c. 1700.* Cambridge: Cambridge University Press, 216–222.

Ly, Abdoulaye. 1955. *L'Évolution du Commerce Français d'Afrique Noire dans le Dernier Quart du* XV *$^e$ Siècle. La Compagnie du Sénégal 1673 à 1696.* Bordeaux: Thèse pour le Doctorat ès Lettres, Université de Bordeaux.

Machat, J. 1906. *Documents sur les Etablissements Français de l'Afrique Occidentale au* XV *$^e$ Siècle.* Paris: Éditions Augustin Challamel.

Marees, Pieter de. 1605. *Description et Récit Historiale du Riche Royaume d'Or de Guinea.* Amsterdam.

McWhorter, John. 1995. "Sisters under the skin: A case for genetic relationship between the Atlantic English-based creoles." *Journal of Pidgin and Creole Languages* 10:289–333.

McWhorter, John. 1997. "It happened at Cormantin: Locating the origin of the Atlantic English-based Creoles." *Journal of Pidgin and Creole Languages* 12:59–102.

McWhorter, John. Forthcoming. *Towards a New Model of Creole Genesis.* New York: Peter Lang.

Mettas, Jean. 1975. "La traité des Noirs française." *Revue Française d'Histoire d'Outre-Mer 62,* 19–46.

Mettas, Jean. 1978, 1984. *Répertoire des Expéditions Négrières Françaises au* XV *$^e$ Siècle.* Vol. 1–2. Paris: Société Française d'Histoire d'Outre-Mer.

Mufwene, Salikoko. 1996. "The founder principle in creole genesis." *Diachronica* XII:83–134.

Ogot, B. A. (ed.). 1992. *General History of Africa 5: Africa from the Sixteenth to the Eighteenth Century.* Paris: Unesco.

Parkvall, Mikael. 1994. "On the input components of French Creole genesis." Paper presented at the 10th Biennal Conference of the Society for Pidgin and Creole Linguistics and the Society for Caribbean Linguistics, University of Guyana, Georgetown, August 1994.

Parkvall, Mikael. 1995a. "A Dual Approach to French Creole Genesis." MS, Stockholm: Institutionen för Lingvistik.

Parkvall, Mikael. 1995b. "Is Afro-Genesis possible in the case of French Creoles?" Paper presented at the Second Westminster Creolistics Workshop, April 1995.

Parkvall, Mikael. 1995c. "On the role of St. Kitts in a new scenario of French Creole genesis." In Baker (ed.), 41–62.

Parkvall, Mikael. In press. "Feature distribution and genetic relationships among the Atlantic creoles." In Magnus Huber and Mikael Parkvall (eds.), *Spreading the Word: Papers on the Issue of Diffusion of Atlantic Creoles.* London: University of Westminster Press.

Postma, Johannes Menne. 1990. *The Dutch in the Atlantic Slave Trade 1600–1815.* Cambridge: Cambridge University Press.

Pottier, Bernard. 1966. "La formation des parlers créoles." 5_ Coloquio internacional de estudios lusobrasileiros. Coimbra: Officina da Gràfica.

Rice, Frank A. (ed.). *Study of the role of second languages in Asia, Africa, and Latin America.* Washington: Center for Applied Linguistics.

Saugnier. 1792. *Voyages to the Coast of Africa by Mess. Saugnier and Brisson...* London: G. G. J. and J. Robinson.

Savigny, J. B. Henry & Alexandre Corréard. 1818 [1968]: *Narrative of a Voyage to Senegal...* 1968 edition: London: Dawsons of Pall Mall.

Smith, Norval. 1987. *The Genesis of the Creole Languages of Surinam.* Dissertation, Universiteit van Amsterdam.

Sprengel, M. C. & L. F. Ehrmann (eds.). 1803. *Bibliothek der Neuesten und Wichtichsten Reisebeschriebungen... 9.* Weimar: Verlage des Landes-Industrie Comptoirs.

Stein, Robert Louis. 1979. *The French Slave Trade in the Eighteenth Century. An Old Regime Business.* Madison: The University of Wisconsin Press.

Stein, Robert Louis. 1988. *The French Sugar Business in the 18th Century.* Baton Rouge: Louisiana State University Press.

Stewart, William A. 1962. "Creole languages in the Caribbean." In Rice (ed.), 34–53.

Stewart, William A. 1971. "Sociolinguistic factors in the history of American Negro Dialect." In W. Wolfram & N. Clarke (eds.), *Black-White Speech Relationships.* Washington: Center for Applied Linguistics, 74–89.

Tardieu, M. Amedée. 1847. *Sénégambie et Guinée.* Paris: Firmin Didiot et frères.

Taylor, Douglas. 1961. "New languages for old in the West Indies." *Comparative Studies in Society and History* 3:277–288.

Taylor, Douglas. 1963. " The origin of West Indian creole languages: Evidence from grammatical categories. American Anthropologist 65:800–814.

Thompson, Robert Wallace. 1961. "A note on some possible affinities between the creole dialects of the Old World and those of the New." In LePage (ed.), 107–113.

Thornton, John. 1992. *Africa and Africans in the Making of the Atlantic World 1400–1680.* Cambridge, New York & Victoria: Cambridge University Press.

Usner, Daniel. 1992. *Indians, Settlers and Slaves in a Frontier Exchange Economy. The Lower Mississippi Valley before 1783.* Chapel Hill: University of North Carolina Press.

Voorhoeve, Jan. 1972. "Historical and linguistic evidence in favor of the relexification theory in the formation of creoles." *Language in Society* 2:133–145.

Wadström, Carl Bernard. 1791. *Anmärkningar Rörande Slaf-Handeln på Kusten af Guinea.* Norrköping: A. F. Raam.

Whinnom, Keith. 1956. *Spanish Contact Vernaculars in the Phillipine Islands.* Hong Kong: Hong Kong University Press.

Whinnom, Keith. 1965. "The origin of the European-based creoles and pidgins." *Orbis* 14:509–527.

# Chinese-Cuban Pidgin Spanish
## Implications for the Afro-Creole Debate

John M. Lipski
*University of New Mexico*

## 1.  Contact with Afro-European creoles in 19th century Cuba

By the first few decades of the 19th century, anti-slavery movements in Europe were strong, and slaving ships en route to the Americas were routinely intercepted and confiscated. The African slave trade could not provide sufficient workers to satisfy Cuban demands, and laborers from all over the Caribbean were sought. The transshipment of slaves and free laborers from one island to another rose in importance, creating a Caribbean-wide shell game which was difficult to interdict in its entirety. This increased the proportion of plantation workers who had already acquired other Caribbean creoles. The linguistic consequences of these late-arriving workers is of great importance for reconstructing Afro-Caribbean Spanish. Workers were brought in large numbers from individual speech communities, unlike in earlier times, where slaves speaking mutually unintelligible languages found intercommunication difficult. Since these laborers worked side-by-side with African-born slaves, as well as with workers born in Cuba and Puerto Rico, there existed ample opportunities for both of the latter groups to acquire fragments of the imported languages, all of which were Afro-European creoles. These creole languages share many commonalities, particularly in syntax, as well as recurring cognate elements. The creole languages which aided in the formation of Afro-Caribbean Spanish varied according to the time and place. Cuba, the largest sugar plantation colony, naturally received the widest variety of creole languages beginning in the late 18th century; these include Haitian Creole, Jamaican Creole, Papiamento, West African Pidgin English, and Negerhollands (Lipski 1993, 1994, forthcoming c).

## 2.    The Chinese labor force in 19th century Cuba

### 2.1

In addition to the variety of Afro-American linguistic and cultural groups which added to the demographic mix in 19th century Cuba, and which interacted with bozal Spanish as spoken non-natively by African-born slaves and in some circumstances their immediate descendents, another group of imported laborers exercised a significant linguistic influence on late colonial Cuban Spanish. In the second half of the 19th century, Cuba received at least 150,000 Chinese laborers, who worked in the sugar plantations and mills as virtual slaves, side by side with Africans and workers from other Caribbean islands. The linguistic conditions surrounding the lives of Chinese laborers in Cuba closely parallels that of African *bozales*, and according to available evidence, Chinese workers' acquisition of Spanish followed similar paths. Moreover, the linguistic model for Chinese workers was frequently the speech of *bozales* who had already learned some Spanish, as well as the Spanish spoken as a second language by workers from (Afro-American creole speaking) Caribbean territories. Finally, since most of the Chinese were recruited through the Portuguese colony of Macao, where a Portuguese-based pidgin and creole was spoken among the native Chinese population, there exists the possibility that some of the Chinese workers added their knowledge of a Portuguese creole to the already rich mix of creole and creoloid elements present in 19th century Cuba.

### 2.2

Spanish authorities tried a number of sources to obtain workers, including the virtual comandeering of Yucatan natives (Menéndez 1928, 1932). This project did not yield the desired results, and before long the Spanish government turned to a labor source already known in Spanish America through commerce in the Spanish colony of the Philippines: the nearly inexhaustable labor force of China. In the following decades, several hundred thousand laborers would be taken to plantations in Cuba and coastal Peru, where most of them would remain indefinitely. In Cuba, the importation of Chinese laborers began in 1844, spurred by a black slave revolt in Matanzas. The Chinese were recruited through a process known ignominiously as *el enganche* 'the snatch,' whereby Portuguese entrepreneurs in Macao would obtain laborers from neighboring Chinese areas between Macao and Canton, using methods which ranged from flattery and false promises to kidnapping.[1]

2.3

By 1853, Chinese immigration to Cuba was substantial, and the abuse of Chinese subjects increased to scandalous proportions, attracting much international attention, including human rights commissions in the United States (e.g. Cuba Commission 1876). The Chinese government, still embryonic and decentralized, tried to intervene to improve the lot of the *braceros* or laborers, but were only barely effective. Both Portuguese traders in Macao and British traders in Hong Kong participated in the Chinese labor trade to Spanish America, although most of the workers contracted by the British went to the British West Indies.

Once in the New World, the Chinese were not always submissive, especially since unlike African slaves, many Chinese had actually been recruited with promises of high wages and favorable working conditions. Having left their homeland voluntarily, these Chinese were enraged to find themselves working as slaves, deprived of wages and subject to forced confinement and physical abuse. The Chinese quickly developed the reputation for being rebellious and sullen, at the same time as more compliant Chinese were prized for their industriousness and superior intelligence. Revolts of Chinese workers were not uncommon, and many planters began to have second thoughts about continuing the Chinese labor trade. The first revolt occurred in 1847, just a few years after Chinese began arriving in Cuba.

2.4

From the beginning, relations between Chinese and Africans in Cuba were not cordial. Each group regarded the other with hostility and considered itself superior. Africans saw that some Chinese could purchase out their indentured contracts or otherwise 'buy their freedom,' and were technically subject to the same abject slavery as were Africans. Chinese and Africans traded mutual accusations of ignorance and superstition, of unhealthy food practices and living habits, and of savage behavior. Some plantation owners segregated Chinese and African workers in separate *barracones* or slave barracks to prevent conflict and violence, but even in these instances the two groups worked together in the fields, and in many cases also shared living quarters. Most Chinese brought to Cuba were men, and some married African women, thereby initiating the inevitable rapprochement of the two races. Common misery did the rest, and by the time of the Cuban independence wars of the late 1800s, it was a common sight for blacks and Chinese to fight together with Cubans of European origin as *mambises* or rebel fighters. At the same time, after importation of Chinese laborers ceased in 1873, there was a gradual movement away from the sugar plantations. In the first American census taken in Cuba, in 1899, out of a total population of 1,572,797 inhabitants, 14,863 were listed as Chinese, of which there were 49 women and 14,814 men. These figures only refer to Chinese-born subjects, and do not reflect the by then considerable Cuban-born population of Chinese origin. The American military government prohibited further immigration from China, and although subsequent Cuban governments partially lifted the prohibition, relatively few Chinese moved to Cuba in the 20th century.

2.5

Chinese laborers were also taken to many other Caribbean areas during the 19th and early 20th centuries, especially to the English colonies (Guyana, Jamaica, Trinidad, etc.). However, their situation vis-à-vis the African slave labor force was different from what occurred in Cuba (and Peru), and even when demographic proportions between Africans and Chinese were similar to those representing Cuba (Chang 1956), the chances for linguistic interaction were considerably less. Whereas in Cuba and Peru, Chinese laborers were recruited to do the same tasks as African plantation laborers, worked as virtual slaves, and shared all aspects of the oppressive plantation system, in the Anglophone Caribbean Chinese were often brought in as strike-breakers, and were viewed by the white owners as a foil to growing African resistance. Chinese were both physically and psychologically separated from Africans, and there existed neither motive nor opportunity for Chinese workers to absorb detailed aspects of the Africans' approximations to English. As a consequence, Chinese pidgin English in the Anglophone Caribbean appears to bear fewer similarities with the Afro-American creoles, and to more closely approximate the speech of the white colonial population, than in the case of the Chinese in Cuba (cf. Clementi 1915; Crawford 1989; Horton 1941; Jenkins 1981; Kirkpatrick 1939; Look Lai 1993; Sanjek 1990).

## 3.    Linguistic features of Chinese pidgin Spanish

3.1

In comparison with Africans in Cuba, the number of Chinese was small indeed, although once the Chinese moved to urban environments, their pidginized Spanish became nearly as familiar to middle-class Cubans as the speech of African bozales. So familiar was the *habla de chino* 'Chinese talk' to the average

Cuban, that a literary stereotype quickly developed, almost always portraying the Chinese in a somewhat comical but never totally unfavorable light. Matters can be improved somewhat by also considering the small corpus of Peruvian examples of Chinese pidgin Spanish.[2]

## 3.2

The most common single instance of 'Chinese' Spanish is the massive conversion of /r/ to [l] in all positions. This same change was frequently attributed to Africans during several centuries of Afro-Hispanic linguistic contacts in Spain and Latin America (Lipski forthcoming a, forthcoming b). Throughout Latin America, the stereotype of the *habla del chino* is the change of /r/ > [l], and the occasional change of /d/ > [l] (Pichardo (1953: liv). Virtually all texts in the Cuban-Chinese and Peruvian-Chinese corpus make use of this shift; in some cases, this is the only discrepancy with respect to standard Spanish. Although many writers and actors exaggerate the shift /r/ > [l], it is a real part of the interlanguage Spanish produced by speakers of Chinese languages. Nearly all of the Chinese taken to Cuba were speakers of Cantonese, a language which contains only /l/ to represent liquid consonants (Kao 1971). The shift /d/ > [l], as in *miedo* > *mielo* 'fear,' *jodido* > *jolí* 'screwed up,' *emperador* > *empelaló* 'emperor,' *nadie* > *nalie* 'nobody,' etc. appears to have passed through an intermediate stage /d/ > [r], resulting from a short occlusive/flap articulation of intervocalic /d/, which is frequent in many interlanguage varieties of Spanish, and is well known in the United States as a typical mispronunciation frequent among Anglophone learners of Spanish.[3]

## 3.3

Cantonese phonotactics are more complex than some other Chinese languages, particularly as regards the appearance of coda consonants; since Cantonese words are basically monosyllabic, this is equivalent to word-final consonants. However, the consonants which appear in the coda do not fully coincide with Spanish patterns. Cantonese permits /p/, /t/ and /k/ in the coda, often realized as unreleased stops, together with the nasals /m/, /n/ and /ŋ/. Neither /s/ nor /l/ is found in the coda, which leads to the prediction that Cantonese speakers would further weaken the already precarious syllable-final /s/ of Cuban Spanish, and would also weaken syllable-final /l/, and/or add a paragogic vowel. In Cuban Spanish, word-final /l/ usually resists efacement, while preconsonantal /l/ may succomb to loss combined with compensatory lengthening of the following consonant (*algo* > *aggo* 'something'), particularly in western Cuban dialects. The Cuban-Chinese corpus does contain some examples of loss of syllable-final consonants, which combine pan-Cuban traits (e.g. loss of /s/) with pronunciations not commonly found in Cuba (loss of word-final /r/).

3.4

In grammatical terms, there are almost no similarities between Cantonese and any first- or second-language variety of Spanish. Searching for direct grammatical interference from Cantonese is therefore a risky enterprise. There are, however, general tendencies of Cantonese which correspond with most African languages found in Cuba and Peru, and which result in similar configurations in the resulting Spanish pidgin (Norman 1988; Ramsey 1987). For example, Cantonese has no verbal inflexion, using only invariable monomorphemic verbs. There is no noun-adjective agreement, nor are there case-marked pronominal forms. Several Cuban-Chinese examples of undifferentiated pronouns reflect this tendency (also found among several African language families).

3.5

Like Spanish, Cantonese permits null subjects. The manner in which null subjects are licensed is quite different however, given that Chinese languages have no subject-verb agreement, and arguably have no Infl node whatsoever. Subject identification is effected through discourse-level constraints, intimately linked to the possibility for null and non-gap topics, and syntactic binding of null subjects by discourse antecedents (cf. Gilligan 1987; Hermon and Yoon 1989; Huang 1984; Jaeggli and Safir 1989). The high degree of null subjects in Cantonese (which are often preferred over overt pronominal subjects in normal discourse contexts) is often carried over to Chinese pidgin Spanish, a feature which runs against the normal stable/expanded pidgin and creole tendency to employ overt subject pronouns to compensate for loss of verbal inflection.[4] Some examples of null subjects in Cuban pidgin Spanish are:

> ¡Qué late, late, late; si pue, coje y si no, leja! 'What a hassle! If you can catch [them], catch [them], if not, let [them] go' (Feijóo 1981: 145);
> Vete, vete, no puele molí aquí 'Go away, [you] can't die here' (Feijóo 1981: 153).
> Tú, Malena, jabla mucho; no tlabaja, no jase na; to lo día sentá la sillón 'You, Magdalena, talk too much; [you] don't do anything; [you] don't work, [you] sit all day in an easy chair' (Francisco de Paula Gelabert; in Bueno 1984: 459–463);
> yo pue cojé la cocina, tú come y halla sabloso, ¿poqué lice esa cosa ahola?

'I can take care of the kitchen. You eat and find [the food] tasty; why do [you] say those things now?' (Francisco de Paula Gelabert; en Bueno 1984: 459–463)
No quelé tlabajá ... No sabel, capitán ... Yo no sabel ... Chino buenas costumbres. Sel inolante, todo inolante, jué. No sabel nala ... '[I] don't know captain, I don't know. Chinese man [has] good manners. [I] am innocent, judge. [I] don't know anything.' (Bueno 1959: 54–73)

Subject pronouns were used in Chinese pidgin Spanish when contrastive focus or emphasis was needed:

Cuando tu quele pasiau yo compla manta vapó, yo compla uno palasó ... Yo tiene plata en lo Banco, tú pa mi casa mejó. ... 'When you want [to take] a trip I will buy a steamer blanket, I'll buy a parasol ... I have money in the bank ... you'd be better off to marry me' (Santa Cruz 1982: 294)

Tú tlabaja mucho. Tú tumba mucha caña y ganá mucho dinelo ... 'You work hard, you cut a lot of sugar cane and you earn a lot of money' (Feijóo 1981: 153–4)

Aló ta balato ahola; yo ba complá una aloba ... 'Rice is cheap now; I'm going to buy an *arroba* [unit of measure]' (Francisco de Paula Gelabert; in Bueno 1984: 459–463)

Yo no so pícalo, yo so chino honlá ... 'I'm not a scoundrel; I'm an honest Chinese man.' (Francisco de Paula Gelabert; in Bueno 1984: 459–463)

## 4. Possible influence of Macao creole Portuguese

### 4.1

In addition to the influence of Cantonese structures on the pidgin Spanish of Chinese workers in Cuba, there is another factor which makes the Chinese-African contacts in Cuba and the convergence of bozal and Chinese pidgin Spanish of special interest to creole studies. During the Chinese labor trade to Cuba, the major port of exportation from the China coast was the Portuguese colony of Macao. It is not known precisely how many Chinese workers were actually from the Portuguese-held territory, but given the fact that recruitment efforts were normally most successful in rural parts of Canton province, it is probable that few natives of Macao were included among the *culíes* sent to Cuba. At the same time, recruited workers often had to spend several months in Macao, awaiting the ships which would take them to Spanish America.

### 4.2

In Macao, the native Chinese population speaks Cantonese, so that Chinese workers recruited from nearby Canton would have no difficulty in communicating with their compatriots living in the Portuguese colony. The labor trade itself was predominantly in the hands of Portuguese entrepreneurs, as were Macao businesses and the maritime traffic to the Americas. To accomodate the vast linguistic differences between Portuguese and Cantonese, a Portuguese-based pidgin (sometimes learned as a creole in Macao) facilitated communication across ethnic boundaries. The small expatriate Portuguese community in Macao spoke European Portuguese with one another, but those born in Macao or who had lived there for an extended period spoke the local pidgin, which was used when speaking to Macao Chinese. The latter in turn were usually proficient in the Portuguese pidgin, which according to contemporary sources, was sometimes used among Macao Chinese in addition to Cantonese; some examples of Macao creole Portuguese are given in the Appendix.

4.3

By all appearances, Macao Portuguese pidgin did not develop in Macao, but is substantially the result of an already existent Portuguese pidgin imported from the Portuguese colony at Malacca (this pidgin turned creole, known locally as Papia Kristang, is still spoken in rural Malacca; cf. Batalha 1958–9, 1960, 1974; Baxter 1988; Ferreira 1967, 1978, 1990; Gomes 1957; Montalto de Jesus 1926; Rego 1943). Macao creole Portuguese shares many of the patterns common to Afro-European creoles implicated in the formation of Afro-Lusitanian varieties in Cuba and elsewhere in the Caribbean, including Cape Verdean, Papiamento, Palenquero, and more distantly São Tomense and Annobonese. There are also noteworthy parallels with Haitian Creole, Jamaican Creole, Negerhollands and other creoles known or suspected to have been spoken in 19th century Cuba. The implications for the study of *bozal* Spanish are immediate and far-reaching, for if it can be demonstrated that Chinese workers in Cuba brought with them, at least some fragments of Macao creole Portuguese, and added it to the linguistic mix in which *bozal* Spanish was formed in the Caribbean, this provides yet another route of entry of certain creoloid constructions in attestations of Afro-Cuban Spanish. Such a demonstration — whose full realization is as yet beyond the grasp of currently available documentation — would not invalidate claims that *bozal* Spanish derives from an Afro-Lusitanian pidgin originally formed in West Africa and used throughout the Atlantic slave trade. It would, however, reduce the necessity of such a hypothesis.

4.4

In earlier times, pluralization of nouns was effected by simple reduplication: *chino-chino* 'Chinese (pl.),' *coisa-coisa* 'things,' etc. This was eventually replaced by an NP in which plural /s/ was marked only on the first determiner: *as casa* 'the houses,' *três pataca* 'three patacas' [monetary units], *dois mão* 'two hands,' etc. (Batalha 1958: 10). This same pattern is found in Angolan *musseque* Portuguese (Endruschat 1990; Lipski d), in vernacular Brazilian Portuguese (Guy 1981), and in some vestigial Afro-Hispanic enclaves. In the past, literary representations of *bozal* Spanish and Portuguese beginning in the late 17th century depicted this form of pluralization (Lipski forthcoming a, d; Sarró López 1988).

4.5

Macao creole Portuguese uses no definite articles, reflecting the absence of articles in Cantonese. The use of pronominal clitics is quite limited, and several processes combine to reduce the Portuguese pronominal paradigm to a set of invariant forms. For example, direct objects are normally expressed via use of periphrastic constructions using *a*: *ele disse a mim* 'he/she told me,' instead of the (European) Portuguese *êle disse-me*. Direct object pronouns are normally replaced by the corresponding subject pronouns: *nã bate ele* 'don't hit him/her,' instead of *não lhe batas*. This usage is similar to vernacular Brazilian Portuguese, but unlike the latter language, Macao creole Portuguese allows replacement of the first person singular object clitics by *eu*: *ele chamá eu vai alí* 'he/she calls me to go there' (Batalha 1958–9: 15). The Chinese pidgin corpus provides several examples of disjunctive object pronouns being used instead of clitics, as well as of elimination of definite articles.

> tú no da *nosotlo* life, tú no da *pa nosotlo* cásula ... 'You don't give us rifle(s); you don't give us cartridge(s)' (Jiménez Pastrana 1983: 92; Quesada 1892: 130–1)
>
> No señó Capitán, *pa mi* no sentí gente pasá ... 'No sir, Captain, I didn't hear anybody go by' (Jiménez Pastrana 1983: 114)
>
> Si tiene dinelo paga *pala mí* ... 'If [you] have money, pay me' (Chuffat Latour 1927: 63; Jiménez Pastrana 1983: 97)
>
> Comandante Lupelto, *pa mi* no mila ... 'Major Ruperto, I didn't see [anything]' (Feijóo 1981: 145)
>
> come caña hata sábalo y ven dipué, que yo lipachá comía *pa ti* ... 'Eat sugar cane until Saturday and then come, and I'll sell you food' (Feijóo 1981: 153–4)

Mila, Ginilá, coje tlella *pa ti*, dásela otlo gente, que yo no quiele dejá máuse
que tu no lo lá *pa mi* ... 'Look, General, take these stars for yourself, give
them to somebody else; I don't to give up the mauser that you won't let me
have' (Consuegra y Guzmán 1930: 163–4)

4.6

In Macao creole Portuguese, verbs are sometimes omitted, especially when
Portuguese would call for a copula. This reflects the syntactic strategies of
Cantonese: *ele filho tudo crescido já* 'all his/her children are grown up,' *sempre
roupa muito limpo* 'the clothes are always clean,' *eu priguiça subi escada* 'I am
afraid to climb the stairs,' *ela pena* 'she is ashamed,' *ovos caro* 'the eggs are
expensive,' *esta criada bom* 'this maid is good,' *eu fómi* 'I am hungry,' etc. The
Chinese pidgin Spanish corpus contains a few instances of similar constructions.

> Ciudadano cubano tó ... Yo digo, junto tó nosotlo ... 'Cuban citizens, all [of us]
> ... I say, all of us [are] together' (Jiménez Pastrana 1983: 92; Quesada 1892: 130–1)
> Celo ta bueno ... mucho caballelo con dinelo; mucho casa glande; tlabajo
> bueno pa chino ... 'Heaven is good ... [there are] lots of men with money, lots
> of big houses, good jobs for Chinese' (Francisco de Paula Gelabert; in Bueno
> 1984: 459–463)
> Chino olvilalo ... Chino buenas costumbres ... 'Chinese man forgot ...
> Chinese man [has] good manners' (Bueno 1959: 54–73)
> Yo mimito con lifle... 'I [shot the enemy] myself, with a rifle' (Consuegra y
> Guzmán 1930: 163–4)

## 5.   Macao's African connection

5.1

It is known that Malay/Malaccan natives formed the largest foreign-born
population during the formative period of Macao creole Portuguese (Batalha
1974: 27–30), and it appears likely that Malay settlers brought to Macao at least
the rudiments of the Portuguese-based creole formed in Malacca. Batalha
(1974: 21) believes that Macao creole Portuguese was 'uma linguagem já para
aquí trazida em pleno desenvolvimento' [a language taken there fully developed].
Macao was also home to settlers from Portuguese colonies in south Asia, where
Portuguese-based creoles also arose (Batalha 1974: 27). Finally, and most
significantly, there were also black Africans in Macao, brought there by Portuguese traders (Amaro 1980; Batalha 1974; Teixeira 1976).

5.2

Among the linguistic features linking Macao creole Portuguese to Afro-Lusitanian creoles as opposed to other Asian Portuguese creoles is the invariant copula *sã*. This item first made its appearance in the 16th century Afro-Portuguese works of writers such as Gil Vicente, and passed into *bozal* Spanish (usually in denasalized form) shortly thereafter. This copula became a permanent feature of the Portuguese-based creoles of the Gulf of Guinea (São Tomé and Annobón), but is not found in any other other Portuguese creole, in Asia, Africa, or the Americas, with the exception of Macao creole Portuguese.

5.3

Perhaps the most significant single feature of Macao creole Portuguese which draws it into the theoretical discussions on the formations of Afro-Hispanic creoles and the nature of Cuban *bozal* Spanish is the use of preverbal particles to signal tense, mood and aspect: *ta* (continuative), *lôgo* (future/irrealis), and *ja* (anterior/perfective). The first particle, *ta*, has been implicated in nearly all monogenetic theories of Afro-Iberian pidgins and creoles; this particle is found in Cape Verdean creole, in Papiamento, and in Colombian Palenquero. The same particle is also found in most Asian Portuguese-based creoles, including those of India and Sri Lanka, Malacca, and Macao. It is also found in Philippine Creole Spanish (Chabacano), being one of the structural features which draws that language into the monogenetic debate, and which calls into questions the relative contributions of Spanish and (pidgin) Portuguese in its genesis (Lipski 1987, 1992). Significantly, preverbal *ta* is also found in several key Afro-Cuban *bozal* texts, and in one *bozal* text from Puerto Rico. In the Chinese-Cuban corpus, there are several indications of *ta* used as a preverbal particle in a fashion similar to that found both in Macao creole Portuguese and in Caribbean *bozal* Spanish; there are also many instances of *estar* reduced to *ta* as an invariant copula:

Ya poble chino ta jolí ... 'Now the poor Chinese man is screwed' (Piedra Martel 1968: 91)
tó la gente ta qui jabla bonito na má 'All the people here just talk fancy, that's all' (Jiménez Pastrana 1983: 92; Quesada 1892: 130–1)
pa mi no sabe, ta trabajá, quema carbón 'I don't know, [I] was working, burning charcoal' (Jiménez Pastrana 1983: 110)
Glacia, señola. Aquí ta suciando 'Thank you, ma'am. It's dirty here' (Feijóo 1981: 149)
Celo ta bueno ... mucho caballelo con dinelo; mucho casa glande 'Heaven is

nice ... many men with money, lots of big houses ...' (Francisco de Paula Gelabert; en Bueno 1984: 459–463)

Aló ta balato ahola; yo ba complá una aloba ... 'Rice is cheap now; I'm going to buy an *arroba*' (Francisco de Paula Gelabert; en Bueno 1984: 459–463)

Luce Pelanza ta muy macliá 'It seems that Esperanza is very bad-mannered' (Francisco de Paula Gelabert; en Bueno 1984: 459–463)

¿Londi ta Ginilá Maceo 'Where is General Maceo?' (Consuegra y Guzmán 1930: 163–4)

Campo ta mijó '[In] the country it's better' (Loveira 1974: 165)

Nosotlo tá Oliente, nosotlo peleá Oliente ... 'We were in Oriente [eastern Cuba], we were fighting [in] Oriente' (Jiménez Pastrana 1983: 92; Quesada 1892: 130–1)

Yo tá peliá ¡tú tá la casa ...! 'I was fighting; you were at home!' (Jiménez Pastrana 1983: 128; Souza y Rodríguez 1939: 95)

Aguanta poquito, guajilo, que chinito tá quivocá 'Wait a minute, country fellow; the Chinese man has made a mistake' (Feijóo 1981: 148–9)

Mujé tá buena todavía [That] woman is still in good shape' (Feijóo 1981: 152)

## 5.4

In the case of *ta* used as copular verb, reduced from *esta(r)*, there is no reason to assume that Chinese in Cuba learned this construction from any other than native Spanish speakers, or from *bozal* and Cuban-born Africans who had at least correctly acquired this facet of the Spanish verbal system. Examples like *yo tá peliá* and *ta trabajá* cannot be readily explained through imperfect learning of native speaker models, and in fact these constructions are identical both to Macao creole Portuguese and to Afro-Iberian creoles, including some attestations of Cuban *bozal* Spanish. Assuming — as seems overwhelmingly probable — that these similarities are not due to chance, the question remains of how Chinese laborers in Cuba came to acquire the combination of $ta + V_{INF}$ as an invariant form of present or progressive verbs. There are at least three logically possible hypotheses: (1) Chinese workers had acquired Macao Portuguese creole prior to arriving in Cuba, and drew upon their knowledge of this language when attempting to speak Spanish; (2) Chinese laborers learned $ta + V_{INF}$ constructions directly from their Afro-Cuban workmates; (3) both Afro-Cuban and Chinese workers learned $ta + V_{INF}$ constructions from a common external source, such as the groups of Papiamento speakers found in Cuba at the time of the massive Chinese arrivals.

5.5

Although most Chinese workers carried to Cuba were not natives of Macao, and therefore had little lengthy exposure either to Portuguese or to Macao creole, the average period between recruitment in Canton province and arrival in Cuba was usually close to one year. Much of the time was spent in Macao or on shipboard, surrounded by Portuguese traders and sailors who routinely used Macao creole when speaking to Chinese. The conditions were therefore propitious for more experienced Chinese to teach some pidgin Portuguese to their newly arrived compatriots. Whatever Portuguese or creoloid elements the Chinese might have learned, these forms would have been reinforced by contact with Spanish, replete with easily recognizable cognate elements. The frequent reduction of *estar* to *ta* in vernacular Cuban Spanish, and the elimination of final /r/ in verbal infinitives by Afro-Cubans provided ready links to the Macao creole Portuguese verbal system. Moreover, *ta* + $V_{INF}$ verbal constructions were already well known in Cuba, being common among Afro-Cubans and recognized by white Cubans as pertaining to *bozal* language. Thus, unlike some other constructions from Macao creole Portuguese, verbal constructions based on *ta* would be readily interpreted and accepted by white and black Cubans alike.

5.6

There is also some indication that Chinese workers isolated in the more remote *barracones* of the Cuban sugar plantations and condemned to work as virtual slaves surrounded by African slaves and paid laborers picked up much of their Spanish from Afro-Cuban role models. The limited corpus of Chinese-Cuban materials is not extensive enough to scan for other traces of Afro-Cuban language, but a few curious instances of convergence point in the direction of a more profound *bozal* legacy in Chinese pidgin Spanish. One involves the use of *son* as invariable copula, found in a couple of Chinese Cuban texts:

> No, Malía *son* mi mujé, y yo la llamo pa que vea un choque de tlene de su male paliba ... 'No, María is my wife, and I [would] call her so that she could see one hell of a train wreck' (Feijóo 1981: 150–1)
> chino *so* pesona lesente ... Mentila, chino *son* pelsona lecente. 'Chinese man is decent ... [it's a] lie, Chinese man is a decent person' (Feijóo 1981: 152)
> ¿Londi ta Ginilá Maceo, que yo va pleguntá si *son* velá esi cosa? 'Where is General Maceo; I'm going to ask him if that is true' (Consuegra y Guzmán 1930: 163–4)

Svetlana, tú no sabe lo que *son* una ecuación ... 'Svetlana, you don't know what an equation is' (Sánchez-Boudy 1970: 24–5)

Use of invariable *son* was a staple characteristic of Afro-Cuban speech, not only of African-born *bozales* but apparently also of at least the first generation of Cuban-born blacks.

## 6.  Summary and conclusions

The Chinese pidgin Spanish data in themselves represent only a tiny fraction of the non-native Spanish language usage found among slaves and indentured laborers in 19th century Cuba. In addition to the curiosity value afforded by the disclosure of yet another marginalized linguistic community in the forced labor environment of the 19th century Caribbean, the Chinese data have potentially greater significance for the reconstruction of Afro-Caribbean Spanish. First, the Chinese workers brought to Cuba spoke a language whose structural features shared many commonalities with the Afro-European pidgins and creoles already present in the Cuban sugar plantations and slave quarters. These similarities would both facilitate the Chinese workers' learning semi-creolized varieties of Spanish, and reinforce creoloid patterns used among other plantation workers for whom Spanish was not a native language. Some of the Chinese laborers may also have known Macao creole Portuguese, a language which is not only genetically related to Afro-Lusitanian creoles and hence — according to monogenetic theories at least — to some varieties of Afro-Hispanic speech, but which also received a direct African component that bypassed the developmental patterns of Portuguese creoles in other parts of southeast Asia. The presence of Macao Chinese laborers, African-born *bozales*, and creole-speaking blacks from other Caribbean islands in mid-19th century Cuba brings the Euro-creole scenario full circle, creating intriguing possibilities for cross-fertilization and innovation.

The preceding remarks are not intended to diminish the major role played by Afro-Hispanic *bozal* language in 19th century Cuba, nor to undermine other theories as to the relative contributions of African languages, Portuguese pidgins and creoles, Caribbean creoles, and second language acquisition strategies, to Afro-Cuban speech (cf. Lipski forthcoming e, for a summary of the debate). One important lesson to be drawn from the Chinese story in Cuba is that the reconstruction of earlier Caribbean Spanish is a complex endeavor, not all of whose components have yet been uncovered, much less analyzed. These brief comments on Chinese Cuban pidgin Spanish are meant to stimulate interest in the individual and collective contributions of involuntary or unwilling immigrants — whose voices have only been heard, if at all — when their marginality has evolved into comic relief — to the development of Latin American Spanish

## Notes

1. For a composite of the history of Chinese in Cuba, cf. Chang (1956), Chuffat Latour (1927), Corbitt (1971), Deschamps and Pérez de la Riva (1974), Helly (1979), Jiménez Pastrana (1983), Martín 1939), Montalto de Jesus (1926: 399–412), Gomes (1957), Ordas Avecilla (1893), Pérez de la Riva (1966, 1978; Varela (1980). A comparable history of Chinese laborers in Peru is provided by Arona (1891), Bazán (1967), Díaz Canseco (1973), Fernández Montagne (1977), Rodríguez Pastor (1977, 1979, 1989), Sánchez (1952), Stewart (1976), Trazegnies Granda (1994), In Cuba, ethnic Chinese were often referred to as *chino Manila*, since for many Spanish subjects China was identified with the Philippine trade and the Manila Galleon, known as the *Nao de la China*, which brought Chinese merchandise to the port of Acapulco. However, most Chinese laborers taken to Cuba were from the Macao-Canton area, and spoke Cantonese.

2. Despite the fact that few pidgin-speaking Chinese are still to be found in Cuban communities, the stereotype remains, and is widely cultivated in popular culture. For example, the daily Radio Martí broadcasts aimed at Cuba by the U. S. Information Agency/Voice of America include a number of serial comedies produced in the Miami Cuban exile community. In one of these shows, '¿Qué pasa en casa?' [what's happening at home?], Pancho, a Cuban-Chinese neighbor of the protagonist family frequently participates in conversations with a stereotypical 'Chinese' pidgin Spanish. Despite the type-casting, this character is portrayed as both generous and hard-working, and is highly regarded by his acquaintances.

3. In past decades, Cubans enjoyed a radio serial known as 'La serpiente roja' [the red serpent] (Varela 1980: 18), whose main character was a Chinese detective Chan Li Po. His signature phrase was 'Tenga mucha pachencha. Chan Li Po no tiene mielo' [be patient, Chan Li Po is not afraid].

4. The occasional appearance of *mí* as subject pronoun in the Chinese Cuban corpus may represent contact with other creole languages already present in Cuba, e.g. Papiamento, Jamaican Creole, or Negerhollands, all of which use *mi* as first person singular subject. It is also possible that the Chinese laborers used the Chinese Pidgin English pronoun *mi* (which, however, was usually pronounced [ma], given the widespread use of Chinese pidgin English at the time.

## References

Amaro, Ama Maria. 1980. *Um Jogo Africano de Macau: A Chonca*. Macau: Separata do Nº 1 da Revista da Facultade de Ciências Sociais e Humanas da UNL.

Arona, Juan de. 1891. *La Inmigración el el Perú*. Lima: Imprenta del Universo, de Carlos Prince.

Batalha, Graciela Nogueira. 1958–9. "Estado actual do dialecto macaense." Revista Portuguesa de Filologia 9.177–213.

230     JOHN M. LIPSKI

————. 1960. "Coincidências com o dialecto de Macau em dialectos espanhóis das ilhas Filipinas." Boletim de Filologia 19.295–303.

————. 1974. *Língua de Macau*. Macau: Imprensa Nacional.

Baxter, Alan. 1988. "A grammar of Kristang (Malacca creole Portuguese)." Canberra: Department of Linguistics, the Australian National University (Pacific Linguistics Series B, No. 95).

Bazán, Armando. 1967. "Marfil chino. Lima en la narración peruana," ed. Elías Taxa Cuádroz, 27–36. Lima: Editorial Continental.

Bueno, Salvador (ed.). 1959. "Los mejores cuentos cubanos, tomo II." La Habana: Segundo Festival del Libro Cubano.

————. 1984. "Cuentos populares cubanos, tomo I." Santa Clara: Universidad Central de Las Villas.

Chang, Ching Chieh. 1956. *The Chinese in Latin America: A Preliminary Geographicl Survey with Special Reference to Cuba and Jamaica*. Tesis doctoral inédita, University of Maryland.

Chuffat Latour, Antonio. 1927. *Apunte Histórico de Los Chinos en Cuba*. La Habana: Molina.

Clementi, Cecil. 1915. *The Chinese in British Guiana*. Georgetown: Argosy.

Crawford, Marlene. 1989. *Scenes from the History of the Chinese in Guyana*. Turkeyen: Historial Society, University of Guyana.

Consuegra y Guzmán, Israel. 1930. *Mambiserías: Episodios de la Guerra de Independencia 1895–1898*. La Habana: Imprente del Ejército.

Corbitt, Duvon Clough. 1971. *A Study of the Chinese in Cuba, 1847–1947*. Wilmore, Kentucky: Asbury College.

Cuba Commission. 1876. "Chinese emigration: report of the commission sent to China to ascertain the condition of Chinese coolies in Cuba." Shanghai: Impreial Maritime Customs Press.

Deschamps Chapeaux, Pedro y Juan Pérez de la Riva. 1974. *Contribución a la Historia de la Gente sin Historia*. La Habana: Editorial de Ciencias Sociales.

Díaz Canseco, José. 1973. *Duque*. Lima: Biblioteca Peruana, Ediciones Peisa.

Endruschat, Annette. 1990. *Studien zur Portugiesischen Sprache in Angola*. Frankfurt am Main: Verlag Teo Ferrer de Mesquita.

Feijóo, Samuel (ed.). 1981. "Cuentos populares cubanos de humor." La Habana: Editorial Letras Cubanas.

Fernández Montagne, Ernesto. 1977. *Apuntes Socio Económicos de la Inmigración China en el Perú (1848–1874)*. Lima: Universidad del Pacífico.

Ferreira, José dos Santos. 1967. "Macau sã assí." Macau: Tipografia da Missão do Padroado.

————. 1978. "Papiá cristám di Macau." Macau: n.p.

————. 1990. "Doci papiaçám di Macau." Macau: Instituto Cultural de Macau.

Gelabert, Francisco de Paula. 1984. "Un chino, una mulata, y unas ranas." Costumbristas cubanos del siglo XIX, ed. Salvador Bueno, 459–463. Caracas: Biblioteca Ayacucho.

Gilligan, Gary. 1987. *A Cross-linguistic Approach to the Pro-drop Parameter.* Ph. D. dissertation, University of Southern California.

Gomes, Artur Levy. 1957. "Esboço da história de Macau 1511–1849." Macau: Repartição Provincial dos Serviços de Economia e Estatística Geral.

Guy, Gregory. 1981. "Parallel variability in American dialects of Spanish and Portuguese." Variation omnibus, ed. by David Sankoff and Henrietta Cedergren, 85–96. Edmonton: Linguistic Research.

Helly, Denise. 1979. *Idéologie et Ethnicité: Les Chinois Macao à Cuba 1847–1886.* Montréal: Les Presses de l'Université de Montréal.

Hermon, Gabriella and James Yoon. 1989. "The licensing and identification of *pro* and the typology of AGR." CLS 25/1.174–192.

Horton, V. P. Oswald. 1941. *Chinese in the Caribbean.* Kingston: V. P. O. Horton.

Huang, C.-T. James. 1984. "On the distribution and reference of empty pronouns." Linguistic Inquiry 15.531–574.

Jaeggli, Osvaldo and Kenneth Safir. 1989. "The null subject parameter and parametric theory." Jaeggli and Safir (eds.), 1–44.

Jenkins, Edward. 1871. *The Coolie: His Rights and Wrongs.* New York: G. Routledge & Sons.

Jiménez Pastrana, Juan. 1983. *Los Chinos en la Historia de Cuba: 1847–1930.* La Habana: Editorial de Ciencias Sociales.

Kao, Diana. 1971. *Structure of the Syllable in Cantonese.* La Haya: Mouton.

Kirkpatrick, Margery. 1939. *From the Middle Kingdom to the New World: Aspects of the Chinese Experience in Migration to British Guiana.* Georgetown: Margery Kirkpatrick.

Lipski, John. 1987. "The construction *ta* + infinitive in Caribbean *bozal* Spanish." Romance Philology 40.431–450.

————. 1992. "Origin and development of *ta* in Afro-Hispanic creoles. Atlantic meets Pacific: a global view of pidginization and creolization," ed. Francis Byrne y John Holm, 217–231. Amsterdam: John Benjamins.

————. 1993. "On the non-creole basis for Afro-Caribbean Spanish." Research Paper No. 24, Latin American Institute, University of New Mexico.

————. 1994. "A new perspective on Afro-Dominican Spanish: the Haitian contribution." Research Paper No. 26, University of New Mexico Latin American Institute.

————. Forthcoming a. "Literary 'Africanized' Spanish as a research tool: dating consonant reduction." Romance Philology.

————. Forthcoming b. "El lenguaje afroperuano: eslabón entre Africa y América." Anuario de Lingüística Hispánica (Valladolid).

————. Forthcoming c. "Contacto de criollos en el Caribe hispánico: contribuciones al español *bozal.*" América Negra.

————. d. "Portuguese language in Angola: luso-creoles' missing link?" Presented at annual meeting of the American Association of Teachers of Spanish and Portuguese, San Diego, August 9, 1995.

————. Forthcoming e. "Español *bozal*. El estudio de las lenguas criollas de base lexical española y portuguesa en América," ed. by Matthias Perl and Armin Schwegler. Frankfurt: Vervuert.

Look Lai, Walton. 1993. *IndenturedLlabor, Caribbean Sugar: Chinese and Indian migrants to the British West Indies 1838–1918*. Baltimore: Johns Hopkins University Press.

Martín, Juan Luis. 1939. *De dDónde Vinieron los Chinos de Cuba*. La Habana: Editorial Atalaya.

Menéndez, Carlos. 1928. *Historia del Infame y Vergonzoso Comercio de Indios Vendidos a los Esclavistas de Cuba por los Políticos Yucatecos, desde 1848 hasta 1861*. Mérida: Tallers de la Compañía Tipográfica Yucateca, S. A.

————. 1932. *Las Memorias de D. Buenaventura Vivó y la Venta de Indios Yucatecos en Cuba*. Mérida: Tallers de la Compañía Tipográfica Yucateca, S. A.

Montalto de Jesus, C. A. 1926. *Historic Macao*. Macao: Salesian Printing Press and Tipografia Mercantil.

Norman, Jerry. 1988. *Chinese*. Cambridge: Cambridge University Press.

Ordas Avecilla, Federico. 1893. *Los Chinos Fuera de China: El Antagonismo de Razas*. Havana: A. Miranda y Cª.

Ortega, Antonio. 1984. "Chino olvidado." En Bueno (ed.), 54–73.

Pérez de la Riva, Juan. 1966. "Demografía de los culíes chinos en Cuba (1853–74)." Separata de la Revista de la Biblioteca Nacional "José Martí," Año 57, Nómero 4.

————. 1978. "El barracón: esclavitud y capitalismo en Cuba." Barcelona: Editorial Crítica, 2ª ed.

Pichardo, Esteban. 1953. *Pichardo Novísimo o Diccionario Provincial casi Razonado de Vozes y Frases Cubanas*. Edición a carga de Esteban Rodríguez Herrera. La Habana: Editorial Selecta.

Piedra Martel, Manuel. 1968. *Memorias de un Mambí*. La Habana: Instituto del Libro.

Quesada, Gonzalo de. 1892. *Mi Primera Ofrenda*. New York: Imprenta de EL POR-VENIR.

Ramsey, S. Robert. 1987. *The Languages of China*. Princeton: Princeton University Press.

Rego, Antonio da Silva. 1943. *Apontamentos para o Estudo do Dialecto Portugués de Malacca*. Lisbon: Agéncia Geral das Colónias.

Rodríguez Pastor, Humberto. 1977. *Los Trabajadores Chinos Culíes en el Perú: Artículos Históricos*. Lima: n. p.

————. 1979. *La Rebelión de los Rostros Pintados*. Lima: Instituto de Estudios Andinos.

————. 1989. *Hijos del Celeste Imperio en el Perú (1850–1900)*. Lima: Instituto de Apoyo Agrario.

Sánchez, Luis Alberto. 1952. "Los chineros en la historia peruana." Cuadernos Americanos 11(2).220–222.

Sánchez-Boudy, José. 1970. *Alegrías de Coco*. Barcelona: Bosch, Casa Editorial.

Sanjek, Roger (ed.). 1990. *Caribbean Asians: Chinese, Indians, and Japanese Experiences in Trinidad and the Dominican Republic*. Flushing, New York: Asian/African Center at Queens College, CUNY.

Santa Cruz, Nicomedes. 1982. *La Décima en el Perú*. Lima: Instituto de Estudios Peruanos.

Sarró López, Pilar. 1988. "Notas sobre la morfosintaxis del habla de las negras de Lope de Rueda." Actas del I Congreso Internacional de Historia de la Lengua Española, ed. by M. Ariza, A. Salvador, A. Viudas, t. I, 601–610. Madrid: Arco.

Souza y Rodríguez, Benigno. 1939. "Discursos leídos en la recepción pública, la noche del 29 de junio de 1939." La Habana: Imprenta "El Siglo XX."

Stewart, Watt. 1976. *La Servidumbre China en el Perú*. Lima: Mosca Azul.

Teixeira, Manuel. 1976. "O comércio de escravos em Macau." Boletim do Instituto Luís de Camoes (Macau) 10(1–2).5–21.

Trazegnies Granda, Fernando de. 1994. "En el país de las colinas de arena: reflexiones sobre la inmigración china en el Perú del S. XIX desde la perspective del Derecho, tomo I." Lima: Pontificia Universidad Católica del Perú.

Varela, Beatriz. 1980. *Lo Chino en el Habla Cubana*. Miami: Ediciones Universal.

# Monogenesis Revisited

## The Spanish Perspective

### Armin Schwegler
*University of California, Irvine*

> The Portuguese were the inaugurators of the [slave] trade and almost through-
> out the trade's long, tragic history continued to be important carriers.
>
> *The Transatlantic Slave Trade,*
> Rawley (1981:429)

## 1. Introduction

Granda (1978, 1985, 1988, 1991, 1994) and a small group of followers
(Megenney 1984, 1993; Otheguy 1973; Perl 1989, 1990; Schwegler 1993b,
1996a, 1996b)[1] have long claimed that several phenomena found in Afro-
Caribbean Spanish (Cuba, Dominican Republic, Puerto Rico, northern Venezuela
and Colombia, see Map 1, p.239) point to the prior existence of a uniform pan-
Caribbean Spanish pidgin or creole. The ultimate source of this contact vernacular presumably was the pidgin Portuguese "reconnaissance language" that arose
in the fifteenth century along the West Coast of Africa.[2] As Lipski and others
recognize, this sweeping monogenetic claim, if substantiated, would totally
reshape our understanding of the formation of American Spanish:

> The impact of the creole Portuguese hypothesis o[n] Spanish dialectology is
> obvious, for in its most radical form, this theory claims that a SINGLE creole
> underlay virtually all Afro-Hispanic speech over a period of more than three
> centuries, and was more important than the strictly African element in deter-
> mining the characteristics of Bozal Spanish and its possible repercussions in
> general Latin American Spanish. The focus of Afro-Hispanic studies thus
> shifted partially, away from the search for direct African-American links to the

postulate of an intermediate pan-Hispanic creole stage ...

*This is a sweeping claim, which if substantiated would totally reshape our understanding of the formation of Latin American Spanish in vast areas of the Caribbean and coastal South America.* The African contribution to Latin American Spanish would then be twofold: not only the direct transfer of Africanisms, but also an intermediate transfer from an Afro-Hispanic creole, whose characteristics had already solidified among the African population in Latin America. (Lipski 1994: 112–13; my italics)

Lipski and the majority of Hispanists[3] have, however, rejected the monogenetic hypothesis because, as they rightly point out, none of the evidence traditionally adduced in favor of a widespread Afro-Hispanic pidgin or creole convincingly resists alternative analyses (e.g., spontaneous innovation or peninsular origins).[4] Similar conclusions to those of Lipski are reached, independently and generally on the basis of external data alone, by creolists like Goodman, who, in a seminal article on the Portuguese influence on the American creoles, concludes that in the New World the Afro-Portuguese pidgin (and its various varieties)

does not appear to have been widely or regularly used as an African inter-ethnic lingua franca outside of certain coastal areas [of Africa], and, therefore, was probably known to very few slaves prior to captivity, since these were largely drawn from the hinterland, away from where the Portuguese-speaking communities were located, and where their language served as an important medium of contact between Africans and Europeans" (Goodman 1987: 366).[5]

Among creolists, the monogenetic Afro-Portuguese hypothesis[6] and the various issues related to it continue to be a "hot" topic,[7] yet the Spanish Caribbean perspective (as opposed to the French or English) has never fully been taken into account.[8] This is regrettable for at least two reasons. First, as recent field work in Palenque, the Dominican Republic, Western Colombia (Pacific Lowlands), and highland Ecuador reveals,[9] a closer examination of synchronic data from Afro-Hispanic areas may help validate (or, if reason so dictates, ultimately reject) a hypothesis that clearly remains key to an understanding of how Afro-American speech varieties evolved. Second, as Goodman (one of the premier scholars on the issue at hand) himself recognized almost a decade ago, the unmistakably Portuguese items in Palenquero — a creole spoken just outside of Cartagena — strongly suggest that an Afro-Portuguese speech variety did indeed reach the Spanish Caribbean, and that therefore the question "requires additional investigation" (Goodman 1987: 397–98). In his view, the closeness of the Portuguese and Spanish languages (which approach mutual intelligibility) was such that in Spanish-controlled areas like those of Cartagena, the Afro-Portuguese pidgin "might have served as a lingua franca between the two races, particularly in view of the fact that the Spanish acquired nearly all of their slaves from the Portuguese until 1640" (Goodman 1987: 397–98).

Concentrating on Palenquero (Colombia), Chota (highland Ecuador), and Bozal Spanish (Cuba, Puerto Rico, and so on), this article seeks to rectify the relative neglect of Afro-Hispanic vernaculars in the monogenetic controversy. Intended to offer a lone but unusually valuable piece of UNEQUIVOCAL evidence in favor of the monogenetic pidgin/creole theory, this study argues for a once widespread, possibly pan-Caribbean, Afro-Iberian pidgin or creole by examining a series of third person pronouns (or person/number markers) that are all reflexes of the Afro-Portuguese pronouns *ele* (< Port. *ele* 'he' and *eles* 'they'). As shown in examples (1)–(3) below, these formally similar reflexes share a morphological feature that is strikingly pidgin or creole in flavor in that they are all invariant (they signal neither gender nor case, and are, therefore, quite different from their Spanish counterparts *él, ella, ellos, ellas,* and *le, les*).

(1) **Bozal Spanish** (19th c.):[10]　　　　　　　　　　(Cuba/Puerto Rico)
　　　　ELLE estaba en un mortorio.　'THEY were at a funeral'.
　　　　ELLE solito con su espá ...　'HE alone with his sword...'.

(2) **Chota** (highland Ecuador):[11]
　　　　ELE, él ta allí.　　　　　　　'HE/SHE is there'.
　　　　¡Yo! Con ELE no fuera.　　　'I! With HIM/HER I would not go'.
　　　　ELE no les quiero dar　　　　'I don't want to give it to HIM/HER'.

(3) **Palenquero** (Colombia):[12]
　　　　ELE a-ta kumé ku ELE.　　　'HE/SHE is eating with HIM/HER'.
　　　　ELE tan miní akí. (archaic)　'THEY will come here'.

Having already examined in considerable detail the origins and current use of Pal. *ele* in other publications (Schwegler 1993a, 1993b), in this paper I shall make reference to the Colombian form only in passing. Special attention will here be paid to the (heretofore undocumented) Chota *ele*, and to Cuban and Puerto Rican bozal *elle* — a form that has recently been characterized as an element with "no plausible source" (Lipski 1994: 116). For reasons of space, no attempt will be made here to investigate in detail the multiple and rather complex functions of these items in the respective languages, for my primary concern here is to simply document the existence of Portuguese-derived pronouns in several widely dispersed Afro-Hispanic regions. My overriding purpose in presenting the data is to support the claim that in colonial times an Afro-Portuguese-based contact vernacular must have existed in many parts of Black Latin America.

## 2.  Theoretical and practical preliminaries

Before examining the Afro-Hispanic pronouns in greater detail, it may be useful to offer some theoretical considerations which illustrate the extraordinary significance of the data to be analyzed. First, it must be recognized that "deep" grammatical features such as pronouns are particularly useful to prove genetic relationships or genetic origins. This is so because, as Arlotto (1972) and others have noted, deep features are rarely borrowed, and if so only in intense and prolonged contact situations:

> In point of fact it is very rare that pronouns are borrowed, which is one of the reasons that comparative linguists often look first to pronouns when seeking to establish genetic relationships. (Arlotto 1972: 188)

Second, as argued in Schwegler (1993b, 1996b), *the discovery of even a single* DEEP *grammatical Afro-Portuguese feature in Caribbean Spanish automatically validates the monogenetic theory.* This line of reasoning is based on multiple considerations, most important among them are the following:

(a)  the Portuguese never settled the Caribbean in sufficient numbers to transfer "deep" Lusitanian features into American Spanish;[13]
(b)  there currently is no plausible alternative hypothesis that could account for a "deep" Portuguese feature in New World Spanish.

When advancing claims as far-reaching as the ones made in this paper, one typically seeks to adduce language-internal as well as language-external evidence (from language history or history of the slave trade, and so on.). In this instance, however, we may be content with predominantly internal proof for the following reasons. First, external evidence about the transshipment of thousands of slaves from Portuguese-controlled African territories to Spanish America (including all of the areas examined in this paper) is readily available[14] so that the question of how Afro-Portuguese features could have reached the Americas is not of immediate concern. Second, and more importantly, at this stage it seems clear that the discussion and, perhaps, eventual resolution of the Afro-Portuguese monogenetic controversy rests crucially on the discovery of **unequivocally** Afro-Portuguese features. Put differently, skeptics will always welcome additional external documentation (similar to that provided by the Jesuit priest Alonso de Sandoval 1987 [1627]:140), but only incontestable internal evidence will convince them of the validity of the monogenetic hypothesis.

## 3.   Data sources and speech areas to be discussed

The data for this paper come from three areas: Bozal speech of Puerto Rico and Cuba (Lipski 1993a, 1994), Palenquero (Schwegler 1993a and fieldwork), and the Chota in highland Ecuador (from a corpus of recordings and field notes gathered *in situ* in 1993). The speech areas discussed (Puerto Rico, Cuba, Palenque, Chota — see Map 1) may comfortably be characterized as Afro-Hispanic. Spanish has been the dominant language in each of these regions for several centuries, and Black (or mulatto) speakers constitute a numerically significant or even dominant portion of the overall population. However, important cultural and linguistic differences among them should be taken into account in the arguments introduced below. A brief examination of these differences serves both to present the sociolinguistic context in which pronominal *ele* and *elle* are used, and to introduce a region — the Chota Valley — that has never figured prominently in Creole or Latin American studies.

Cuba, Puerto Rico, and Palenque are areas where Lowland Spanish (with its characteristic aspiration or loss of syllable final [s]) is spoken. Chota Spanish, on

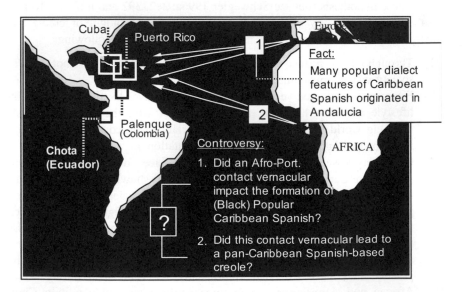

Map 1. *Afro-Hispanic speech areas (Cuba, Puerto Rico, Palenque, Chota) highlighted in this study*

the other hand, belongs to the generally more conservative Andean highland dialect cluster, in which deletion of syllable-final [–s] is atypical (Lipski 1982, 1986, 1987a, 1988b). Chota Spanish is, therefore, closer to standard American Spanish[15] than are any of the Caribbean popular Spanish varieties.

Situated in a bilingual region (Quechua/Spanish), the almost exclusively Black Choteños, who from the 17th century onward formed a society apart, are monolingual speakers of Spanish. They rarely mix (and only rarely intermarry) with the Quechua-speaking *indios* or with whites living in nearby towns. Found vestigially among older black *choteños* are a few morphosyntactic and phonological configurations that differ conspicuously from typical highland Spanish. Lipski, the only scholar to have analyzed the Spanish spoken in the Chota Valley, characterizes these special features as suggestive of earlier and more Africanized stages of the language (Lipski 1982, 1986, 1987a, 1994: 129–30). It is important to note, however, that some of the most salient features of Chota speech — including the retention of the pronoun *ele* and the consistent omission of the synthetic plural markers [–s] or [–es] in nouns (cp. *tres pastel y dos pan* = *tres pasteles y dos panes*)[16]–received no attention in Lipski's pioneering investigations. Thus potentially tangible evidence in favor of the pidgin or creole origin of Chota speech has yet to be considered in discussions of the Afro-Portuguese hypothesis (but see Schwegler 1996a: 282, 392 and *n279*).[17] To give further credence to my claim that an Afro-Portuguese pidgin or creole was instrumental in the formation of Choteño speech, I note the following:

(1) Throughout its formative period (17th-18th century), the Chota Valley society was overwhelmingly Black.[18]

(2) For over two hundred years Black male Chota slaves lived a plantation-like lifestyle and thus had only minimal contact with the outside Spanish-speaking world (male slaves almost invariably worked on labor-intensive Jesuit-owned *latifundios*–mostly sugar plantations).

(3) Chota slaves were purchased in a variety of places, most prominent among which were Cartagena, Popayán, and Ibarra;[19] as shown on Map 2, the latter two received the majority of its Black slaves from Cartagena — the most likely place in Latin America to receive Afro-Portuguese-pidgin-speaking slaves.

(4) In the Chota, Jesuit *haciendistas* apparently preferred importing Bozal rather than Creole slaves because the former were less expensive to acquire and more amenable to discipline (Jurado Novoa 1992: 149; see also Coronel 1988).[21] This practice may have extended significantly the time span during which African and Afro-Portuguese features could enter and condition Chota speech.[22]

(Map adapted from Schwegler 1996a: 282)

Map 2. *Localization of the Chota Valley and principal routes (in order of importance) by which Black slaves reached this tropical Andean valley during the 16th and 17th centuries.*[20]

## 4.    Importance of social pressures on Chota and Palenquero speech

Choteños as well as Palenqueros have long suffered from deep-seated racial stereotyping, ridicule of their "strange" local "African" traditions, and the widespread sentiment that theirs is a backward place. This has contributed to making the Afrochoteños and Palenqueros guarded and reserved individuals who routinely adjust their speech and behavior in the presence of outsiders. This is an important point, for it helps explain how in some Afro-Hispanic communities outside pressures can conspire over time to squeeze out speech forms — for instance *ele*–that have an unmistakable local and, therefore, Black flavor.[23] The

combined effect of these same long-term pressures may also lead to the wholesale abandonment of a local creole, as is currently happening in Palenque where
the youngest generations are now monolingual Spanish speakers. Today only
about half of the Palenquero community has an active command of the creole,[24]
which contrasts sharply with the situation Friedemann & Patiño Rosselli encountered in the middle of the 1970s when the community was still fully bilingual
(Schwegler 1996a: 42–46, 1998). Such abrupt recession of a strictly local
vernacular differs from that found in gradually dying languages in that a wide
range of proficiency is normally not encountered. As a result, certain "dying"
native elements (for instance pronominal *ele*) may be lost not so much because
younger speakers no longer recall how to use them, but rather because younger
generations *in toto* may sever themselves from the cultivation, practice and even
promotion of linguistic skills that were traditionally considered key to the
indigenous culture. I argue below that there is evidence that the history of Pal.
*ele* is currently being conditioned significantly by such sudden rejection and
neglect of the language.

## 5.    Authenticity of Black speech in Bozal texts

Nothing precise is known about the linguistic pressures under which the Bozal
slaves lived in the first few centuries of Latin American colonization (in Latin
America, the African presence lasted for almost 400 years). Even less is known
about the exact nature of 16th to 18th-century Bozal speech. A handful of 17th-
century poems and songs do attempt to represent that type of speech, but they
are little more than a mimicry of the *habla de negro* of Golden Age Spain
(Lipski 1994: 101). More abundant and more useful attestations (for the linguist)
of Afro-Hispanic speech in Latin America are found in the 19th century. It
should be noted, however, that according to Lipski, most of these Bozal Spanish
texts do not suggest the prior existence of a uniform pan-Latin American Spanish
pidgin or creole, and that "recurring features of Bozal language can be explained
as spontaneous independent developments or as natural learner's errors" (1994: 11;
see also Lipski 1998).

Today it is impossible to determine with rigor whether any of the Bozal
texts indeed contain authentically Afro-Hispanic language.[25] Many works are
replete with stereotyping, and, as Lipski observes correctly, "the most egregious
cases of exaggeration and distortion involve the lexicon, not to mention plot
lines" (1994: 97).

## 6. The comparative data: Origins and use of *ele* and *elle* in four non-contiguous speech areas

### 6.1 *Palenque (Colombia)*

Pal. *ele*, generally articulated [éle] or [éli], is typical of unhurried articulation (other variants include the Spanish-derived *e*, or the apocopated *el'* < Port. *ele*). Earlier investigators correctly identified *ele* as the prototypical 3rd-person genderless singular pronoun (cp. ELE a degobbé también 'he/she also returned'), but they failed to recognize that the same word occasionally has an archaic third-person PLURAL function (*ELE era ma suamo* ... 'THEY were the owners ...' [Schwegler 1993a: 155]). In light of the low frequency of this PLURAL form (2 tokens in a corpus containing over 250 third person plural pronouns), this oversight might at first seem inconsequential. As it turns out, from a historical perspective its dual function (i.e., 3rd singular AND plural) is, however, of considerable relevance. As mentioned earlier, Granda (1978: 438, 1988: 26), Friedemann & Patiño (1983: 162), and Megenney (1983: 557) have adduced 'singular' *ele* as a rare but critical link between Palenquero and the putative Afro-Portuguese contact language from which the creole is said to have originated. Such an argument could, however, be potentially weakened by the fact that a simple paragoge of Span. *él* > *ele* could also have yielded *ele* (from an "African" perspective, this paragoge would have offered the more favorable open syllable pattern *e-le*).[26] As argued in Schwegler (1993a: 154), attestations of PLURAL *ele* do, however, provide conclusive evidence against the Spanish hypothesis since paragoge of Span. *ellos* 'they' (or its feminine counterpart *ellas*) could not possibly give rise to Pal. *ele*. Discounting for the moment word-final *-s* (which is regularly dropped in Palenquero), Port. *eles* [éles ~ élis] 'they' is, moreover, homophonous and synonymous with Pal. *ele ~ eli,* which further suggests that Afro-Portuguese played a crucial role in the formation of the Palenquero pronominal paradigm.

A fully bilingual community since the beginning of the 18th century (Friedemann & Patiño 1983: 45, Schwegler 1996a: 26–27), Palenque has always maintained systematic distinctions in the third-person pronouns, that is, just as the creole code in general has been kept separate from local or regional Spanish,[27] so too Creole and Spanish pronouns like *ele* 'he, she', *suto* 'we', *ané* 'they', and Span. *él* 'he', *ella* 'she', *nosotros* 'we', *ellos/ellas* 'they', respectively, have always been associated with a distinct code. In Palenque, strict separation of co-existing languages has, therefore, prevented a potential phonetic or grammatical coalescence of the two pronominal systems (this situation contrasts sharply with that of Bozal Spanish, examined below). It is not unreasonable to assume that, due to the current rapid recession of the Palenquero creole, Pal. *ele* may disappear before it ever becomes affected by language-mixing.

The fact that the (Afro-) Portuguese derivation of Pal. *ele* is irrefutable leads to the simple but, especially for the Chota and Bozal data, important conclusion that (at least some) African slaves did indeed bring Portuguese pronouns to the Spanish Caribbean. This immediately raises the question, however, whether Palenque was an exception (as has traditionally been argued), or whether the creole pronominal system and the speech variety to which it belonged were more widespread. Sections 6.2–6.3 examine this issue, and offer comparative evidence that strongly favor the latter scenario.

## 6.2  *Chota (Ecuador)*

Used exclusively in the town of Chota — culturally and linguistically the most conservative locale among the eleven Afro-Hispanic communities of the Chota Valley — the forms presented below have never before been reported. Chot. 3rd-person *ele*, rarely used in the presence of outsiders, is similar to Pal. *ele*:

(a)  it is undifferentiated for gender and/or case (see examples 4a to 4e below);
(b)  it has a singular as well as plural function (see 4a–c vs. 4d–4g), and
(c)  it may be articulated [éle] (4a–f) or [éli] (4g).

Here are the relevant examples (4a, b, f are repeated from 2 above):[28]

(4)     a.   ELE, *él* ta allí.
             '**He**, (he) is there'.
        b.   ¡Yo! ¡Con ELE no fuera!
             'I! With **him** I would not go!'
        c.   ELE *el guagu* a se torció el pie.
             '(**He**) the kid twisted his ankle'.

        d.   ELE *ese* ya le chancó al puerco.
             '(**He**) this one already killed the pig'.
        e.   ELE *ellas* se van a pasear.
             '(**They**) they (fem.) are going for a walk'.
        f.   ELE no *les* quiero dar.
             Lit. '(**To) them** not to them I want to give = I don't want to give (it) to them'.
        g.   ELI *los pescados* se han muerto.
             '(**They**) the fish have died'.

Chota *ele* differs from its Palenquero counterpart in a number of ways, only some of which will be examined here. First, unlike Pal. *ele*, Chot. *ele* has a distinctively archaic flavor. Not surprisingly, it is found predominantly in the speech of older generations, and Choteños readily characterize the particle as "something that older folks used to say here all the time" (informant). Second, it is employed sporadically at best, that is, it is never used consistently in any extended stretch of speech (even older speakers routinely give preference to *ele*'s functional Spanish counterparts *él, ella, ellos, ellas*).[29] Third, in addition to being a "simple" third person pronoun like Pal. *ele*, the Chota form can also hold a coreferential and topicalizing function (see (4a, c) above, where co-referenced items have been underlined).[30]

The etymological arguments advanced earlier for Pal. *ele* are also valid for Chot. *ele* — a form which cannot be related plausibly to Span. *él, ella, ellos* or *ellas*.[31] If the Portuguese 3rd-person pronouns *ele* (singular) and *eles* (plural) were indeed brought to the Ecuadorian highland by Black slaves, and if word-final *-s* was in fact subject to deletion (as we must assume it was, based on contemporary evidence [Lipski 1988b]), then Chot. *ele* is a perfectly logical outcome, both phonetically and semantically. The discovery of the 3rd-person marker *ele* in highland Ecuador is, therefore, of extraordinary significance because, as in the case of Pal. *ele*, its phonetic shape and especially its dual function (singular/plural) require its connection to an (Afro-) Portuguese rather than a Spanish source. What is more, the articulatory alternation between *ele* and *eli* is found in many Portuguese dialects. The observed phonetic instability of the Chota and Palenquero forms (i.e., *ele* vs. *eli*) may thus be accounted for by something other than the sporadic vowel closure that converts unstressed [e] to [i] (such closure is otherwise atypical in Chota Spanish).[32]

Having established the Portuguese connection of the Chota pronoun and referential clitic *ele*, an earlier observation deserves to be reiterated: no part of Ecuador was ever inhabited by any numbers of Portuguese, but slaves originating from Portuguese-controlled African ports did end up in the distant and isolated regions of highland Ecuador. Logic dictates, therefore, that these slaves were the only ones who could have introduced Lusitanian features into the Chota Valley.

One noticeable trait is that, in the plural function, Pal. *ele* and Chot. *ele* are never articulated with a final [–s] (i.e. *\*eles*). While the absence of such an [–s] in Pal. *ele* < Port. *eles* may be considered a logical consequence of Caribbean Spanish articulatory habits (regarding [–s] deletion in Lowland Spanish, see above), the same cannot be said of Chot. *ele* < Port. *eles*. One of the characteristic features of Portuguese and Andean Spanish (including that of the Chota) is precisely the RETENTION of syllable-final consonants (including [–s]), whence

*eles* rather than *ele* would be the expected outcome. Two mutually complementary explanations offer themselves: (1) in the Chota, deletion of [-s] in *ele* <
*eles* could have resulted from the tendency — undoubtedly common among
*Bozales* — to favor open syllable structures; or (2) slaves sold into the Ecuadorian highland from the Cartagena region may have brought with them articulatory
habits reflective of popular Caribbean Spanish and/or Afro-Hispanic contact
vernaculars akin to those found in Palenque.

We have already had occasion to remark that Chota and Palenquero *ele*
have long coexisted with the functionally similar Span. *él, ella, ellos* and *ellas.*
Not surprisingly, in both speech communities, *ele* has acquired a strongly local,
and, therefore, ethnic (i.e., Black) flavor, which, in turn, has made it into one of
those elements that are adjusted routinely in the presence of outsiders (in
Palenque, this adjustment manifests itself in that the entire creole — rather than
a given word or selected grammatical or phonetic features — is shunned in the
presence of strangers). As is well known, superstratal pressures can have the
most diverse effects on such ethnically marked, normally non-standard forms. In
the case of *ele,* at least four different outcomes may be envisioned: (1) Simple
coexistence with standard forms (no effect), (2) gradual abandonment, (3) rapid
abandonment, and (4) cross-fertilization (blending of non-standard with standard
forms). The first (simple coexistence) reflects the situation found in Palenque
prior to the 1970s, in which *ele* seemingly was retained unchanged, despite
centuries of pressure from adstratal Spanish third-person pronouns. "Gradual
abandonment" best describes the Chota circumstances. Rapid abandonment of *ele*
currently occurs in Palenque due to the abrupt wholesale recession of the creole.
Cross fertilization (or, to use a now less-favored term, interference) — appears
to have occurred in Bozal Spanish. It is this fourth, more complex possibility that
we shall now examine.

## 6.3 *Bozal Spanish (Cuba and Puerto Rico)*

### 6.3.1 *Preliminaries*
For some scholars, Bozal Spanish refers to the Afro-Hispanic speech of slaves
born in Africa (it is, therefore, by definition not a mother tongue). To others, the
same term can also refer to restructured, non-standard, and possibly native
varieties of Spanish spoken by American-born black slaves.[33] The 19th-century
texts from which the data presented in this section have been taken are similarly
ambiguous in that it is not always clear whether a given example of Cuban or
Puerto Rican Bozal Spanish is supposed to represent the speech of an African-
born or, American-born slave. This does not, however, reduce the weight of the

evidence to be presented, since the primary aim of this article is to document the former existence of Portuguese-derived pronouns in ANY variety of Black Latin American Spanish.

In Section 3 above I mentioned that it is impossible to determine with rigor whether any of the extant Bozal texts indeed contain authentically Afro-Hispanic language. This general problem of authenticity does not, however, in any way affect the validity of the pronominal data to be discussed. This is so because these forms, although limited to relatively few Afro-Caribbean texts, are attested with enough frequency and consistency across time and space so as to leave no doubt about their actual existence in 19th-century Bozal speech (for a representative selection, see Lipski 1993a: 14–15, 1994: 116). They cannot, therefore, be explained away as a fanciful invention by writers, nor as second-language errors.

### 6.3.2 *Attestations of (n)elle*

If one projects, as I have done based on synchronic evidence from Palenquero and Chota Spanish, that undifferentiated 3rd-person pronoun *ele* was a deep feature of an early widespread Afro-Portuguese contact vernacular, one would expect that traces, however tenuous, of similar constructions could also be detected in Caribbean Bozal Spanish. Evidence of precisely this nature has been brought together recently by Lipski, who, in a paper on the supposed non-creole basis of Afro-Caribbean Spanish, qualifies the undifferentiated 3rd-person pronouns we are about to examine as "one of the more clearly creoloid features of Latin American Bozal Spanish" (1993a: 14).

The Afro-Caribbean texts from Cuba and Puerto Rico to which I refer exhibit occasional third-person pronouns — most often *elle* or *nelle* (articulated [éye] and [néye], respectively) — that are strikingly similar (but never identical) to those encountered in Afro-Iberian creoles, where the singular variant has the general form *e(le)* (Lipski 1994: 116; Bartens 1995). Representative Bozal examples are given in 5–6 below. Note that, parallel to Pal. and Chot. *ele,* these forms are morphologically non-complex pronouns in that they are undifferentiated for gender and case (this is atypical of Peninsular speech varieties but consistent with patterns of creole languages).[34] Employed pleonastically, they hold a co-referential or topicalizing function that is strikingly similar to that of Chot. *ele* (cp. 6f to 6g, where co-referenced items are once again underlined). As is the case with Chota *ele,* they seem to occur in free variation with alternate Spanish forms (*él, ella, ellos, ellas)*:

(5)  a.  ELLE estaba en un mortorio.                              (Cuba)
         'HE was alone in a mortuary'.                    (transl. Lipski)
     b.  Dentra Tondá, ELLE solito con su espá, coge dos.        (Cuba)
         'Tondá entered, alone, HE grabbed two of them'.
                                                          (transl. Lipski)
     c.  yo to be da un medalló pa que tu luse con EYE.          (Cuba)
         'I am going to give you a medallion so that you'll
         look good with IT'.                              (transl. A.S.)
     d.  yo no quisió di con ELLE.                             (P. Rico)
         'I did not want to go with HER'.                 (transl. A.S.)

(6)  a.  NELLE son mala cabesa.                               (P. Rico)
         'He is a bad head = he is a bad person'.         (transl. A.S.)
     b.  noté quie jabla con NELLE ...                          (Cuba)
         'I noticed who was speaking with/to him ...'     (transl. A.S.)
     c.  yo pué casá CUNELLE.                                   (Cuba)
         'I then married HER'.                            (transl. A.S.)
     d.  si yo lo tené uno niño como NELLE, yo va murí
         de cuntentamienta.                                     (Cuba)
         'If I had a child like HER, I would die of happiness'.
                                                          (transl. Lipski)
     e.  eso mimo quiere yo, NELLE lo mimo, vamo pa
         la engresia.
                                                               (Cuba)
         'That's just what I want, SHE does too, let's go to the church'.
                                                          (transl. Lipski)

**Pleonastic *(n)elle* with a co-referential or topicalizing function:**
     f.  y NELLE lo *muchachito* va pendé su Paña de nuté.      (Cuba)
         'And THEY the boys are going to depend on your Spain?'
                                                          (transl. Lipski)
         (Examples from Lipski 1993a: 14–15 and 1994: 116)

**Compare to pleonastic Chot. *ele*:**
     g.  ELI *los pescados* se han muerto.
         (repeated from 4g above)                             (Chota)
         '(THEY) the fish have died'.

6.3.3 *Origin of elle*
While the Afro-Portuguese origin of Pal. and Chot. *ele* is beyond doubt, the same
cannot be said of Boz. *elle*, *nelle*, or *cunelle*. Lipski, after reviewing Álvarez

Nazario's etymological proposal, concludes that "there is no plausible source in the case of *nelle* ...", and that, therefore, "*elle/nelle* may thus be a spontaneous Afro-Hispanic development which arose in the nineteenth-century Caribbean" (1994: 116). The etymological problems posed by *(n)elle* or similar forms (e.g., *nella, porelle, dielle*) are indeed complex but not without solution. No attempt will be made here to address all the issues surrounding the trajectory of *(n)elle*. Comments will, therefore, be limited almost exclusively to matters directly relevant to the putative link between Caribbean Bozal Spanish pronouns and Afro-Portuguese *ele(s)*.

Álvarez Nazario (1974: 190), in the first analysis of the Bozal forms under review, states unhesitatingly that *elle* is a cross between Afro-Creole *ele* 'he, she' and Spanish *ella* 'she'. Implicit in this explanation is the assumption that the palatal glide [y] in *elle* and *nelle* is derived from Span. *ella* [éya] (see Figure 1).[35] Since neither standard Portuguese *ele* nor corresponding Afro-Lusitanian creole forms contain the glide in question, Álvarez Nazario's explanation is indeed plausible, but weakened somewhat by the fact that *Bozales* generally ignored gender distinctions (masculine rather than feminine forms were typically employed as genderless pronouns), whence *ella* may not have figured prominently enough in early Afro-Hispanic speech to condition the articulation of Afro-Port. *eye*.

Although not stated explicitly, it seems clear that Álvarez Nazario felt that Span. *ella* rather than *él* intervened in the formation of *elle* because *ella* alone exhibits the palatal glide -ll- (phonetically [y]). As will become apparent, the now expanded corpus of information (i.e., Pal. *ele*, Chota *ele*, and the Bozal forms under discussion), and especially the recognition that *ele* held both a singular and a plural function strengthen the argument that [éye] (with its palatal glide) eventually came to replace [éle] in Bozal speech.

The fact that both Palenquero and Chota *ele* today have singular as well as plural meanings suggests that, in the Caribbean, *Bozales* captured in Portuguese-controlled African territories must have also used *(n)elle* with a dual singular/plural function.[36] If this was so (as one must assume), then the palatal glide [y] was likely to originate not from one but three different (but related) sources, namely, Span. *e_lla_, e_llos_,* and *e_llas_* (additional pressure may have also been exerted by *e_llo_* 'it'). Figure 2 illustrates the process.

The fact that *(n)elle* has both a singular and plural function once again provides key information: it permits ruling out Span. *elle* as a possible source for PLURAL *(n)elle*, while offering a simple, purely phonetic explanation for the word-final vowel of both Boz. *elle* (< (Afro-Port. *ele*) and Boz. *elle* 'they' (< Afro-Port. *eles*). Naturally, if *elle* 'he' figured in the speech of some Spanish immigrants to Cuba or Puerto Rico, this regional form may have furthered the

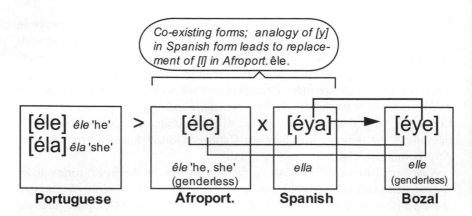

Figure 1. *Álvarez Nazario's proposal*

Note that "singular" Span. *ella* alone was supposed to have provided the pressure for the replacement of [l] by palatal [y] in the Bozal form. An oversight (misreading of Álvarez Nazario) led Lipski (1993a: 15) to reject this proposal.

acceptance, in Bozal speech, of *elle* 'he, she, they'. However, demographic and language-internal considerations (some of which I have mentioned above) suggest that language contact rather than straight language transmission must be the primary cause for the existence of *elle* in certain varieties of Afro-Caribbean speech.

The realization that four sources (i.e., *ella, ellos,* and *ellas,* and, perhaps dialectal Span. *elle*) rather than a single source (i.e., *ella*) may have contributed to the acceptance of the palatal glide in *(n)elle* is important because it could explain why bozal *elle* [éye] rather than the standard Spanish pronouns displaced the originally Portuguese *ele* [éle]. Pronouns like Span. *ella, ellos,* and *ellas* — all of which contain a palatal glide — enjoy a very high frequency of use. Due in part to this high frequency, Bozal speakers may have come to recognize the glide as a standard feature of 3rd – person pronouns. This scenario may help explain why [y] was extended to a form — *elle* [éye] 'he' — whose phonetic shape could not otherwise be explained by the convergence of masculine Span. *él* 'he' and Port. *ele.*

It is impossible to determine with certainty why speakers of Bozal Spanish ultimately blended Afro-Portuguese *ele* with *ella, ellos,* and *ellas.* It may have been the case, however, that they recognized functional benefits in adopting Portuguese rather than Spanish 3rd-person pronoun endings. As shown in the right-hand column of Figure 2, the creation of the Bozal 3rd-person pronouns (i.e., *elle* 'he, she, they') removed the inflectional complexity of standard Spanish

| Form | Spanish | Std. Port. | Interference Spanish Afro-Port.[a] | Bozal result |
|---|---|---|---|---|
| singular (fem.) | ella [éya] | ele | [**éya**] x [éle] elle | [**éye**] *analyzed in Fig. 1* |
| plural (masc.) | ellos [éyos] | eles | [**éyos**] x [éle] elle | [**éye**] *Álvarez Nazario* |
| plural (fem.) | ellas [éyas] | elas | [**éyas**] x [éle] elle | [**éye**] *did not consider* |

Figure 2. *Expanded hypothesis*

(a) Regular loss of word-final -*s* is assumed here. Afro-Lusitanian creoles and Chota Spanish strongly suggest that such a loss did in fact occur. Furthermore, loss of final /-s/ was and continues to be a regular feature of Caribbean Spanish. Also, gender distinctions are assumed to have been eliminated.

pronouns by neutralizing gender and number in consistent fashion. It seems then that, on the one hand, Caribbean Bozales were "willing" to accept Spanish phonetic material (i.e., the [y] glide in *elle*) but resisted adopting the morphologically more complex endings of Span. *ella* (FEM. SG), *ellos* (MASC. PL) and *ellas* (FEM. PL).[37]

### 6.3.4 *Etymology of* nelle

Explanations offered thus far have attempted to elucidate the origin of *elle*, but as yet nothing has been said about the word-initial nasal element of the variant *nelle*. In Spanish, several prepositions including the frequent *en* 'in, at', *con* 'with', and *sin* 'without' feature a word-final -*n*. The frequent juxtaposition of such prepositions with the definite article *el* (e.g., *con EL libro*) or the 3rd-person pronouns *él, ella, ellos, ellas,* coupled with phonotactic and other factors that need not be detailed here, could readily lead to false word divisions. Constructions like *con él, con ellos* and *en ella, en ellas* were, therefore, subject to be reanalyzed as *co nél, co nellos* and *e nella, e nellas,* respectively. Such reanalysis could be facilitated further by the tendency — apparently strong among Afro-Hispanics — to articulate certain Portuguese-derived prepositions without a final nasal (e.g., Boz. *kunelle* 'with him/her' [Lipski 1993a: 14]; Pal. *ku* 'with' < Port. *com o* 'with the' [Schwegler 1993b: 675]).

## 7.   Conclusions

The data examined in this study invite us to accept the following statements about *ele* (Palenque and Chota) and *(n)elle* (Bozal):

(1)   they cannot plausibly be linked to a common Spanish source;

(2)   they are too similar in form and function to be considered spontaneous (i.e., unrelated) innovations;

(3)   they cannot be explained away as foreigner talk (i.e., imperfect acquisition by Bozales of Spanish forms);

(4)   they can be shown to be connected phonetically and functionally to Port. *ele* (sing.) and *eles* (pl.);

(5)   they have a distinctively creole flavor (i.e., they are morphologically simplified, and phonetically and functionally similar to Palenquero and other Afro-Iberian 3rd-person creole pronouns); and

(6)   they are found in geographically non-contiguous Afro-American areas where Portuguese have never settled. (See Map 3.)

If all this is true, then the Afro-Portuguese pidgin or creole hypothesis offers the only logical sociolinguistic explanation for the presence of *ele* and *(n)elle* in Spanish America.

At the outset of this article I argued that the discovery of even a single deep grammatical Afro-Portuguese feature in Caribbean Spanish automatically validates the monogenetic theory. I believe that the pronouns examined here constitute such a feature, and are, therefore, uniquely helpful in proving the genetic relationship between the putative Afro-Portuguese pidgin/creole and the Antillean and Ecuadorian speech varieties in which they are found.

If — and perhaps most importantly — pronouns are indeed "deep features" that are not spread casually, it is safe to infer that *slaves could not have implanted* ele *in Chota, Palenque, Cuba or Puerto Rico without also having a fairly extensive command of other domains of (Afro-) Portuguese grammar and lexicon.* It must be assumed, furthermore, that if Antillean slaves had been acquainted with Afro-Portuguese in a merely superficial way, regionally "strange" forms like *ele* or *elle* would have been leveled rather quickly in favor of their functional Spanish equivalents.

It is, of course, true (as opponents of the monogenetic hypothesis will be quick to point out) that the undifferentiated third person pronouns we examined do not characterize all or even most Latin American Bozal texts, and that their attestation is rather limited in time and space. But while I agree that this limited distribution of Afro-Portuguese-derived pronouns in Latin America does not offer conclusive proof of the claim that a stable Afro-Hispanic creole was established over ALL OF THE CARIBBEAN (including the Dominican Republic, northern Venezuela, and so on), nonetheless their existence does provide indisputable evidence that an Afro-Portuguese contact vernacular was used in the New World. Furthermore, contemporary sociolinguistic evidence from Palenque

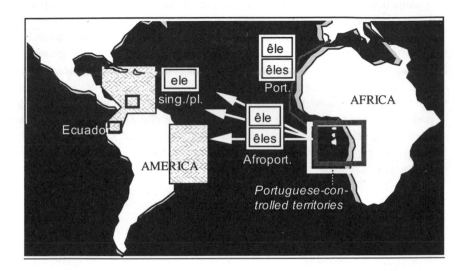

Map 3. *Approximate areas in America where AfroPort.* ele *and* eles *may have been in use by slaves and their descendants (marked by* >>>> *). In the Caribbean, loss of syllable-final [-s] reduced* ele *and* eles *to a single, morphologically non-complex form, i.e.,* ele *'he, she, they' and 'him, her, them').*

and the Chota is unambiguous about the extent to which negative attitudes towards "Black" speech and superstratal pressures from adstratal (standard or regional) Spanish conspire to drive out local speech forms (including *ele*). Since there is good reason to believe that such pressures have likewise been operative in other Afro-Hispanic areas of Latin America, one ought not be surprised at the extremely scant survival of indisputably Afro-Portuguese elements (this sobering point is reinforced by the observation that both Pal. and Chot. *ele* too are likely to become extinct before the middle of the next century).

In making my claims, I have said nothing about the exact nature of the Afro-Portuguese contact vernacular (a pidgin or a well established creole?) that presumably circulated among Afro-Hispanic slaves. This question cannot be answered satisfactorily here since so much remains to be done in terms of additional field work, analysis of Bozal texts, refinement of existing hypotheses, etc. At the same time, the discovery of Portuguese pronouns in four widely separated Afro-Hispanic areas, and, *inter alia*, the existence of a full-fledged Spanish-Caribbean creole (Palenquero) for which an Afro-Portuguese origin can be established incontrovertibly, favor the theory that Caribbean Bozal Spanish was a stable creole with Afro-Lusitanian roots.

The previous observations and data, coupled with other striking creole-like features (e.g., double negation of the type *NO hablo inglés NO*) in the grammars of Palenquero and certain Caribbean Spanish dialects (Schwegler forthcoming a), make it incumbent upon opponents of the Afro-Portuguese hypothesis to account for the established facts. Whatever the eventual conclusion, discussion of the hypothesis should remain in the forefront of Creole and Spanish studies, for an answer to the (similarly disputed) question of the African contribution to the formation of popular Caribbean Spanish crucially depends on the resolution of the monogenetic controversy.[38]

## Notes

1. For additional references to pertinent publications by these and other authors, see Lipski (1993a, 1994), or Schwegler (1996b).

2. On the use of an early Afro-Portuguese pidgin in coastal West Africa, see, for instance, Couto (1993), Goodman (1987), Holm (1989: 259–84), Clements (1992, 1993a) and Perl (1990).

3. Including Alpízar Castillo (1987, 1989), Bachiller y Morales (1883), López Morales (1980, 1992), Martínez Gordo (1982), Valdés Bernal (1978, 1987), and Zamora Vicente (1974 [1960]).

4. For a recent overview and analysis of Caribbean Spanish features traditionally used to bolster the monogenetic hypothesis, see Lipski (1993a: 12–14, 1994: 113–17). It should be pointed out that Lipski does consider at least one Afro-Hispanic element — the preverbal particle *ta* – as potential evidence for an earlier widespread Afro-Hispanic creole language (Lipski 1987c, 1987d, 1993a: 12, 15, 1993b, 1994: 177–22). However, he attempts to trace the source of that verbal construction to the importation of Papiamento-speaking laborers from Curaçao to Puerto Rico and Cuba at the beginning of the nineteenth century. Granda (p.c.), Perl (p.c.) and other proponents of the monogenetic hypothesis (including myself) consider this type of diffusion an unlikely scenario.

5. For a similar position, see Ferraz, who admits that some Afro-Portuguese pidgin-speaking slaves may have come to the Americas, but that "the numbers of such slaves must have been scant" (1987: 339). For an opposite view, see Martinus (1989). Other creolists who reject monogenetic explanations include Laurence (1974), Mintz (1971) and Rickford (1987: 46–50, 53–56).

6. It should be noted here that the monogenetic hypothesis is by no means a unified theory since many differing versions (some stronger than others) have been proposed — often by the same author (e.g. Granda 1978, 1985, 1988, 1991, 1994). The arguments presented in this study, however, are not affected by differences among the various monogenetic theories.

7. Witness, for instance, the recent heated exchanges between Naro (1993) and Clements (1993b).

8. Goodman's seminal 1987 article on the Portuguese element in the American creoles constitutes the only serious attempt to evaluate the Afro-Portuguese controversy from a fully cross-linguistic perspective. This is, however, merely reflective of a wider tendency in creole circles to neglect data from Afro-Hispanic areas (witness, for instance, Mufwene's otherwise excellent

(1993) edition *Africanisms in Afro-American Language Varieties,* where Latin America is ignored altogether).

9. See Schwegler 1991b, 1996 (and recent studies of Palenquero cited therein), and forthcoming a.

10. Examples from Lipski (1994: 116).

11. Examples collected *in situ* by the author.

12. Examples collected *in situ* by the author.

13. I am fully aware of the presence of Portuguese merchants and settlers in Cartagena and other metropolitan areas of Latin America (Schwegler 1996a: 20 *n*15; Böttcher 1995). Starting in 1593, in Cartagena and elsewhere these Portuguese were obliged to pay "composiciones" ('fees') to the King of Spain. Especially with the assault on the city by Drake, the Portuguese merchants were viewed with suspicion (many supposedly collaborated secretly with the English), and the governor of Cartagena apparently intervened on multiple occasions to have them expelled from the region (Borrego Pla 1983: 435–438). For these and other reasons (e.g., the historical antagonism between Portuguese and Spaniards), Portuguese immigrants to Cartagena were likely to veil their origin by adopting Spanish rather than Portuguese as their every-day means of communication.

    It should also be kept in mind that, although relatively important for the early economic development of Latin America, these Luso-Iberian contingents of merchants constituted no more than a small fraction of the total Spanish-speaking population. Hence they could not have introduced deep grammatical features into popular varieties of Caribbean Spanish.

14. See, for instance, Borrego Plá (1983), Del Castillo (1982), King (1939), Rout (1976), Sandoval (1987 [1627]), Sharp (1976), Palacios (1973), and Rawley (1981).

15. As found, for instance, in the *habla culta* of Bogotá, Lima, or Mexico City.

16. For additional examples, see Schwegler (1996a: 282, 392 and *n*279).

17. I am currently preparing a more extensive study of the internal and external language history of Chota Spanish that examines Chota pronouns and substantival pluralization in greater detail.

18. Local Indians were forced to complement the Black labor force, which remained small througout the initial settlement period (1575–1700). The indigenous population apparently resented the new presence of Blacks, which led some Indians to relocate to neighboring towns (Jurado Noboa 1992: 147).

19. Smaller contingents of slaves were also purchased in Portobelo (Panama). Coba (1980: 31) maintains that all Chota slaves were imported directly from Africa and Jamaica, but offers no evidence for his implausible claim.

    The Chota slaves were of varied ethnic and linguistic background. Chota last names like Carabalí, Lucumí, Congo, Anangonó, Chalá, or Minda (Coba 1980: 30–31 and my own field notes) attest to this early mix — a mix which was unlikely to have differed significantly from that of other predominantly Black areas of northern and northwestern South America (e.g., the Cartagena area or the Pacific Lowlands of Colombia and Ecuador). Early as well as subsequent Afro-American communities of the Chota Valley must, therefore, have included sizable numbers of Bozales from the Portuguese-controlled coasts of Central West Africa (Angola, Congo, São Tomé, etc.).

20. Today, as in the past, there is no direct social contact between the Chota Valley and the distant jungles of the Pacific coast, where the vast majority of the Afro-Ecuadorian population resides. This and other considerations suggest that route #2 probably never played a significant role in

the importation of Black slaves to the Andean highland. Thousands of slaves were, however, supplied via the well-known Cartagena-Honda-Popayán-Pasto route, which was also the principal route by which Bozales and Criollos alike were sent to other parts of Western South America (Ecuador, Peru, and so on).

21. The basis of this practice [i.e., the importation of Bozales rather than creoles] was the early Spanish law which was meant to exclude Peninsular slaves from the Indies, who were considered to be mischief-makers.

22. For additional information on the social and economic history of the Chota, see Coronel (1988), Jibaja Rubio (1988), Naranjo (1989), Obando (1986), and Savoia, ed. (1990, 1992). Although focusing on the history of COASTAL Black Ecuador, Jurado Noboa (1990) and Whitten (1974), are also useful sources.

23. With time, members of historically oppressed communities often adopt the negative linguistic attitudes held by outsiders. This is clearly the case in Palenque, for instance, where some residents have become agents of their own oppression. During my multiple stays in Palenque (1985–1995), I was told more than once that "eso [la "lengua"] no vale pa' nada" ('this [our creole language] is good for nothing'). On similar attitudes towards pidgins and creoles elsewhere, see Rickford and Traugott 1985.

24. There is a sharp generational cut-off: those 25 to 30 years of age and younger no longer speak the language (with exceptions, of course). Those below 15 years of age don't speak it at all. In the ten years I have done field work there, the change has been dramatic.

25. The problem with them is that they leave out (almost systematically) certain features, such as double negation. However, they ARE useful in that they do include other features, more or less systematically, and in this respect they are rather reliable, since (1) the features occur in multiple sources, and (2) the features are also attested in current Afro-Spanish or Spanish-based creoles.

26. Pal. *sere* (< Span. *ser* 'to be') and *dioso* (< Span. *Dios* 'God') (Megenney 1986: 118) demonstrate that paragoge is not unusual in Palenquero. Compare Alleyne (1980: 46ff) for parallels in English-based creoles.

27. Despite earlier claims to the contrary, in Palenque, code-mixing (interference) but not code-switching is a relatively rare phenomenon (cp. Schwegler 1996a: 45–46). Put differently, Palenqueros are able to switch constantly between the Spanish and Creole grammars, but keep them virtually free of influence from each other.

28. Care must be taken to distinguish pronominal *ele* from a homophonous exclamatory element whose main function is to signal surprise (in some instances, the stress in exclamatory *ele* is shifted from the initial to the final syllable: [éle] → [elé]; such a shift never occurs in pronominal *ele*). Examples from my corpus include: ¡ELE! ¡ya le mojé! 'GEE! I already got him wet!; ¡ELE! ¿Ele él dónde va dí? 'GEE! Where is he going?'. Jaramillo de Lubensky's *Diccionario de ecuatorianismos en la literatura* (1992: 74) makes clear that the exclamatory usage of *ele* is of Quechua origin, and is used in many parts of Ecuador (surprisingly, Siebenäuger's *Quechuismen im Spanischen Südamerikas* [1993] makes no reference to exclamatory *ele*). Providing the examples given below, my Quechua informant Virginia Tocagón (native of Otavalo) immediately confirmed the Amerindian origin of exclamatory *ele*, but rejected vehemently any such connection between pronominal *ele* and an undetermined Quechua source.

*Quechua examples of exclamatory* **ele**

| Quechua | Spanish translation | English translation |
|---|---|---|
| [elé wási urmarka] | ¡Elé! Se cayó la casa! | Gee! The house has already crumbled! |
| [ele muti̯á čirká'ne] | ¡Ele! Ya le mojé! | Gee! I already got him wet! |

29. A good example of the functional equivalence of *ele* and Spanish *ellos* is found in *la mamá d' ell[os] ... d' ELE con mi mamá eran hermanas,* where hesitation (here indicated by "...") led the speaker to substitute *ellos* with *eli.*

30. In my corpus, this pleonastic *ele* occurs with greater frequency than the strictly pronominal *ele.*

31. Quechua influence can be ruled out a priori for a variety of reasons. Suffice it to say here that (a) outside of the Chota, none of the highland Spanish dialects (many of which are found in bilingual Quechua/Spanish speaking areas) exhibits pronominal *ele,* and (b) phonetically, the Quechua third-person singular pronoun [pái̱] cannot possibly be the etymon of *ele.*

32. Seen in this light, Chota constructions like *deli* 'dale' (field notes) are best analyzed as having originated from *da + eli* lit. 'da (a) él' rather than *da + le.*

33. For an extensive discussion of this terminological ambiguity, see Lipski (1998).

34. Gender distinctions shown in the translations of *(n)elle* 'he, she' are invariably inferred from context.

35. As Lipski (1993a: 15) notes, in a few texts, *nella* is occasionally found alongside *nelle.* An explanation for the origin of the initial [n-] in *nella* and the more common *nelle* is offered in § 6.3.4. below.

36. In Portuguese-controlled African territories, Port. *ele* 'he' **and** *eles* 'they' undoubtedly figured in the contact vernacular Europeans and Africans used to communicate. Brought to the Spanish-speaking Caribbean, *ele* and *eles* converged into a single form due to the regular loss of syllable-final [-s].

37. The history of Boz. *(n)elle* is actually considerably more complex than outlined here. Due to limitations of space, I have, for instance, omitted discussing here that some Peninsular Spanish dialects (e.g., Asturian and Leonese) did indeed feature a 3rd singular pronoun *elle* 'he', a fact that has been overlooked in earlier investigations of Bozal *elle* (for Span. *elle,* see Menéndez Pidal 1958: 252, Rodríguez Castellano 1952: 122, 129–130, Zamora Vicente 1974 [1960]:170, or Holtus, Metzeltin & Schmitt 1995: 564–618, esp. 573). As I will show in a future contribution, language-internal and external considerations do, however, oblige one to reject a "dialectal" explanation of straight linear descent, thus leaving the Afro-Portuguese hypothesis as the only plausible model. In the same future study I intend to present synchronic and diachronic data from Portuguese (e.g., *eis* 'they') that offer additional insights into the origins of the palatal glide in Boz. *elle* [éye] and *nelle* [néye].

38. The most recent assessment of the African impact on Latin American Spanish is Lipski (1994, Chap. 4), which contains extensive references to earlier works on the subject (complemented further by Lipski 1987b, 1988a, and Schwegler 1996b).

# References

Alleyne, Mervyn C. 1980. *Comparative Afro-American: An historical-comparative study of English-based Afro-American dialects of the New World.* Ann Arbor: Karoma.

Alpízar Castillo, Rodolfo. 1987. Un curioso documento lingüístico del siglo XVIII cubano. *Anuario de L/L* 18: 3–17.

———. 1989. *Apuntes para la historia de la lingüística en Cuba.* Havana: Editorial de Ciencias Sociales.

Álvarez Nazario, Manuel. 1974 (1961). *El elemento afronegroide en el español de Puerto Rico*. San Juan: Instituto de Cultura Puertorriqueña.

Arlotto, Anthony. 1972. *Introduction to historical linguistics*. Lanham, MD: University Press of America.

Bachiller y Morales, Antonio. 1883. Desfiguración a que está expuesto el idioma castellano al contacto y mezcla de razas. *Revista de Cuba* 14: 97–104.

Bartens, Angela. 1995. *Die iberoromanischen Kreolsprachen*. Frankfurt am Main: Peter Lang.

Borrego Plá, Carmen. 1983. *Cartagena de Indias en el siglo XVI*. Sevilla: Escuela de Estudios Hispano-Americanos de Sevilla.

Böttcher, Nikolaus. 1995. *Aufstieg und Fall eines atlantischen Handelsimperiums. Portugiesische Kaufleute und Sklavenhändler in Cartagena de Indias von 1580 bis zur Mitte des 17. Jahrhunderts*. Frankfurt: Vervuert Verlag.

Byrne, Frank & John Holm, eds. 1993. *Atlantic meets Pacific: A global view of pidginization and creolization*. Amsterdam: John Benjamins.

Clements, J. Clancy. 1992. Foreigner talk and the origins of Pidgin Portuguese. *Journal of Pidgin and Creole Languages* 7: 75–92.

————. 1993a. A contribution by an old creole to the origins of pidgin Portuguese. In Byrne & Holm, eds., 1993: 145–61.

————. 1993b. Rejoinder to Naro's Arguing about Arguin. *Journal of Pidgin and Creole Languages* 8: 119–24.

Coba Andrade, Carlos Alberto G. 1980. *Literatura popular afroecuatoriana*. Otavalo: Editorial Gallocapitán.

Coronel, Rosario. 1988. Indios y esclavos negros en el valle del Chota colonial. In Savoia, ed., 1988: 171–87.

Couto, Hildo Honório Do. 1993. The genesis of Portuguese Creole in Africa. In Byrne & Holm, eds. 1993: 381–89.

Del Castillo, Nicolás. 1982. *Esclavos negros en Cartagena y sus aportes léxicos*. Bogotá: Instituto Caro y Cuervo.

Ferraz, Luiz Ivens. 1987. Portuguese in the New World, West Africa, and Asia. In Gilbert, ed., 337-60.

Friedemann, Nina S. De & Carlos Patiño Rosselli. 1983. *Lengua y sociedad en el Palenque de San Basilio*. Bogotá: Instituto Caro y Cuervo.

Gilbert, Glenn, ed. 1987. *Pidgin and creole languages. Essays in memory of John E. Reinecke*. Honolulu: University of Hawaii Press.

Goodman, Morris. 1987. The Portuguese element in the American creoles. In Gilbert, ed., 361–405.

Granda, Germán De. 1978. *Estudios lingüísticos hispánicos, afrohispánicos y criollos*. Madrid: Gredos.

————. 1985. *Estudios de lingüística afro-románica*. Valladolid: Universidad de Valladolid.

————. 1988. *Lingüística e historia*. Valladolid: Universidad de Vaylladolid.

————. 1991. *El español en tres mundos. Retenciones y contactos lingüísticos en América y África.* Valladolid: Universidad de Valladolid.

————. 1994. *Español de América, español de África y hablas criollas hispánicas. Cambios, contactos y contextos.* Madrid: Editorial Gredos.

Holm, John. 1989. *Pidgins and creoles: Volume 2. Reference survey.* New York: Cambridge University Press.

Holtus, Günter, Michael Metzeltin & Christian Schmitt, eds. 1995. *Lexikon der Romanistischen Linguistik. Vol. II, 2: Die einzelnen romanischen Sprachen und Sprachgebiete vom Mittelalter bis zur Renaissance.* Tübingen: Niemeyer.

Jaramillo De Lubensky, María. 1992. *Diccionario de ecuatorianismos en la literatura.* Quito: Casa de la Cultura Ecuatoriana.

Jibaja Rubio, Leopoldo. 1988. Casos de compra y venta de esclavos en la Sierra ecuatoriana (1778–1838). In Savoia, ed. 1988: 189–92.

Jurado Noboa, Fernando. 1990. *Esclavitud en la Costa Pacífica. Iscandé, Tumaco, Barbacoas y Esmeraldas. Siglos XVI al XIX.* Quito: Ediciones ABYA-YALA.

————. 1992. Una visión global sobre el Chota. In Savoia, ed., 1992: 145–54.

King, James F. 1939. Negro slavery in the Viceroyalty of New Granada. Dissertation, University of California, Berkeley.

Laurence, Kemlin. 1974. Is Caribbean Spanish a case of decreolization? *Orbis* 23: 484–99.

Lipski, John M. 1982. El Valle del Chota: enclave lingüístico afroecuatoriano. *Boletín de la Academia Puertorriqueña de la Lengua Española* 10: 21–36.

————. 1986. Sobre lingüística afroecuatoriana: El Valle del Chota. *Anuario de Lingüística Hispánica* 2: 153–76.

————. 1987a. The Chota valley: Afro-Hispanic language in Highland Ecuador. *Latin American Review* 22: 155–70.

————. 1987b. African influence on Hispanic dialects. In *Current trends and issues in Hispanic linguistics,* ed. L. Studerus, 33–68. Arlington: Summer Institute of Linguistics.

————. 1987c. The construction _ta_+ infinitive in Caribbean Bozal Spanish. *Romance Philology* 40: 431–50.

————. 1987d. Sobre la construcción *ta* + infinitivo en el español 'bozal'. *Lingüística Española Actual* 8 (1986): 73–92.

————. 1988a. Contactos hispano-africanos en África y el Caribe. In *Studies in Caribbean Spanish dialectology,* ed. R. Hammond & M. Resnick, 50–65. Washington: Georgetown University Press.

————. 1988b. Reduction of /s/ in Spanish: The Afro-Hispanic connection. In *On Spanish, Portuguese and Catalan linguistics,* ed. John J. Staczek, 4–16. Washington: Georgetown University Press.

————. 1993a. *On the non-creole basis for Afro-Caribbean Spanish.* Research Paper Series no. 24 (Feb. 1993). Albuquerque, NM: University of New Mexico.

————. 1993b. Origin and development of *ta* in Afro-Hispanic creoles. In Byrne & Holm, eds. 1993: 217–31.

————. 1994. *Latin American Spanish*. New York: Longman.

————. 1998. Perspectivas sobre el español Bozal. In Perl & Schwegler, eds., 1998: 293–327.

López Morales, Humberto. 1980. Sobre la pretendida existencia y pervivencia del criollo en Cuba. *Anuario de Letras* 18: 85–116.

————. 1992. *El español del Caribe*. Madrid: Editorial Mapfre.

Martínez Gordo, Isabel. 1982. Lengua 'bozal' como lengua criolla: un problema lingüístico. *Santiago* 46: 47–53.

Martinus, Frank. 1989. West African connection: the influence of the Afro-Portuguese on the Papiamentu of Curaçao. In *Estudios sobre español de América y lingüística afroamericana*, (no editor), 289–99. Bogotá: Insituto Caro y Cuervo.

Megenney, William W. 1983. La influencia del portugués en el palenquero colombiano. *Thesaurus* 28: 548–63.

————. 1984. Traces of Portuguese in three Caribbean creoles: evidence in support of the monogenetic theory. *Hispanic Linguistics* 1: 177–89.

————. 1986. *El palenquero. Un lenguaje post-criollo de Colombia*. Bogotá: Instituto Caro y Cuervo.

————. 1993. Elementos criollo-portugueses en el español dominicano. *Montalbán* 25: 149–71.

Menéndez Pidal, Ramón. 1958. *Manual de gramática histórica española₆*. Madrid: Espasa-Calpe S. A.

Mintz, Sidney W. 1971. The socio-historical background to pidginization and creolization. In *Pidginization and creolization of languages,* ed. Dell H. Hymes, 481–88. Cambridge: Cambridge University Press.

Mufwene, Salikoko S., ed. 1993. *Africanisms in Afro-American language varieties*. Athens: University of Georgia Press.

Naranjo, Marcelo V., ed. 1989. *La cultura popular en el Ecuador (tomo 5: Imbabura)*. Quito: Centro Interamericano de artesanías y artes populares.

Naro, Anthony. 1993. Arguing about Arguin. *Journal of Pidgin and Creole Languages* 8: 109–18.

Obando, Segundo. 1986. *Tradiciones del Chota*. Quito: Ediciones ABYA-YALA.

Otheguy, Ricardo. 1973. The Spanish Caribbean: A creole perspective. In *New ways of analyzing variation in English,* ed. Charles-James N. Bailey & Roger W. Shuy, 323–39. Washington: Georgetown University Press.

Palacios Preciado, Jorge. 1973. *La trata de negros por Cartagena de Indias (1650–1750)*. Tunja: Universidad pedagógica y tecnológica.

Perl, Matthias. 1989. Zur Präsenz des kreolisierten Portugiesisch in der Karibik — Ein Beitrag zur Dialektologie des karibischen Spanisch. *Beiträge zur romanischen Philologie* 28: 131–48.

————. 1990. A reevaluation of the importance of early pidgin/creole Portuguese. *Journal of Pidgin and Creole Languages* 5: 125–30.

Perl, Matthias & Armin Schwegler, eds. 1998. *América negra: panorámica actual de los estudios lingüísticos sobre variedades hispanas, portuguesas y criollas* Frankfurt: Vervuert.

Rawley, James A. 1981. *The transatlantic slave trade*. New York: W. W. Norton.

Rickford, John R. 1987. *Dimensions of a creole continuum: History, texts, and linguistic analysis of Guyanese Creole*. Stanford, CA: Stanford University Press.

Rickford, John R. & Elizabeth Closs Traugott. 1985. Symbol of powerlessness and degeneracy, or symbol of solidarity and truth? Paradoxical attitudes towards pidgins and creoles. In *The English language today*, ed. S. Greenbaum, 252–61. Oxford: Pergamon.

Rodríguez-Castellano, Lorenzo. 1952. El pronombre personal en el asturiano. *Boletín del Instituto de Estudios Asturianos* 15: 119–30.

Rout, Leslie B. 1976. *The African experience in Spanish America*. New York: Cambridge University Press.

Sandoval, Alonso De. 1987 (1627). *De instauranda aethiopum salute. Un tratado sobre la esclavitud*. Introduction and translation by Enriqueta Vila Vilar. Madrid: Alianza Editorial.

Savoia, Rafael, ed. 1988. *Actas del primer Congreso de Historia del Negro en el Ecuador y Sur de Colombia (1988)*. Quito: Centro Cultural Afro-Ecuatoriano.

————. 1990. *El negro en la historia. Aportes para el conocimiento de las raíces en América Latina*. Quito: Centro Cultural Afro-Ecuatoriano.

————. 1992. *El negro en la historia. Raíces africanas en la nacionalidad ecuatoriana*. Quito: Centro Cultural Afro-Ecuatoriano.

Schwegler, Armin. 1991a. Zur Problematik der afroportugiesischen Kontaktsprache in Amerika: Neues aus El Palenque de San Basilio (Kolumbien). *Lusorama* 15: 54–79.

————. 1991b. El habla cotidiana del Chocó (Colombia). *América Negra* 2: 85–119.

————. 1993a. Subject pronouns and person/number in Palenquero. In Byrne & Holm, eds. 1993: 145–61. Amsterdam: John Benjamins.

————. 1993b. Rasgos (afro-)portugueses en el criollo del Palenque de San Basilio (Colombia). In *Homenaje a José Pérez Vidal,* ed. Díaz Alayón, 667–96. La Laguna, Tenerife: Litografía A. Romero S. A.

————. 1996a. *Chi ma nkongo: lengua y rito ancestrales en El Palenque de San Basilio (Colombia).* 2 vols. Frankfurt: Editorial Vervuert.

————. 1996b. Lenguas criollas en Hispanoamérica y la contribución africana al español de América. *Contactos y transferencias lingüísticas en Hispanoamérica.* In *Signo y Seña* 6: 295–346. Instituto de Lingüística, Universidad de Buenos Aires).

————. 1998. Palenquero. In Perl & Schwegler, eds., 1998: 218–291.

————. Forthcoming. La doble negación dominicana y la génesis del español caribeño. *Lingüística* 3. [Also in *Hispanic Linguistics* 8: 246–315 (1996)].

Sharp, William Frederick. 1976. *Slavery on the Spanish frontier: the Colombian Chocó, 1680–1810.* Norman: University of Oklahoma Press.

Siebenäuger, Gerhard Philip. 1993. *Quechuismen im Spanischen Südamerikas.* 1993. Bern: Peter Lang.

Valdés Bernal, Sergio. 1978. Las lenguas africanas y el español coloquial de Cuba. *Santiago* 31: 81–107.

————. 1987. *Las lenguas del África subsaharana y el español de Cuba.* La Habana: Editorial Academia.

Whitten, Norman E. Jr. 1974. *Black frontiersmen: A South American case.* Cambridge, MA: Schenkman Publishing Company.

Zamora Vicente, Alonso. 1974 [1960]. *Dialectología española.* Madrid: Gredos.

# PART C

## Attitudes and Education in Creole Communities

# Changing Attitudes towards
# Australian Creoles and Aboriginal English

Diana Eades
*University of Hawai'i at Mānoa*

Jeff Siegel
*University of New England, Armidale*

## 1. Introduction

One of Charlene ('Charlie') Sato's important contributions to linguistics has been her work on creoles and nonstandard dialects of English, focussing in particular on Hawai'i Creole English (Sato 1985, 1989, 1991). She promoted greater acceptance of these 'minority varieties' by showing how misconceptions about them and misunderstanding of them have led to their speakers' disadvantage, particularly in education.

Like speakers of Hawai'i Creole English, speakers of Australian creoles and Aboriginal English are similarly disadvantaged, due to negative attitudes. There are two creole languages in Australia, both lexified by English. Kriol is the name given to the creole spoken by Aboriginal people in the Northern Territory and the northern part of the state of Western Australia. It is the fastest growing indigenous language in Australia. Torres Strait Creole (TSC), also known as 'Broken', is a distinct creole language, spoken mainly in the Torres Strait Islands and the northern tip of Cape York Peninsula in the state of Queensland.

Aboriginal English (AE) refers to the varieties of English spoken by Aboriginal people which differ from Standard Australian English (SAE) in systematic ways. There is considerable variation in the AE spoken throughout the country, ranging from the so-called 'heavy' varieties which are closest to Kriol, to the 'light' varieties which are closest to SAE (see Sandefur 1991; Shnukal 1991; Malcolm and Kaldor 1991 for a brief introduction to these varieties and further references).

During her brief time in Australia, Charlie took an active interest in these minority varieties and the rights of their speakers. For example, at the Australian Linguistic Institute in 1994, she was co-organizer of a well attended workshop on pidgins, creoles and nonstandard varieties in education. In this paper in her honor, we felt it would be appropriate to describe briefly some of the recent developments which give cause for optimism in showing greater awareness and acceptance of these varieties in Australia. After looking at some current speaker attitudes to the creoles and AE, we'll talk about some of the developments in education and the legal system which we think are evidence of changing attitudes to these varieties in Australian society more generally (see Romaine, this volume, for evidence of changing attitudes to Hawai'i Creole English).

## 2.    Attitudes of speakers

The long history of the denigration of AE and creoles in Australia has always had some impact on the complex way in which speakers themselves view their own language. As described in other countries (see e.g. Rickford and Traugott 1985: 252 and also Reynolds, this volume and Romaine, this volume), there is a "paradoxical combination of negative and positive attitudes". Some speakers of a creole or AE still feel that they are speaking "bad English" while others are proud of their own distinctive ways of talking. For example, in a small scale survey of attitudes to Kriol in the Halls Creek area of Western Australia, one speaker called Kriol "lazy English" while another said it is "an Aboriginal language" (Sefton 1994).

On the other hand, many indigenous people combine both a pride in their own distinctive ways of speaking with a fear that recognition of AE or Kriol or TSC, in the school system particularly, may lead to their children being denied the opportunity to learn the language of power, namely SAE. With regard to education, for example, half of the speakers Sefton (1994) surveyed in the Halls Creek study thought that children should speak and read and write in Kriol at school, while the other half were strongly opposed to this (see Romaine, this volume, for similar ambivalence about the role of Hawai'i Creole English in the classroom).

In the Torres Strait, Shnukal (1992: 4) noted that people are "reluctant to accept the use of creole as a formal medium of instruction in their schools, seeing it as a method of depriving them of instruction in the kind of English that white people use, and thus condemning them to permanent underclass status". However, in an earlier paper Shnukal (1983: 32) had shown how attitudes of speakers towards TSC "are constantly being renegotiated on an individual as well as societal level". A new direction began early in 1995 when community meetings at Bamaga on Cape York Peninsula decided to support a proposal for a Home Language Program involving preschool and first year pupils whose home language is the local variety of TSC. After further consultation, and assurances that the majority of parents were in favor, this program commenced in mid-1995 at the Injinoo Campus of the Bamaga State School.

To start off the program, children's own stories in Creole were recorded, written down and used as the basis for teaching initial literacy. English translations were also used, where appropriate, to teach English literacy. It was the community's idea to have, as they put it, "the two languages walking together": that is, to have children learn literacy in both Creole and English, and also the appropriate contexts for each. The initial report from the teacher indicated that the children's increased self-esteem led to "a very confident and positive attitude to reading in Creole", which carried over to English (PACE 1995: 15).

This and other positive developments come at a time when more indigenous people than ever before, including a large proportion of speakers of AE, Kriol and TSC, are undertaking teacher training, and are participating in national and state education, government and policy decision making. Through such participation, these people are publicly acknowledging the validity of their ways of speaking in forums where they cannot be ignored by policy makers. For example, Aboriginal students undertaking teacher training through the Australian Catholic University have on several occasions raised the issue of the validity of their AE as a dialect of English, and have provided the catalyst for the education of academic staff on this issue.

Hitchen's (1992: 68) study of perceptions of AE among a small group of Aboriginal teacher trainees in Moree in New South Wales found that most of them "reported a pride in having a distinctive dialect and/or feeling comfortable speaking a distinct dialect at home". However, a number also reported that they felt self conscious or embarrassed hearing or using AE when communicating with certain non-Aboriginal people. One of these teachers also pointed out that AE is serving an increasingly important role as an identity marker among Aboriginal people who do not speak a traditional language or creole and often find it impossible to tell from physical characteristics whether new people they meet, for example, at a conference or sports event, are Aboriginal.

For less traditionally-oriented Aboriginal people, such as these trainee teachers, AE is often regarded as a tangible aspect of their distinctive Aboriginality. For example, Daphne Wallace, a young tertiary-educated Aboriginal woman from western New South Wales and the first Curator of Aboriginal Art at the Art Gallery of New South Wales, told a journalist that this is how she reacts to people who comment on her Aboriginal English 'accent': "I just say: 'Look that's my accent and it's all I've got left of my culture. I'm not going to lose it for anyone. If I change the way I speak, what's the good of me doing what I'm doing?'" (*Sydney Morning Herald* April 15, 1994).

Since the initial formulation of Australia's language policy (Lo Bianco 1987), the Australian government has committed funds to the maintenance of indigenous languages. Discussions at all levels continually include the role of AE and the creole languages in the demise of the 'traditional' languages on the one hand, and in the Aboriginal or Torres Strait Islander identity of their speakers on the other. The Aboriginal and Torres Strait Islander Languages Initiatives Program and its precursor, the National Aboriginal Languages Program, have enabled the establishment of over twenty regional Aboriginal language centers and committees run by local Aboriginal people.

While the major work of these language centers and committees is on the maintenance of 'traditional' languages, the Katherine Regional Aboriginal Language Centre (KRALC) in the Northern Territory has led the way in the recognition of Kriol as a valid language. This centre has now included Kriol in its languages 'brief' as the result of a vote at its 1993 Annual General Meeting. According to Denise Angelo (personal communication):

> It was agreed that Kriol is an Aboriginal language (i.e. its speakers are Aboriginal); that virtually no services are easily accessible to Kriol speakers (education, law, health, social security, etc); and that KRALC move to secure recognition of Kriol and services for Kriol speakers (ie interpreting).

Some of the positive outcomes which have resulted from this decision will be seen below.

Every year the 'Aboriginal Languages Fortnight' is an important part of the course of studies for some of the Aboriginal and Torres Strait Islander students at Batchelor College in the Northern Territory. During this time students do work on a language of their choice, usually their own traditional languages. In 1995, for the first time, nine urban students from the town of Katherine who speak English as their mother tongue decided to focus on Kriol for their language studies. This is a significant change, as attitudes of Aboriginal speakers of English towards Kriol have typically been quite negative. No doubt this decision to include Kriol in the 'Aboriginal Languages Fortnight' was influenced by the incorporation of Kriol as one of the languages being 'taken care of' by the KRALC.

## 3.     Attitudes of non-speakers

Recognition of the need to address language and communication issues affecting speakers of AE and the creole languages is developing along with the greater public voice of their speakers. Given the demographic and political minority position of indigenous people in Australia, it is arguably not their own attitudes to these stigmatized language varieties, but those of non-indigenous Australians which will have the greatest impact. The areas in which we see the most positive developments are education and the law, and we will highlight some of these positive developments in the rest of this paper.

## 3.1 *Education*

We will report separately on four kinds of developments in education: special materials and training for teachers, training for people who work with speakers of AE, educational materials for all Australian school students and training of interpreters.

### 3.1.1 *Materials and training for teachers*

Sato (1989: 264) called for inservice training for teachers to promote 'additive bidialectalism' in the classroom- in other words, teaching the language of power without repressing the students' minority varieties. This call is reiterated by Hawai'i teacher, Susan Reynolds, in her contribution to this volume. In Australia, the most comprehensive initiative in this area has been the 1994 publication and widespread use of the FELIKS kit: *Fostering English language in Kimberley schools: Professional development course for primary schools*. Developed by the 'Language Team' of the Catholic Education Office in the Kimberley Region of Western Australia, the FELIKS kit is designed for running in-service courses to train teachers about Kriol and AE so that they can effectively teach SAE to speakers of these varieties. The kit contains all the material needed for the two-day (seven session) in-servicing of teachers: a manual for presenters, audio and video tapes, masters for overhead transparencies, participants' booklets and games handouts.

FELIKS starts by showing participants that Kriol is a valid language and AE is a valid dialect of English; they are not just 'poor English'. Later, it illustrates some of the systematic semantic, phonological and grammatical differences between each of these varieties and SAE, and of the potential for miscommunication when these differences are not understood. Participants also learn some basic sociolinguistic terms such as *pidgin, creole* and *speech continuum*. But more significantly, the course emphasizes the importance of students having control of both SAE and Kriol/AE. Teachers come to understand that each of these varieties can be used appropriately in different contexts, and that children need to be able to switch between them if they want to participate in both Aboriginal and non-Aboriginal Australian society.

Interest in the FELIKS program has been strong among both Catholic and Government schools in the Kimberley. It has also been adapted to the local situation in Barunga in the Northern Territory, where there has been a Kriol-English bilingual program since 1977 (see Siegel 1993). To develop teachers' understanding of issues raised in the FELIKS program and to support them in the use of suitable classroom activities, the FELIKS team has begun to produce a newsletter, *FELIKSnews*. It contains reports and stories from teachers, games and other ideas for classroom activities, and other useful information for teachers of Kriol-speaking students.

Education departments in a number of states are developing materials for teachers of AE speaking children. It is noteworthy that many of these were initially inspired by specially funded projects during the International Year of Literacy (1990). For example, in September 1995 the New South Wales Board of Studies published an Aboriginal Literacy Resource Kit which originated initially from action research undertaken by teachers in a number of inner city schools on AE in their classrooms.

This kit includes a 48-page book titled *Aboriginal English* which explains to teachers issues such as the origins of AE, the role of AE in Aboriginal identity, and features of the grammar, phonology and vocabulary of AE in New South Wales, as well as important aspects of Aboriginal communicative style, such as the use of silence, particularly as they effect classroom interaction. An important part of the preparation of this book was the input from Aboriginal teachers and education department officials, all speakers of AE, as well as the circulation of a nearfinal draft to all regional Aboriginal Education Consultative Groups in the state.

In the state of South Australia the ELA (English Language Acquisition for Aboriginal Students) program began in 1991. Like FELIKS, this program informs teachers about the nature of AE and its differences from SAE. The program is now widely used in Aboriginal schools in South Australia and is spreading into other schools.

As part of the public awareness campaign component of the Australian Language and Literacy Policy, the federal Department of Employment, Education and Training (DEET) produced a 32 page color booklet in 1994 titled *Langwij comes to school: Promoting literacy among speakers of Aboriginal English and Australian Creoles*. The main purpose of this booklet is (1994: 4):

> to help teachers to assist young Aboriginal and Torres Strait Islander students achieve proficiency in Standard Australian English (SAE) through a better understanding of the diversity and validity of the language backgrounds of these students.

The booklet defines terms such as *pidgin, creole* and *dialect*, provides some information about origins of AE and Australian creoles, and describes some linguistic features of AE. A number of current school programs are featured in the booklet, including the FELIKS course, the Kriol-English bilingual program at Barunga in the Northern Territory, the ELA program in South Australia, and the acceptance of AE in a New South Wales community school at Toomelah. The appearance of *Langwij comes to school* was widely reported in the media, sparking a great deal of interest. There were both positive and negative responses from the public to the statement from the Federal Minister for Schools, Education and Training, who said at the launch of the booklet that AE and indigenous creoles should be recognized as legitimate forms of expression, so that teachers can use methods which "encourage self-esteem and lead to higher levels of achievement overall, especially in English literacy". In some cases, however, media reports were inaccurate, for example, one carrying the headline "Schools to use Aboriginal English", or made serious mistakes, for example, one saying that Aboriginal children in Brisbane speak Kriol. The booklet itself has been criticized by some teachers and linguists for not being clear enough in distinguishing varieties of AE and creoles.

As more people develop an understanding about AE, there is finally a recognition that it is a part of Australia's language situation which should be understood by all teachers, not just those who teach Aboriginal students. In the Year of Indigenous People, the national Primary English Teachers Association (PETA) commissioned a pamphlet in their PEN (*Primary English Notes*) Series on Aboriginal English.

### 3.1.2 *Training for people who work with speakers of AE*

In recent years many professions, government departments and other organizations have become more aware of communication difficulties their employees have with their Aboriginal co-workers or clients, even when all parties speak English. In order to try to overcome these difficulties, and more adequately address access and equity goals in relation to Aboriginal people, workshops have been organized with the goal of facilitating more effective communication. Participants in these workshops range from those who are keen to develop more effective cross-cultural communication to those whose employer has told them to attend. Using a non-threatening interactive approach which focuses on recognizing language and cultural differences, these workshops introduce all participants to some basic understandings about AE, and ways in which it is different from other varieties of English in Australia. The workshops have been run in several states and participants have included teachers, lawyers, youth workers, social workers, council workers, prison warders, volunteer church workers, field officers with courtordered community service programs, National Parks officers, domestic violence workers, trainer of police, doctors, a magistrate, museum workers, disability services employees, and public servants working in a wide range of areas, including health, welfare, housing, employment, disability, corrective services, community services.The fact that follow-up workshops are frequently requested is one indication that there is a greater acceptance of the need for awareness about AE in a wide range of Australian work places.

### 3.1.3 *Educational materials for all Australian school students*

The Australian Indigenous Languages Framework is a national curriculum project, under the direction of the Senior Secondary Assessment Board of South Australia, which is devising a new Year 11-12 subject on Aboriginal languages. In 1996 the subject was trial-tested in a small number of schools, and in 1995 in the state of Victoria it was a final year subject with the name 'Australian Indigenous Languages'. The subject is designed so that the first half teaches students about the indigenous languages of Australia and the second half requires them to do an indepth study of a particular language. The textbook for the first half of this subject, which is currently near completion, has one of its 12 chapters on 'Aboriginal English and Australian creoles'. It describes the nature of AE, Kriol and TSC using conversational examples. It also describes the origins of creole languages in general and of Kriol and TSC in particular. Some other creoles around the world are mentioned, and attitudes towards creoles are discussed.

### 3.1.4 *Training of interpreters*

Courses in Kriol interpreting have been run for two years now at three places in the Kimberley region of Western Australia and last year at the Katherine Regional Aboriginal Language Centre (KRALC) in the Northern Territory. Several Aboriginal students have already been accredited at the para professional level by NAATI (National Association for Accreditation of Translators and Interpreters). These courses are partially funded by the federal department of Employment, Education and Training and the Attorney General's department.

For both courses, special teaching materials have been developed. In the case of Western Australia, the materials are written in English for teaching interpreting in Kriol and other Aboriginal languages as well. In the KRALC course, the materials have been developed in Kriol, with the emphasis on Kriol-English interpreting in legal and medical contexts, and perhaps in other areas, such as land claims. Trainees in the KRALC course have been involved in work experience such as travelling with a speech therapist on community visits and working in the Supreme Court in Darwin. The speech therapist has also been successful in getting funds from the Northern Territory Health Department for a parttime Kriol interpreter to assist with diagnoses.

In the lead up to the interpreting course, KRALC received a grant from the Department of Primary Industry's Rural Access Program for a project to produce illustrative word lists to help in interpreting. Six booklets were to be printed on the following topics: personal finance, health, law, education, social security and Aboriginal organizations.

## 3.2 Legal contexts

The serious over-representation of Aboriginal people in the criminal justice system has been the focus of much public attention, especially since the Royal Commission into Aboriginal Deaths in Custody (1991) found that an Aboriginal person is more than twenty times more likely than a non-Aboriginal person to be taken into custody, and fifteen times more likely to be imprisoned.

Much of an individual's treatment by the justice system depends on language use, and a large proportion of indigenous people use a variety of AE or Kriol or TSC. Linguists are becoming increasingly involved in informing the justice system on issues involving these language varieties. This has occurred in relation to the two following concerns:

–   miscommunication involving speakers of AE and the creoles in all stages of the legal process — police interviews, interviews with lawyers, and giving evidence in court; and
–   the lack of recognition of these language varieties and the differences between them and SAE, and the effect of this on the way in which expert linguistic evidence about these minority language varieties is treated by the legal system.

This latter area was one in which Charlene Sato (1991) was involved when she presented evidence about Hawai'i Creole English (HCE) to the legal system in Hawai'i. In doing so she focused the spotlight on how HCE was 'on trial'. In Australia AE has been 'on trial' since the Stuart case in 1959 when expert linguistic evidence about AE was first given. In this case, and in the Condren case in 1987, AE was not recognized by the law (Eades 1995a).

Judicial attitudes in the Condren case precipitated the writing of a handbook for lawyers which was funded and published by the Queensland Law Society (Eades 1992). Titled *Aboriginal English and the Law*, this handbook is also used in other parts of the country in a number of other contexts. In explaining the origins and features of AE specifically in terms of how it is used and misunderstood in the legal system, the handbook addresses both of the main concerns outlined above. Following from this publication, workshops and public lectures on the topic of Aboriginal English and the law have been requested by a number of legal organizations, including the 1993 annual conference of the judges of the Supreme Court of NSW.

In November 1993, the Appeal Court of Queensland in Brisbane accepted linguistic evidence about the communicative style of a speaker of 'light' AE in the much publicized appeal of an Aboriginal woman, Robyn Kina. As a result of this appeal, Kina, who was serving a life sentence for murder, had her conviction quashed and was released from jail. The sociolinguistic evidence showed how Kina's lawyers, who were not aware of AE communication patterns, lacked sufficient cross-cultural communication ability to find out her story and to represent her adequately at her trial. As a result, the jury had convicted her in the absence of important evidence which should have been used in her defence (see Eades, 1996).

It appears that the Appeal Court's decision in this case had quite an impact on the recognition of AE on one level, as seen in a strong statement made by the state Attorney-General on a television current affairs show on the day following the decision. Talking about the need for the legal system to 'find ways to make special provisions frequently for Aboriginal witnesses', the Attorney-General said that 'the problem of cross-cultural communication is one which the legal system needs to have knowledge of and needs to be sensitive to' (*7.30 Report* 30 November 1993).

Yet the optimism following the Kina case was short-lived. In another case, less than 18 months later, a Brisbane court ignored some of the very features of AE communicative style which had been crucial to Kina's appeal. In the so-called Pinkenba case, three Aboriginal boys, who, like Kina, were speakers of 'light' AE, were prosecution witnesses in a committal hearing against the six police officers who had allegedly abducted them. The way in which the boys were cross-examined ignored important differences between AE and mainstream SAE ways of finding out information and of interpreting both silence and the avoidance of eye contact. Linguistic expert evidence on these issues was called but then overruled, so that the magistrate was not informed about the important details of the use of AE in interviews, which were crucial to the accurate interpretation of the boys' answers to questions in their cross-examination. In the absence of this knowledge of AE, the magistrate made strong negative conclusions about the reliability of the boys' evidence. As a result the trial of the police officers could not proceed (see Eades 1995b).

In response to the public outcry over the Pinkenba case, the Criminal Justice Commission has instituted a research project into 'Aboriginal Witnesses' addressing the issue of 'problems in the way Queensland's criminal courts deal with the evidence of Aboriginal witnesses ... in particular ...any cultural or linguistic factors which affect Aboriginal English speakers as witnesses'.

The use of linguistic expertise in cases involving Kriol and TSC speakers has begun to impact on the legal system in several ways in 1995. Firstly, the new interpreter training program in Kriol in Katherine (discussed above) has wasted no time in practical legal applications. On several occasions interpreters have been used to assist Kriol speakers in relation to their matters in the Magistrate's Court and the Family Court. In addition, interpreting students have been called on to assist lawyers in their interviews with accused people before court appearances.

In the Katherine Magistrate's court in August 1995 a KRALC linguist gave evidence that an Aboriginal defendant who broke a good behavior bond, could not have fully understood the bond conditions explained to him and found in the written bond document. As a result of this evidence, the breach of bond charge was dropped. This appears to be the first time in the Northern Territory that a successful defence has been based on expert linguistic evidence arguing that a defendant could not fully understand English (*Katherine Times* 23 August 1995).

In another precedent-making case, expert linguistic evidence was presented in May 1995 in the Supreme Court in Cairns in defence of a TSC speaker charged with attempted murder. The evidence, which was accepted by the court, was an analysis of the accused's understanding of the police interview. It was concluded that the accused did not have sufficient knowledge of English to deal with the complexities of the questions in the interview. The charge was reduced from attempted murder to unlawful wounding (PACE 1995: 15).

## 4.    Conclusion

Like many people who read Charlene Sato's work, studied or worked with her, listened to her talks, or had the opportunity to get to know her, we have been influenced by her strong commitment to addressing the issue of linguistic inequality. In the continuing work of changing attitudes to AE and creole languages in Australia, it is encouraging to see so many positive signs, only some of which have been reported in this paper. Yet much remains to be done.

## References

Eades, Diana. 1992. *Aboriginal English and the Law: Communicating with Aboriginal English Speaking Clients: A Handbook for Legal Practitioners*. Brisbane: Queensland Law Society.

———. 1995a. "Aboriginal English on trial: The case for Stuart and Condren." In Diana Eades (ed.), *Language in Evidence: Issues Confronting Aboriginal and Multicultural Australia*. Sydney: University of New South Wales Press, 147–74.

———. 1995b. "The crossexamination of Aboriginal children in the Pinkenba case." *Aboriginal Law Bulletin* 3(75):10–11.

———. 1996. "Legal recognition of cultural differences in communication: The case of Robyn Kina." *Language and Communication* 16 (3):215–227.

Hitchen, Moy. 1992. *Talkin Up: Aboriginal English in Moree*. Unpublished M.Litt. dissertation, Department of Linguistics, University of New England.

Lo Bianco, Joseph. 1987. *National Policy on Languages*. Canberra: Australian Government Publishing Service.

Malcolm, Ian, and Susan Kaldor. 1991. "Aboriginal English — An overview." In Romaine (ed.), 67–83.

PACE. 1995. *Pidgins and Creoles in Education (PACE) Newsletter* 6. Armidale, NSW: Department of Linguistics, University of New England.

Rickford, John R. and Elizabeth C. Traugott. 1985. "Symbol of powerlessness and degeneracy, or symbol of solidarity and truth? Paradoxical attitudes toward pidgins and creoles." In Sidney Greenbaum (ed.), *The English Language Today*. Oxford: Pergamon, 252–62.

Romaine, Suzanne (ed.). 1991. *Language in Australia*. Cambridge: Cambridge University Press.

*Royal Commission into Aboriginal Deaths in Custody*. 1991. *National Report*. Canberra: Australian Government Publishing Service.

Sandefur, John. 1991. "A sketch of the structure of Kriol." In Romaine (ed.), 204–12.

Sato, Charlene J. 1985. "Linguistic inequality in Hawai'i: the post creole dilemma." In Nessa Wolfson and Joan Manes (eds.), *Language of Inequality*. Berlin: Mouton, 255–272.

———. 1989. "A nonstandard approach to Standard English." *TESOL Quarterly* 23,2: 259–82.

———. 1991. "Sociolinguistic variation and language attitudes in Hawai'i." In Jenny Cheshire (ed.), *English Around the World*. Cambridge: Cambridge University Press, 647–663.

Sefton, Margaret. 1994. "Survey of attitudes to Kriol in the Halls Creek Area." Unpublished paper.

Shnukal, Anna. 1983. "Blaikman Tok: changing attitudes towards Torres Strait Creole." *Australian Aboriginal Studies* 1983/2: 25–33.

———. 1991. "Torres Strait Creole." In Romaine (ed.), 180–94.

———. 1992. "The case against a transfer bilingual program of Torres Strait Creole to English in Torres Strait schools." In Jeff Siegel (ed.), *Pidgins, Creoles and Nonstandard Dialects in Education*. Melbourne: Applied Linguistics Association of Australia (Occasional Paper no.12), 1–10.

Siegel, Jeff. 1993. "Pidgins and creoles in education in Australia and the Southwest Pacific." In Francis Byrne and John Holm (eds.), *Atlantic Meets Pacific: A Global View of Pidginization and Creolization*. Amsterdam: John Benjamins, 299–308.

## Afterword

Since this paper was completed in January 1996, there have been many developments regading attitudes to Australian creaoles and Aboriginal English, and several relevant publications (listed below). Berry and hudson (1998) have written a handbook for teachers based on the FELIKS program, described in Section 3.1.1. Australia's Indigenous Languages (SSABSA 1996) is the textbook referred to in Section 3.1.3. The report of the criminal justice commission research project (Section 3.2) was released (CJC 1996). Turner (1997) gives more details about the Injinoo Home Language Program (Section 2). Eades (1997) discusses a umber of recent developments in legal contexts and Siegal (1998) discusses others in educational contexts.

Berry, Rosalind & Joyce Hudson (1997). *Making the Jump: A Resource Book for teachers of Aboriginal students*. Broome: Catholic Education Office, Kimberley Region.

CJC [Criminal Justice Commission] (1996). *Aboriginal Witnesses in Queensland's Criminal Courts*. Brisbane: Criminal Justice Commission.

Eades, Diana (1997). "Languages in court: The acceptance of linguistic evidence about Indigenous Australians in the criminal justice system." *Australian Aboriginal Studies* 1: 15–27.

Siegel, Jeff (1998). "Literacy in Melanesian and Australian pidgins and creoles." *English World-Wide* 19: 104–133.

SSABSA [Senior Secondary Assessment Board of South Australia] (1996). *Australia's Indigenous Languages*. Wayville, South Australia: SSABSA.

Turner, Christine (1997). "The Injinoo Home Language Program: A positive community response to marginalisation and institutional racism." *Australian Journal of Indigenous Education* 25: 1–9.

# Reactions to Bu

## Basilect Meets Mesolect in Hawai'i

Joseph E. Grimes

*Summer Institute of Linguistics and Cornell University*

## 1. Hu Bu?

The years 1994 and 1995 in Hawai'i were enlivened by one Kaui Hill, who owns a surfing shop in Kailua, on the windward coast of the island of O'ahu. He moonlights as a character extraordinary with the stage name Bu La'ia. Wearing a black fright wig and blacked out tooth, in T-shirt, shorts, and rubber slippers, Bu first appeared on Television Channel 14, a small station. Almost instantly he became known throughout Pidgin-speaking[1] Hawai'i purely by word of mouth. According to one Channel 14 staff member (personal communication), he soon gained them more viewers than any of their other programs. Different people react to Bu differently. The reactions of other Pidgin speakers highlight some linguistic differences in contemporary Pidgin usage in Hawai'i.

In keeping with his counterculture image, Bu's TV scenes were shot with wobbly handheld cameras and bad lighting — and still he pulled in the viewers. Possibly because he identifies with surfers, he picked up sponsorship from Hawaiian Island Creations, a major retailer of sports clothing, and Billabong, a surfing clothes manufacturer. He brought in guest stars well known both in the Hawaiian community and outside it, including the late Israel Kamakawiwo'ole, recently voted Musician of the Year, and Sunny Garcia, world surfing champion.

In 1995 Channel 5, which has many more viewers on average than Channel 14, took over Bu's program. Their studio people reran some of his old scenes, edited slightly to make them more palatable to urban viewers. They appear to have put their own camera crew on the new scenes that they shot. Bu continued on Channel 5 for several months, then went back to Channel 14 for a while in reruns, until he dropped out of sight as a regular television fixture.

## 2.    Persona

Bu La'ia's stage name fits his persona. It is a pseudo-Hawaiianization with a glottal stop inserted into *bulaia* 'liar', from *bulai* 'tell lies'.[2] His stock in trade is tall tales: his genealogy, for example, jumps from Adam to Michael Jordan to the Hawaiian chieftain's line of Kamehameha[3], and he refuses to go surfing unless the waves at Makapu'u are at least thirty feet high. In his counterculture stance Bu goes out of his way to kick urban sacred cows: he kisses his dog; he eats cat food; he dresses up as a *tutu* (Hawaiian: 'grandmother'), and he drools copiously. He keeps a whole deep freeze full of plastic bags of *poi*, a traditional Hawaiian staple food.[4] He gets his money by picking up aluminum cans along the road. He drags a surfboard behind him down the sidewalks of Waikiki and Las Vegas.

Bu clearly identifies with the ethnic Hawaiian community; many of them also identify with him. He lives in Waimanalo, a part of O'ahu heavily populated by Hawaiians. He encourages the Hawaiian sovereignty movement, although so far he has not taken the part of any particular group. He has done a lot for ethnic Hawaiian pride through goofy ploys such as billing himself as "the Hawaiian Superman[5] and advising Hawaiians to "it da laulau (a popular local dish)[6] nat da big maek" ('eat laulaus, not Big Macs') so that, he claims, they can become strong like him and take back their lands.

Some of his promotions aimed at ethnic Hawaiians have had quite a positive effect: one television spot that ends "Don't be a fool; stay in school!" carries a strong message.

Bu also made public appearances at surfing meets to award prizes. He participated in various commercial promotions. A cartoon of him, for example, appears in an ad in the local newspaper (*Honolulu Advertiser* August 18, 1995), with the caption "Da bestest deals on da bestest wheels! ... No worry, Pacific Nissan Can Get You Financed!"[7]

The place where Bu attracted the widest public notice, however, was in politics. He entered the 1994 primary election as a Democratic candidate for governor of the state. He was taken off the ballot because he was under the required age. The official who pronounced him disqualified was then Lieutenant Governor Ben Cayetano, himself a candidate, who then won the primary and the regular elections for governor. The anomaly of having one's opponent be the one legally responsible for kicking him out of the race was a natural source for comedy material.[8] Although Bu could not run, the ballots had already been printed. In the primary he got 5,754 votes, more than nineteen other candidates (Price 1994), and second only to Cayetano.

## 3.  Language usage

Bu's use of Pidgin fluctuates between the fairly basilectal form one often hears on the Leeward Coast of O'ahu, and the mesolectal kind associated with the capital, Honolulu. For example, his lead into a program aired in June of 1994 begins like this:

> Wazap evribadi! Tude wi in daun taun Honolulu bra. Da staz, wea da staz haeng aut. Wi ste, wan big lagshri hotel bra. Wea Izrael Kamakawiwo'ole, da Hawain, av Makaha Sanz a Ni'ihau. Aen wi gon hia baut sam'm, go vizit him, e. Bai da we, ... ai no hi wan San a Makaha, so ai went daun dea, hi wazan dea, den a wen Ni'ihau. A kawl ma baws ova dea, wen Ni'ihau aen da baga wazan dea ida. So. A fainli faun aut, daet dis wea hi liv, bra. Lagshri hotel, bat hi no liv, da kain ...
>
> What's up, everybody! Today we are in downtown Honolulu, brother. The stars, where the stars hang out. We are in a big luxury hotel, brother. Where Israel Kamakawiwo'ole, the Hawaiian, of the Makaha Sons of Ni'ihau.[9] And we'll hear about something, we'll pay him a visit. By the way ... I know he's a Son of Makaha, so I went there, and he wasn't there; then I went to Ni'ihau (a privately owned island off the western coast of Kaua'i, which has a large population of native Hawaiians). I called my boss over there, went to Ni'ihau, and the bugger wasn't there. Then, I finally found out that this is where he lives, brother. A luxury hotel, but he does not live luxuriously ...

There are plenty of basilectal Pidgin markers in this short bit: *bra* and *e* tagged on to sentences, verbless sentences, *go* to show initiative differing from the collateral (or future) auxiliary *gon*, *wan* as the nonspecific (or indefinite) article and *da* as specific (or definite), *da kain* as generalized pro-form. In other samples he uses other forms typical of basilectal Pidgin: *no mo* as the negative of *get* 'existential, have', with *neva haev* as the backgrounded or anterior of the same; *ste* 'durative'; *kam* + nominal or adjectival complement 'become'.

As the piece continues, however, more and more English-based and urban-oriented forms appear that are not common in the more basilectal Pidgin-speaking community: *av* 'of' for a group affiliation, *bai da we* 'by the way' as a conjunction and *fainli* 'finally' and *ida* 'either' as adverbs, inflected *went* alternating with *wen* as main verb and *wazan* 'wasn't' and *faun aut* 'found out'. These forms, especially the English-inflected forms of the most common strong verbs, occur in the speech of other basilectal speakers, but it seems characteristic of Bu that they go up in frequency after he begins to talk. Before long, instead of sounding like a Waimanalo boy, he comes across as someone from one of the English-dominant areas: Honolulu, Kailua, or Kaneohe.

The same pattern shows up in vocabulary choices. There are plenty of urbanisms such as "supplement yo' income", "I would give you my phone numbah", "get involved in da restoration of da Hawaiian Nation" that show direct English influence. On the other hand, the rhymed phrasal doublets that are dear to the hearts of Pidgin speakers come through frequently: "no worries beef curries", "wass da scoops, hula hoops?", "relax tampax", "false crack, medivac", "get on it, grommet".

There are a number of polysyllabic English words not current in Pidgin that Bu pulls into Pidgin for deliberate comic effect. The words preserve their English meanings but they are infixed with -ama-, occasionally with a change in a neighboring consonant: *edumacated* ejamaketid or "edgimated" ejametid 'educated', *gradgimate* graejamet 'graduate', *congradgamalations* kangrae-jamaleshinz 'congratulations', *origimanated* arijamanetid 'originated', *speciamalized* speshamalaiz 'specialized', *hesimate* hezamet 'hesitate', *stratemy* shtraetami 'strategy', *inspamational* inspameshanal 'inspirational', and even *Pidginomology* pijinamalaji 'Pidginology'. There is a variation from the -m- pattern with *instinctiously* instinkshasli 'instinctively'.

## 4.    Reactions

Bu La'ia is widely perceived as a person associated with rural ethnic Hawaiians who highlights in a humorous way issues that are of real concern to them. Both in the persona he projects and in his constant use of Pidgin, he seems to distance himself from *haoles* (Hawaiian: 'foreigner', now simply Caucasians), who control most of the economy and the media in the Islands (see also Romaine, this volume). He positions himself a little closer to other non-*haole* ethnic groups, especially to those individuals who do not wholly follow the *haole*-dominated view of life. For example, he has had a local Japanese sumo wrestler on his show, and in another scene he tries to convince a local Samoan bus driver to let him take his surfboard on the bus.

He serves, in effect, as the exaggerated symbol of a counterculture that in many ways prefers maintaining relationships with people — especially kin — to advancing up the social ladder at the cost of relationships, individual control of time to fitting into a schedule, acting macho to behaving in a conventionally acceptable way, giving and receiving help within a social network rather than saving up money so you won't need to bother anyone else if you have a special need.[10] To use a term that has occasionally been applied technically to the culture Bu represents, he is Local, with a capital L. His role seems to be widely understood and accepted, including by people whose life styles are very different from Bu's and who are turned off by the way he does things.

To a linguist, however, one of the most interesting things about the situation I describe is that it does not quite match the reactions some Pidgin speakers have to Bu's kind of Pidgin. It is a truism that Pidgin is the carrier language for Local culture. As such, it cuts across ethnic ties and reinforces cultural ties. Yet not everybody in the Local culture identifies with the way Bu talks.

The reaction of one friend from the outer island of Hawai'i (locally called the Big Island) to Bu's book (Bu La'ia 1995b) was the tipoff that people who are full participants in the Local culture react in more than one way to his speech. She pointed out that even though he clearly acts like a Local person and talks Pidgin, it is a decreolized Pidgin that she finds hard to relate to. She reported this in connection with a remark she heard in an O'ahu K-Mart store from a group of teenagers from Kalihi who were looking at Bu's book: "e, no nid rid daet, ony ingalish" 'Hey, there's no need to read that. It's only English.'

Most of what I have examined of Bu La'ia's speech, spoken or written, points in the same direction. The framework is clearly Pidgin, but it is more like the decreolized Pidgin of Honolulu than like the more conservative Pidgin of the Leeward Coast or the Outer Islands. It appears to resonate more with people who speak mostly English and use Pidgin on the side than with the people who use Pidgin as their mother tongue in everyday life, and may or may not interact much with English.

The least basilectal Pidgin that I have encountered is that used among recreational groups of men in their thirties. These are well educated professional men who speak English all day at work and at home; then they get together for basketball or volleyball. Afterwards, over coffee, the Pidgin flows freely as the language of social solidarity. In all the kidding and joking, it's mainly the sounds of Pidgin that one hears. The selection of words, the grammar, and the discourse sequencing are mainly standard English, interspersed with occasional Pidgin vocabulary markers like *no mo* 'there isn't any' or *laik* + VP with no explicit complementizer 'want to'.

The most basilectal Pidgin I have encountered is that of the Leeward Coast of O'ahu, where I live. Independently of Hawaiian, Samoan, Filipino, Japanese, Chinese, or mixed ethnicity, such basilectal speakers tend to use Pidgin in the home from childhood onwards, with friends and relatives or in the neighborhood. They make use of uninflected verbs[11] with auxiliaries like *wen* 'background information, anterior sequencing' and *gon* or *goin* 'collateral information' and aspectual preverbs like *ste* 'durative' and *go* 'intentional'. Such speakers distinguish sharply between identificational sentences with no verb and *bi* sentences with an intentional meaning 'make the effort to be something'. They choose words and phrasal lexemes more by their place in the Pidgin semantic system than as equivalents of English expressions. They organize the time sequence of discourse iconically with the events, with exceptions for claims of causality that need to be highlighted, and they reidentify referents much more frequently than in English.

Nobody there (or anywhere else I have found), however, speaks a pure basilect. They slip in some English words even when there are perfectly good Pidgin expressions available, though if asked they have a sharp sense of which is which. They use inflected forms of common verbs freely but not exclusively. Yet when asked to judge whether sentences formed with inflected verbs sound better or more appropriate than equivalent sentences on the Pidgin model, their choice overwhelmingly supports the Pidgin model.[12]

People refer to the Pidgin spoken on the Leeward Coast as "hevi kain pijin" 'deep Pidgin'. Other entertainers such as Andy Bumatai (1981), who graduated from Wai'anae High School on the Leeward Coast, represent it quite accurately when they control their own scripts. It is also compatible with the Pidgin of the Outer Islands, except for localisms and the frequency of variants of things like the *wen* ~ *bin* ~ *haed* auxiliary.[13]

If the heaviest, most basilectal Pidgin were rated as 10 and the Pidgin-flavored English of the recreational groups in Honolulu were 1, Bu La'ia's overall speech might come in around 3 or 4, mainly because of the strong Pidgin phonology. This suggests why speakers whose own performance would rate above 6 on the same scale might react to his speech as close to Standard English.

## 5. Discussion

There is evidence that some people whose life style fits the Local culture pattern and who use Hawai'i Pidgin English as the vehicle for their closest relationships distinguish between people like themselves and people who speak Pidgin as their secondary language, ancillary to English, or at least whose Pidgin falls into an urban mold. This reaction might show that there is a limit to the amount of recognizably English usage the everyday Pidgin speakers tolerate willingly. In the other direction, it might be due to insufficient weight of signals that say "This is Pidgin, not English". It might even be based on knowledge or assumptions about the person speaking. There are undoubtedly other factors I have not singled out yet. I also have no grasp yet on whether the perceptions in the opposite direction match. But it seems clear that there is a distinction; perhaps we can work out from there to understand its implications.

# Notes

1.  What linguists know as Hawai'i Creole English is universally called Pidgin by those who speak it. I accept their autonym; linguists are well aware that the real pidgins of the early plantations are long gone. I write spoken Pidgin here using the transcription attributed to Carol Odo. *ae* and *aw* stand for monophthongal low front and low back vowels, respectively. ' is the glottal stop. *D* represents an apical tap. *r* indicates a rhotacized mid central vowel, either as a syllable nucleus or as a consonant. Other symbols are taken with their usual phonetic values. Long and short vowels are not distinct, even in expressions and place names from Hawaiian that do distinguish length. Examples from written materials follow English spelling norms more or less, and are given in double quotes. All the written examples cited are from Bu La'ia (1995b).

2.  I have also heard it etymologized as *Bu* 'brother' plus *La'ia* 'sunfish', but my sources are inconclusive on the issue of whether anybody actually understands it that way.

3.  In another account he claims "100 percent Hawaiian, 10 percent Chinese, 5 percent Haole [Caucasian], an' 3 percent Samoan."

4.  Pounded taro root (*poi*) is getting hard to find, hence the deep freeze; rice has replaced *poi* in most people's diets.

5.  From a song about the Hawaiian demigod Maui, made popular by Israel Kamakawiwo'ole.

6.  Pork and butterfish steamed in taro leaves inside a ti leaf wrapper.

7.  The subtext, that people like Bu are going to have trouble getting financing, is undoubtedly not appreciated in the Pidgin-speaking community, and is probably not true. A flyer by the same company for mid January of 1996 has an even more negative message: next to Bu's picture, the caption in English reads "Bad Credit? Hassle Free Credit Approvals."

8.  A blurb on the cover of Bu La'ia (1995b) says, "Wow! If I knew this young Hawaiian was so full of wisdom, I would have voted for him myself!" — Ben Kai Otano. In the English credits for his 1995 recording *False Crack???* Bu thanks Cayetano "for letting me make fun of him. Without you I wouldn't have anyone to tease."

9.  A singing group that disbanded a few years ago when Kamakawiwo'ole branched out on his own. The others stayed together as the Makaha Sons, and Kamakawiwo'ole died in 1997. For many, Ni'ihau is a symbol of the pure Hawaiian culture.

10. The values Bu La'ia symbolizes are strikingly like the kind Eckert (1989) finds among the social networks labelled "burnouts" in the Detroit high school scene.

11. Nonstative verbs are inflected with *-ing* 'progressive' (and possibly 'gerund') in all varieties of Hawai'i Pidgin English. By "uninflected" I mean lack of English style inflection for third person singular agreement, past tense including strong verb stem changes, and the past participle.

12. The statements in this paragraph cry out for explicit quantification; but I've been working in participant observer mode, mainly on the lexicon, and don't have the kind of samples that could give a representative idea of the actual frequencies. This means that what I say here is not proof that the situation is as I say it is. Nevertheless, as happens generally with participant observation by trained observers, it would be surprising if the quantitative results turned out radically different from my description.

13. *haed* as the background information auxiliary for any verb alternates freely with *wen* on the Big Island and Kaua'i, and is distinct from *haed* = *wen* + *get* in the existential sense of *get*.

## References

Bu La'ia. 1995a. *False crack???* Honolulu: Pig Poi Records.
———. 1995b. Ask Bu. Honolulu: Keefah Productions.
Bumatai, Andy. 1981. *Andy Bumatai's Ohana: A Scrapbook.* New York: Lee Publications
    Group.
Eckert, Penelope. 1989. *Jocks and Burnouts: Social Categories and Identity in High School.*
    New York: Teachers College Press.
Price, Larry. 1994. "Smear Campaigns Muddy The Issues." *MidWeek.* September 28.

# Changing Attitudes to Hawai'i Creole English

## Fo' find one good job,
## you gotta know how fo' talk like one haole

Suzanne Romaine

*Merton College, University of Oxford*

## Introduction

My title is deliberately ambiguous. I will discuss both the ways in which attitudes to Hawai'i Creole English (hereafter HCE) are changing as well as ways in which linguists might help to bring about change in attitudes. At first glance this dual purpose might seem to mix illegitimately the concerns of description and prescription, which linguists have traditionally argued were distinct. However, the discipline of sociolinguistics emerged at least partly in response to educational problems surrounding the use of non-standard varieties. With it came the recognition that negative attitudes towards such varieties were at least as, if not more, important than structural differences between them and the standard varieties when it came to measuring academic achievement. In the forefront of such research were linguists like Labov (1982) who urged commitment on the part of sociolinguists to the communities which served as research sites. Others such as Wolfram (1993) have developed language awareness programs, while Baugh (1995) has stressed the importance of sociolinguistic research in high school teacher education.

Inspired by similar sentiments about the empowerment of minority groups through education and research, I began teaching a summer course called "Pidgin and Creole Languages" at the University of Hawai'i at Hilo as a way of raising consciousness about Hawai'i Creole English. For many years Charlene Sato had been teaching a similar course at the University of Hawai'i's main campus at Mānoa. The majority of students taking the course at the Hilo campus were born in Hawai'i and a number of them are enrolled in the education program, or are already teachers in public schools. The course covers the history and structure of HCE, its uses and functions in contemporary society, as well as its relationship with other Pacific pidgins and creoles.

For many of the students it is a revelation that HCE can be regarded as a language in its own right and that the study of pidgin and creole languages constitutes a legitimate academic discipline. Many of the local students grew up speaking HCE as their native language and were corrected at school for speaking "bad English". Indeed, some came to school having been corrected at home by parents and grandparents. Despite the fact that HCE is the first language of the majority of locally born children and the first language of somewhat less than half the State of Hawai'i's population of just over a million, like most of the world's pidgins and creoles, it has no official recognition. It is instructive for the students to consider cases elsewhere in the world such as in the Caribbean, West Africa and Papua New Guinea, where pidgins and creoles are used across an even wider spectrum of public domains than HCE is in Hawai'i.

Since 1992 I have given students in my class a fieldwork assignment in which they have to conduct interviews in the local community to investigate people's attitudes towards "pidgin", the name given locally to HCE. I focussed this exercise on attitudes towards the use of creole in education since this is the public setting within which children are often first exposed to negative attitudes to HCE. Day (1980), for instance, using a matched guise experiment, has shown how kindergarten children from low income areas preferred HCE over Standard English, but first graders already had negative attitudes to HCE and preferred standard English. After providing a brief history of HCE, I discuss the results of attitude surveys the students conducted between the years 1992–1995.

## 1.    Brief History of Hawai'i Creole English

Pidgin English in Hawai'i was the outcome of contact between Hawaiians, Europeans (primarily English speakers, who contributed most of the vocabulary to the pidgin), and the various immigrant groups (e.g. Chinese, Japanese, Filipinos, etc.) brought to Hawai'i to work as indentured laborers on plantations. Reinecke (1969) provides a good socio-historical account of the formative period of the creole variety. Drechsel (this volume) and Roberts (this volume) discuss the antecedent stages to the development of Hawai'i Pidgin English. While Hawai'i Pidgin English still exists, it is spoken only by the oldest generation of immigrants to the plantations and is now dying out. Its descendant, Hawai'i Creole English, is the first language of probably the majority of children in

Hawai'i. Thus, although varieties of Hawai'i Creole English are locally called 'pidgin', most of them are technically forms of creole English since they function as the native rather than second language of most of their users.

My discussion of attitudes in class with the students focuses on how speakers of Hawai'i Creole English have been discriminated against through education in a school system which originally was set up to keep out those who could not pass an English test. In this way it was hoped to restrict the admission of non-white children into the English Standard schools set up in 1924, which were attended mainly by Caucasian children, locally called haoles (from Hawaiian 'foreigner). By institutionalizing what was essentially racial discrimination along linguistic lines, the schools managed to keep creole speakers in their "place" and maintain distance between them and English speakers until after World War II (see Sato 1985 and 1991). Ironically, as Sato (1985: 265) has pointed out, the relative isolation of creole speakers from speakers of mainstream varieties of English actually strengthened Hawai'i Creole English for a time. Normally, schooling in the colonial language accelerates decreolization (see e.g. Romaine 1992).

Now, however, the great extent of decreolization affecting HCE, particularly since World War II and the political incorporation of the islands into the United States as the 50th state have left the boundaries between standard English and HCE fuzzier than elsewhere in the Pacific, e.g. Papua New Guinea. This too has decreased the autonomy of HCE.

## 2.    Attitudes to Hawai'i Creole English based on survey data 1992–1995

While most of those interviewed are currently resident on the island of Hawai'i (locally called the Big Island), a number were born elsewhere in the islands, and a few are currently resident in Honolulu. The only restrictions on participation in the survey are that the students interview someone they do not know personally and that the person should have attended school in Hawai'i. Although the resulting interviews still represent a judgement rather than a strict random sample, over a period of four years the students in the various classes have managed to cover a great cross-section of the population, as evidenced by the age, ethnicity and occupations of the men and women they surveyed. Altogether they interviewed a total of 211 people, 122 (57%) of whom were women and 89 (42%), men, ranging in age from 13 to 86. A number of the students have been very enterprising in their search for and choice of subjects. For example, one woman made an appointment with the mayor of the Big Island to obtain his

views on the subject. Another woman who had to attend a bridal shower for her
niece in Honolulu took the opportunity of interviewing her niece's friends.
Others deliberately chose teachers, or retired plantation workers, and some
stopped passers-by in local malls, eating places, or at the beach.

The students had to ask several questions of each respondent. The first of
these aimed at finding out whether people thought pidgin was acceptable for oral
and written communication at school. Interviewees were asked if they thought
children should be allowed to speak pidgin and to write pidgin in the classroom.
The second question asked for information whether the interviewees recalled
children being corrected in school for speaking pidgin. The term 'pidgin' was
deliberately used since the term creole and the label HCE are not widely
understood or applied locally. Indeed, as one respondent put it after being told
about the term 'creole', "I thought creole was only spoken in Louisiana".

Table 1 summarizes the responses in each of four years from 1992 to 1995
given by 211 persons whom the students interviewed.

Table 1: *Replies to questions about attitudes 1992–1995*

| YEAR | 1992 | 1993 | 1994 | 1995 | TOTAL | |
|---|---|---|---|---|---|---|
| Question 1 SPEAKING | N | N | N | N | N | % |
| Yes | 17 | 15 | 20 | 12 | 64 | 30 |
| Sometimes | 3 | 16 | 15 | 14 | 48 | 23 |
| No | 22 | 33 | 19 | 24 | 98 | 47 |
| No response | | 1 | | | | |
| WRITING | | | | | | |
| Yes | 6 | 8 | 11 | 5 | 30 | 14 |
| Sometimes | 1 | 16 | 14 | 8 | 39 | 19 |
| No | 34 | 41 | 29 | 35 | 139 | 66 |
| No response | 1 | | | 2 | 3 | 1 |
| Question 2: CORRECTION | | | | | | |
| Yes | 26 | 41 | 34 | 30 | 131 | 62 |
| No | 15 | 17 | 14 | 20 | 66 | 31 |
| Can't remember | | 7 | 5 | | 12 | 6 |
| No response | 1 | | 1 | | 2 | 1 |
| TOTALS | 42 | 65 | 54 | 50 | 211 | |

## 3.   Speaking and writing HCE: Fo' find one good job, you gotta know how fo' talk like one haole

The results clearly indicate that people expressed more positive views about the spoken rather than written use of HCE in the classroom. Table 1 shows that overall a slight majority (53%) of interviewees think that spoken pidgin should be allowed in at least some contexts at school. Nearly a third (30%) replied with an unqualified yes, and 23% said "sometimes". A total of 47% replied negatively.

Respondents base their negative views on perceived linguistic inadequacies or the economic and social limitations of HCE vis-à-vis standard English. Most of the respondents who said "no" stressed the economic advantages to standard English. One woman who worked as a receptionist said: "That's why you go to school for, so you don't write pidgin English". (EKm, 1992).[1] *Pidgin to da Max* (Simonson 1981), a collection of cartoons illustrating some common local expressions and one of the most popular works today, illustrates aptly the all too real economic and social advantages to standard English by juxtaposing pictures of a woman standing over a stove cooking and a businessman with suit and tie seated at his desk. Underneath the picture of the woman the caption reads: "Fo' find one good job, you gotta know how fo' talk like one haole", while under the man, it says: "To get a high-paying position, one must be able to speak good English". The examples are intended to illustrate the differences in complementation structures in HCE, which makes use of *fo*, and English, which uses the infinitive *to*.

A 45 year old Filipino male who works as a Hawaiian Airlines cargo employee expressed similar sentiments when he said, "No, speaking pidgin in the classroom should never be allowed because this is an English-based world where success is measured by knowledge of it. Writing pidgin is also out of the question because it will handicap kids for future advancement if they never learn Standard English (JHf, 1992)".

Others offered answers reflecting the limited currency of HCE, such as a 63 year old woman of Portuguese ethnicity, who said, "byembye when da kids go to da mainland they're going to feel shame if they don't speak proper English". (CK-Sf, 1993). One young male truck driver said students should not speak pidgin in the classroom because "bambai wen they go mainland, nobody going understand dem wen they talk." (SHf,1993).

Many of those who expressed negative attitudes towards the use of both spoken and written pidgin in the classroom offered the familiar reasons such as it is "slang" or "broken" English. One 32 year old woman of part-Hawaiian ethnicity said "No, because it is not proper English" (RHf, 1992). Many were quite emphatic in their beliefs, such as one 59 year old Portuguese/ Caucasian woman employed at a rental car agency at Hilo airport, who said:"No way, I wouldn't want it, speaking or writing" (AMf, 1992).

Respondents who spoke out in favor of spoken HCE emphasized that teachers also used pidgin themselves to some extent, which made pidgin-speaking children feel more comfortable. One 64 year old Hawaiian, a retired cowboy from Parker Ranch told how he hated school because he was made to feel dumb. "When da teacha only speak haole, da kids tink dat da teacha is more betta dan dem. But if da teacher speak to dem in pidgin the kids dey feel like "Oh" dis teacha is juss like us. Den dey like go class and learn because dey no feel juss like scaed". He himself left school in the fifth grade. "I was corrected so often dat I neva even talk any more, I hated school so much all I wanted to do was stay on the ranch with my fada because nobody correct me all the time dea." (CK-Sf, 1993). One 33 year old Hawaiian raised on the Big Island, said pidgin should be allowed in classrooms because "that's what we all know... Our teachers like fo us speak up in class, join in discussions and didn't correct us fo speaking da kine, cuz den we clam up. Mo betta we participate." (CMf, 1995).

Not surprisingly, the question about writing in HCE gave rise to the most negative responses with 2/3 (66%) of the interviewees saying that they did not think it was acceptable for children to write in pidgin in school. Overall only 14% of interviewees gave an unqualified affirmative response to the question about writing and slightly more (19%) said it could be allowed in some contexts, e.g. creative writing.

There are many reasons why this question attracted more negative replies. Like most pidgin and creole languages, HCE has not been standardized. This gives rise to the popular belief in Hawai'i and elsewhere that pidgin cannot be written. For example, one 37 year old male of Hawaiian, Japanese and German descent raised in Hilo immediately said "no", but then asked: "How do you do that?" (KSm, 1995).

Although linguists have for some time been using a phonemic orthography developed by Carol Odo (1975), it has no wider recognition. Anyone who wants to write in pidgin has to work out an ad hoc system. Despite the lack of written norms and standardization in Hawai'i Creole English, however, there are some writers who have attempted to use it as a medium for poetry, short stories and drama by adapting English spelling to represent some of the features characteristic of speech varieties in Hawai'i. Two examples of this can be seen in the contributions by Eric Chock and Darrell Lum to this volume.

Because it has no distinctive writing system of its own, HCE is represented as if it were a deviant or non-standard variety of English (see Romaine 1994a and b for further discussion). This in turn reinforces popular beliefs that HCE is not a language in its own right. Even those who were tolerant to some extent about the use of spoken pidgin especially if it is the child's only way of communicating, were negative about writing, such as a female teacher at one of Hilo's elementary schools who said pidgin should not be written because it had no grammar.

Various alterations to standard orthography (e.g. *neva* for *never*, *tink* for *think*, *bruddah* for *brother*), together with the use of contracted forms common to most casual conversation (e.g. *wanna* instead of *want to*, etc.) and overdone 'eye' dialect (e.g. *wat* instead of *what*, *sez* instead of *says*, etc). strengthen stereotypes that written pidgin is but bad or broken English in need of correction. These visual alterations to spelling send a strong message to readers about the non-standard status of HCE. The over-use of apostrophes suggesting elided consonants and vowels (e.g. *'um* for *him* or *them*) also fosters the view that HCE is simplified and reduced by comparison with the standard. The fact that until relatively recently HCE was not really seen as a vehicle for serious artistic expression leads many people to think that the only appropriate domain for written pidgin, if there is one at all, is in popular songs and comic entertainment.

Although positive responses were very much in the minority as far as writing is concerned, they were nonetheless interesting. One young Japanese male, a full-time student at the University of Hawai'i at Hilo, said that children should be allowed to use both spoken and written pidgin because they could express their thoughts better that way. He even insisted that children learn to write in pidgin. He himself wrote poetry in pidgin (KTm, 1994). One young Japanese woman employed as an elementary school counselor in Hilo voiced similar sentiments when she said, "As a school counselor, I view the expression of thoughts and feelings by children as a means of fostering inquisitiveness. This, in turn, motivates children to grow and to learn, to search for answers to their questions. Rather than stifle children by insisting that they speak in standard English, perhaps we need to be flexible enough to incorporate the use of pidgin in the classroom." (SAMf, 1994).

Similarly, a 63 year old retired housewife of Samoan/Hawaiian/ Caucasian descent said that pidgin could be used in the classroom for speaking and writing as a tool for teaching standard English. Children could be bilingual; by beginning with what they knew, they would feel a sense of accomplishment and pride instead of shame at what they did not know. (SAMf, 1994). She herself had been made to feel stupid in school because she spoke 'heavy pidgin'.

## 4.   Correction: How many times I tol' you, no talk li' dat

The pervasiveness of correction is underlined in *Pidgin to Da Max*, whose back
cover shows a mother figure saying "How many times I tol' you, no talk li' dat."
Not surprisingly our survey also revealed that the majority of interviewees,
(66%) recalled having teachers or parents correct them or others for the use of
HCE. One 18 year old Hawaiian man employed in his father's pyrotechnics
business recalled, "me and my bruddahs were corrected jes' 'bout every day"
(WAWm, 1992), while a 55 year old Caucasian woman employed as a book-
keeper remarked, "Kids like me were punished every day". (KTm, 1994). As the
daughter of plantation workers, she came to school knowing only pidgin. A 62
year old retired saleswoman of Portuguese ethnicity even told of teachers who
formed "Pidgin patrols" and gave demerits and detention to students whom they
caught speaking pidgin (YKf, 1993). Another elderly woman, also a retired
salesclerk, reported that children answering the teacher in pidgin were sent
outside to pull weeds (SHf, 1993). These latter two women attended school in
rural areas of the Big Island, but respondents who attended school on O'ahu also
reported getting detention in high school for speaking pidgin.

While some respondents had little to say about correction, many offered
stories about specific incidents which revealed the deep embarrassment many felt
at being corrected. One male student attending the University of Hawai'i at Hilo
talked about how one fellow student at Konawaena School on the leeward coast
of the Big Island was corrected. The student asked the teacher, "I can go
batroom?" The teacher insisted that the student repeat the question over and over
again in front of the class until he produced it in standard English (KCf, 1995).
A female school counselor recalled a teacher who would thank students for
telling her something in pidgin but not respond to their questions unless they
asked them in standard English. In response to a question such as "I can borrow
pencil?", she would reply: "I don't know, can you?" (SAMf, 1994).

Others commented on how badly they felt when a written assignment was
returned covered with the teacher's corrections in red. For many respondents
writing Standard English was especially difficult. As one male interviewee put
it "Haoles got lotta small kine words dat go all ova da place. I git twisted, by n
by, when try fo puttem in der place." (CMf, 1995)

In addition to revealing some of the strategies used by teachers in correcting
children, some respondents offered their perceived reasons for correction. Some
said that the teachers were upholding authority and enforcing rules. One man in
his mid 70s commented that he had called his son's teacher periodically to
remind them of the importance of Standard English, adding that he did not allow

his grandchildren to speak pidgin when they visited his home (RMm, 1992).

Others, such as a 40 year old man of Portuguese and Hawaiian descent who worked for the County of Hawai'i, recognized the motivations behind correction, but objected to them. He recalled how "My teacher had correc me in front da whole class, pau, I kill fight awreddy. I no like tawk awreddy. She told me afta she wasn't making fun of me. She just wanted me to understand that not everybody would understand the way we locals tawk, but I was shame awreddy! I get it now, what my teacher was trying to do for me then. Our teachers were all local those days. They were just trying to help, but that turned me off to school for a long time" (CSf, 1992). When CS told him she was doing the survey as part of a class at the university, he was pleased that "someone finally got da balls to study and prove this stuff is okay so our keeds won't have to suffer the humiliation I did. Sheesh, it really was a haranging experience for me. That's how we lose a lot of kids in the system we have now." (CSf, 1992)

At the same time, some of the interviewees recognized the futility of correction. As one 29 year old man of Hawaiian, Japanese and Caucasian descent who had lived on the Big Island all his life put it, "Kids gonna talk pidgin, no matta what. You can't stop 'em, stupid fo' try. It's what dey hear from small kid time, how you gonna change dat... We all know English too, so we handle.... Just cus I speak pidgin neva mean I stupid" (CMf, 1995). Another young man of part Hawaiian background related how although children always got scoldings for speaking pidgin, it didn't make them want to stop speaking it (SRf, 1994). One woman in my class recalled how she had been corrected by her boss for speaking pidgin over the public address system. Although her boss habitually spoke 'heavy pidgin', he told her she represented the company and had to present a good image.

The futility of correction of non-standard language use in the classroom also receives support from academic research such as that of Piestrup (1973), who found that children's use of African-American English increased in direct proportion to how much they were corrected. In classrooms where teachers corrected children, the more they used non-standard speech. Reading scores were also low in such classrooms, compared to classrooms where children were allowed to express themselves and read orally in African-American English. In addition, studies show an increase in the use of non-standard speech varieties among ethnic minority groups such as West Indians in Britain as children approach adolescence, indicating the effects of peer group allegiance.

While it seems at first glance paradoxical that HCE and other stigmatized varieties persist despite correction and negative public opinion, it is well known that speakers attach positive value to creole and other non-standard varieties as a marker of solidarity and intimacy. Using a matched guise technique in Guyana, Rickford (1983) showed that although standard English was rated more favorably along the status and power dimensions, creole was valued more highly for friendship and solidarity (see also Rickford and Traugott 1985, and Trudgill's 1972 distinction between covert and overt prestige). Those who opt for standard English risk ridicule from their HCE-speaking peers for being too "haolified". One Caucasian student in my class commented that she had been around pidgin speakers all her life, but her father did not allow her and her brother to use pidgin at home. However, for "survival's sake", as she put it, they had to learn it and did so at school from their peers (TBf, 1995).

## 5.    Discussion

The tension between public and private attitudes in Hawai'i has long been present, but until recently the prevailing public opinion was not seriously challenged. Attitudes towards HCE regularly become part of public controversy in Hawai'i, particularly when the annual achievement test results are announced. "Pidgin" is often blamed for the poor performance of Hawai'i's students on the verbal ability section of the SAT. The "pidgin problem", as it is often called in educational circles, erupted in a very forceful way in 1987 when the State of Hawai'i Board of Education drafted a policy which would officially ban pidgin from the classroom, and sanction the use of Standard English only. A heated debate broke out and was carried out in newspapers, radio, TV, as well as Board of Education meetings. The original policy statement declared that "Standard English [will] be the mode of oral communication for students and staff in the classroom setting and all other school related settings except when the objectives cover native Hawaiian or foreign language instruction and practice" (cited in Watson-Gegeo 1994: 108).

An outpouring of public and professional sentiment against the strong version of the policy in the form of testimony to the board by linguists such as Richard Day, Michael Forman and Charlene Sato, teachers, and letters to the editor, modified the position of some Board members. When the policy came to a vote, the Board of Education approved a much watered down policy which endorsed what was already educational practice. The school staff was supposed to give high priority to English and to encourage and model the use of oral English in all school-related settings. The local newspaper carried articles for three days running entitled "Talking 'Da Kine'. The Pidgin Story" (September 28, 29, 30, 1987).

A survey reported by the *Honolulu Star Bulletin* done in 1988 in the wake of the policy controversy revealed a significant split between the attitudes of students attending Hawai'i's public and private schools (Verploegen 1988). A slight majority (54%) of those attending public schools were in favor of some use of pidgin in the classroom, while only 26% of those in private schools responded favorably. The split is indicative of a long standing division between public and private education. Hawai'i has the highest percentage of students attending private institutions in the US.

The responses to the survey show that the Board's 1987 proposal flew in the face of widespread public feeling that spoken pidgin was appropriate for the classroom in some circumstances. Language planners of course stress that policy makers should conduct such attitude surveys in advance of decision making. A famous case where policy was largely out of touch with grass roots feelings was the law establishing compulsory Irish instruction in schools in the Irish Republic. While Irish people had very positive attitudes to the language, most opposed compulsory Irish. In fact, only a very small number of Irish people are willing to express negative attitudes to Irish. As one Irish person said to Hindley (1990), "although we are all FOR Irish as we are for cheaper bus fares, heaven and the good life, nobody of the masses is willing to make the effort."

As far as policy making is concerned in Hawai'i, the State's Department of Education has acknowledged that Hawai'i Creole English constitutes a language in its own right with a structure distinct from English, but this recognition has not resulted in any concrete action in the classroom. A teacher who took my class wrote that one of the major problems she had encountered over her 15 years in the public school system was that the issue of the needs of HCE speakers had never been seriously addressed. She noted also that the Department of Education also needed to be honest in recognizing the "pidgin problem" as a political problem, and not simply hide behind the excuse that it is a language problem. (SRf, 1994).

In 1994 the "pidgin" issue erupted again after a conference took place in Honolulu on the topic of language rights. One woman wrote to the editor of the *Honolulu Advertiser* (Oct. 16, 1994), "I wonder if anyone else felt as uneasy as I did after reading the article about a conference at which speakers supported the use of and respect for pidgin." The Sunday *Honolulu Advertiser* responded with a series of special focus articles (Oct. 9, 16, 30, 1994) entitled "Revisiting pidgin: If it's 'garbage, so is Shakespeare." The debate was also carried out in student newspapers at the two main branches of the University of Hawai'i at Mānoa and Hilo. I was pleased when one of the students who had taken my class, wrote a letter to the editor to point out many of the misconceptions about HCE.

In 1995 the debate continued in the newspapers with *Honolulu Weekly* (January 4, 1995) carrying as its main feature the story "Wot, Da Kine Talk Boddah You?", followed a few weeks later by the lead article series in the *Honolulu Advertiser* entitled "Pidgin:Da Kine Dispute" (January 29, May 14, May 15, August 14 1995). One of the articles appearing on August 14, 1995 reported the results of a survey done by SMS Research for the Hawaii Democracy Forum as part of its Community Dialogues project. One of the questions was whether standard English should be the only language used in classrooms: 65% said yes, although 503 respondents were almost evenly split on whether pidgin should be forbidden: 47% said it should be forbidden, but 44% said that no rules about pidgin should be made. Only 3% said teaching in pidgin ought to be promoted in schools.

Many of the students, both local and no-local, who conduct the interviews, find some of the attitudes of their respondents surprising. Some expect to find that older people will have more negative attitudes than younger people, but find instead that many older people are very positive and many younger people quite negative. While it would be necessary and interesting to do a more systematic investigation with a sample more carefully controlled for age, sex, ethnicity and other factors such as place of birth, school attended, etc., my impression from the analysis of these results is that negative and positive attitudes can be found among all sectors of the community. I have tried to illustrate that by giving some of the details of respondents' backgrounds when citing their replies to the questions.

Many students also report that their own attitudes change as a result of taking the course and are therefore somewhat dismayed at the negative attitudes they encounter among the community at large. One student of Japanese ancestry from the US mainland wrote (MSm, 1995): "When I first came to Hawaii I have to admit that I thought that the creole English spoken here was a form of broken English, and that it was the language used by lazy and uneducated people". After working with a variety of people who spoke creole to him in the mistaken assumption that he was local, he realized that creole speakers were not lazy or uneducated, but that HCE served important functions as a marker of solidarity. This particular student happened to interview two young people, both of whom spoke in creole to him at the same time as they said children should not be allowed to use HCE in the classroom. He, along with others not local to Hawai'i, expressed surprise at how negative local attitudes were to the creole. This same student wrote, "the more I learned about HCE, the more I began to understand that suppressing people from speaking the language they grew up with, is a form of discrimination (MSm, 1995).

An African American woman from the US mainland wrote, "I do believe there has been a change in my thinking due to what I have learned in this course. A month ago I think I would have answered "no" to whether I thought pidgin should be spoken in the classroom, and I'm sure I would have answered "no" to whether I thought pidgin should be written in class. Now that I know the history of pidgin languages and its importance to past and present cultures, I would be in favor of allowing children to speak and (possibly) write their first language in class." (LJ, 1995).

A local student wrote, "Prior to taking this class in Pidgin and Creole Languages, "pidgin" was always something I thought I had to apologize for because my parents and teachers always corrected my "bad English.... I was so brainwashed by the "no pidgin allowed" idea that I passed it on one generation further to my son. He grew up confused when the so-called "correct" way of speaking made him the joke of many situations. When he would say "Helocopter", his friends would laugh at him because they said it was helicoptah. He ran home crying. He also thought that "spatula" was supposed to be spatuler.... Today I am proud of my "pidgin" background thanks to the facts provided by this class. It is deeply rooted in our Hawaiian history, first as Hawaiian Pidgin, then Hawaiian Pidgin English. ... I never will apologize for speaking "pidgin" again." (JHf, 1992).

One male student of part-Hawaiian ethnicity wrote: "I myself am very obstinate against the insistence ... that I and the people I identity with conform to a standard set thousands of miles away by a people I do not identify with. I am very comfortable with the fact that I am multilingual. I readily use my Hawaiian, HCE and SAE [Standard American English] abilities in situations I feel are appropriate and my ability to make the switch between each is effortless. To insist that I give up one or more of my languages is to ask that I biologically change my own ethnicity and color of skin; neither is possible or desirable." (KSm, 1995).

A woman, at the time a student teacher, commented "when I began this project, I was hoping to find some answers to the pidgin dilemma. Should pidgin be allowed in the classroom? But as I now know, there is no quick answer. What I've learned is that, as a teacher I will not correct a student for speaking pidgin in class. I now know that this is their language and I need to show respect for it. Also I believe that if I can't understand a student that is talking in Hawaiian Creole English, it is my responsibility to learn it." (TNFf,1993).

A high school social studies teacher in the class wrote "I allow students to use HCE in the classroom when they are speaking to me or when they are speaking to each other.... However, I expect students to use "standard English in most written assignments; there are no restrictions imposed in their journal writing.... Even those of us who believe HCE is a language have ambivalent feelings.... Our attitude may not be totally negative, but our ambivalence may be communicated powerfully to our students." (EOf, 1993).

## Notes

1.  I have identified the sources of these citations by initials of the student interviewer, followed by f[=female] or m[=male], and the year when the interview was conducted.

## References

Baugh, John. 1995. "Sociolinguistic research and high school teacher education." Paper presented at NWAV, Philadelphia.

Day, Richard R. 1980. "The development of linguistic attitudes and preferences." *TESOL Quarterly* 14:27–37.

Drechsel, Emanuel J. this vol. "Language contact in the early colonial Pacific: Evidence for a maritime Polynesian jargon or pidgin."

Hindley, Reg. 1990. *The Death of Irish. A Qualified Obituary.* London: Routledge.

Labov, William. 1982. "Objectivity and commitment in linguistic science: the case of the Black English trail in Ann Arbor." *Language in Society* 11:165–201.

Odo, Carol. 1975. *Phonological Processes in the English Dialect of Hawaii.* Ph.D. dissertation. University of Hawai'i at Mānoa.

Piestrup, A. 1973. *Black Dialect Interference and Accommodation of Reading Instruction in First Grade.* Berkeley: Monographs of the Language Behavior Research Laboratory.

Reinecke, John E. 1969. *Language and Dialect in Hawaii. A Sociolinguistic History to 1935.* Honolulu: University of Hawai'i Press.

Rickford, John R. 1983. "Standard and non-standard language attitudes in a creole continuum." *Society for Caribbean Linguistics Occasional Paper* No. 16. Trinidad: University of the West Indies.

Rickford, John R. and Traugott, Elizabeth C. 1985. "Symbols of powerlessness and degeneracy of symbol of solidarity and truth? Paradoxical attitudes towards pidgins and creoles." In Sidney Greenbaum (ed.), *The English Language Today.* Oxford: Pergamon, 252–62.

Roberts, Sarah Julianne. this vol. "The TMA system of Hawaiian Creole and diffusion."

Romaine, Suzanne. 1992. *Language, Education and Development: Urban and Rural Tok Pisin in Papua New Guinea.* Oxford: Oxford University Press.

———. 1994a. "Hau fo rait pijin." *English Today* 38:20–24.

———. 1994b. "Hawai'i Creole English as a literary language." *Language in Society* 23:527–554.

Sato, Charlene J. 1985. "Linguistic inequality in Hawai'i:the post creole dilemma." In Nessa Wolfson and Joan Manes (eds.), *Language of Inequality*. Berlin: Mouton, 255–272.

————. 1991. "Language attitudes and sociolinguistic variation in Hawai'i". In Jenny Cheshire (ed.), *English Around the World*. Cambridge: Cambridge University Press, 647–663.

Simonson, Douglas. 1981. *Pidgin to da max*. Honolulu: Bess Press.

Trudgill, Peter. 1972. "Sex, Covert Prestige and Linguistic Change in the Urban British English of Norwich." *Language in Society* 1:179–95.

Verploegen, Hildegaard. 1988. "Pidgin in classroom stirs spirited debate by seniors." *Honolulu Star Bulletin*. June 1.

Watson-Gegeo, Karen A. 1994. "Language and Education in Hawai'i: Sociopolitical and economic implications of Hawai'i Creole English." In Marcyliena Morgan (ed.), *Language and the Social Construction of Identity in Creole Language Situations*. Los Angeles: UCLA Center for African American Studies, 101–120.

Wolfram, Walt. 1993. "Ethical considerations in language awareness programs". In J. Plummer (ed.), *Issues in Applied Linguistics* 4:225–255.

# Mutual Intelligibility?

## Comprehension Problems between American Standard English and Hawai'i Creole English in Hawai'i's Public Schools

Susan Bauder Reynolds

*Pa'auilo School, Hawai'i*

## Introduction

For the past thirteen years, I have been observing the language of the students in my fifth grade classroom at Pa'auilo School on the island of Hawai'i (locally called the Big Island because it is the largest in the Hawaiian island chain). This school is part of the statewide system of public education based in Honolulu, on the island of O'ahu. Many of the children on the Big Island, as well as other rural areas around the state, speak what is commonly known throughout the state as "Pidgin" as their first language, learned at home. This is the language linguists know as Hawai'i Creole English (HCE).

Most public school students in rural Hawai'i have limited exposure to American Standard English (ASE) due to their geographic and historic isolation from mainland American culture and language. Traveling to any other island requires air travel costing roughly $100 round trip. Many Big Island students have never been to the state capital, Honolulu, which is 200 miles away on the island of O'ahu. All of the towns and villages on the Big Island could be described as rural. Only two towns, Hilo (on the eastern or windward side of the island) and Kailua-Kona (on the western or leeward side) have populations that approach 35,000, including outlying areas. While exposure to ASE through various forms of public media may give HCE-dominant children some receptive competence in ASE, they do not automatically acquire the ability to switch between HCE and ASE easily (see e.g. Purcell 1984). At the same time, there are other children in the public school system whose first language is ASE, who have limited exposure to HCE, and who are unable to switch between ASE and HCE easily.[1]

There is also a local variety of standard English, which can be called Hawai'i Standard English (HSE). An example of this type would be the speech of sportscasters such as Robert Kekaula on local television, and radio personalities such as Larry Price. This variety can be thought of as the most acrolectal form of HCE. "HSE is ASE with a local flavor" (Joseph Grimes, personal communication). HCE and ASE/HSE are closely related so that they have been described as two ends of a continuum, with HCE on one end and HSE/ASE on the opposite end. As is generally the case in such a continuum, adjacent varieties are usually mutually intelligible. However, the varieties on end points (ASE at its most literary form and HCE at its most local form) are as mutually unintelligible as two different languages would be. Grimes (1994) gives a number of common, specific examples of communication problems that involve people in Hawai'i who are not bidialectal and whose speech is on the opposite ends of the continuum.

HCE is commonly thought of, and often overtly labeled, as "bad English", while ASE is thought of as "good English", both in educational circles and by the general public (see Romaine, this volume). This classification reflects an attitude that is common throughout the world when comparisons between a standard language and a related nonstandard variety are made (see Eades and Siegel, this volume, for evidence from Australia). Negative value judgments about a particular form of language have far reaching effects; they determine curriculum decisions, and are "likely to hinder the design and implementation of adequate educational policies" (Craig 1985: 280).

Even though the first language of most people in Hawai'i has never been ASE, it is significant that Hawai'i's education system has had ASE as the official medium of instruction for over one hundred years (Sato 1985). Ignoring the existence of HCE in language planning and policy has, in fact, tended to be accepted in Hawai'i. Valuing bidialectalism has never been considered seriously as an option by educational institutions. In my conclusion I suggest some new directions for educational policy.

Despite institutional and societal pressures, many speakers of HCE have not bowed to assimilation pressures. Holm (1989: 523) and others have pointed out that a minority language like HCE is "maintained as a symbol of local identity and solidarity in the face of the growing threat of inundation by the mainland's cultural norms." Eastman and Stein (1993: 193) characterize such actions and attitudes as "ethnic retreat," a means to preserve to some extent a culture under attack.

## 1. Comprehension of HCE and ASE at school

The HCE-dominant child entering school may have difficulty comprehending and producing the kind of Standard English used in the classroom for all written material, television and computer programs. Most island children have grown up listening to television and radio which use ASE almost exclusively, and that may be their only resource for hearing ASE as it is actually used by fluent speakers outside of the classroom (Carr 1972; see, however, Grimes, this volume, for a rare example of broadcasting in HCE). Spoken and written ASE differ in formality as well as in other dimensions, so that even some measure of receptive competence does not necessarily prepare a child adequately for the language of the classroom, nor literacy in Standard English more generally.

Students who know only ASE may be disadvantaged in a different way than monolingual HCE speakers because the inability to switch limits social interaction. Outside the classroom, within relaxed peer group settings, the use of HCE is expected. Although ASE speakers may be able to function academically because their own language is used in that domain, responding in socially appropriate ways with their HCE-speaking peers may be difficult. If they have any competence at all, it may be limited to the receptive mode. Students who are not able or choose not to use HCE may be ridiculed for being too *haole*. This term originates from the Hawaiian word for 'foreigner'. It is now applied to Caucasians, or as an insult to a person of any race who is acting unbearably pompous.

The following facts are further indications that there are language difficulties under the present educational system administered by the Department of Education (DOE) in Hawai'i:

1. 50% of Hawai'i public school students living in rural, poorer economic areas regularly score below average on the SAT (Stanford Achievement Test) reading test (Honolulu Star Bulletin 1991, 1992, 1993, 1994; *Honolulu Advertiser* 1990).
2. A much greater percentage of HCE speakers than the DOE's statewide estimate of 60% come from these same areas (State of Hawai'i 1991; Actouka and Lai 1989).
3. These HCE speakers are still told they must learn under an English only policy dating back to 1894 that has never seriously been assessed, with the exception of a few short-lived, geographically limited and now defunct federally-funded programs (Petersen et al. 1969; State of Hawai'i Department of Education 1976, 1988a, 1988b, 1994).

## 2. Research on Big Island Students' Comprehension of HCE and ASE Text

In order to clarify the extent to which comprehension is presently a problem for fifth grade students on the Big Island of Hawai'i, I conducted field work with 418 students from the fifth grade level in public school classes in Hawai'i and among a control group in Texas. For the purposes of this article I will be referring only to the results of a subset of this population. Every school reported that the classes were a heterogeneous, random mix of fifth grade students as characterized by that school's population. Aside from the SAT, the present study has by far the largest sample of any language related study using fifth grade public school students in Hawai'i, and it is the only one I know to have used a control group from another state. The data in this study were gathered during the first two weeks of November 1995.

Because HCE is primarily used orally, students do not usually have the opportunity to read it. Therefore, I chose listening rather than reading comprehension as the appropriate assessment tool. Ching (1963), Speidel (1979) and Speidel et al. (1985) specifically link listening and reading skills using HCE and ASE (see further in 4).

In order to assess and compare the students' comprehension of oral HCE and ASE, I prepared two audio tapes based on a story written by a fifth grader, Michelle Slape, published by Houghton Mifflin in a new fifth grade reading textbook in 1996 (Cooper and Pikulski 1996: 468469). The tape recordings were produced in the sound studio of radio station KBIG in Hilo by a professional disk jockey. Both tapes featured the voices of the same two speakers, both fluent in HCE and HSE who were able to switch between the varieties. A female native HCE speaker read the story, and a male HSE speaker read a series of questions relating to the story. On one tape the story and questions were in HCE; on the other tape the same story and questions were in ASE.

Originally, the introduction, instructions, story, and questions were written in ASE. They were then translated into HCE. A pilot version of the instructions, story, and 31 questions were field tested, then revised several times, with the help of nine native HCE speakers and four native ASE speakers in grades 6–8 in one of the seven schools in this study. Ultimately, the final version contained ten questions that all of the older students could answer with 100% accuracy when the story and questions were given in their native language. Each participating group was given either the HCE tape or the ASE tape. Both versions and the questions are included in the appendix to this article.

The same explicit written instructions were given to each teacher regarding what to say to students and what to do before, during, and after the test, regardless of which version the students heard. Side one of the answer sheet provided for each student asked for information about what language(s) the student speaks and where the student speaks them. These questions were completed as a group, with the classroom teacher reading off the choices and the students reading along and writing their answers on their own answer sheets.

Later, in analyzing the data, the answers given by the students to these questions were used as one way to calibrate students' dominant language, i.e. in accordance with each student's perception of the language he/she used best. The choices were HCE, ASE, and Other, with a space to name the other language. First, students were asked to put an X by all of the languages that they spoke. Second, students were asked to put an X by what language they spoke the most in five specific domains: at home, with friends or relatives, at school, on the school playground, and at the beach or in a park. Again, the choices were HCE, ASE, or Other.

After students indicated their language usage, the tape was turned on with each class receiving either the ASE or HCE tape. First came the introduction explaining the purpose for the study (i.e. "the researcher wants to know what kind of language is easy or hard to understand" on the ASE tape), followed by a brief sample story that included two sample questions. Next, the female voice on the tape asked students to turn over their answer sheets to side two and start the real story with the questions that were to be tabulated for this study.

As the woman read the story, the male voice asked questions at appropriate places on the tape. Questions were interspersed with text rather than at the end of the tape in order to control for the memory factor. The classroom teacher was instructed to push the pause button to stop the tape long enough for students to write their short answers on the answer sheets that were provided. Teachers were explicitly instructed not to repeat any words from the story nor from the questions, but to continue playing the tape after students had stopped writing answers to each question.

## 3. Results

For the purposes of this study, correct short written answers to questions relating to the text are considered to be indications of good comprehension. This seems to be an appropriate measurement, since it follows a common procedure for evaluating students' comprehension in the classroom. These questions were all of the kind that elicit factual answers, not the yes/no variety that encourage people to take stabs in the dark. All the answers were tabulated on a correct/incorrect basis. For example, "Why did she hold the rope?" got answers like "to hold the cow" that were obviously correct, and others like "high in the tree" that showed lack of understanding. Answers that couldn't be evaluated were extremely rare. There was no penalty for faulty spelling or grammar.

The modal number of errors for students tested in their own language is always one, and for students tested on the other language it is always two. This pattern held true for native HCE and for native ASE speakers alike. By itself, this observation might be nothing but a curious coincidence; but it provides a way to characterize the two error patterns shown to be distinct by the contingency test.

Since a total of 10 questions were asked, the range of possible errors was 0–10. For those students hearing the HCE version, regardless of which language they claimed proficiency in, the range of actual errors made was 0–10. Only one student, who had just moved to Hawai'i from the mainland, answered all 10 of the questions incorrectly on the HCE version; the rest of the Hawai'i students hearing the HCE version had a range of 0–7 errors. Those students from Texas who heard the HCE version had errors ranging from 0–8. Those in Hawai'i who heard the ASE version had a range of 0–6 errors; those from Texas who heard the ASE version had a range of 0–7 errors.

Figure 1 shows the number of errors made by Hawai'i students from each of the native language categories placed according to their own assessment of language dominance: B (balanced), P (Pidgin-dominant), and S (Standard English-dominant).[2] Although students were instructed to choose which language they used most, some students put down more than one X in each domain. All X marks were counted. The P language category comprises students who had more than one half of their X marks under the category "Pidgin" on the language self-assessment portion of the answer sheet. The S language category includes students who had more than one half of their X marks under the category "Standard English" on their answer sheets. On pooling columns from the right until all cells in the {P, S} X {0, 1, …} matrix attain a count of 5 or more, the probability that the chi square statistic for the p test could be as large as it is by chance (i.e. if P speakers and S speakers really belonged to the same population) is only .007 (2 degrees of freedom, n = 91), and thus, below the .02 threshold. This shows that the comprehension differences between HCE-dominant and ASE-dominant speakers who listened to an HCE tape were statistically significant.[3]

The arrow draws attention to the higher modal number of errors made on the HCE version of the text by students who consider themselves ASE-dominant. Nevertheless, the errors were quite spread out, suggesting that some ASE

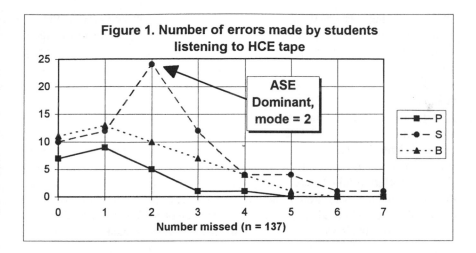

Figure 1. Number of errors made by students listening to HCE tape

speakers have considerably more trouble than others in understanding HCE. This may help to explain why there can be acute problems for ASE speakers who try to comprehend teachers or fellow students who are speaking HCE. As noted earlier, this may put ASE-speaking students at a social disadvantage, since HCE is the acceptable language in many social situations, particularly in rural areas of the Hawaiian islands.

The same analysis using the students' self-evaluation of their dominant language was made for the classes that heard the ASE tape, but the probability is too high for significance. Here p (chi square) = .176 (4 d.f., n = 111). One might suggest that five years of classroom exposure to ASE have indeed made some of the HCE-dominant students more capable of handling Standard English, so that as a group their behavior is only marginally distinct from that of the English-dominant students. However, the errors are again spread out, indicating that there are some students do not automatically acquire proficiency in ASE.

The teachers were also asked to assess each student's language competence based on their personal interactions in the classroom. There was quite a discrepancy between the students' self-assessment of their language-dominance and that given by the teachers for each of the same students. Regardless of the test language, 75% of the teachers tended to classify many more students as balanced between HCE and ASE than the students themselves did. For example, with HCE as the test language, teachers put a majority (53%) into the Balanced category, while only 33% of the students classified themselves as such. In addition, teachers classified only 12 students (9% of the seven classes) as Pidgin-dominant. Such a small number certainly seems unrealistic compared to those same students' self-evaluations, which was 23 (17%), or nearly twice as many. Possibly the teachers counted as Pidgin-dominant only the most basilectal speakers.

Teachers also classified nearly half of the students who listened to the ASE tape as ASE-dominant. As shown in Figure 2, there is a sharply diverse pattern of response compared to the results calculated by using the scores of the students who considered themselves ASE-dominant. Although the mode was one error for those students labeled ASE-dominant by their teachers, there is a cluster of students who made three errors, which is unexpected. The data are statistically significant. Here p (chi square) = .000 (<.02), 3 d.f., n=124). Again, we can see that some students who are on one end of the HCE/ASE continuum are unable or unwilling to switch adequately to the other language. The modal number of errors for students tested in their dominant language is again one, and for students tested in their non-dominant language, it is two.

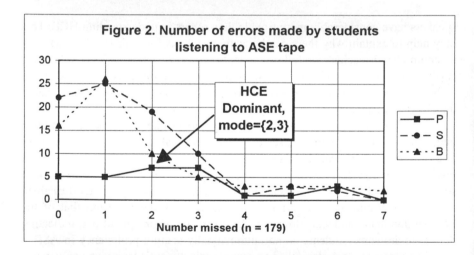

Figure 2. Number of errors made by students listening to ASE tape

There is at least one other notable observation in the results of this study. There were only two classes, from opposite ends of the island, with a mode of three errors out of ten questions. Not surprisingly, they were from exactly the same schools where students tend to be close to one end of the language continuum or the other, rather than balanced in their competence. In one of the classes the teacher said there was only one student who was a native ASE speaker, but none of the students rated themselves as ASE-dominant. The fact that their mode was three errors on the HCE test shows quite strikingly that comprehension is at least as difficult for ASE-dominant students listening to HCE as it is for HCE speakers listening to ASE. However, the status difference between the two languages dictates that speakers of HCE understand and use ASE. Thus, the fact that lack of mutual intelligibility is a problem faced by both groups is usually overlooked.

To put these findings into a different perspective, the Summer Institute of Linguistics, a prominent Bible translation organization, considers that translation is warranted for a speech variety if there is a 90% or lower comprehension rate with surrounding speech varieties. The students who missed three or more answers in this study had a comprehension rate of 70% and below. The modal pattern shown in the results of this study, i.e. missing one answer when listening to one's dominant language and missing two answers when listening in the non-dominant language (whether HCE or ASE) indicates that a great number of students in our public schools are below the 80% comprehension line.

## 4. Conclusion

The finding that students on either end of the HCE/ASE continuum consistently make one error in their dominant language and two errors on their non-dominant language indicates that without explicit assistance in switching, there are some students even at the fifth grade level, who have not been able to 'pick up' competency in the non-dominant language. These difficulties affect all levels of language (from the word to the discourse level, including syntax, phonology, morphemes, and graphemes) and all modalities (listening, speaking, reading, and writing). When a mismatch between the home language (HCE) and the school language (ASE) occurs, there are academic difficulties, particularly in reading for students who must operate in an "English only" school environment. This point has been well documented with children in the elementary grades in Hawai'i (Speidel 1979; Ching 1963; Day et al. 1974 and 1975; Speidel et al. 1985; Choy and Dodd 1976).

My own experience has revealed that when I am not trying to snatch away the language of my students, they do not feel that they have to hang onto it so tightly. Instead, the more we talk and play and practice with both HCE and ASE, the more interested we all become in both languages, and the more willing we all are to take risks and add another dialect to our linguistic repertoire (Reynolds 1991, 1995).

Possibly as a result of bidialectal language-related activity in the fifth grade, the Pa'auilo sixth graders consistently scored better than their peers on the state-mandated SAT test. This test is normed so that nationally 23% of all students score in the below average range, 54% in the average range, and 23% in the above average range. However, Pa'auilo School sixth graders had reading scores of 17% below average in 1992 and only 4% below average in 1994. In culturally comparable HCE-speaking areas elsewhere in the state, 50% or more of the sixth graders regularly scored in the below average range (Honolulu Advertiser 1990; *Honolulu Star Bulletin* 1991, 1992, 1993, and 1994).

A detailed discussion of the changes needed in Hawai'i's educational system is beyond the scope of this paper. However, I will conclude by suggesting some new directions for educational policy which could ensure that HCE and ASE speakers would be served appropriately:

1.    DOE and University of Hawai'i cooperation.
Each institution has strengths that need to be shared with the other. For example, the university has access to recent worldwide research in literacy and related disciplines, and personnel who can be used in teacher training, as well as in conducting original research. The DOE can provide sites and subjects for that research, the structure for disseminating pertinent results to teachers and can give practical insights from the field.

2.    Trained teachers.
Knowing and being able to use and teach the markers of HCE/ASE at the word, sentence, and discourse levels should be part of the teacher training program at the university level, and mandatory for currently employed teachers. (Romaine 1988 and Labov 1970 are good places to begin). Bowie and Bowie (1994) found that the attitudes of prospective teachers of Black English speaking students changed when they began to realize that miscues, or 'goofs' as Dulay (1972) called them, were themselves a reflection of a legitimate, rule governed, alternative spoken dialect, and not merely a faulty grammar system. There is an obvious parallel with HCE.

3.    A user-friendly employment policy.
The DOE should employ teachers who know both the traditional language of education (ASE) and the language of their students (HCE). This is particularly true in rural areas where HCE is likely to be the home language of a majority of the students.

4.    Use current DOE paradigm shifts.
    a.      The shift away from central control and toward school-based management can assist in support above the school level in the development and delivery of new, language-appropriate, child-centered strategies that value

bidialectalism. Schools with a predominately HCE or ASE population base would benefit from such curriculum options.

b.    The shift away from teacher as disseminator of all knowledge toward teacher as colearner and facilitator can help promote a language policy change that includes reading and writing in HCE at times, as well as in ASE. Cooperative learning strategies and *ohana* (Hawaiian: 'family') style class management are culturally appropriate, since they emphasize personal relationships, teamwork, and unity, which are positive values in the local culture, rather than competition or an emphasis on individuals, which are negative local values (Gallimore et al. 1974; Boggs 1985; Watson-Gegeo and Boggs 1977). Currently in the United States there are a number of useful models that elicit an abundance of natural language practice for the purposes of real, not artificial communication. Among these are the Wright Group (Williams 1992, 1993), the International Reading Association (Heath and Mangiola 1991), and the "Experience-Text-Relationship" (ETR) strategy suggested by Au (1979) and used in a current school text (Cooper and Pikulski 1996).

c.    There is a shift away from separate classes for reading and writing toward an integrated language arts curriculum which includes listening, speaking, reading, and writing in all content areas and a related paradigm shift toward talking about appropriate language in specific contexts (see Heath 1986; Cazden et al. 1992; Freeman and Freeman 1992; Stubbs 1986; Cambourne 1988; Graves 1983). We need to extend our vision of this whole language paradigm to include both HCE and ASE in all four modes of communication.

5.    Use models from around the world. We need to study, adapt, and use the best programs that have as their goal adding a new dialect to the students' linguistic abilities (UNESCO 1953; see Hamers and Blanc 1990:Ch. 8 for a summary of a number of programs).

6.    Disseminate and help teachers to use existing DOE documents and materials that value bidialectalism and are practical to use in the classroom (Good 1991; Good and Higa 1993; State of Hawaii 1991, 1992–93).

Now is the time to choose 'additive bilingualism' (Lambert and Tucker 1972), a positive, new direction in language policy, even if complex language and cultural attitudes make it difficult for educational institutions to devalue remediation and subtractive bidialectalism, and even if it means reconsidering a one hundred year old "English-only" monolingual policy. If one of the goals of education is for students to consider literacy as part of their everyday lives, then policy must make it possible for all students to use the language(s) of their everyday lives in literacy-related activities inside the classroom. If one of the goals of education is for students to become equipped with appropriate literacy skills, then policy must make it possible for all students to build on and expand the linguistic skills they bring from home, whether those skills come in the form of HCE or ASE, or some other language.

In building a sound educational policy, as in architecture, form should follow function. If the desired function is to have Hawai'i's students using appropriate literacy skills and participating fully in the pluralistic state of Hawai'i, then the educational form that would follow includes training students to use and value both HCE and ASE. Such a policy would also put Hawai'i on the "cutting edge of reform" in education (Stephen Walter, 1994, International Literacy Coordinator, Summer Institute of Linguistics, personal communication). This paper is intended to be a step in that direction.

## Acknowledgments

I would like to express my appreciation of Charlene Sato whose 1989 article was my first realization that others in the world were seeing what I was observing in my own classroom. She had the classroom experience and linguistic knowledge to be able to articulate what I could not. Through her work and her writing she expanded my knowledge and made me want to know even more, the mark of a true teacher. I would also like to thank Dr. Joseph Grimes, of Cornell University and the Summer Institute of Linguistics, for his help with the design and statistical interpretation of the experiment, for his insightful comments on various versions of this paper, and for his tireless encouragement, without which this experiment would not have been accomplished. Thank you, too, to Dr. Suzanne Romaine of Oxford University who has been a mentor, friend, and a great help on this paper. I would like to acknowledge the help of Dr. Nancy Hadaway of the University of Texas at Arlington; various participating fifth grade public school teachers and students on the Big Island and at Goodman Elementary School in Dallas, Texas; Cynthia (Cindy) Juan and Nelson Ray Parker for volunteering their time and talent to make the audio tapes; and my husband, Dr. Elsbery W. (Jerry) Reynolds, for his love and support.

## Notes

1. An increasing number of immigrant students speak neither HCE nor ASE as their mother tongue. The Hawaiian language is the first language of very few students, although there is a small number of newly created Hawaiian language immersion schools, where Hawaiian is used exclusively.

2. Omitted from Figures 1 and 2 are the data from the students who had incomplete answer sheets (N = 26), students identified by their teacher or by themselves as Other dominant (i.e. did not fit the three categories of P = pidgin-dominant, B = balanced or S = Standard English-dominant). My calculations also do not distinguish between HSE and ASE speakers since these two varieties differ only in surface features.

3. Two groups of data are set to one side in the chi square calculations because they are not useful in discriminating between the two languages, HCE and ASE:

    i.    the answers by students (N = 114) who indicated they were balanced (B) between HCE and ASE (i.e. had an equal number of X marks in the HCE and ASE spaces on the language assessment sheet). They could not be used to discriminate between the two speech communities because they participate in both. Thus, it makes no difference which tape a group of Balanced students heard; the modal number of errors is one — the same score obtained by students who heard the tape in their dominant language.

    ii.    the control group of Texas students (N = 74), who all claimed ASE as their first and dominant language. Their data serves, however, to authenticate the general pattern for the response profile: students tested in their own language peak at 1 error while students tested in their non-dominant language peak at 2 errors in a similar distribution.

## Appendix: HCE and ASE versions of story

HCE Story Script *You Tink Dis Jus One Odda Day?*

    Get strange tings happen in one small town, especially when you stay in da country. Taking care da cattle main ting, but helping da madda deliver one calf, boy, das something else, awready.

    One day, I had go wid my fadda fo' check all his cattle. (1. *How come da girl had go wid her fadda?*) We wen start our truck and head for da pascha. Some quiet was. Only da cows mooing sometimes. Get da new bales hay. Some sweet dey smell. Da wifas smell good in da breeze.

Get some choke cows in dis pascha. When dey had hear my fadda's truck, dey wen run togedah to one place in da pascha. Dad wen pak da truck. Den he wen climb ovah one rusty, ol' bab wia fence for check all da cattle up close. (2. *How come da fadda had climb ova one bab wia fence?*) When almos' pau, he wen spak one young cow trying for give birt'.

    Dad had tell, "How can? We going help her. Bumbye we gotta pull da calf."

    My fadda wen rope da cow, but some strong da buggah. She wen jump da fence and run to da end of da small pascha. We wen walk down to da cow. My fadda had grab da rope from around her neck and tie da odda end to da tree. Me? I wen hol da end of da rope so no can slide off da tree. (3. *How come she wen hold da rope?*) "No let loose da rope", Dad wen warn me. (4. *Dad had warn her for what?*)

    "Some soah my hands was when I wen hol' em tight!" I stay grumbling to him.

    "Still yet, no let go da rope!" Dad wen tell me again. (5. *What had Dad tell again?*)

    For real man, I was some scared! (6. *How she had feel?*) Pitcha dis one tousan' pound cow, if she like, she just go charge into me, lidat.

    Finally, wen da cow had come quiet, my fadda wen start fo' pull on da keiki's foot. Den, he wen get one smaller rope and tie 'em around da hoofs. Some hard he wen pull. (7. *How he wen pull em?*) And e'ry time he wen pull da rope, could see some moa of da calf. (8. *What wen happen e'ry time he had pull da rope?*) Finally, da cow wen lie down, and my fadda had pull out da calf, easy.

    When he had pull out da calf, no could breathe, so my fadda had clean out da mouth. (9. *How come Dad had clean out da mouth?*) Den da madda cow had get up, and we wen take da rope off da neck. Den da cow wen turn around. She wen smell and lick da calf. Still yet, she was in da wrong pascha. For move her, my fadda had pick up da calf an' carry her. Da madda cow only follow.

    Before dat day, I nevah know pulling one calf was some hard work. (10. *What lesson she wen learn dat day?*) What you tink? Easy? O kay den, I like see you try um!

ASE Story Script *Just Another Day?*

    Weird things happen in small towns, especially when you live in the country. Tending to cattle is one thing, but delivering a calf is another.

One day I went with my dad to check his cattle. (1. *Why did the girl go with her father?*) We started our truck and headed for the pasture. It was very quiet unless one of the cows mooed. The sweet smell of freshly baled hay floated around in the cool breeze. There were about sixty cows in this pasture. When they heard my dad's truck, they all went running to one part of the pasture. Dad had to park our truck and then climb over an old, rusty barbed wire fence to check all the cattle closely. (2. *Why did Dad climb over the barb wire fence?*) When he was almost finished, he spotted a young cow trying to have a calf.

Dad said, "She can't have the calf by herself, so we'll have to pull it."

My dad roped the cow, but she was so strong that she jumped the fence and ran to the end of a small pasture. We walked down to the cow, and my dad grabbed the rope that was tied to her neck and tied it to a tree. I had to hold the end of the rope so that it wouldn't slip off the tree. (3. *Why did she hold the rope?*) "You'd better hold on to that rope tight!" Dad cautioned me. (4. *Why did Dad caution her?*)

"It hurts my hands to hold on tight!", I whined.

"You'd better not let go!", Dad repeated. (5. *What did Dad repeat?*)

I was quite scared. (6. *How did she feel?*) Just imagine a thousand pound cow that could come charging at you any time!

When we finally got the cow still, my dad started pulling the calf's hooves out. Then he got a smaller rope and tied it to the hooves. My dad had to pull really hard. (7. *How did he pull them?*) And every time he pulled the rope, a little more of the calf came out. (8. *What happened every time he pulled the rope?*) Finally the cow lay down, and my dad pulled the calf right out.

When he pulled the calf out, my dad had to clean its mouth so it could breathe. (9. *Why did dad clean out the mouth?*) Then the mama cow got up, and we took the rope off her neck. The cow then turned around and started smelling and licking her calf. We still had to get her back in the right pasture, so my dad picked up the calf and carried her and the mama cow followed.

That day I learned that pulling a calf is much harder than people think. (10. *What lesson did she learn that day?*) If you don't believe me, go try it yourself!

# References

Actouka, Melody and Morris Lai. 1989. *Project Holopono Evaluation Report 1987–1988.* Grant No. G008425026. College of Education. University of Hawai'i.

Au, Kathryn. 1979. "Using the experience-text-relationship method with minority children." *Reading Teacher* 32:677–679.

Boggs, Stephen. 1985. *Speaking, Relating, and Learning: A Study of Hawaiian Children at Home and at School.* Norwood, NJ: Ablex Publishing.

Bowie, Robert and Carol Bowie. 1994. "Influencing Future Teachers' Attitudes Toward Black English: Are We Making a Difference?" *Journal of Teacher Education* 45,2: 112–118.

Cambourne, Brian. 1988. *The Whole Story: Natural Learning and the Acquisition of Literacy in the Classroom.* New York: Scholastic TAB Publications.

Carr, Elizabeth. 1972. *Da Kine Talk: From Pidgin to Standard English in Hawaii.* Honolulu: University of Hawai'i Press.

Cazden, Courtney, Patricia Cordeiro, Mary Ellen Giacobbe, Marie M. Clay, and Dell Hymes. 1992. *Whole Language Plus: Essays on Literacy in the United States and New Zealand*. New York: Teachers College Columbia University.

Ching, Doris. 1963. "The effect of a six-month remediation program in oral writing and reading skills of third grade Hawaiian bilingual children." *Journal of Experimental Education* 32:133–145.

Choy, S. J. and D. H. Dodd. 1976. "Standard English-speaking and nonstandard Hawaiian-English speaking children: Comprehension of both dialects and teachers' evaluations." *Journal of Educational Psychology* 68:184–193.

Cooper, J. David and John Pikulski (eds.). 1996. *Explore: Invitations to Literacy*. Palo Alto: Houghton Mifflin.

Craig, Dennis. 1985. "The sociology of language learning and teaching in a Creole situation." In Wolfson and Manes.

Day, Richard, Stephen Boggs, Roland Tharp, Ronald Gallimore, and Gisela Speidel. 1974. "The Standard English Repetition Test (SERT): A measure of Standard English performance for Hawaii Creole English-speaking children." Technical Report No. 15. Honolulu: The Kamehameha Early Education Project.

Day, Richard, Roland Tharp, C. Kim, M. Sloat, and Gisela Speidel. 1975. "The Teaching of English to HCE-Speaking Children." Technical Report No. 29. Honolulu: The Kamehameha Early Education Project.

Dulay, Heidi. 1972. "Goofing: an indicator of children's second language learning strategies." *Language Learning* 22:235–252.

Eades, Diana and Siegel, Jeff. this vol. "Changing attitudes towards Australian creoles and Aboriginal English."

Eastman, Carol and Roberta Stein. 1993. "Language display: Authenticating claims to social identity." *Journal of Multilingual and Multicultural Development* 14, 3:187–202.

Freeman, David and Yvonne Freeman. 1992. "Strategies for promoting the primary languages of all students." *The Reading Teacher* 46,7:552–558.

Gallimore, Ronald, Stephen Boggs, and Cathie Jordan. 1974. *Culture, Behavior, and Education: A Study of Hawaiian Americans*. Beverly Hills: Sage Publications.

Good, Elaine. 1991. "Inservice and preservice training: Language modules final revision." Produced for the Native Hawaiian Special Education Project. Honolulu: State of Hawai'i Department of Education.

Good, Elaine and Marion Higa. 1993. "Pidgin, Standard English and language teaching in the multicultural classroom in Hawaii." Produced for the Native Hawaiian Special Education Project. Honolulu: State of Hawai'i Department of Education.

Graves, Donald. 1983. *Writing Teachers and Students at Work*. Portsmouth, NH: Heinemann.

Grimes, Barbara. 1994. "Evaluating the Hawaii Creole English Situation." *Notes on Literature in Use and Language Programs* 39:39–60. Dallas: Summer Institute of Linguistics.

Grimes, Joseph E. this vol. "Reactions to Bu: Basilect Meets Mesolect in Hawai'i."
Hamers, Josiane and Michel Blanc. 1990. *Bilinguality and Bilingualism*. New York: Cambridge University Press.
Heath, Shirley Brice, and Leslie Mangiola. 1991. *Children of Promise: Literate activity in Linguistically and Culturally Diverse Classrooms*. Washington, DC: National Education Association Center for the Study of Writing and Literacy and the American Educational Research Association.
Heath, Shirley Brice. 1986. "Sociocultural contexts of language  development." In California State Department of Education, *Beyond Language: Social and Cultural Factors in Schooling Language Minority Students*. Los Angeles: National Evaluation, Dissemination, and Assessment Center, California State University, 166–170
Holm, John. 1989. *Pidgins and Creoles*. Volume II. *Reference Survey*. New York: Cambridge University Press.
*Honolulu Advertiser*. 1990. "Stanford Achievement Test Scores Reported School by School." Dec. 21:C:6.
Honolulu Star Bulletin. 1991. "Complete School By School List of  Stanford Achievement Test Series Results in Hawaii Public  Schools." Dec. 27:A:4.
———. 1992. "Complete Stanford Achievement Test  Scores for Hawaii Public Schools." Oct. 2:A:8.
———. 1993. "Complete SAT Scores in Hawaii Public Schools." (Chart). Oct. 8:A:6.
———. 1994. "Complete SAT Scores in Hawaii Public Schools." Nov. 18:A:6.
Labov, William. 1970. *The Study of Nonstandard English*. National  Council of Teachers of English and The Center for Applied Linguistics.
Lambert, Wallace and Richard Tucker. 1972. *Bilingual Education of Children: The St. Lambert Experiment*. Rowley, MA: Newbury House.
Petersen, Robert, Harry Chuck and Arthur Coladaraci. 1969. *Teaching Standard English as a Second Dialect to Primary School Children in Hilo, Hawaii*. Final Report No. 1. U.S. Department of Health, Education and Welfare. Bureau of Research. No. 5–0692. Contract No. OE10–176.
Purcell, April K. 1984. "Code shifting Hawaiian style: Children's  accommodation along a decreolizing continuum." *International Journal of the Sociology of Language* 46:71–86.
Reynolds, Susan Bauder. 1991. *Switching: Teaching Standard English to Hawaii Creole English Speakers, Using Television as a Resource*. M.Ed. Thesis. Heritage College.
———. 1995. "The 'pidgin problem' and some possible solutions for Pa'auilo School." Unpublished paper.
Romaine, Suzanne. 1988. *Pidgin and Creole Languages*. London: Longman.
———. this vol. "Changing attitudes to Hawai'i Creole English:Fo' find one good job, you gotta know how fo' talk like one haole."
Sato, Charlene J. 1985. "Linguistic inequality in Hawaii: the postcreole dilemma." In Wolfson and Manes (eds.), 255–272.

————. 1989. "A nonstandard approach to standard English." *TESOL Quarterly* 23, 2:259–282.

Speidel, Gisela. 1979. "Psycholinguistic abilities and achievement in children speaking nonstandard English." Technical Report No. 91. Honolulu: Kamehameha Early Education Project.

Speidel, Gisela, Roland Tharp, and Linda Kobayashi. 1985. "Is there a comprehension problem for dialect speaking children?: A study with children who speak Hawaiian English." Honolulu: Kamehameha Early Education Project.

State of Hawai'i Department of Education. 1976. *HEP Handbook* (Hawai'i English Program). TAC 761598. Honolulu: Honolulu District Office.

State of Hawai'i Department of Education. 1988a. "Language Arts Program Guide." RS 884–889. Honolulu.

State of Hawai'i Department of Education. 1988b. "Literature Review: Research Findings on Students' Use of Hawaii Creole (Pidgin) English and Relationships with Standard English and School Achievement in Hawaii." (Revised). Honolulu.

State of Hawai'i Department of Education. 1991. OIS Language Section, "Project Akamai Oral Communication Strategies." Honolulu.

State of Hawai'i Department of Education. 1992–93. "Project Narrative, Chapter I, Kaunakakai School." (Moloka'i). Honolulu.

State of Hawai'i Department of Education. 1994. "Hawaii writing assessment field test II SY '94–'95." Honolulu.

Stubbs, Michael. 1986. *Educational Linguistics*. New York: Blackwell.

UNESCO. 1953. "The use of vernacular languages." Paris: United Nations Educational, Scientific and Cultural Organization.

Watson-Gegeo, Karen and Stephen Boggs. 1977. "From verbal play to talkstory: The role of routines in speech events among Hawaiian children." In Susan Ervin-Tripp and Claudia Mitchell Kernan (eds.), *Child Discourse*. New York: Academic Press.

Williams, Rebel. 1992. *Launching a Love of Literature: Integrated Learning Workshops*. Bothell, WA: The Wright Group.

————. 1993. *Launching Literature Circles: Integrated Learning Workshops*. Bothell, WA: The Wright Group.

Wolfson, Nessa and Joan Manes (eds.). 1985. *Language of Inequality*. Berlin: Mouton.

# PART D

# Creole Discourse and Literature

# Beyond Grammar

## Teaching English in an Anglophone Creole Environment

Velma Pollard

*University of the West Indies, Mona, Jamaica*

## Background

The complexity of the linguistic environment of the Anglophone Caribbean has come to be appreciated as a result of descriptions provided by linguists over the last thirty years or so. The official language, English in which the formal motions of the societies are carried out, operates side by side with creoles of English lexicon spoken by the majority of the people. On two islands (St. Lucia and Dominica) there is a vibrant creole of French lexicon as well. English is perceived to be the language of instruction in the region but the ease with which teachers switch from English to Creole (and not necessarily in situations where classroom simulation requires it), makes that statement only half true.

The teacher of English is held responsible for preparing students to pass tests in English Language and to write answers in all other subject areas. Because the content of English Language as a subject area at the high school level has always been vague, and because Grammar has historically had a high profile, teachers have traditionally taught Grammar and have considered it the means of effecting improvement in the students' spoken and written English. The fact that some of them spoke English before they ever heard of Grammar and that all of them speak the creoles without knowing the grammar does not affect that perception.

Exposure to second language teaching techniques and to other modern methods of teaching English has accounted for somewhat of a lessening of the emphasis on Grammar since the decade of the seventies. But the current failure of school children to pass English Language examinations and the panic that has accompanied it has pushed many teachers back into a mode which sees the teaching of Grammar as a panacea for all language learning ills. The pundits in the societies, educated in the early part of the century, have gladly found a scapegoat for the failure in English in the decrease in the teaching of Grammar. Everybody feels competent to write in the press about language and specifically about the teaching of English.

This paper looks at errors in scripts of children writing a "Basic English" examination with a view to identifying some of the areas of difficulty the teacher needs to be aware of in order to help students improve their writing in English. There is no attempt here to amass large quantities of data. The intention is to indicate error type rather than frequency of occurrence. No attempt has been made either, to locate errors in terms of Caribbean territory or to imply that certain speech communities are likely to foster a particular error although that is indeed a fact in the situation. The examples have all been taken from scripts submitted for the Caribbean Examinations Council (CXC) English examination at the Basic Level across the region during one sitting.

A word about that examination is in order. While the Basic level certificate is not considered adequate to allow its holder to qualify for entrance to a tertiary level institution or to be competitive for a job requiring expertise in English, it does indicate that its holder has mastered at least the skills of writing and comprehension (if not of speech) in English. This should allow him/her to function competently in lower level clerical jobs and should prepare him/her for acquiring skills the finer points of which may only be available in books written in English.

The concerns of this paper need to be seen against the background of the expectations of the society for the holders of the certificate in Basic English as well as the expectations of students themselves for their own future in a society where English is the official language and where the inability to use it effectively can get in the way of many otherwise achievable goals.

The official language is not heard much in the communities of our concern. The creoles are the languages of regular usage. But everywhere (expect in Belize) people respond to the question "What language do you speak?" with "English." The errors presented here are largely the result of unfamiliarity with the language of the teacher's expectation if not of his/her usage. The fact that the creoles are English **related** adds to the confusion for the creole-speaking learner.

## Categories of Error

Examples of errors are given here within four categories determined by the aspect of language to which the particular error seems to be related: Phonology,

Lexicon, Grammar, or Idiom. Some comment on the possible causes of error within the categories is followed by suggestions of strategies which teachers might try in an attempt to help students understand the nature of the errors and ways to correct them.

Errors placed in the Lexical and Phonological categories are in a sense new errors since teachers have tended to regard them as spelling errors in a situation where analyses of the creoles are relatively rare, as are methods associated with these analyses. That the examples are taken from scripts written by people who have spent at least four years in secondary institutions and who were, presumably, considered able to pass, if not do well in, an examination in Basic English, indicates how grave the classroom problems are.

## Category I: Errors associated with Phonological/Spelling inaccuracy

*Examples*

a. I enjoyed the SUMMOND (sermon)
b. The same day Sam visited the man and told him that he has a SUMMOND for him to be in court a week from today (summons)
c. That was the week of the Grenada INVERSION (invasion)
d. "Do you take this Mary as your wedded wife?" He answered, "Yes I do," and the same question VICEY VERSAL. (Vice versa)
e. You are CO-ORDINALLY invited to attend the reception (cordially)
f. My brother and I attended the BASULAR party (bachelor)
g. I decided to go to the city to earn an EARNEST living (honest)
h. They will OWN extra pocket money (earn)
i. I came in town that THEY (day)
j. I was finished and was back THEY with my bird. (there)
k. We WHEN THROW it (went through)
l. Suppose Miss have lost it or someone have TAKING it. (taken)
m. The crowd became thicker and their excitement SEIZED (ceased)
n. On reaching the market Dave became A WHERE of where he was going ... That day they skirted the town looking for Dave but he was KNOW where to be seen (aware; nowhere)

*Discussion*

This category of errors whose origins are thought to be related to phonological phenomena is, in this sample of errors, the largest. While this may be the result of chance in terms of which scripts the researcher examined, the greater likelihood is that these errors are in fact most numerous. They are the result of the effect of the Creole pronunciation of English words in different Caribbean territories on the written language of the students. Research in Caribbean languages very early in its existence identified obvious differences between the standard pronunciations of certain English words and those prevailing in some Caribbean territories.

As early as 1961 Cassidy detailed those differences which he had noticed in the speech of Jamaicans (some of which had been commented on by Russell 1898!). More recently Winer (1983, 1986), analyzing errors in the writing of secondary school children in Trinidad, includes errors associated with phonological inaccuracies in her "Spelling" category. Two of her examples are RIVA (river) and SONG (sound). These she attributes to "Transfer Phonology" which is one aspect of a more general category of error attribution labeled "Transfer," accounting for those errors which result from "... inappropriate application of L1 items and rules to the target language." (1986: 95)

In terms of the classroom and the problems faced by teachers of English where children from Caribbean speech environments are the pupils, the teaching of what is traditionally regarded as Grammar can be of little help where this kind of error is at issue.[1]

It seems that what is required first is the teachers' awareness of the differences between the standard and non-standard pronunciations and the decision not only to indicate these to students but to help them appreciate the appearance on the page of the words they use. In other words, students need to be able to recognize the words in newspapers and books and to see them not as strange words but as words which already are part of their own working vocabularies. The student in one of my classes, a trained teacher with more than five years experience, who did not recognize CELOTEX on the page because in her mind it was SALITEX, that being her pronunciation and presumably that of her hardware merchant, is not so rare.

The teacher of English is not required to be a teacher of speech and is not trained to be that. But she/he can initiate discussions on a variety of subjects requiring a wide range of vocabulary items. Students can be asked to report these discussions in writing and so be made to reproduce words they have used in discussion on the page. The teacher as facilitator can make a point of indicating what the troublesome words should look like on the page. Students from these communities share with speakers from Standard English speaking environments the errors normally associated with problems of spelling homophones like THERE and THEIR. The situation is compounded however, by words which may be regarded as false homophones like those in the examples in this category.

A striking one is the item SUMMOND in examples Ia and Ib used to mean both "sermon" and "summons". Note also examples Ii and Ij where THEY represents both "day" and "there". Somewhat more frightening in terms of the teacher's recognition of the learner's meaning is the kind of error represented by example Ik where the sentence might have to be spoken aloud for the sense to emerge. Context, is of course paramount.

The task of classifying errors into their appropriate categories may itself present a problem for the teacher who has to decide, with little or no advance training, to which category a particular error belongs. Note in this regard that example l in category I is also placed in Category III (example IIIh). If the error is judged to be phonological, then a grammatical explanation (which I have heard given) involving present and past participles can do very little good. The difference in pronunciation between TAKEN and TAKING must be addressed.

The importance of Reading to the child's educational advancement has been greatly emphasized in discussions on second language learning. The reading of texts, not only in the content areas but in areas having to do with children's experience and their interests, is important here. There can be no excuse for a Jamaican schoolboy, for example, to have to write RICKET (which is one pronunciation on the playing field) for WICKET at a time when so much has been written about cricket in fiction and when reports on matches are so common in the local newspapers. Those teachers who make the newspaper a part of the normal classroom fare help students to relate experience to expression in English.[2]

## Category II: Errors associated with Lexical inaccuracies

*Examples*

a. Days after days TRODDING the same plains he got nothing. (treading, walking through)
b. The mob SIGHTED* Mr. Banday running (saw; noticed)
c. I onced asked a man where he worked and he said some words IRREPEAT-ABLE and the crowd laughed like hell.
d. After his BETTERMENT he decided to continue his journey (recovery)
e. The animals belongs to people of my village who have become NEG-LETTERS of their animals (neglecters)

*Discussion*

Most of the comments I have made concerning errors associated with Phonology may well be applied to errors associated with Lexicon. In fact other teachers of English might make one category of the phonological and lexical categories suggested here especially since the lexical category is small in this sample. Again the size may be the result of the chance selection of scripts. If the sample had favored territories where French Creole is spoken, earlier studies suggest that this category might have been large.

What is interesting here however, is the fact that two of the five examples (TRODDING, SIGHTED) are words from the vocabulary of Rastafari (see Pollard 1994: 5), a philosophical movement which has in the last two decades spread from its place of origin, Jamaica, to the Eastern Caribbean and indeed to metropolitan cities where significant numbers of Black people reside. With regard to the words from the vocabulary of Rastafari the teacher will need to discuss quite openly and without prejudice (if possible), the need to use the forms of items expected in an English exercise except where verbatim reports are given.[3]

With regard to "sighted" (sentence IIb) a colleague has suggested that the popular use of "sight" for the English "see" is as much a feature of the age of satellites as it is of the influence of Rastafari. And perhaps it is. In any case there is the need for the child to be able to distinguish between "seeing" and "catching sight of". Examples IIc, IId, and IIe are all the result of generalizing a principle which applies in the formation of certain English words. Example IIe however requires special comment because it is an addition to a list of items (formed by adding agentive *-er* to a verb or noun) which seems to be growing at a very fast rate. Some other (even more egregious) items are:

> *liver*: one who lives/resides ("You are not a liver here?"[are you?])
> *typewriter*: one who types/typewrites ("The youngest one is a typewriter")

Although these may seem like logical extensions of the word-formation process that yields *baker* from *bake*, they are not conventional English words, at least not with these meanings. ("Neglecter" is rare as an agentive, but it is at least a conventional form.) English is not perfectly logical or consistent in this regard. The teacher has to treat each new item as it appears and indicate why it needs to be rejected.

### Category III: Errors associated with Grammatical inaccuracy

*Examples*

a.  An old time friend of mine brought an invitation to attend his wedding which WOULD TOOK PLACED the evening at 4 o'clock
b.  We had WALKEN for an exact three hours when all of a sudden the rain

POUR down heavily.

c. When it was at the bottom of the loop, that was fine but when we went up in the air and then was STUCKED UPSIDED down for about 1 minute that was the worst part of all.

d. I ONCED asked a man where he worked.

e. The pastor then asked the couple to cut the cake then feed THEIR ONE ANOTHER

f. The place WERE very beautiful and nice and a lot of people were there to attend the wedding. Music WERE playing loudly and the people were dancing.

g. I DIDN'T NOT take notice of NOTHING

h. Suppose Miss HAVE lost it or someone HAVE TAKING it.

i. Sometimes drivers are VERY HURRY and HAS a very high speed limit and by the time they BRAKES at fast rate the vehicle can either TURNED over and KILLED whosoever is in THEIR or TURNED the car right around.

## Discussion

This is the category of error which results from misapplication of the rules of English grammar and so the category which should be most amenable to elimination as a result of the intervention of the teacher who favors the explicit teaching of Grammar. The examples here illustrate a variety of problems. Since more than half of them have errors connected in some way to the expression of past events or states, that problem deserves special comment. Past time expression is particularly troublesome to the creole-speaker who tries to speak/write English. In most creoles the onus of time marking does not rest on verb endings but on adverbials, verb stativity, and the context of the activity under review. It is difficult for the creole-speaking child to internalize the notion of the primacy of marking the verb morphologically for expression of time.

Example IIIa suggests that the student has learned the past tense forms of "will" and "take" but not the details of their application. A rule is here generalized to include even "place" which is not recognized as part of the verbal unit "to take place". In example IIb a rule which applies to one verb list (which includes "take") is applied to a verb ("walk") from a different list. No attempt is made to mark the pastness of the second verb "pour." The unmarked verb used to represent past actions or events is a commonplace in creoles. This error is therefore predictable. To the extent that teachers get greater knowledge about how the system works, they should be able to point to predictable errors before they occur.

Example IIIc illustrates the double marking sometimes given verbs in the past tense. So "stick" becomes STUCK(ED). Another verb frequently treated this way is "pack" which becomes PACKTED. While "upsided" is an example of the generalization of marking beyond verb to adverb, it is also a form commonly used in the past environment. The teacher might well predict this error and so prevent it. Generalizing the rule to "once(d)" in example IIId is less predictable. Both however illustrate the lack of distinction in the mind of the student between items with different functions as well as a certain lack of clarity about the system of marking for past time.

Example IIIf illustrates another kind of generalization. There is acceptance here of the fact that "were" is the past tense (plural) form of the verb "to be." "Place"and "music" are forced into the mold into which the other subjects fit easily and accurately.

I do not think that any old-fashioned drilling of the past tense form of the English verb is likely to correct this kind of error. The marked forms are all strange to the creole-speaker whose language may use the same form no matter what time frame is indicated. Opportunities have to be provided for students to use these unfamiliar forms in the classroom and the relationship between the spoken word and its written representation has to be clearly established.

Any form that is not creole is regarded by the student as English. Hyper-corrected forms like those appearing in example IIIa are probably heard as the best English produced by some adults in the society in situations requiring the formal language. The formal situation in the Caribbean invariably requires English. Teachers need to be aware of the trauma students undergo when they produce what they have heard in formal situations, and learn from the teacher, or her/his red-ink pen markings, that it is incorrect. This is particularly difficult where the rationale is articulated by the teacher in terms related to a rule of grammar which is likely to be illogical.[4]

The requirement that the past tense form of the verb be used where past event or state is expressed may well seem unreasonable where some other indication of pastness is already in place. English is in fact redundant in this respect. This is immediately clear if you examine the adverbials which the learner has to include in the sentence after he/she has altered the verb.

In example IIIe "one another" functions like a noun (perhaps "partner" here) and so is accompanied by a possessive adjective. This example will be considered again in Category IV.

Example IIIg illustrates usage common in early standard and in contemporary non-standard English — the double negative (here a triple negative). The intention is to represent the positive. The writer has to be made to understand that the fact that the statement seems logically defensible does not make it correct for English.

Example IIIh, which was partly treated within Category I (see II), also illustrates the difficulty with the parts of the auxiliary verb required to express the perfective. The verb "to have" for some reason poses as many difficulties as does the verb "to be".

Example IIIi illustrates several error types. The first two errors link it to example IIIe in terms of idiom and we will return to that aspect later. The verb "has" for the English " have" is part of the confusion mentioned above of parts of the verb "to have". The past tense verbs later in the sentence are part of the hypercorrection also discussed before. Past tense forms of the verb in creoles where the verb is usually unmarked, are frequently found in hypercorrected utterances which label speech "English" in the minds of the speaker.

## Category IV: Errors associated with Idiomatic inaccuracy

*Examples*

a.    THEIR ONE ANOTHER (see IIIe above)
b.    VERY HURRY.... BRAKES (see IIIi above)
c.    The airport was not as beautiful as Barbados OWN but you could still appreciate it
d.    The only way we can get rid of the dogs is if ME AND YOU gang up together and the whole society even the health department and discuss the problem

*Discussion*

Examples IVa (=IIIe) and IVb (=IIIi) are relevant to this category as well as the preceding one. "THEIR ONE ANOTHER" is a translation into English of "dem wan aneda" the Jamaican Creole equivalent of the English "each other". "VERY HURRY" is considered to be English by the Trinidadian student who says "yu tuu hori" in Trinidad Creole ("you (are in) too (much of a) hurry"). To "BRAKES," which translates into English as "to apply brakes" is common throughout the Anglophone Caribbean. "OWN" (example IVc) is the equivalent of the possessive as in "Barbados own," "John own," "my own" where English would have "Barbados'," "mine," and "John's." "ME AND YOU" (example IVd) where English would have "You and I" is particularly common in Jamaica where the pronoun "me" functions both as subject and object.

These are examples of idiomatic inaccuracy which survive in students' writing long after they have conquered plural nouns and past time verbs in English. Frank comparison and contrast between the relevant creole and English seem to be the only route open to the teacher here.

There are classroom tasks which can make translation a pleasant and exciting assignment as well as a useful teaching strategy. These include classroom skits in Creole to be played with English sub-titles in much the same way that Kung Fu movies appear on local screens.

## Conclusion

What the suggestions in this paper have in common is that they require the teacher's acceptance of the fact that the teaching of Grammar as it has traditionally been understood has failed to correct the errors exemplified here and will continue to fail to do so. Teachers need to experiment with imaginative methods triggered by the more precise linguistic analyses now available. Shields' (1989: 52) comment on the task of language educators is to the point:

> What is certain is that if all that is established is a return to the formal teaching of English via traditional text-book rules, the same misinterpretations which were initially responsible ... will be reinforced.

In a later paper the same writer mentions concrete alternatives suggesting the exploitation of all aspects of the media in the classroom. Note for example her comment that:

> The new emphasis will be on developing active rather than passive learner/participants who... have the opportunity to critically evaluate, modify and transform the offerings they receive through discussion and constant practice. (Shields-Brodber 1995: 27)

There are no simple answers to the difficulties confronting the teacher in the English classroom in a complex linguistic situation. Efforts are being made by individual educators to deal with those problems they consider most immediate at any particular grade level. But there is need for a more general and a more comprehensive attempt to find solutions. The placing into the categories recommended here of errors which might all have been considered errors of either "grammar" or "spelling" under the old system, seems a reasonable point at which to begin.

## Notes

1. Notice that several of the sentences in the examples are structurally correct in much the same way as Lewis Caroll's famous lines which begin "Twas brillig and the slythe toves/Did gyre

and gimble in the wabe..." are correct.

2. Shields' (1989)comments on competing models of Standard English in Jamaica and Pemagbi's (1995) remarks with regard to the sometimes doubtful English of newspapers in Sierra Leone suggest that teachers might want to give informed preamble to the use of newspapers without entirely negating their usefulness.

3. Even in the language of educated speakers in the Caribbean, words from the Rasta vocabulary are now being used quite unselfconsciously. I believe that in the standard varieties of Caribbean English the form TROD for example (see sentence "a") will entirely replace TREAD and join that list of verbs (including "put" and "cut") whose present and past forms are identical. Until this happens however, the teacher needs to indicate to the student the preferred English form. For more on this see Pollard 1994.

4. The present tense is an even greater challenge for the creole speaker. The rule that a singular subject takes a singular verb is difficult to defend when examples like the one below are given:
   I do not drink milk
   She does not drink milk
   They do not drink milk

# References

Cassidy, F. G. 1961. *Jamaica Talk-Three hundred years of the English language in Jamaica.* Kingston: Institute of Jamaica.

Pemagbi, J. 1995. Using Newspapers and Radio in English Language Teaching: The Sierra Leone Experience. *English Teaching Forum* 33. 3.

Pollard, Velma. 1994 *Dread Talk-The language of Rastafari.* Kingston, Jamaica: Canoe Press,

Russell, T. 1868. *The etymology of Jamaican grammar by a young gentleman, M. DeCordova* Kingston, Jamaica.

Shields, K. 1989. Competing models of Standard English in Jamaica. *English World Wide* 10. 1.

———. 1995. The Media and the demise of Standard English in Jamaica or Where have our trusty English language models gone? *Journal of English Teachers* (Jamaica). Special Anniversary Issue, November 1995.

Winer, L. 1986. An analysis of errors in written compositions of Trinidadian Secondary School students. *Caribbean Journal of Education* 13, 1 and 2.

# PART D

# Creole Discourse and Literature

# On the Marking of Temporal Sequencing in Vernacular Liberian English

John Victor Singler

*New York University*

*Feni/Finish* forms part of the tense-mood-aspect system of Kru Pidgin English, Nigerian Pidgin, and Vernacular Liberian English.[1] It occurs post-clausally in the first two of these varieties, as can be seen in (1) and (2).[2]

(1)     Kru Pidgin English
        a go tu ma rum, a lɔk  ma rum,  put ma drɛs, put ma ta *feni*,
        I go to my room I lock my room put my dress put my tie
        go shɔ.
        go shore
        'I went to my room and locked the door. After I had put on my
        uniform and tied my tie, I went ashore.'          (Ghana Steward)

(2)     Nigerian Pidgin
        a (dɔn) wɔsh plet *finish*.
        I      wash plate
        'I have already washed (the) dishes' or 'I have finished washing
        (the) dishes.'                                 (Faraclas (1989: 430))

Vernacular Liberian English (VLE), the pidgin continuum that spans all of Liberia's nonstandard varieties of English except Settler English and Kru Pidgin English (Singler 1997), displays *feni* (occasionally *fenish*) both post-clausally (as in (3)) and preverbally (as in (4)).[3] (Henceforth all examples come from VLE unless otherwise noted.)

(3)    afta yu skrash di ras *fenish*, wɛn ɛni gras en e, yu tra tu
       after you scratch the rice          when any grass in it you try to
       hɔl e aw.
       haul it out
       'Once you have planted the rice, then you weed the field.'

                                                            (Fanima Boatman)

(4)    wɛn yu go, yu brɔsh di bush. yu *feni* brɔsh e, yu kɔt di
       when you go you brush the bush you          brush it you cut the
       stek.
       stick
       'When you go, you cut the brush. Once you have cut the brush
       completely, then you chop down the trees.'          (Fanima Painter)

In VLE, *feni* occurs far more often preverbally than post-clausally. Indeed, in a
VLE corpus of over seventy hours, *feni* shows up post-clausally only in a small
portion of the sample, its occurrence limited to the speech of elderly speakers in
Robertsport, a coastal town sixty miles northwest of Monrovia.[4]

Because the West African pidgins referred to thus far have most likely
descended from a single older West African English-lexifier pidgin, it seems
likely that *feni/finish* developed in post-clausal position, its move to preverbal
position in VLE occurring after that variety had developed its own separate
history. Guyanese Creole English (GCE) *don* also occurs both post-clausally and
preverbally. Bickerton (1975) makes a case there too for a scenario in which *don*
originated post-clausally and then moved to preverbal position.[5]


## 1.   The semantics of *feni*

The first point to be made with regard to the semantics of *feni* is that, as part of
its grammaticalization as an auxiliary, it has undergone semantic bleaching such
that it now refers not simply to an action's or state's end-point but to its entirety.
Examples where an event is virtually instantaneous and, therefore, not readily
dissectible into temporal units illustrate this (as in (5)) as do instances where *feni*
marks the duration of a stative verb rather than any change produced by its
cessation (as in (6)). (Ordinarily while *feni* co-occurs with a bare main verb in
basilectal VLE, it co-occurs with a main verb bearing the suffix *-en* (< *-ing*) in
the mesolect, as in (5) and (6). The suffix bears no imperfectivity here; presumably, *feni V-en* is modelled on Standard English *finish V-ing*, the fundamental
differences notwithstanding between the construction's meaning in Standard

English and in VLE.)

(5)    ... hya hen dɛ   na,   de   *feni* kelen   hen fɔ ran-pɛn
        here him there now   they        kill-ing him for round-pan
        kɔrɔshən.
        corruption
        '... Just look at him. They killed him for 'round-pan' [i.e. rampant]
        corruption.'                                              (Patience)

(6)    a *feni* leven    tu gbanga.
        I        live-ing to Gbarnga
        'I remained in Gbarnga,' not *'I stopped living in Gbarnga.'
                                                                  (Shorty)

The meaning of *feni* shows strong parallels to the meaning of African American
Vernacular English (AAVE) *done* and Guyanese Creole English (GCE) *don*.[6]
Like them, it ordinarily expresses Completive, Perfect, and/or Intensive. Given
this array of meanings, it is not surprising that there are competing semantic
analyses, specifically as to which elements of an auxiliary's meaning are primary
and which derivative. Labov et al. (1968) see distinct components as competing
and equally primary, namely Perfective (as in (7)) and Intensive (as in (8)).[7]

        African American Vernacular English
(7)     You don't have it, 'cause you *done used* it in your younger age.
                                                              (1968: 265)

(8)     I forgot my hat! I *done forgot* my hat! I *done forgot*!
                                                              (1968: 266)

They comment:

> The meaning of *done*, like so many elements of the central grammatical
> system, is inevitably disjunctive. It has a perfective meaning, and with it there
> is usually associated an intensive meaning. But there are occasions when the
> intensive sense occurs without a perfective sense, and then *done* is seen as
> perfectly appropriate. This is equally the case when a non-intensive perfective
> situation occurs.... This is part of the general process by which meanings
> cluster, overlap, but never perfectly coincide (1968: 266).

Seeking to unify the elements of *done*'s meaning, Bickerton (1975) argues that,
for GCE *don* as well as AAVE *done*, there is an underlying semantic unity, and
it is expressed by the feature (and feature value) [+ Completion]. Thus, rather
than saying that *done* is sometimes Perfective and sometimes Intensive, Bickerton says that the sense of *done* can in all cases be expressed by paraphrases

involving 'complete,' 'completed,' or 'completely.' Along these lines, paraphrases for the AAVE sentences in (7)–(8) are given in (9)–(10).

(9)     Paraphrase of (7)
        You don't have it because you used it up **completely** in your
        younger age.

(10)    Paraphrase of (8)
        I forgot my hat! I **completely** forgot my hat! I **completely** forgot it!

In a similar effort to unify the various elements of *don*'s meanings, Rickford
describes GCE *don* as an "Emphatic Perfect" (1987: 125).

While 'Emphatic Perfect' may describe *don*, it does not hold for *feni* in that
there are instances of *feni* that are Completive and Intensive but not Perfect.
Examples (11) and (12) are cases in point.

(11)    de  se  kɔpugai wɔn tan, di  mɛ  *feni* klin  di  mɛ  he.
        they say corporal one time the man      clean  the man head
        'They called the corporal, and he came immediately and shaved off
        all the man's hair.'                                  (Nimba Cook)

(12)    di  pɛsɔn  wa  kɔt di  rop, a *feni* flash di  pipi    ɔn hez fes, ɔ.
        the person what cut the rop I      flash the peepee on his face all
        'The person who cut the rope, I urinated all over his face.'

                                                          (Fanima Builder)

McCoard (1976) argues that Completive is not a necessary component of Perfect
and should not be considered a core part of the definition of Perfect, even for
telic events. He offers (13) as an example of a sentence where a Perfect-marked
telic verb is not complete; in this case, the "persuading" has not taken and is
hence incomplete.

(13)    American English
        I have persuaded him once already, but he may have lost heart and
        need another talking to.                         (McCoard 1976: 150)

Without exception in VLE, however, the Perfect uses of *feni* are Completive.
Whether *feni* is Intensive or not, whether it is Perfect or not, it is Completive. As
such, Completive seems the most important element of *feni*'s meaning.[8] (A more
detailed analysis of the meaning of *feni* and kindred VLE auxiliaries is given in
Singler (1984).)

I have presented evidence from auxiliaries in other languages because these
auxiliaries seem to share a fundamental congruence. Still, it is also true that the
semantics of these auxiliaries are by no means identical across languages. (Cf.

Edwards' (1995) discussion of crucial differences between GCE *don* and AAVE *done*). Dayton (1996) sees AAVE *done* as encompassing two types of Perfect, experiential and resultative, with "counterexpectation" and possibly disapproval underlying both types of Perfect. In VLE, on the contrary, it is quite clear that counterexpectation — to say nothing of disapproval — is completely at odds with how *feni* is used. As will be discussed in the next section, in the VLE basilect *feni* occurs most often to mark the expected, not the unexpected.

## 2.    The Function of *feni*

In what follows I will be making use of continuum terminology, specifically "basilect" and "mesolect." It is therefore appropriate to note that, while a given speaker ordinarily occupies a range across the continuum rather than a single point, in the Liberian case there are clear social correlates of a speaker's range, namely whether or not a speaker began the acquisition of VLE as a child or as an adult, how much western education the speaker had, and where the speaker acquired VLE (whether in Monrovia, elsewhere on the coast, or in the interior). The correlation between these factors and linguistic behavior vis-à-vis the continuum is discussed and demonstrated in Singler (1984, 1987a, 1988, 1997).

One of the cornerstones of Bickerton's prototypical creole TMA system is the anterior tense (Bickerton 1980; Singler 1990). Bickerton states: "A marker of anterior aspect indicates past-before-past for action verbs and simple past for state verbs" (1980: 5). In subsequent work Bickerton refines his definition. In *Roots of Language*, anterior is described as being "prior to the current focus of discourse" (Bickerton 1981: 91). In his model, anteriority provides the tense component of the TMA triad of the creole prototype. Following Gibson (1982), I wish to recast anteriority in the light of Traugott (1975). Traugott distinguishes between temporal sequencing, on the one hand, and tense, on the other:

> Temporal sequencing, also called serial ordering or serialization, involves the relation of two events, A and B, as overlapping, preceding, or following each other.... [S]equencing and tense should not be confused since tense involves speaker deixis, while sequencing involves the anchoring of events with respect to each other, but not necessarily to the speaker (Traugott 1975: 208).

From this perspective, it can be seen that anteriority falls under temporal sequencing, not under tense. That is, anteriority marks the **disruption** of temporal order.

By introducing Traugott's terminology, I do not mean to suggest that there

is some far-reaching difference in this area between her and Bickerton. Bickerton (1979), for example, is quite close in spirit to Traugott (1975). I am introducing Traugott's terminology here because the term "temporal sequencing" is
especially apt for what I wish to discuss.

In presenting Guyanese *don*, Bickerton notes that it occurs frequently in
process descriptions, such as accounts of how to grow rice, and infrequently
elsewhere. In fact, with reference to the rice-growing texts, Bickerton comments
that "[w]ithout these texts, the incidence of *don* would have been so low that it
could conceivably have been overlooked in analysis" (1975: 40).

Though not perhaps so extreme, the distribution of *feni* in the Liberian
English basilect is similar. Most of its occurrences are in procedural texts (as in
(14)), narratives (as in (15)), or hypothetical examples (as in (16), hypothetical
examples being a frequently used rhetorical device in Liberian speech).

(14)    a procedural text
        yɔ   go en di  bush, deg sɔn   ho.  dɛn *feni* deg da   ho   deg
        y'all go in the bush  dig some hole then       dig that hole dig
        da ho,  dɛn yu  put dɛt ova e.
        that hole then you put dirt over it
        'You go into the forest and dig a hold. Dig the hole very, very deep
        and cover it with [leaves and] dirt.'                    (Gedeh Childminder)

(15)    a narrative
        dɛn  a tek  da  wɔn shelen. a gev da  mɛ.  put mi ensad da  ples.
        Then I take that one shilling I give that man put me inside that place
        wɛn  de   *feni* tek  di  lod,  put e ensad da  ples, lɔk  e, bo! di
        when they       take the load put it inside that place lock it bo  the
        tren muv  aw.
        train move out
        'Then I took that one shilling and gave it to the man, and he put me
        inside the train. Once they had taken the load and put it in the train,
        they locked the car, and bo! the train moved out.' (Fanima Builder)

(16)    a hypothetical example
        ɛn du-gu   nɛva mek sɔnbadi   bi yu   frɛn. yu kɛn kɔn
        and do-good never make somebody be your friend you can come
        hya, a tek des ho     drenk hya, a gev e tu yu, yu *feni* drenk,
        here I take this whole drink here I give it tu you you       drink
        dɛn  yu  go.
        then you go
        'And good actions toward someone never makes that person be your

friend. You can come here, and if I take this whole drink here and give it to you, you might drink it and leave.'    (Lofa Shopkeeper)

What these three discourse types have in common is the nature and centrality of their temporal organization. Each is structured along a time-line.

To measure the distribution of *feni* quantitatively, I classified occurrences first according to whether they occurred in a procedural text, narrative, hypothetical example, or none of these three.[9] An illustration of "none" is given in (17).

(17)    [the speaker, asked to answer a vexing riddle, says:]
        a *feni* ɛnsa    ɛva sens o. a se  e sɔ vɛri had.
        I     answer ever since    I say it is very hard
        'I answered a long time ago. I said it's very hard.'
                                                    (Lofa Shopkeeper)

Reported speech within, for example, a narrative was placed in the "none of these three" category. This is because reported speech can depart from the narrative's basic time line and perhaps has a time line of its own. For comparison of basilect to mesolect, social criteria were used, with a speaker considered a basilectal speaker if the speaker had little or no formal western education, had begun the acquisition of VLE (or any form of English) as an adult, and had not grown up in the environs of Monrovia. If any of the three did not hold for a speaker, then the speaker was considered to be a mesolectal speaker.

In the basilect, 82% of all the occurrences of *feni* were in narratives, procedurals, or hypotheticals (54/66), while only slightly more than half of *feni*'s occurrences among mesolectal speakers were within these discourse structures, 54% (36/67).

Given that there is a strong tendency in the basilect for *feni* to show up in one of these three temporally ordered discourse events, one must next ask what *feni* is doing there. That is, when it shows up, what does it signal? It is my contention that, for the basilect, when *feni* shows up in a temporally ordered discourse event, its function is to **reinforce** the underlying temporal sequence. When *feni* occurs, it is ordinarily in one of the two sequences given in (18), where the order of the clauses matches the chronological order of the events they describe.

(18)    $V_i$–*feni* $V_j$–$V_k$
        $V_i$–*feni* $V_i$–$V_j$

The first strategy is illustrated in (15) and (16) above, and the second in (4) and (14). An example of a use of *feni* that fits neither of these strategies — and that goes against the claim being made here — is given in (19).

(19)    na   wi  ste  en di  ro   wɔn, di  wɔn mek  tu,  wi  rish  tu di
        now  we  stay in the  road one   the one  make two  we  reach to the
        mɛ  kɛn,  tu bɛlɛbu.  heeee! wi rish  dɛ,   de   *feni* bɔn  hez
        man  camp  to Bellehbu        we reach there they       burn his
        tan   ɔ;  hez has    o,  ɔ!
        town  all his  house o  all!
        'We were on the road a full day, and on the second day we reached
        the man's camp in Bellehbu. Heeee! When we got there, [we saw
        that] they had burned his town to the ground — his house, every-
        thing!'                                                (Nimba Cook)

In (19), the burning had occurred prior to the men's arrival; the sequence of
clauses thus fails to match the sequence of events, and this example is exception-
al. It is *feni* acting solely as an intensive marker rather than *feni* as preserver of
temporal sequencing. Of the 54 occurrences of *feni* in temporally ordered
discourse events, 50 conform to one of the order-preserving strategies presented
in (18), a rate of 93%. In contrast, the rate in the mesolect is 56% (20/36). In the
mesolect, on the other hand, far more than in the basilect, *feni* serves to mark the
Perfect without necessarily preserving temporal order. (For present purposes,
Comrie's (1976: 52) "continuing present relevance of a past situation" can be
used as a definition for the Perfect.) While only 61% percent of the basilectal
occurrences of *feni* fit this definition of the Perfect, 88% percent of the mesolectal occurrences do.

    The data in (20) summarize the distributions under discussion:

(20)    What percentage of all uses of *feni* occurs in temporally ordered
        discourse events, i.e. narratives, procedurals, or hypotheticals?

        Basilect              54/66 82%   Mesolect              36/67 54%

        Of those occurrences in *feni* that occur in a temporally ordered
        discourse event, how many of them conform to one of the order-
        preserving sequences presented in (18)?

        Basilect              50/54 93%   Mesolect              20/36 56%

        Of all uses of *feni*, how many of them are Perfect?

        Basilect                          Mesolect
        order-preserving      26/50 52%   order-preserving      16/20 80%
        not order-preserving  14/16 88%   not order-preserving  43/47 91%
        total                 40/66 61%   total                 59/67 88%

These results show that, in the basilect in particular, again and again the event marked by *feni* occurred after the event described in the previous clause — or was a recapitulation of it — and occurred before the event in the subsequent clause. For the mesolect, on the other hand, *feni*'s primary function seems to be different, namely that of marking the Perfect.

Earlier, I made reference to Traugott's discussion of temporal sequencing, and I suggested that anteriority signalled the **disruption** of temporal sequencing. VLE has no marker of anteriority, no signal of temporal disruption. Rather, it has *feni*, which is precisely the opposite: that is, the presence of *feni* signals the **preservation** of temporal order.

It may seem unusual for a language to have a marker that reinforces temporal order when there is no marker to signal the disruption of temporal order. In that respect, GCE seems less remarkable. That is, I wish to suggest that GCE *don*, like Liberian *feni*, signals the observance of temporal order. A review of a limited amount of GCE data supports the idea that most occurrences of *don* fit into one of the sequences outlined in (18), as illustrated in an example like that in (21), taken from Rickford (1987):

(21)   GCE

... wel ii — wen di mongkii len om, wen ii *don* piil am, di reezo brok.
'Well he — when the monkey lent him [a razor], and he had finished peeling it [a coconut], the razor broke.'

(Rickford 1987: 130)

In this regard, Winford (1993), responding to an earlier version of the present article, endorses my suggestion that "a typical function of *don* is to signal the observance of temporal order, in a way similar to Liberian English *feni*" though he notes that it "... is not restricted to contexts such as narratives and procedural accounts, ... but can be found in other contexts involving temporal sequencing or resultative meanings, where the notion of completion is appropriate" (1993: 51). In a footnote, Winford cites a personal communication from George Huttar calling attention to "a similar use of *kaba/kaa* 'finish' in the Surinamese creoles" (p. 51n.).

To return to VLE, the question remains as to why *feni* came to assume its function as a signal of preservation of temporal ordering. The answer would seem to lie — in part, at least — in the substrate. In Kru languages, as in VLE and perhaps all languages, the expected order in narratives and procedurals is one in which the sequence of clauses parallels the chronological order of the events described in those clauses. Marchese (1978, 1984) shows that narratives and procedurals in Kru languages are rich with cues that reinforce the obvious temporal order. Recapitulative clauses in particular — like those in (4) and (14)

— recur with remarkable frequency. Quite often in Kru languages, the recapitulative clause contains a *'finish'* + V construction. The gloss of one of Marchese's sentences, given in (22) with recapitulative clauses in italics, illustrates this.

> (22)    'And then you build a shelter. *If you have built a shelter*, then you and your wife, you will pull out the grass. *If you have finished pulling out the grass*, then the rice will sprout. *If the rice has sprouted ...*'                                                              (Marchese 1978: 71)

Western Kru languages are spoken along most of Liberia's coast. These languages, particularly Bassa, are probably the most important substratal languages in the Liberianization of the more general West African pidgin that arose in the eighteenth century. While Marchese's articles deal with Godié, an eastern Kru language, she makes the point in her 1984 article that the phenomenon of multiple marking of the usual temporal order obtains in western Kru languages as well.

I wish to argue that the Kru data reflect a culture-based notion as to what it takes to tell a story well or to describe a process clearly. It is metalinguistic and not tied to a speaker's first language. Consequently, it would "go with" speakers as they acquired additional languages. It is thus that a word derived from English 'finish' comes to be used in the way that it is, i.e. as one more agent of reinforcement for temporal order. Certainly, the fact that VLE English is a pidgin of long standing and one characterized by long contact with Kru languages makes even more likely this type of transfer of cultural expectations; but, particularly if they represent an areal phenomenon of some magnitude, such expectations would also seem to be especially likely candidates to survive physical displacement and to persist in the Caribbean creoles. Discourse-based phenomena stand as especially salient sites for substratal influence upon creole languages.


## 3.    The Multifunctionality of *feni*

As a final note, I wish to consider what looks to be an expansion of *feni*'s domain. Labov et al.'s analysis of *done* is sometimes referred to as the "adverbial analysis" of *done*, e.g. by Dayton (1996). (This characterization might more aptly fit Bickerton's analysis than Labov et al.'s.) In the case of VLE, an "adverbial analysis" of *feni* is fully apropos inasmuch as Intensive *feni* has expanded its categorial membership and now shows up as adverb as well as auxiliary, particularly among Monrovians. The examples in (23) and (24) make this point.

(23)    Mason:
oma,    wɛn  sɔnbadi    fɔlo    yua  mɛ, yu    hat    kɛn bɔn?
old ma  when  somebody  follow  your man  your  heart  can burn
Lakpazee Bassa Grace:
bɔ  a *feni* o    na.
but I    old now
Mason:
Old ma, when a woman chases your husband, does it upset you?
Lakpazee Bassa Grace:
I'm too old for that.

(24)    a se  di  mɛ  ho    su  wə  *feni* ɔrɛnj.
I say the man whole suit was      orange
'I say the man's whole suit was completely orange (from blood).'

(Comfort)

For some creoles, there has been ongoing debate as to whether "predicate adjectives" are adjectives at all or are a class of stative verb instead. In VLE. the adjectival status of "predicate adjectives" is inarguable (Singler 1984, 1987a). Thus, *feni* in (23) and (24) is an adverb modifying a predicate adjective, not an auxiliary modifying a stative verb.

It is not clear whether or not *feni* is able to occur pre-adjectivally within an NP; there are no occurrences of it there in more than seventy hours of VLE data. Moreover, speakers reject the use of *feni* pre-adverbially, as in (25) (but do not reject the analogous sentence in (26) where *feni* is pre-adjectival).[10]

(25)    *de    bit   hen *feni* fan.
they beat him      fine
'They beat him severely.'

(26)    di  we  de   bit   hen wə  *feni* fan.
the way they beat him was      fine
'The way they beat him was severe.'

While there are limits on *feni*'s ability to function as an adverb — for now, anyway — the grammaticality of sentences like (23), (24), and (26) establishes *feni*'s ability to function as an intensifying adverb. In its occurrence as a main verb, an auxiliary, and now as an adverb, *feni* displays the multifunctionality that Voorhoeve (1980), among others, identifies as a common creole phenomenon.

## Acknowledgments

A preliminary version of this article was presented at the Thirteenth NWAVE meeting at the University of Pennsylvania. In preparing this work, I benefited from discussions with Roger Andersen, David Peewee, Henry Salifu, Samson Tiklo, Walter Wiles, and Lynell Marchese Zogbo. John Mason and Boakai Zoludua conducted interviews that provided some of the data; I am grateful to them, to other members of my research team (J. Hosea Kanmoh, Tamba Mayson, Dubel Nyankun, and Tinisi Saytue), and to all those who were willing to be interviewed.

## Notes

1. The data come from sociolinguistic interviews carried out in 1980–81 and 1988, the latter carried out under a Fulbright African Regional Fellowship. The orthography used in this article is that used in Fyle and Jones (1980), Todd (1982), and Singler (1984). A nasalized vowel is written as ⟨Vn⟩.

   If a speaker's pseudonym contains an occupation, that means that the speaker acquired VLE (or Kru Pidgin English, in the case of Ghana Steward) as an adult and did not have western education. On the other hand, if the pseudonym contains a personal name or nickname, the speaker acquired VLE as a child and/or had extensive western education. For some speakers, a place name is part of the pseudonym: it refers to where they are from. "Lakpazee" is a neighborhood in Monrovia, and "Fanima" is a neighborhood in Robertsport, a coastal town not far from Monrovia. All the other Liberian toponyms refer to regions away from the coast.

2. A post-clausal form *fini* also shows up in Français Populaire d'Abidjan, as illustrated in (a) below. The lexical source in this case is presumably French *finir*.

   a.   Français Populaire d'Abidjan
        il      mangé *fini*.
        he/she eat
        'He/She has already eaten.'                                    (Yero Sylla, p.c.)

3. Settler English is the language of the descendants of the African Americans who immigrated to Liberia in the nineteenth century (cf. Singler 1989), while Kru Pidgin English is the language of Kru mariners and migrant workers (cf. Singler 1988).

4. The same VLE speakers who use *feni* post-clausally sometimes place it in a separate clause instead, as in (a):

   a.   wayt pipo bed d ɔ dɛ has, e *feni* na, di mɔni kɔn na.
        white people build that all their house it now the money come now
        'When the whites had built all their houses, then they paid us.' (Fanima Painter)

5. Indeed, Bickerton suggests that "*don* initiated as an innovation in Africa, possibly as a calque on a form in some as-yet undetermined indigenous language" (1975:54). In Singler (1983), I present one such African source, namely Bamana[Bambara]-Malinke-Dyula (BMD), the chain of Northern Mande dialects widely spoken in the western half of West Africa. There, the verb *bàn*, meaning 'finish', functions like a perfect marker, as in (b).

   Bamana
   a.   N' y' à      ye.
        1SG-PAST-3SG see
        'I saw him/her.'

b. N'y'à ye kà bàn.
to finish
'I've already seen her/him.'

Similar constructions, involving a form of the verb meaning 'to finish' and conveying the notion of 'already,' show up in the Liberian Mande languages Loma and Māniyakā (Cutler 1981 and Dwyer 1981, both cited in Singler 1984). (Māniyakā is a part of the BMD chain.) The link is not a surprising one and can be expected to show up in other Niger-Congo languages in the region as well.

6. Settler English, like AAVE, descends from nineteenth century African American Vernacular English, and makes use of *done*. In modern Liberia, *done* stands as an affective badge of Settler identity and is not found in VLE. On the other hand, VLE does have an analogous auxiliary, *na*. In Singler (1987b) I present the phonological sequence by which *na* probably evolved from *done*.

7. In Singler (1984) I argue that "Completive" and "Perfective," seemingly different in what they emphasize, overlap in practice and are virtually interchangeable in the analysis of *feni*, *done*, *don*, and similar auxiliaries. In VLE there are rare cases where an auxiliary is Completive but not Perfective but none where it is Perfective but not Completive.

8. An analysis of *feni* in which Completive is the central element of its meaning is parallel to Winford's assessment of GCE *don*: "it seems best to retain the label 'Completive' for *don* while allowing that it has secondary foci such as 'terminative' and 'resultative'" (1993: 50).

9. Only speakers with five of more tokens of *feni* were included.

10. Given the restrictions on the distribution of *feni* qua adverb, it might seem plausible to hypothesize that *feni* used to modify predicate adjectives at a stage in VLE's history when these adjectives were actually verbs and that when they took on the status of true adjectives *feni* continued to be able to precede them. There are, however, a number of problems with such a hypothesis, not least that the sequence *feni* Adj shows up overwhelmingly in the speech of Monrovians, who are innovators in VLE, not laggards (cf. Singler 1987a).

# References

Bickerton, Derek. 1975. *Dynamics of a creole system*. Cambridge: University Press.

———. 1979. The status of *bin* in the Atlantic creoles. *Readings in creole studies*, ed. by Ian F. Hancock, 309–314. Ghent: Story-Scientia.

———. 1980. Creolization, linguistic universals, natural semantax and the brain. *Issues in English creoles: Papers from the 1975 Hawaii Conference*, ed. by Richard Day, 1–18. Heidelberg: Groos. (Originally published 1974 in University of Hawaii Working Papers in Linguistics 6(3).125–141.)

———. 1981. *Roots of language*. Ann Arbor: Karoma.

Comrie, Bernard. 1976. *Aspect: An introduction to the study of verbal aspect and related problems*. Cambridge: University Press.

Cutler, Sue, with David J. Dwyer. 1981. *A reference book of Māniyakā*. East Lansing: Michigan State University, African Studies Center.

Dayton, Elizabeth. 1996. *Done*: An element of the VAAE aspectual system. Paper presented at the annual Linguistic Society of America Meeting, San Diego.

Dwyer, David J. 1981. *A reference handbook of Lorma*. East Lansing: Michigan State University, African Studies Center.

Edwards, Walter. 1995. A sociolinguistic exploration of the usage of the aspectual marker *done* in AAE in Detroit. Paper presented at the Twenty-Fourth Annual NWAVE Meeting, University of Pennsylvania.

Faraclas, Nicholas G. 1989. *A grammar of Nigerian Pidgin*. University of California at Berkeley Ph. D. dissertation.

Fyle, Clifford N., and Eldred D. Jones. 1980. *A Krio-English Dictionary*. London: Oxford University Press.

Gibson, Kean A. 1982. *Tense and aspect in Guyanese Creole: A syntactic, semantic and pragmatic analysis*. Ph. D. dissertation, University of York.

Labov, William, Paul Cohen, Clarence Robins, and John Lewis. 1968. *A study of the Non-Standard English of Negro and Puerto Rican speakers in New York City*, Vol. I. New York: Columbia University.

Marchese, Lynell. 1978. Time reference in Godié. *Papers on discourse*, ed. by J. E. Grimes, 64–75. Dallas: SIL.

––––––. 1984. On the role of conditionals in Godie procedural discourse. Paper presented at the Symposium on Discourse Relations and Cognitive Units, Eugene, Oregon.

McCoard, Robert. 1976. *Tense choice and pragmatic inference: A study of preterit/perfect oppositions in English*. Ph. D. dissertation, University of California, Los Angeles.

Rickford, John R. 1987. *Dimensions of a creole continuum*. Stanford, CA.: Stanford University Press.

Singler, John Victor. 1983. Liberian English *feni*: AUX and ADV. Paper presented at the Annual Linguistic Society of America Meeting, Minneapolis.

––––––. 1984. *Variation in tense-aspect-modality in Liberian English*. Ph. D. dissertation, University of California, Los Angeles.

––––––. 1987a. The city, the mesolect, and innovation. *Journal of Pidgin and Creole Languages* 2.119–147.

––––––. 1987b. Where did Liberian English *na* come from? *English World-Wide* 8.69–95.

––––––. 1988. The homogeneity of the substrate as a factor in pidgin/creole genesis. *Language* 64.27–51.

––––––. 1989. Plural marking in Liberian Settler English, 1820–1980. *American Speech* 64.40–64.

––––––. 1990. Introduction: Pidgins and creoles and tense-mood-aspect. *Pidgin and creole tense-mood-aspect systems*, ed. by John Victor Singler, vii-xvi. (=Creole Language Library, 6.) Amsterdam: John Benjamins.

––––––. 1997. The configuration of Liberia's Englishes. *World Englishes* 16. 205–231.

Todd, Loreto. 1982. *Cameroon*. (Varieties of English Around the World, T1.) Heidelberg: Groos.

Traugott, Elizabeth. 1975. Spatial expressions of tense and temporal sequencing: A contribution to the study of semantic fields. *Semiotica* 15.207–220.

Voorhoeve, Jan. 1980. Multifunctionality as a derivational problem. *Generative studies on creole languages*, ed. by Pieter Muysken, 25–34. Dordrecht: Foris.

Winford, Donald. 1993. *Predication in Caribbean English creoles*. (=Creole Language Library, 10.) Amsterdam: John Benjamins.

# Temporal Frames in
# Spoken Papiamentu Discourse

Roger W. Andersen

*University of California, Los Angeles*

## 1. Introduction

Unlike most creoles, Papiamentu, the Spanish-, Portuguese-, and Dutch-based creole spoken in Aruba, Bonaire, and Curaçao, appears to have an absolute tense-aspect system which distinguishes 'perfective' *a*, 'past imperfective' *ta'a* (and variants *ta'ata* and *tabata*), and 'present' *ta*.[1] *Ta*, *ta'a*, and *a* are illustrated in (1), in which a woman (Mrs. T.) is talking to her grandson.

> (1)     Mrs. T. (B11b:304–309)[2]
>
> *si. mi no [ta] korda    ku [ta'a] tin   mas   ruman.*
> yes. I   not IMP remember that IMP-P exist more sibling
> 'Yes. I don't remember if there were more brothers and sisters.'
>
> *Johan .. [a] kasa   .. ku   .. un mucha mué .. [tabata] yama Ana.*
> Johan .. PFV marry .. with .. a   girl       .. IMP-P call Ann
> 'Johan married a girl … her name was Ann.'

However, Papiamentu 'present' *ta* occurs in a number of contexts besides the typical 'present' situations. One frequent use of *ta* is in past habitual contexts as in (2), from an interview with an 87–year old man (I=Interviewer, M=Man). Here *ta* is used in both a 'present' context (*awor aki* 'now') and a distant past context (expressed by *tempunan di nos* 'our times', *tempunan ei* 'that time', *tempunan aya* 'those days'). The explicitly past-marked Papiamentu imperfective *tabata* (*ta'ata*, *tabatin*) is only used in the first two clauses to establish the past time frame.[3]

(2)    First Communion (T3:91–118)

M: ***Tempunan di nos** [ta'ata]      tempu*
   time-PL    of we  IMP-P-COP  time
   'Our time was the time'

*ku   dios [ta'ata]    aki  bou   huntu   ku   nos.*
that God  IMP-P-COP  here below together with us
'that God was down here with us.'

***Tempunan ei**     bo   [ta] bai...*
time-PL       there you IMP go...
'Those days you go ...'
='Those days you would go...'

*bo  [Ø] tin   ku  risibí   ku   djesdos aña, no promé.*
you       have that receive with twelve  year not before.
'You have to receive (first communion) at the age of 12, not before'
='You had to receive (first communion) at the age of 12, not before'

I: *ai, ta   **awor aki**  nan [a] but' e seis, shete  aña.*
   oh  FOC  now  here they PFV put  it six   seven year
   'Oh, yah, they have only recently changed it to six or seven.'

M: *nan [ta] pon' é ku    seis ku    shete **awo**.*
   they  IMP put it with six  with seven now
   'They make it six or seven now.'

I: *shete   aña, sí,   sí*
   seven  year yes yes
   'Seven, yes, yes.'

M: ***Tempunan aya,   no**.*
   time-PL     there not
   'But not in those days.'

I: *djesdos aña.*
   12        year
   'Twelve.'

M: *djesdos aña.*
   12       year
   'Twelve.'

*bo  n'  [Ø] por [Ø] risibí   promé ku   djesdos aña.*
you not    can     receive before than 12        year
'You can't receive communion before you are twelve.'
='You couldn't receive communion before you were twelve.'

I: *antó, [ta] konformá mesora    tambe?*
   then  IMP  confirm    same-time  too
   'Then are you confirmed at the same time, too?'
= 'Then, would you be confirmed at the same time, too?'

This understanding of how the Papiamentu tense-aspect system actually works in natural spoken discourse prompted me to argue, in Andersen (1990a, 1990b), for the necessity of studying creole (and other) tense-aspect systems within a discourse framework. The discourse in (2) sets up two temporal frames (*tempunan ei* 'those days' and *awor aki* 'now, these days') and the temporal reference of each token of *ta* is easily interpretable as belonging in one or the other of these frames.

The purpose of this paper is to show how mutual recognition of these temporal frames by all participants in the discourse is critical to communicative success. In doing this, I rely on a diverse literature on frames, schemas, scripts, themes, topics, and related notions in pragmatics and discourse analysis (e.g., Brown & Yule 1983; Chafe 1980, 1987, 1994; Givon 1983; Goffman 1974; Hanks 1990; Keenan & Schieffelin 1976; Schegloff 1972; Shank & Abelson 1977; Tannen 1979, 1993). As my focus is primarily on the empirical establishment of how Papiamentu speakers use temporal frames in ways I assume all humans do, a more detailed treatment of the different theoretical approaches to this question is a topic for a different paper. This paper is meant to be a contribution to our understanding of creole languages, providing a more accurate account of the day-to-day use of one creole language, and also to general linguistic theory in that it offers an account of how speakers of any language rely on temporal frames in discourse.

## 2.    The role of temporal frames in interpreting *ta* in discourse

### 2.1 *Frames*

I assume that in a viable theory of comprehension in spontaneous verbal interaction, successful communication requires that participants be able to mentally construct a frame within which any situation is assumed to hold or any event to unfold. When one participant begins a new discourse topic (or sub-topic), other participants must be able to associate that topic with a pre-established frame or a new one. I assume that such a frame minimally includes locative, temporal, and human attributes. For example, in (2), both speakers must be able to agree on one frame that includes the moment of speaking and another frame whose temporal coordinates are in a distant past.

When speakers draw on their own experiences in such verbal interaction (see Chafe 1980, 1987, 1994; Labov 1972; Labov & Waletzky 1967; among others), the experiences they access in their memory obviously have temporal and locative coordinates. In one of the data sets used for this study, a private conversation between two brothers, one of the brothers, Angel,[4] initiates a new discourse topic with the statement *ami mester a hari e dia swa* 'I had to laugh that day, man.' After this recording had been transcribed and edited, I asked Angel to clarify a number of points, including what day he was referring to here. He replied: *Un dia ku ami tin den mi kabes na e momentu ei ku mi ta papiando ku David. E suseso ku mi ta bai konta David a sosodé riba e dia ei* 'A day that I have in my head at the time that I'm talking with David. The event that I am going to tell David happened on that day.'

Angel mentions the day (in his original statement, *ami mester a hari e dia swa*) with a definite article (*e* 'the'), because for him it is already an established referent, even though this is the first mention of it. It appears that a comment by his brother a couple of turns earlier provided a series of associations that called to mind this episode. So the first chance he gets, he tells the story that is on his mind.

## 2.2 *Multiple frames*

It is commonplace in daily turn-by-turn discourse to move rapidly from one time frame to another. As long as the participants in the discourse are tuned into the same frames, including the temporal attributes of each frame, the discourse flows effortlessly. In one short segment of another conversation between Angel and David (C1a:201–328), consisting of 127 clauses or clause fragments, the two brothers pursue a particular discourse topic that cuts across seven different frames. Angel and David are talking in their parents' home, where David still lives and where Angel has recently arrived for a visit. David had visited Angel six months earlier. The seven time frames (and relevant participants) are: (1) the time of speaking (including both Angel (A) and David (D)); (2) before David went to visit Angel (only D included in frame); (3) when David was visiting Angel (D and A); (4) the time period from when David returned up to the moment of speaking (D only); (5) the day David took film from his trip to be developed (D only); (6) Angel at home after David left (A only); and (7) a projected future period when Angel would go back home (A only).

The brothers shift back and forth among these temporal frames with great ease, as would any two speakers who know each other well. For such a discourse exchange, it appears that Papiamentu is similar to Spanish and English in obligatorily marking speech time [ST][5] (and an indeterminate period preceding and following, but containing, speech time) with 'present' *ta*. Verbs with reference time prior to speech time are marked with Perfective *a* for bounded situations and Imperfective Past *ta'a* for unbounded situations. Verbs with reference time after speech time are marked with *ta* in certain circumstances and, in others, an explicit 'future' form, usually *ta bai* (similar to English 'be going to'). Throughout this paper, I will follow Reichenbach's (1947) formulations, in which the 'present' = Event Time [ET] and Reference Time [RT] coinciding with Speech Time ($ET=RT=SR$), the 'past'= Event Time coinciding with Reference Time and preceding Speech Time ($ET=RT>ST$), the 'future'= Speech Time preceding Event Time which coincides with Reference Time ($ST>ET=RT$), the 'pluperfect' = Event Time preceding Reference Time preceding Speech Time ($ET>RT>ST$), and the 'perfect'= Event time preceding Reference Time coinciding with Speech Time ($ET>RT=ST$).

However, these markers alone are not sufficient to establish and keep clear the various temporal frames involved. For the brothers to locate a referent in the ongoing discourse, they must be able to place each clause or sequence of clauses in their respective frames. In this segment, which is too long to reproduce here, a sentence-based grammar could possibly 'account' for the use of each preverbal tense-aspect marker, but only in terms of reference time being prior (*ta'a*, *a*), concurrent with (*ta*), or subsequent to (*ta bai*) speech time. We would still need the notion of frames to understand how each participant can locate referents in each of the various 'past' (and one future) time frames and thus make sense of the conversation.

## 2.3   *Sentences without frames*

Most linguistic studies of tense-aspect construct sentences to support their argument or illustrate an analysis, for example: *The students built a float during the noon hour yesterday* (Smith 1991: 55). Many of these sentences have built into them temporal frame information that would be available only in the larger discourse in natural spoken discourse. For other sentences there is usually a default interpretation. For example, the time of speaking is always an available reference time, which can be resorted to when there is no information to the contrary (Comrie 1985). In (3), which is a real sentence extracted from its full context, it is easy to reconstruct the correct temporal frame in which $ET=RT=ST$.

(3)     Mrs. T. (B11b:284)
        *bo   [ta] korda?*
        2SG IMP remember
        'Do you remember?'

In examples 4–8, however, taken from fuller contextualized segments displayed later in this paper, the default ET=RT=ST temporal frame makes sense in isolation (as in sentence-based grammars) but is wrong in each instance. 'Present' *ta* does not have a 'present' temporal frame in these cases.

(4)     Mrs. T. (B11b:442–3)
        *ora   niun hende  no  [ta] mira.*
        when no    person  not IMP look
        'when nobody is looking.'

(5)     Mrs. T. (B11b:1979–83)
        *.. e    [ta] keda awe   te     sink'or',*
        3SG IMP stay  today until five.o.clock
        '… He is staying today until five o'clock,'

(6)     Mrs. T. (B11b:550–560)
        *ultimo yu    n'  [ta] kasa   bai laga  mama    so.*
        last    child not IMP marry go  leave Momma alone.
        'The last child doesn't marry and go off and leave her/his mother
        alone.'

(7)     Two Brothers (B9:190–206)
        *e     hombernan [ta] para*
        the man-PL       IMP stop
        'The men stop'

(8)     Frankamente (T96a:77)
        *bo   [ta] lanta,*
        2SG IMP get.up
        'You get up,'

## 3.    The multiple lives of *ta*

*Ta* lends itself well to the study of the contribution of temporal frames to the interpretation of speakers' intentions because it occurs in a large number of discourse contexts, only one of which corresponds to its traditional name, 'present.' In this section I show how the temporal frame in which each token of *ta* occurs is critical to the success of the discourse. I will discuss seven 'contexts' in which *ta* occurs: (1) as a copula; (2) the 'present' (reference time includes speech time); (3) in subordinate clauses in which past time reference comes from the main clause; (4) in indirect discourse (a special case of 3); (5) in past habitual contexts, where *ta'a* would also be appropriate in certain registers; (6) the Historical Present; and (7) hypothetical situations.

## 3.1  *Copula*

The copula *ta* is identical to the tense-aspect auxiliary *ta* (compare English copula *is* and the auxiliary *is*). Neither the 'present' auxiliary *ta* nor the Perfective *a* can co-occur with the copula (see example 9). For past time reference, if explicitly marked, only the Imperfective Past *ta'a* (and variants) can precede the copula, as in (10). Indeed, *ta'a* itself can occur as the Imperfective Past form of the copula. This suggests an alternative analysis: 'Copula' *ta* is really the auxiliary *ta* preceding a nonverbal predicate. This also accounts for why neither *ta* nor *a* can precede the 'copula': The preverbal auxiliaries *ta*, *ta'a*, and *a* are mutually exclusive.

> (9)  Two Brothers — Photos 'N Stuff (C1a:65–67)
> A: *e  joke [ta]     bon si.*
> the joke IMP=COP good yes
> 'The joke IS good!'

> (10)  Two Brothers — Walking (C1b:463–470)
> H: *kon e  pan  [ta'ata.]*
> how the bread IMP-P-COP
> 'How was the bread?'
>
> A: *bon. e n' [ta'a]     malu no.*
> well. it not IMP-P-COP bad  no
> 'Well. It wasn't really BAD!'

## 3.2  *'Present'*

In discussing example (3), *bo ta korda*? 'Do you remember?' it was pointed out that the default interpretation of [*ta*] in a main clause without any clarifying context is that ET=RT=ST. Thus, Mrs. T. is asking her grandson at that moment if he remembers something. In (11) we find another common use of *ta* that is characterized as 'present' — to refer to a generic statement that holds in all time frames.

(11)    Mrs. T. (B11b:911–912)
     *ku    bo  [Ø] trata un hende  malu*
     that/if 2sg     treat a  person bad
     'If you treat a person bad'

     *e   n'  [ta] sigi     bini.*
     3sg not imp continue come
     'he doesn't keep coming over.'

If most time frames are limited to one particular moment or period located with respect to speech time, a generic time frame can be seen as encompassing all time. Even though (11) was uttered with respect to events in a particular distant past time frame, as a general truth it is not restricted to that frame.

## 3.3 *Ta in dependent clauses*

Maurer (1988: 160) states that in Papiamentu multiclause sentences in a time frame in which reference time is prior to speech time, tense can be neutralized in the dependent clause if the reference time of the dependent clause is simultaneous with that of the main clause. Thus *ta* in the second clause in (12) could be replaced by the Imperfective Past *ta'a*, but is not necessary because the temporal reference of the main clause extends to the dependent clause.

(12)    Mrs. T. (B11b:442–3)
     *e   tábata sa   bini  pero ora   niun hende  no  [ta] mira.*
     3sg imp-p mod come but  when no   person not imp look
     'He used to come but when nobody is looking.'
     ='but when nobody was looking.'

As we will see later, however, while this is a valid description of isolated complex sentences of this sort, in which the only clue to the temporal reference of the sentence lies in the tense-aspect auxiliary of the main clause, this characterization errs in treating as a syntactic phenomenon what is in reality a discourse phenomenon. As we already have seen in example (2) and will see in further examples, what is really involved here is that once the speaker is confident that the *time frame* is shared by all participants in a conversation, the speaker can suspend explicit marking of time (i.e. 'tense') in subsequent clauses, regardless of whether the clauses are independent or dependent.

## 3.4 *Ta* in indirect discourse

Papiamentu, like many other languages, does not obligatorily copy the temporal marking associated with the verb of saying to the clause containing an indirect quote. In a direct quote, the speaker says what the person being quoted is assumed to have said at that time. Orthographically we indicate this as in (13), by setting off the direct quote between quotation marks. In (13) a change of pronoun from *e* 'him' *to bo* 'you', both with the same referent, makes it clear that this is meant to be a direct quote. The verb of saying, *di* 'said' is an irregular perfective form and the verb in the quoted speech, *tin* 'have', is marked appropriately as a case of ET=RT=ST, but with the time of *di* as 'speech time' and not the time when *mi di kun e* was uttered.

(13)    Frankamente (T96c:16–17)
    I: *mi di    kun e: 'si bo   tin   mester di un kos,'*
    1SG said to   3SG 'if 2SG have need   of a   thing,'
    'I said to him, 'If you need something,' '

In (14) *mi no ta bai nunka mas* could be either a direct quote or an indirect quote. As we have seen, Papiamentu does not require that the verb in the subordinate clause be explicitly marked for tense. In cases such as (14) where the subject of both clauses is the same (*mi* here) only prosodic features of the actual flow of talk provide clues as to whether the subordinate clause is a direct or indirect quote. This is a direct quote.

(14)    Mrs. T. (B11b:460–1)
    T: *m' a    bisa, mi   no [ta] bai nunka mas.*
    1SG PFV say  1SG not IMP go  never  more
    'I said I am not going any more.'
    = 'I said I wasn't going any more' [as indirect quote] or
    'I said, 'I am not going any more.' [as direct quote]

Again, participants in such a conversation identify the time reference of verb phrases like *ta bai* by placing it in an appropriate time frame.

    In (15) we can see that lack of explicit tense-marking in dependent clauses and in indirect discourse is indeed a consequence of the speaker *mentally putting herself into the scene she is remembering*: (15) is a case of indirect discourse with the subordinator ku 'that' at the beginning of the second clause, making it clear that this is indirect discourse and not a direct quote. However, in the following clause the use of *awe* 'today' reveals that she is now reporting the speech of the head of the school as if she were right there. She has thus mentally placed herself within the time frame of that event. The pragmatically derived information that the speaker is now in her seventies and was a young girl at the time this event took place is all that keeps us from taking the time frame to be the time of the recording. Even the first clause *e kabes di skol ... a bisa mi* could be interpreted as meaning 'the head of the school has told me,' since *a* can be interpreted as perfective or perfect.

(15)  Mrs. T. (B11b:1979–83)
    *en todo kaso an - uhm- e   kabes di skol   .. [a]  bisa mi*
    anyway       th- uhm- the head of school .. PFV tell 1SG
    'Anyway th- uhm- the head of the school .. told me'

    *ku mi [Ø] tin ku bai sinta den klas ei,*
    that 1SG have to go sit in class there
    'that I   have to go sit in that  classroom,'
    'that I had to go sit in that classroom,'

    *.. e   [ta] keda awe  te    sink'or',*
    .. 3SG IMP stay today until five.o.clock
    '.. He is staying today until five o'clock,'
    ='.. He was staying today until five o'clock,'

    *.. I   si sink'or'   mi no .. [a] pidi    despensa,*
    .. and if five.o.clock 1SG not .. PFV ask.for pardon
    '.. and if (at) five o'clock I haven't apologized,'
    '.. and if (at) five o'clock I hadn't apologized,'

    *.. anto e   [ta] bai laga  mi.*
    .. then 3SG IMP go  leave 1SG
    '.. then he is going to leave me'
    ='.. then he was going to leave me.'

## 3.5  *Past habitual*

In (16) Mrs. T. anchors the story she is telling in a distant past time frame by using the Imperfective Past auxiliary *tábata*. She again uses this form (the variant *ta'a*) in the third clause from the end and the last clause. These three cases mark the time frame as different from the time frame within which the recorded conversation is taking place. However, all the other clauses can be interpreted as taking the perspective from within this distant time frame.[6] That is, the first clause establishes the time frame, allowing Mrs. T. to then mentally place herself within that frame.

(16)   Mrs. T. (B11b:550–560)
*.. ora   mi   [tábata] bai kasa,*
.. when 1SG IMP-P   go   marry
.. 'When I was going to get married,'

*tur mi   rumannan [a]  kasa   kaba*
all 1SG sibling-PL PFV marry already
'All my brothers and sisters had already married'

*anto ami    ku   mi   mama   só   [ta] biba na kas   aki.*
then 1SG.OBJ with 1SG Momma alone IMP live in house here
'So only me and my mother live in this house.'
='So only me and my mother lived in this house.'

*anto    .. uh - e   tempunan ayá bo no [ta] kasa   -*
then    .. uh - the time-PL   there 2SG IMP marry -
'Then   .. uh - those days you don't marry -'
='Then .. uh - those days you didn't marry -'

*ultimo yu   n' [ta] kasa   bai laga   mama   so.   huh?*
last   child not IMP marry go  leave Momma alone. OK?
'The last child doesn't marry and go off and leave her/his mother alone. OK?'
='The last child didn't marry and go off and leave her/his mother alone. OK?'

*i   aki [ta'a] tin   un kas,*
and here IMP-P exist a   house
'and there was a house here,'

*mi   mama   [ta] biba aden*
1SG Momma IMP live  inside
'My mother lives inside (it).'
='My mother lived inside (it).'

*dus mi   mama   [tábata] ke   pa mi   kasa   keda biba aki.*
so 1SG Momma IMP-P   want for 1SG marry stay live here
'So my Momma wanted me to get married and stay living here.'

Mrs. T. is providing orientation for the full narrative that will soon follow. In doing so, she uses *ta* for past habitual and past descriptive situations, apparently resorting to past-marked *tábata* and *ta'a* to continue to establish this time frame as distinct from the one in which she is conversing with her grandson.

In this example as well as in the previous examples of 'present' *ta*, *ta* in dependent clauses, and *ta* in indirect discourse, the speaker is in some sense getting into the scene being retrieved from memory and reconstructed through speech and thus relating elements of the information from the perspective of the time frame of the situation being narrated. Thus the notion of *time frame* is critical to understanding why a non-past auxiliary like *ta* would appear so frequently in past contexts. Once the speaker has begun to create the frame, she/he can take a perspective either internal to that frame or a perspective from the speech time and thus external to the narrated frame. Thus the use of *ta* in both 'present' and 'past' contexts follows from the same principle: Assume a vantage point and talk about what you 'see' and 'hear' from that vantage point. In the case of 'present' *ta* the vantage point is the speech time. In the case of various 'past' context uses of *ta*, the vantage point is within the frame being reconstructed by the conversation.

### 3.6 *Historical present*

The historical present has frequently been treated as a sort of 'stylistic device' that speakers can use to make a narrative more vivid, more real, telling the story as if it were happening before the listeners' eyes. From Labov and Waletzky's (1967) first characterization of real-life personal narratives to work by Wolfson (1979), Schiffrin (1981), Silva-Corvalán (1983) and Fleischman (1990), this notion of vividness has been much debated. Fleischman (1990: 124) especially has explained the use of 'present' verb forms within past narrative in terms of the narrator taking a 'story-now' perspective intead of the 'speaker-now' perspective. The 'speaker-now' perspective takes speech time as the reference time, so that 'present' forms constitute ET=RT=ST and 'past' forms constitute RT and ET both being prior to speech time. The 'story-now' perspective places the narrator into the story frame.

This explanation accounts for the use of historical present in Papiamentu discourse, as exemplified in (17). As in previous examples (not involving historical present), the speaker shifts back and forth between a speech time perspective (Fleischman's speaker-now), requiring Imperfective Past auxiliaries (the two cases of *ta'a* in (17)) to establish the time frame as prior to speech time, and story-now perspective, viewing the situation from within the time frame — all cases of *ta* and [Ø] in (17).

(17)    Two Brothers (B9:190–206)
        D:   *Boneriano[7] hom'. ... e gai ayá,*
             Bonairian man. ... the guy there
             'Bonairian, man. ... That guy,'

e   gai ku   [ta'a] keda seka Richard tambe [ta]        un - Axel.
the guy that IMP-P stay  near Richard also    IMP=COP a -  Axel
'The guy that was staying with Richard also is a - Axel.'

A:   ahan si, Axel. sè.  'Oh yes, Axel. Yah.'
D:   e   hom' t- ..[ta]  kore riba vèlt  hunga bala,
     the man i- .. IMP run  on   field play  ball
     'The man runs/is running on the field playing ball,'

     e   hombernan [ta] para
     the man-PL     IMP stop
     'The men stop'

     'Boneriano .. ba'   fe'i   vèlt.'
     Bonairian  .. get.off from field
     'Bonairian .. get off of the field!'

     .. hopi tristu 'om'.
     .. very sad   man
     '.. Really sad, man.'

     e   gai [ta'a] hunga bon   bon.
     the guy IMP-P play   good good
     'The guy was playing really good.'

A:   ta   tenta nan [Ø] ke   tent'é    no.
     FOC tempt they    want tempt 3SG CHK
     'What they want to do is tempt him, y'know.'

The 'vividness' created by taking a 'story-now' perspective is not a special stylistic device but a consequence of viewing the unfolding event from within the event.

### 3.7   'Present' that is not present and 'past' that is not past: *ta* and *a* to convey Hypothetical Situations

The notions 'past' and 'present' are general human notions similar to 'then/now', 'yesterday/today' and similar lexical and semantic contrasts that provide very general terms for relating events and memories to the current moment of consciousness. The term 'past' refers to something being completed, over with. But such terms fail to capture the complexity of how people use the grammatical device that traditional grammars label as 'past' and 'present'. In (18), from a private conversation between two people, the speaker is presenting his side of the story in a case where he got involved in a family squabble after waking up his alcoholic wife after she got drunk and fell asleep outside their house. He very effectively brings his conversational partner into the dilemma by creating a hypothetical situation where the listener is temporarily turned into the wife with the problem (see *bo* 'you' in lines 10–14).

(18) Frankamente (T96a:61–101)

1. *wel ... ami .. ta esaki mi [Ø] ke sak' afo'.*
   well 1SG.OBJ FOC this 1SG want bring out
   'Well, ... I .. this is what I want to bring out.'

2. *mi [Ø] ke ... mi [Ø] ke pa un 'ende bisa mi .. no?*
   1SG want 1SG want for a person tell 1SG CHK
   'I want ... I want somebody to tell me .. ok?

3. *.. frankamente.*
   '.. frankly.'

4. *un hende no [ta] haña .. ku un muhé*
   a person not IMP find that a woman
   'A person doesn't think .. that a woman'

5. *ku [ta] bebe, bebe, bebe, bebe,*
   that drink
   'who drinks and drinks and drinks and drinks'

6. *.. tur dia e mué [tabata] bebe*
   .. every day the woman IMP-P drink
   'Every day the woman was drinking'

7. *tur dia e mué [tabata] bebe*
   every day the woman IMP-P drink
   'Every day the woman was drinking'

8. *bo [t'] 'aña e kos [ta] bon?*
   2SG IMP find the thing IMP=COP good
   'Do you think the thing is good?'

9. *bo [ta] aña -*
   2SG IMP find
   'Do you think -'

10. *bo [ta] lanta, bo [ta] bebe ron, .. bai drumi .. riba stupi.*
    2SG IMP get.up 2SG IMP drink rum go sleep on front.step
    'You get up, you drink rum, .. go and sleep .. on the front step.'

11. *ku m' [a] lagá bu drumi ei riba, no,*
    if 1SG PFV let 2SG sleep there above CHK
    'If I let [past] you sleep up there, no,'

12. .. *ku b'  [a]  'ña.*
    if 1SG PFV find
    '.. if you found.'

13. *por 'empel, m'  [a]  lagá bu  drumi riba,  n'  ta       bèrdè?*
    for example 1SG PFV let   2SG sleep above not IMP=COP true
    'For example, I let [past] you sleep there, right?'

14. *awor ku bo   [ØØ] muri eiribanan,  kiko nan [ta] bisa? .. e?*
    now  if 2SG IRR  die  there.above what 3PL IMP say   CHK
    'Now if you die there, what are they going to say? .. Huh?'

15. *.. ta - nan ta - .. ta  ami      nan [ta] bin     kulpa.*
    ?   3PL ?    FOC 1SG.OBJ 3PL IMP RES/come blame
    '.. It's - they a- .. It's me they're going to blame.'

16. *ami     ku ta     su      kasá   (XXX) ke    men di.*
    1SG.OBJ that IMP=COP 3SG.POSS spouse      want mean say
    'Me, who is her husband, I mean.'

17. *m'  [a]  lant'  é.*
    1SG PFV get.up 3SG
    'I got her up.'

18. *.. m'  [a]  'ña mi  den e   ko'  'i chombon      ei.*
    .. 1SG PFV find 1SG in   the thing of great.difficulty there
    '.. I found myself in a really big mess.'

19. *ku   mi  [a]  lag' é    drumi,*
    that/if 1SG PFV let  3SG sleep
    'If I had let her sleep,'

20. *m'  [a]  'ña mi  den un otro     ko'  'i chombon.*
    1SG PFV find 1SG in   an different thing of difficulty
    'I would have found myself in a different mess.'

21. *... awo' ki   bo  [Ø] ke   mi  'asi? ...*
    ... now what 2SG     want 1SG do
    '... Now what do you want me to do? ...'

The first five lines and lines 8–9, and 21 are 'present' — cases of ET=RT=ST or generic statements. Lines 6–7 (with *tabata*) and 17–18 (with *a*) are 'past' — ET=RT>ST. But most of this excerpt sets up a hypothetical situation in which both 'present' *ta* (10, 14–16) and 'past' *a* (19–20) are used. But labels like 'present' and 'past' (or equivalent formalization following Reichenbach) do not handle what the speaker is actually trying to accomplish with this type of discourse. In lines 10 to 20 the speaker is setting up two hypothetical *frames*, both of which begin the same, but each ending somewhat differently. From 15 on he slips back into a first-person narration, losing the very effective use of *bo* 'you', but he is still within this set of hypothetical frames. And telling the story from within the frame makes the verb forms resemble cases of Historical Present.

In 17–18 he uses Perfective *a* to refer to the real event and in 11–13 and 19–20 he uses *a* in the hypothetical frames. It is not the particular auxiliary, *ta* or *a*, which sets off the time frame, but the mental representation of the frame itself, which both speaker and addressee must reconstruct for this conversational ploy to work. And it does appear to work.

## 4.    Beyond morphosyntax — temporal frames and speakers' perspectives

Fleischman was dealing with (especially) medieval French narratives, Wolfson, and Schiffrin with English narratives, and Silva-Corvalán with Spanish. Their focus was on the especially intriguing cases of historical present. Fleischman's story-now and speaker-now solution is partially constrained by this particular focus. As we have seen, however, the use of *ta* in cases where the speaker is adopting a frame-internal perspective, whether this frame happens to be cotermi-nous with speech time or prior to or subsequent to speech time, or even a hypothetical frame, follows naturally from Fleischman's story-now characteriza-tion. It is important, however, to separate this explanatory framework from narrative and, with a more detailed and explicit notion of temporal frame, expand the story-now/speaker-now framework in such a way that it accounts adequately, as it indeed does, for cases like Papiamentu. I assume that such a framework would account too for other creoles, where a tradition of sentence-level grammar has kept us from understanding how grammaticized devices like tense-aspect markers serve speakers' purposes by allowing them to take different perspectives on events and situations in discourse.

## Acknowledgments

I gratefully acknowledge support for the research on which this study is based, from the National Science Foundation (BNS-8812750), UCLA Academic Senate Research Committee, UCLA Latin American Center, UCLA International Studies and Overseas Programs, and the Latin American Center of the University of Texas, Austin.

# Notes

1. See, for example, Bickerton (1981), Goilo (1972), Maurer (1988), and Muysken (1981, 1988) In Andersen (1990a) I concluded that *ta* is a tense-neutral imperfective marker.

2. See Appendix for Transcription Conventions.

3. [Ø] indicates 'zero' marking for verbs that do not permit *ta* or allow either *ta* or 'zero' for 'present' contexts, to indicate to the reader that no past form has been used in contexts where *a* or *tabata* could be used. Single quotes provide a temporally literal translation and double quotes a temporally more natural English translation.

4. All names of speakers as well as all names mentioned in examples are pseudonyms. Other information that might facilitate identification of participants is omitted or altered in ways that do not affect the interpretation of the example for purposes of this paper.

5. Following Reichenbach (1947) — "present": Event Time and Reference Time = Speech Time (ET=RT=SR), "past": Event Time = Reference Time and precede Speech Time (ET=RT>ST), "future": (ST>ET=RT), "pluperfect": ET>RT>ST, "perfect": ET>RT=ST.

6. Nevertheless, *e tempunan ayá* in the fourth clause places this in a distant time frame.

7. *Boneriano* = 'someone from the more sparsely populated and isolated island of Bonaire.'

# Appendix

1. *Recordings from which examples are taken*:
Selected spontaneous conversation between family members or between friends or acquaintances, selected from over 200 hours of audio and video recordings.

| | |
|---|---|
| B9 | Two Brothers |
| B11b | Mrs. T. (talking to her grandson) |
| C1a | Two Brothers — Photos 'N Stuff |
| C1b | Two Brothers — Walking |
| T3a | First Communion (talking to an acquaintance about the past) |
| T96c | Frankamente (lively spontaneous conversation on street) |

2. *Transcription conventions*: (Adopted, with apologies, in simplifed format from Sacks, Schegloff, and Jefferson (1974).)
In original transcripts, each line contains a single clause or clause fragment, to facilitate study of verbs and auxiliaries. In examples, one-clause-per-line format usually retained; in some cases clauses are combined on one line, for ease of exposition.

| | |
|---|---|
| .. | short pause |
| ... | more noticeable pause |
| - | self-interruption |
| , | non-final intonation |
| . | final intonation |
| ? | rising intonation |
| n' | *no* with vowel not uttered ( ' represents missing vowel) |

Papiamentu orthography is a phonemic adaptatation of the IPA, with certain exceptions, often from Dutch orthography (e.g., *dj* in *djesdos* like 'j' of 'jeep', Dutch-origin vocabulary often retains Dutch pronunciation). Word stress is penultimate when ends in vowel (*aña* = [áña]), final when ends in consonant (*mester* = [mestér]); otherwise indicated with stress mark (*antó*).

3. *Symbols used for glosses*:

| | | |
|---|---|---|
| *ta* | IMP | Imperfective (tense-neutral) |
| *ta* | IMP-COP | Same as IMP, but with 'copula' function |
| *ta'a* | IMP-P | Imperfective Past |
| *tá*bata | ' | |
| *ta'ata* | ' | |
| *a* | PFV | Perfective |
| *ØØ* | IRR | Irrealis (in certain subordinate clauses) |
| *bin* | RES | resultative (*bin* 'come') |
| *ta* | FOC | focus |
| *no* | CHK | checking device |
| *mi* | 1SG | 1st person singular pronoun 'I/me/my' |
| *ami* | 1SG.EMPH | emphatic version of *mi* |
| *bo* | 2SG | 2nd person singular pronoun 'you/your' |
| *abo* | 2SG.EMPH | emphatic version of *bo* |
| *e* | 3SG | 3rd person singular 'he/she/it;him/her' |
| *su* | 3SG.POSS | 3rd singular possessive 'his/her' |
| *nan* | 3PL | 3rd person plural 'they/them/their' |
| *nan* | PL | noun plural suffix |

# References

Andersen, Roger W. 1990a. "The papiamentu tense-aspect system, with special attention to discourse." In John Singler (ed.), *Pidgin and Creole Tense-Mood-Aspect Systems*. Amsterdam: John Benjamins, 59–96.

Andersen, Roger W. 1990b. "Verbal virtuosity and speakers' purposes." In Patricia Rounds & Hartmut Burmeister (ed.), *Variability in Second Language Acquisition*. Eugene, Oregon: Department of Linguistics, University of Oregon, 1–24.

Bickerton, Derek. 1981. *Roots of Language*. Ann Arbor: Karoma.

Brown, Gillian, and George Yule 1983. *Discourse Analysis*. Cambridge: Cambridge University Press.

Chafe, Wallace. 1980. "The deployment of consciousness in the production of a narrative." In Wallace Chafe (ed.), *The Pear Stories: Cognitive, Cultural, and Linguistic Aspects of Narrative Production*. Norwood, N.J.: Ablex, 9–50.

Chafe, Wallace. 1987. "Cognitive constraints on information flow." In Russell Tomlin (ed.), *Coherence and Grounding in Discourse*. Amsterdam and Philadelphia: John Benjamins, 21–51.

Chafe, Wallace. 1994. *Discourse, Consciousness, and Time*. Chicago: University of Chicago Press.

Comrie, Bernard. 1985. *Tense*. Cambridge: Cambridge University Press.

Fleischman, Suzanne. 1990. *Tense and Narrativity: From Medieval Performance to Modern Fiction*. Austin: University of Texas Press.

Givon, Talmy. 1983. *Topic Continuity in Discourse: Quantified Cross-Language Studies*. Amsterdam and Philadelphia: John Benjamins.

Goffman, Erving. 1974. *Frame Analysis*. New York: Harper & Row.

Goilo, Enrique R. 1972. *Papiamentu Textbook*. 4th ed. Aruba: de Wit Stores, N. V.

Hanks, William F. 1990. *Referential Practice: Language and Lived Space among the Maya*. Chicago: University of Chicago Press.

Keenan, Elinor O., and Bambi Schieffelin. 1976. "Topic as a discourse notion: A study of topic in the conversations of children and adults." In Charles Li, (ed.), *Subject and Topic*. New York: Academic Press, 335–84.

Labov, William, and Joshua Waltezky. 1967. "Narrative analysis: Oral versions of personal experience." In June Helm. (ed.), *Essays on the Verbal and Visual Arts: Proceedings of the 1966 Annual Spring Meeting of the American Ethnological Society*. Seattle: University of Washington Press, 12–44.

Labov, William. 1972. *Sociolinguistic Patterns*. Philadelphia: University of Pennsylvania Press.

Maurer, Philippe. 1988. *Les Modifications Temporelles et Modales du Verbe dans le Papiamento De Curacao (Antilles Neerlandaises)*. Hamburg: Helmut Buske Verlag.

Muysken, Pieter. 1981. " Creole tense/mood/aspect systems: The unmarked case?" In Pieter Muysken (ed.), *Generative Studies on Creole Languages*. Dordrecht: Foris, 181–99.

Muysken, Pieter 1988. "Are creoles a special type of language?" In Frederick J. Newmeyer (ed.), *Linguistics: The Cambridge Survey. II Linguistic Theory: Extensions and Implications*. Vol. 2. Cambridge: Cambridge University Press, 285–301.

Reichenbach, Hans. 1947. *Elements of Symbolic Logic*. New York and London: The Free Press and Collier-Macmillan.

Sacks, Harvey, Schegloff, Emanuel, and Jefferson, Gail. 1974. "A simplest systematics for the organization of turn-taking in conversation." *Language* 50: 696–735.

Schank, Roger C., and Robert P. Abelson 1977. *Scripts, Plans, Goals and Understanding: An Inquiry into Human Knowledge Structures*. Hillsdale, N. J.: Lawrence Erlbaum.

Schegloff, Emanuel A. 1972. "Notes on a conversational practice: Formulating place." In David Sudnow (ed.), *Studies in Social Interaction*. New York: Macmillan, 75–119.

Schiffrin, Deborah. 1981. "Tense variation in narrative." *Language* 57: 45–62.

Silva-Corvalán, Carmen. 1983. "Tense and aspect in oral Spanish narrative: Context and meaning." *Language* 59: 60–80.

Smith, Carlota S. 1991. *The Parameter of Aspect...* Dordrecht, Boston, & London: Kluwer Academic Publishers.

Tannen, Deborah. 1979. "What's in a frame? Surface evidence for underlying expectations." In Roy O. Freedle (ed.), *New Directions in Discourse Processing*. Norwood, N. J.: Ablex.

Tannen, Deborah, ed. 1993. *Framing in Discourse*. New York: Oxford University Press.

Wolfson, Nessa. 1979. "The conversational historical present alternation." *Language* 55: 168–182.

# Exploration of the Trinary Components in Creole Discourse

## Universals, Substrata, and Superstrata

Hirokuni Masuda

*University of Hawai'i at Hilo*

## 1. Introduction

This paper explores the interaction of three convergent influences on the genesis and development of discourse processes in Hawai'i Creole English (HCE), i.e. universals, substrata, and superstrata. These are the trinary components referred to in my title. Since the monumental works on the integration of the Universalist and the Substratist theories (Muysken & Smith 1986; Mufwene 1993a) were released, the so-called Complementary Hypothesis (Mufwene 1986, 1993b) has attracted the attention of quite a few researchers. This hypothesis is regarded as a promising framework in accounting for the complex mechanisms of pidgin/creole languages. I pursue in this article the possibility of finding those factors in "discourse" or in the organization of structures beyond the sentence level.

Referring to research findings in discourse analysis as well as to those in pidgin/creole linguistics, I will first determine and then describe a particular discourse process in each of the Trinary components in question by utilizing data from HCE as a case study. First, topicalization is presented as evidence of "universals", i.e. biological innate linguistic principles. Second, T[heme] S[cheme] R[heme] formation is claimed to be from the "Substratum", i.e. the transfer of linguistic features from an ancestral language Japanese through a pidgin, in this case Hawai'i Pidgin English (HPE), to a creole (HCE or perhaps directly from the ancestral language to the creole). Third, line-predication is introduced to demonstrate a "superstratal" influence from the lexifier language, English, in the creole.

## 2.    The Trinary Components

First of all, a question arises about whether there could be such a thing as innate properties of creole discourse, created by universal principles in the human language faculty. Syntactically, the surface manifestations of sentences reveal many shared characteristics across creole languages of the world (Romaine 1994). According to Bickerton (personal communication 1992), these shared characteristics derive from situations whenever the universal syntax meets a depleted lexicon. Among them, such variables as the lack of morphology, serial verb formations, Tense-Mood-Aspect system, and preverbal negation, are well-known universal features found across the world.

If it is the case that syntax is created by an inherent human language faculty, why then can't it also be so for discourse? Based on evidence in a number of creoles, I argue that there are some manifestations of possible universal principles in constructing supersentential structure as well.[1] When engaged in constructing a spoken discourse, it is necessary for a speaker to establish that the discourse is structurally organized and rhetorically coherent. Converting sentences into larger units or texts, does not automatically mean that a well-formed discourse is established. In other words, there must be some preferred strategies for speakers to link utterances in a coherent flow so that those utterances can be properly connected in the construction of a structural sequence. Furthermore, a well-formed discourse requires certain formal connections between utterances, and "any formal feature of a text which has a cohesive function" is called a "cohesive feature" by Fairclough (1989: 130).[2] Here I discuss topicalization as evidence of one such cohesive feature in discourse. Escure (1988) argues that topicalization is a basic innate property of creole languages built into the human organism.

Secondly, with respect to substratal influence, I suppose that creole languages inherit some aspects of discourse structure from their pidgin predecessor. Masuda (1995a, 1996a) argues that pidgin discourse retains the linear structuring of narrative organization to compose coherent information by means of a particular tactic called Verse-Projection Strategy. In addition to the process of discourse substratal influence via the pidgin to the creole, there is also the possibility of the transference of features directly from a substratum language to a newborn creole. I present as evidence of substratal transfer a particular discourse process in HCE that I call "TSR Formation" (Masuda 1995a). The analysis is carried out within the framework of Schema Theory.

Thirdly, in addition to the universal principles that organize discourse structures and the substratal transfer from the ancestral languages, it is highly likely that the superstrate language (English) in its capacity as lexifier language also provides some input to HCE the latter. Such extensive input into the lexicon might very well affect the organization of other aspects of the linguistic structures, including discourse. Moreover, English is socially a more dominant linguistic variety than HCE, which in turn affects the consciousness of its speakers such that they switch towards English. Despite the fact that HCE discourse has been heavily influenced by Japanese, frequent use of Line-predication (clauses with predicate verbs in lines) in HCE is a result of the superstrate influence from English. In this analysis I use V[erse] A[nalysis] (see also Masuda 1995b, 1996a), originally invented by Hymes (Hymes 1981, 1983, 1987, 1990a, 1990b, 1992).

In the following sections I carry out an analysis for each of the three components. Although HCE is analyzed as a case study here, I expect this framework to be applicable to discourse structures of other pidgin/creole languages as well. The data utilized in this research have been taken from interviews forming part of projects completed by The Center for Oral History at the University of Hawai'i at Mānoa (Center for Oral History 1984a, b, c; 1985a,b; 1988a, b, c; 1989a, b; 1991a, b). The corresponding recorded tapes have also been examined to provide linguistically detailed transcriptions.

## 3.   Universals: Topicalization

Escure (1988: 173) observes that:

> The priority of topics in language universals is confirmed by the increasing emergence of topic structures observed not only in the acrolects of English Creole continua, but also in the non-standard varieties of non-topic prominent languages such as English. ... the universally preferred strategy happens to be topic prominence."[3]

The widely understood main function of "topic" is to convey given information or to relate to the interlocutor's "assumed familiarity" at the time of the utterance (Gundel 1988: 212). That is, the topic enables a speaker to obtain the hearer's attention with regard to what he/she is going to hear in a given context. A topic associates the addressee's consciousness with his/her relevant knowledge, which can constitute one of the coherence construction strategies in discourse. In creolization it is reasonable to assume that children have to make an extra effort to make discourse coherent with a less structured syntax and the insufficient lexicon of a pidgin language as input. In such contact situations, topicalization must have played an important role in the comprehension/production of effective discourse.[4]

Escure (1988) explored the possibility that topic structures may constitute a such universal feature of natural languages. She classified the topic structures into six subcategories: topicalization; duplication; dislocating and clefting; pseudo-clefts and free relatives; presentative morphemes; and relatives. She obtained evidence from five English-based creoles: Belizean Creole English, Gullah, Jamaican Creole, Providencia Creole, and San Andres Creole. Furthermore, in their summary of information structure in HCE, Sato and Watson-Gegeo (1992) present nine different types of topicalizations in the language: topic-comment; left-dislocation; pseudo-cleft; left-dislocation pronoun; left-dislocation gap; right-dislocation; right-dislocation gap; elaborated topic; and elaborated comment. These scholars convincingly show that topicalization is a quite common linguistic feature in creole languages.

There is another interesting fact to be added here. Corne (1987) discusses the left-preposing of a verb that he calls 'verb-fronting' in Isle de France Creole and Atlantic creoles. He concludes that verb-fronting must reflect African substratal influence. This can be looked at from a different angle, that is, from a viewpoint of topicalization. For instance, Corne relates verb-fronting in the creoles in question to a corresponding construction in Japanese. However, the Japanese example that he (Corne 1987: 105) provides is, in fact, a contrastive topic-comment structure because: 1) each of the nominalized fronted verbs carries a topic marker /wa/ (Kuno 1973), which usually conveys old/ understood information; 2) it is clear that the predicate parts (*wakaru* 'understand' and *hanasenai* 'can't speak') are more focused in meaning than the fronted-verb parts (*wakaru no wa* 'as for understanding' and *hanasu no wa* 'as for speaking'); and 3) the sentence is a left-dislocated structure in which what is given must be stated before what is new in relation to it (Gundel 1988: 229). My English translation of the example in (1) differs from that of Corne, but I believe that my version is closer to the meaning of the Japanese structure.

(1)    *Wakaru    no wa  wakaru;    keredo, hanasu no wa  hanasenai.*[5]
       understand CP TOP understand CONJ    speak  CP TOP can't speak
       'As for understanding, I can understand; however, as for speaking,
       I cannot speak'.

What interests me is that Corne refers to several languages that have verb-fronting such as Russian, Yoruba, as well as Japanese, and he finally concludes that there might be "a certain universality, such that if verb-fronting in Creole arises through transmission, the substratal verb-fronting structures may have been 'favored' in some way in the emergence of the various creole languages". It seems to me that the wide range in use of topicalization suggests that there can be innate (not transmission-related) universal principles operating in the process.[6]

One might reason that topicalization would function as a connector between semantic representations and linguistic (discourse) representations.

Recent research in brain science convincingly shows that discourse representations are independent of syntactic representations in human language faculty. When syntactic representations are transferred to discourse, the first thing is to construct coherence. It is precisely at this time, when topicalization functions as a link and combines utterances into linguistic forms beyond the sentence level, that cohesion is established. Thus, topicalization performs an important task in the fundamental process in the representative as well as communicative system of language establishing a linear sequence of the linguistic production process. For all these reasons, I endorse the claim that topicalization is realized by a universal principle in the human language faculty; it is not necessary to appeal to substratum in order to account for its presence in creoles.

Since all the types of topicalizations discussed earlier share parallel characteristics, I will merge these into three types: left-preposing, duplication and dislocation. I offer additional data here from several speakers of HCE, following Sato and Watson-Gegeo (1992). In the data given below, the initials stand for the subjects' names, and Ø for the gap; topics are in bold.

*Left-preposing*
In left-preposing the topic is merely fronted, which entails gapping in the comment, as in (2) through (6).

(2)     **The bones like that,** *he would give Ø.*                          AB

(3)     **That,** *I don't know Ø.* **That,** *I never hear, too Ø.*          MM

(4)     **How he got out,** *I don't know Ø.*                                RC

(5)     **Vienna sausage,** *we buy one case Ø.*                             RC

(6)     *But,* **certain homes,** *I never did go Ø.*                        BE

*Duplication*
Duplication is a simple copying of a constituent which involves a full or partial repetition of the topic in its logical position, as in (7) through (11).

(7)     **The old man,** *he was the sheriff before.*                        AB

(8)     *And then,* **the hapai ko** [Hawaiian: 'carry cane'] **men,** **they** *got to go get that.*          MM

(9)     *But although,* **some plantations, they** *get cane cutter.*        MM

(10)    **Plantation, the managers, and the lunas** [Hawaiian: 'above', i.e. 'overseer'] *like that,* **they** *were just like kings.*          RC

(11)    *And then in **the area that's now Koloa Post Office**, **that** used to be the
        Koloa ball park.*                                                        BE

*Dislocation*

Dislocation is related to duplication in that both structures involve copying a
topic. However, dislocation requires movement, as in examples (12) through
(16), whereas duplication does not.

(12)    *And **places like McBryde**, I'm sure **they**'re looking at other things,
        even they're looking at offices.*                                        AB

(13)    *In fact, for **the other wood**, in those days, we had to buy **the wood**.*
                                                                                 RC

(14)    *So, as far as **eggs**, oh, we had all the **eggs** we could eat.*       RC

(15)    *Especially, like **the Filipinos**, I think when **they** first came to Hawai'i,
        they all intended to go back to the Philippines.*                        RC

(16)    *Then **Lihu'e Plantation**, we had some **there**.*                      RC

## 4.    Substratum: TSR Formation

Some time ago Sato (1985: 250) observed that:

> The Japanese language naturally retained its vitality in such a supportive
> environment. No doubt this mother tongue retention had the effect of increas-
> ing the amount of Japanese features that became conventionalized in HPE
> because there were so many of these speakers around.

Masuda (1995a) argues that there is a particular utterance structure in HCE, the
so-called "Dollar Utterance", which can be attributed to Japanese influence. In
this utterance, which is syntactically deviant with respect to Standard English,
two semantically heterogeneous nouns are directly connected by a copula verb *be*
as in "Plænteishen waz stil dala a dei." (i.e. 'The payment rate on the plantations
was still a dollar a day'). Further examples are given in (17) through (21):

(17)    *Da faloin dei iz mai braDa.*                                            VS
        'The following day is my brother'.

(18)    *Eitiin tawnz a siks kaz.*                                               MM
        'Eighteen tons are six cars'.

(19)    *1970 waz chrii dalaz.*                                                  TK
        '1970 was three dollars'.

(20)  *Ai æm Eiprol 2.*                                           TK
      'I am April 2'.

(21)  *Doz deiz waz naniwa-bushi.*                                MN
      'Those days was naniwa-bushi'.

Even though these utterance structures may seem awkward to English speakers, they reflect a unique discourse process in HCE that I have named "TSR Formation", in which three representations; 'theme,' 'scheme,' and 'rheme' interact. The most important among the three is scheme, an entity that exists not in the utterance itself but in a larger linguistic 'discourse' unit, or more generally, within the mental representation of background knowledge. The theme, on the other hand, has to appear in the surface form of the utterance, while the rheme serves as the focus of the utterance to provide more information about the theme.

In the extract in (22) a new discourse topic is introduced by the interviewee, RC, who says "Doz deiz, ai tink dei yustu pei foti sents fo a kaki pænts." Thus, "pei" now exists in the discourse as an overt scheme. The theme is "plænteishen", and the rheme is "dala a dei".

(22)  RC: *Doz deiz, ai tink dei yustu pei foti sents fo a kaki pænts. Yu no, tu*
          *so wan av doz. Ænd a wulen pænts, hi wud pei wan dala.*
          'Those days, I think they used to pay forty cents for a khaki
          pants. You know, to sew one of those. And woolen pants, he
          would pay one dollar'.
      WN: So she was making like, if she made three a day, she could
          make like a dollar twenty...
      RC: *Dala twenti, dala siksti, yæ.*
          'Dollar twenty, dollar sixty, yeah.'
      WN: Which is more than what they were making on the plantation...
      RC: *Oh, yæ, plænteishen waz stil dala a dei. Laik a wulen pænts,*
          *leita, ai lrnd hau tu so, ænd ai kud so kaki pænts o wulen pænts.*
          *Bat wid mii, ai kud jast so wan wulen pænts a dei, dæts it.*
          'Oh, yeah, plantation was still dollar a day. Like a woolen
          pants, later, I learned how to sew, and I could sew khaki pants
          or woolen pants. But with me, I could just sew one woolen
          pants a day, that's it'.

Table 1 shows the frequency of occurrences of "Dollar utterances" in the narratives of nine speakers born on Kaua'i, where the first plantation was established in 1835. These people represent the older generation who would have been more likely to have retained the original HCE features than their younger

Table 1: *Number of Dollar utterances produced by nine speakers*

| Speaker | Age | Occupation | Dollar utterances/mins. |
|---------|-----|-----------------------|-------------------------|
| KMRC | 73 | suit seller, tailor | 2/90 |
| PMAM | 67 | sugar company worker | 0/60 |
| GFEV | 82 | school teacher | 0/60 |
| LFKV | 78 | house-maid | 0/60 |
| HFVS | 69 | pineapple company worker | 7/60 |
| JMBE | 74 | auto-parts salesman | 4/60 |
| JMMM | 82 | plantation laborer | 5/90 |
| JMTK | 76 | barber | 7/80 |
| JMMN | 81 | plantation laborer | 9/90 |

The four capital letters in the first column represent the following: ethnicity (K=Korean, P=Portuguese, G=German, L=Polish, H=Part-Hawaiian, J=Japanese), sex, initials of the speakers's first and last name.

counterparts would. The likelihood that Japanese served as the substratum model for TSR formation can be supported with both linguistic and the sociohistorical evidence. Japanese exhibits a particular type of utterance, a so-called "Eel Sentence" (Okutsu 1983), in which semantically heterogeneous nominals are connected by the topic marker /wa/ and the copula /da/ as in *Watashi wa hikoki da* (literally: 'I am an airplane') with the meaning of 'I will take an airplane'. The "Eel sentence" is thus constructed in the same manner as the HCE "Dollar Utterance". In example (23) *boku* 'I' is the theme, the scheme is 'transportation', and the rheme is *hikoki* 'airplane'.

> (23)  X:  *Kochira wa nan de kimashita ka?*
>             'How did you come here?'
>        Y:  *Watashi desu ka?*
>             'Oh, me?'
>             *Shinkansen de mairimashita.*
>             'I came by bullet train'.
>             *Nishizaka-san wa?*
>             'What about you, Mr. Nishizaka?'
>        X:  *Boku wa hikoki desu.*
>             'I am an airplane'. (Jorden & Noda 1987: JPA 107: #5)

With respect to the sociohistorical evidence, a careful examination of the chronological and demographic data reveals that it was around 1880 when both Chinese and Portuguese laborers started to work on the plantations together with indigenous Hawaiians. Reinecke's (1969) claim to the effect that "'pidgin' had not been formed until after Portuguese came" entails that 'pidgin creation' had begun only eight years before Japanese first immigrated in 1888. This does not seem to be enough time for a mixed jargon to formalize its linguistic system to the extent that it can be called a 'pidgin' language as a fixed communicative tool among different ethnic groups. My hypothesis is that HPE had not been fully developed yet when the Japanese language was introduced to the community of the plantation laborers.

Masuda (1995a, 1996a) also argues that the chronological and demographic figures show that the Japanese overwhelmingly comprised the majority of workers during the supposed creolization period between 1890 and 1920 in Hawai'i. Andersen et al. (1975: 12) says that the Japanese accounted for 50% of the population on Kaua'i between 1900 and 1920, which means that one out of every two speakers was speaking the Japanese language. Adams (1925) and Schmitt (1977) show that the entire population of Japanese in the state of Hawai'i constituted 40% overall. Roberts (1993) states that the ratio of Japanese plantation workers in the labor force reached 64.2% in 1892, and continued to increase to 72% in 1900. This clearly demonstrates that the Japanese were dominant in terms of population size, which in turn presents a strong case for their possible influence on HCE discourse. Masuda (1995b, 1996a) argues further that the numbering preferences for three in lines and verses, as well as the frequent use of verse-final markers, are also derived from Japanese discourse. Yet, as I will show next, HCE verse structure has also been influenced by English.

## 5. Superstratum: Line-predication

Here I make reference to two approaches to analyze narrative discourse, F[low] A[nalysis][6] (Chafe 1980, 1995) and V[erse] A[nalysis] (Hymes 1981, 1983, 1987, 1990a, 1990b, 1992). Although these approaches differ in various details, Chafe (1994: 57) notes a correspondence between what he calls an "intonation unit" and what Hymes (1981) calls a line. These two units are considered to be the smallest information units in discourse and usually take a predicate verb as a marker to identify themselves. As far as English is concerned, these minimal units constitute clauses.[7] Nonetheless, it is an open question whether or not clauses are universally the smallest informational units. As Chafe (1994: 70) observes that "the relation of intonation units to clauses needs further study, both within and across languages". In fact, Japanese discourse is structured differently from English discourse. Clancy (1982: 72–3) summarizes Japanese information structure as follows:

In spoken Japanese, a syntactic clause is frequently broken down into a number of smaller units, each of which is preceded by an audible pause and/or other hesitations, has a distinct intonation contour, and often ends with heavy stress and higher pitch on the final syllable of the last word or with a particle such as *ne* or *sa*....Temporal, locative, and adverbial phrases, arguments of the predicate, modifiers, verbal complements, conjunctions, and even hesitations such as the common...*ano ne* 'well uh', were frequently produced as separate units having their own intonation contour.

The key question is therefore whether the basic unit of HCE discourse structure corresponds more closely to the clausal type of units found in English or to the smaller phrasal units characteristic of Japanese. Example (24) illustrates the fragmental nature of discourse units in narrative structure in Japanese. The narrative text has been analyzed and arranged according to Verse Analysis. The notation conventions are as follows: Verse-initial particles are in bold; XX indicates the absence of verse-initial particles; parallel structures are enclosed in square brackets []; predicative phases are enclosed in hash (#) marks; verse-final markers are capitalized. Intervals are marked by parentheses, and backchannels by BC.

(24) *Imin no hanashi*
    Act  Hawai
        SN1  Nihon-jin [Participant]
        ST1  Ex:      Issei no Hito
             V1      L1   **Dakedo**, *imano nihon no sa,*
                    L2   *Nan, [nihon kara kiteiru issei, issei],*
                    L3   *[Nihon kara kiteiru, ima no, issei],*
                    L4   *[Nikkei no issei] ne,*
                    L5   *Minna kurou shita mitai NE.*       (.)
             V2      L6   **So** *yo, so ne,*
                    L7   *Atashi ga ima issho ni shigoto shiteiru hito mo,*
                    L8   *Mo nanaju go YO.*            BC
             V3      L9   *A, #nisei ka, nisei ka#,*
                    L10  *Okasan ga nihon kara kita kara,*
                    L11  *Nisei yo NE.*           (.5)
        ST2  Cm:     Hidoi Seikatsu
             V4      L12  *[**Ano**] ne, #tatami#,*
                    L13  *#[Ano] mukashi ne#,*
                    L14  *[Ano] nante yu NO.*       (.)

      V5       L15  **XX** *Painappuru hatake de hataraiteta desho,*
                L16  *#Minna ayu nihon kara imin,*
                L17  *Satokibi toka painappuru#.*       (.)

      V6       L18  **XX** *So sutto ne,*
                L19  *Hottategoya mitai na koya nan datte NE.*(.)

ST3  Cm:      Kurou
      V7       L20  **Soide** *koyu toko ne,*
                L21  *Minna ita no ue shinbun shiite,*
                L22  *Neta n desutte YO.*       (1.5)

      V8       L23  **XX** *Soyu seikatsu shiteta no yo,*
                L24  *#[Mukashi wa],*
                L25  *[Issei no hito wa NE]#.*       (1.0)

      V9       L26  **Demo** *kurou shite,*
                L27  *Soide kodomo kyoiku sashita kara,*
                L28  *Erai wa NE.*       (.)

An immigrant's story
  Act  Hawai'i
    SN1  Japanese
    ST1  The First Generation
        V1       L1    But, Japanese immigrants, (you see),
                L2    What you call, people from Japan, the first generation, the first generation,
                L3    the first generation from Japan,
                L4    the first generation of the Japanese descent, (you know),
                L5    All seem to have gone through hardships, (you know).

        V2       L6    That's right, that's right,
                L7    A woman that I am working with now, too,
                L8    (She is) Already seventy-five, (I inform you).

        V3       L9    Oh, (she is) the second generation, I guess,
                L10  Her mother was from Japan,
                L11  So, (she is) the second generation, (you know).

    ST2  An Awful Life
        V4       L12  You know, what, (it's) straw mats,
                L13  You know, old times,
                L14  You know, what you call.

| V5 | L15 | (They were) working at pineapple fields, right?, |
|    | L16 | All of them are those immigrants from Japan, |
|    | L17 | (They worked with) sugar cane and pineapples. |
| V6 | L18 | Then what happened, (you know), |
|    | L19 | (It's) a shack or a pen, (you know). |

ST3 Hardships

| V7 | L20 | Then a floor like this, (you know), |
|    | L21 | Everyone put a paper on it, |
|    | L22 | And slept (there), (I tell you). |
| V8 | L23 | (They were) living such a cruel life, (I assure you), |
|    | L24 | (That's) Old days, |
|    | L25 | (That's) People of the first generation, (you know), |
| V9 | L26 | But (they) worked hard, |
|    | L27 | And gave education to their children, |
|    | L28 | So (they were) nice, (you know). |

This text illustrates the kinds of utterances which Clancy (1982) would call "highly fragmental". Utterances containing predicates (i.e. verb, adjectival, or nominal + copula) account for half of the total; namely, L2, L3, L5, L7, L10, L14, L15, L18, L19, L21, L22, L23, L26, and L27. Note that the English translation may not correspond structurally to its Japanese counterpart.

Now let us compare the sample of narrative discourse in HCE in (25) using the same method of analysis.

| (25) | Act | Japan |  |  |
|      | SN1 | Yokohama [Location] |  |  |
|      | [ST1] | Ex | Prologue — Mr. Mashimo |  |
|      |       | V1 | L1 | **So** *after I graduated,* |
|      |       |    | L2 | *I went to Japan.* | (.5) |
|      |       | V2 | L3 | *When I went to Japan, Yokohama,* |
|      |       |    | L4 | *I met my Makiki Japanese School principal,* |
|      |       |    | L5 | *Mr. Mashimo was inside the hotel.* | (.5) |
|      |       | V3 | L6 | **XX** *Hotel, they call it ryokan,* |
|      |       |    | L7 | *Not this kind of a big hotel,* |
|      |       |    | L8 | *It is a ryokan.* | (.) |
|      | [ST2] | Cm: | Lobby |  |
|      |       | V4 | L9 | **XX** *He was right inside the lobby,* |
|      |       |    | L10 | *And sitting down, see.* | (0) |

|       | V5   | L11 | *When he saw me,*                     |      |
|-------|------|-----|---------------------------------------|------|
|       |      | L12 | *First thing was that he called me,*  |      |
|       |      | L13 | *Mr. Yoshimura come.*                 | (.)  |
|       | V6   | L14 | **XX** *I went,*                      |      |
|       |      | L15 | *To see him.*                         | (0)  |
| [ST3] | Cm:  |     | One Good Boy                          |      |
|       | V7   | L16 | **XX** *He said,*                     |      |
|       |      | L17 | *You are good boy, aren't you?*       |      |
|       |      | L18 | *Study hard.*                         | (.)  |
|       | V8   | L19 | *No, I came,*                         |      |
|       |      | L20 | *To play,*                            |      |
|       |      | L21 | *Ah, lose his fight.*                 | (.5) |

In (25) all the lines except for L7 are clauses which include a predicate or a *be*-verb. This English-like pattern of line predication organized around clauses contrasts quite sharply with the Japanese text, where only half the units are of this type. Although some aspects of HCE discourse such as the "Dollar utter-ance" have been heavily influenced by Japanese, the language still retains features of narrative discourse such as line predication structure which parallel English. This indicates that the possibility of superstrate influence cannot be ignored either in explaining the source of discourse structure in creole languages.

## 6.    Conclusion

I have provided evidence in HCE for each of the Trinary components: topicaliza-tion for universals; TSR formation for the substratum; and Line-predication for the superstratum. Although this work is preliminary, it shows promise. More extensive and detailed investigation of discourse structures in other pidgin and creole languages is needed.

## Acknowledgments

I offer my sincere prayer and gratitude to the late Dr. Charlene J. Sato for the hearty guidance she extended to me as my advisor. She provided me with provocative instruction in the study of Hawai'i Creole English in particular, as well as in pidgin/creole languages in general. Some portions of the present paper were written while attending her courses during the spring of 1992 and 1993. Without her stimulating lectures and invaluable advice, I could not have chosen this field of discipline as my lifework. I am also grateful to Suzanne Romaine for her support for my work. Finally, I would like to thank Kent Sakoda for his kind editorial help and suggestions as a native speaker of HCE.

## Notes

1. Fairclough (1989: 130) lists five cohesive features: (1) vocabulary links between sentences, (2) repetition of words, (3) use of related words, (4) connectors making temporal, spatial, and logical relationship, and (5) reference — anaphora and cataphora.

2. Schumann (1987) discusses the similarity between pidgins and interlanguages in their use of topic-comment oriented structures. His research motivation is based on Givón's (1979) speculation that both pidginization and early second language acquisition are manifestations of the presyntactic or pragmatic mode of communication which contrasts with the syntactic mode. Their works reinforce the hypothesis that topic-prominence is a universally preferred strategy.

3. Grimes and Glock's (1970) exploration of the narrative structures of Saramaccan presents an interesting and valuable analysis applicable to discourse analysis of pidgins and creoles. They note that "repetition takes the form of a sentence-initial clause introduced by *di* 'with reference to'." In the *di* clause, "the previous sentence is repeated." The fact that the repetition of a clause functions as a connector between the first and the second paragraph in terms of continuity of semantics is clearly a coherence device in Saramaccan discourse. I can see a functional similarity between *di* structure and some types of topic-comment structures.

4. Abbreviations used in the gloss are as follows: TOP topic marker; CP connecting particle; CONJ conjunction.

5. Bickerton (1981: 51–56) regards verb fronting as part of the bioprogram.

6. This is my term to refer to Chafe's analytical framework.

7. Linde (1993) calls the units in question 'narrative clauses'.

## References

Adams, Romanzo. 1925. *The peoples of Hawaii: A statistical study*. Institute of Pacific Relations. Honolulu:University of Hawai'i.

Andersen, Robert N., Gary R. Vieth, Benjamin J. Seidenstein and Blaine Bradshaw. 1975. *Kaua'i socioeconomic profile*. Center for Non-metropolitan Planning and Development. Cooperative Extension Service and Hawai'i Agricultural Experiment Station. Honolulu: University of Hawai'i.

Bickerton, Derek. 1981. *Roots of Language*. Ann Arbor:Karoma.

Center for Oral History. 1984a. *Kalihi: Place of transition*. Vol.1. Social Science Research Institute. Honolulu:University of Hawai'i.

———. 1984b. *Kalihi: Place of transition*. Vol.2. Social Science Research Institute. Honolulu:University of Hawai'i.

———. 1984c. *Kalihi: Place of transition*. Vol.3. Social Science Research Institute. Honolulu:University of Hawai'i.

————. 1985a. *Waikiki, 1900–1985: Oral histories*. Vol. 3. Social Science Research Institute. Honolulu:University of Hawai'i.

————. 1985b. *Waikiki, 1900–1985: Oral histories*. Vol. 4. Social Science Research Institute. Honolulu:University of Hawai'i.

————. 1988a. *Koloa: An Oral History-History of a Kaua'i Community*. Vol. 1. Social Science Research Institute. Honolulu:University of Hawai'i.

————. 1988b. *Koloa: An Oral History-History of a Kaua'i Community*. Vol. 2. Social Science Research Institute. Honolulu:University of Hawai'i.

————. 1988c. *Koloa: An Oral History-History of a Kaua'i Community*. Vol. 3. Social Science Research Institute. Honolulu:University of Hawai'i.

————. 1989a. *Lana'i Ranch: The people of Ko'ele and Keomoku*. Vol. 1. Social Science Research Institute. Honolulu:University of Hawai'i.

————. 1989b. *Lana'i Ranch: The people of Ko'ele and Keomoku*. Vol. 2. Social Science Research Institute. Honolulu:University of Hawai'i.

————. 1991a. *'Ualapu'e, Moloka'i: Oral histories from the east end*. Vol. 1. Social Science Research Institute. Honolulu:University of Hawai'i.

————. 1991b. *'Ualapu'e, Moloka'i: Oral histories from the east end*. Vol. 2. Social Science Research Institute. Honolulu:University of Hawai'i.

Chafe, Wallace. 1980. *The pear stories: Cognitive, cultural, and linguistic aspects of narrative production*. Norwood,NJ:Ablex Publishing.

————. 1994. *Discourse, consciousness, and time: The flow and displacement of conscious experience in speaking and writing*. Chicago/London:University of Chicago Press.

Clancy, Patricia M. 1982. "Written and spoken style in Japanese narratives." In Deborah Tannen (ed.), *Spoken and written language: Exploring orality and literacy*. Norwood, NJ:Ablex Publishing Company, 55–76.

Corne, Chris. 1987. "Verb fronting in creole: Transmission or bioprogram?" In Gilbert (ed.), 93–129.

Escure, Genevieve. 1988. "Topic structures as language universals." Journal of Pidgin and Creole Languages 3(2):159–176.

Fairclough, Norman. 1989. *Language and power*. London/New York: Longman.

Gee, James P. 1985. "The narrativization of experience in the oral style." *Journal of Education* 167(1):9–34.

Gilbert, Glenn G. (ed.). 1987. *Pidgin and Creole Languages: Essays in memory of John E. Reinecke*. Honolulu:University of Hawai'i Press.

Grimes, Joseph E. and Naomi Glock. 1970. "A Saramaccan narrative pattern." Language 46:408–425.

Givón, Talmy. 1979. *On Understanding Grammar*. New York:Academic Press.

Gundel, Jeanette K. 1988. "Universals of topic-comment structure." In M. Hammond, Edith A. Moravcsik, and Jessica R. Wirth (eds.), *Studies in syntactic typology*. Amsterdam/Philadelphia: John Benjamins, 209–239.

Hymes, Dell. 1981. *"In vain I tried to tell you": Essays in Native American ethnopoetics*. Philadelphia:University of Pennsylvania Press.

————. 1983. "Poetic structure of a Chinook text." In Frederick B. Agard et al. (eds.), *Essays in honor of Charles F. Hockett*. Leiden:Brill, 507–525.

————. 1987. "Tonkawa poetics: John Rush Buffalo's "coyote and eagle's daughter." In Joel Sherzer and Anthony C. Woodbury (eds.), *Native American discourse: Poetics and rhetoric*. London/New York:Cambridge University Press, 17–61.

————. 1990a. "Thomas Paul's SAMETL: Verse analysis of a (SAANICH) Chinook Jargon text." *Journal of Pidgin and Creole Languages* 5(1):71–106.

————. 1990b. "Ethnopoetics." *Text* 10 (1/2):45–47.

————. 1992. "Use all there is to use". In Brian Swan (ed.), *On the translation of Native American literatures*. Washington/ London:Smithsonian Institution Press, 83–124.

———— and Henry Zenk. 1987. "Narrative structure in Chinook Jargon." In Gilbert (ed.), 445–465.

Jorden, Eleanor H. and Mari Noda. 1987. *Japanese: The spoken language part 1: Eaves-dropping Tape*. New Haven/London:Yale University Press.

Kuno, Susumu. 1973. *Nihon bunpo kenkyu [Study of Japanese grammar]*. Tokyo:Taishukan Shoten.

Linde, Charlotte. 1993. *Life stories: The creation of coherence*. New York:Oxford University Press.

Masuda, Hirokuni. 1995a. "TSR formation as a discourse substratum in Hawai'i Creole English." *Journal of Pidgin and Creole Languages* 10(2):253–287.

————. 1995b. "Versification and reiteration in Hawai'i Creole English: *If nomo pailamæn, awrai!*" *World Englishes: Journal of English as an International and Intranational Language* 14(3):317–342.

————. 1996a. "Verse analysis and its theoretical contribution to the study of creole discourse." Paper presented at the Society for Pidgin and Creole Linguistics. January 5–6, 1996, San Diego, CA.

————. 1996b. "Ellipsis as a turn-allocation technique in Japanese discourse." Paper delivered at the Center for Japanese Studies, School of Hawaiian, Asian, and Pacific Studies, University of Hawai'i at Mānoa. March 6, 1996.

Mufwene, Salikoko S. 1986. "The universalist and substrate hypotheses complement one another." In Muysken and Smith (eds.), 129–162.

————. (ed.). 1993a. *Africanisms in Afro-American language varieties*. Athens/ London:The University of Georgia Press.

————. 1993b. "Introduction." In Mufwene (ed.), 1–31.

Muysken, Pieter and Norval Smith (eds.). 1986. *Substrata versus universals in creole genesis*. Amsterdam/Philadelphia: John Benjamins.

Okutsu, Keiichiro. 1983. *Boku wa unagi da no bunpo. [The grammar of I am an eel]*. Tokyo:Kuroshio Publishing.

Reinecke, John E. 1969. *Language and dialect in Hawaii : A sociolinguistic history to 1965*. Honolulu:University of Hawai'i Press.

Roberts, Sarah J. 1993. "The transformation of Hawaiian Plantation Pidgin and the emergence of Hawai'i Creole English." Handout distributed at the Society for Pidgin and Creole Linguistics held on June 11, 1993 at Amsterdam, the Netherlands.

Romaine, Suzanne. 1994. Language in society: *An introduction to sociolinguistics*. New York: Oxford University Press.

Sato, Charlene J. 1985. "Linguistic inequality in Hawai'i: The post-creole dilemma." In Nessa Wolfson and Joan Manes (eds.), *Language of Inequality*. Berlin:Mouton, 255–272.

Sato, Charlene J. and Karen A. Watson-Gegeo. 1992. "Information structure in Hawai'i Creole English." Handout presented at Friday Lecture Series on May 8, 1992. Department of English as a Second Language. Honolulu: University of Hawai'i at Mānoa.

Schmitt, Robert C. 1977. *Historical statistics of Hawaii*. Honolulu: University Press of Hawai'i.

Schumann, John H. 1987. "Utterance structure in basilang speech." In Gilbert (ed.), 139–160.

Roberts, Sarah J. 1995. "The transformation of Hawaiian Pidgin: the emergence of Hawai'i Creole English." Paper presented at the Society for Pidgin and Creole Linguistics held on June 17, 1995 at Amsterdam, the Netherlands.

Romaine, Suzanne. [illegible] *Language in society: An introduction to sociolinguistics*. New York: Oxford University Press.

Sato, Charlene J. [illegible] "[illegible] The post-creole dilemma." In [illegible] *Language of Hawaii* [illegible]. Berlin: Mouton, [illegible].

Sato, Charlene J. and [illegible] "[illegible] structure in the [illegible] Hawaiian [illegible]" [illegible]

Schumann, [illegible]

Schumann, [illegible] "[illegible] In [illegible], 139–[illegible]

# Comprehension and Resonance
## English Readers and English Creole Texts

### Lise Winer
*McGill University*

The literature of English Creole speakers — whether written in English or Creole or both — is generally considered to belong to the literary domain of 'English.' But, despite the extensive lexical overlap between English and Creole, can Creole writers and English readers be considered part of the same literary discourse community? What kinds of understanding and resonance are lost or muted when recognition of Creole elements does not occur within the reader?

Readers construct from text not only meaning, but membership in a discourse community comprising both writers and readers. Readers of 'foreign' texts, even in translation, generally recognize the possibility of misunderstanding based on limitations of linguistic and/or cultural competence. Words such as *kimono* in Japanese are not usually translated into something English, these being considered either familiar enough to English readers to be included in standard dictionaries, and there being no good equivalent in any case. Such words may be contextually explained, but are generally used without elaborate notes. A more culturally distant or presumably unfamiliar word may remain untranslated and marked, as in italics, throughout an entire novel such as Tanizaki's *The Makioka Sisters*: "They might as well forget about this *miai*. What of future ones?" (1957: 357). The reader is given considerable information about *miai* 'an arranged formal meeting between prospective marriage partners,' because this is a primary focus of the novel. Some of the details might now be as unfamiliar to a young modern Japanese person as to a foreigner, and would need discussion, explanation, or notation in Japanese, much as the vocabulary and cultural conventions of the Victorians, let alone the Elizabethans, need elucidation for modern English speakers.[1]

It is always a challenge for a writer to determine how much explanation, overt or covert, should be provided for potential readers who might be unfamiliar, to varying degrees, with the vocabulary and cultural content the writer uses. In the case of writers addressing an audience primarily supposed to consist of their cultural and linguistic counterparts, less such support needs to be given, as with any intra-group communication. However, sometimes authors are very much aware that they are writing for audiences of readers that will include many, if not a majority of, (semi-)outsiders. For example, in Maxine Hong Kingston's *The Woman Warrior*, a book about growing up Chinese-American, there are many references to Chinese items, e.g.:

> This document has eight stamps on it ... one, the red seal of Dr. Wu Pak-liang ... one, my mother's seal, her chop marks larger than the president's and the dean's. (Kingston 1975: 68)

The word *chop*, derived from Hindi and associated with the India and China trade, has become a well established loan-word in English, but readers unfamiliar it could either ignore it, or suppose that it is synonymous or metonymous with 'seal' and 'stamp.'

In other instances, all the words are English, but the cultural importance of a particular custom is so powerful that if the reader does not get the reference, considerable impact is lost, e.g.:

> Then I get bitter: no one supports me; I am not loved enough to be supported. That I am not a burden has to compensate for the sad envy when I look at women loved enough to be supported. Even now *China wraps double binds around my feet*. (Kingston 1975: 57, emphasis added)

This sentence refers not only to the traditional Chinese practice of female foot-binding; it also refers to the psychological 'double bind' the narrator feels in trying to accommodate two opposing cultural pressures. Thus it is not by chance that these 'double binds' are wrapped around the narrator's feet, rather than, say, her heart.

Traditionally and currently, Creole writers keep in mind a potential mixed audience, comprising both local and regional readers who are native speakers of Creole and English, *and* foreign native speakers of English. Some authors, particularly poets, such as Louise Bennett and Paul Keens-Douglas, are clearly more oriented towards local than foreign readership — or listenership, as much of their work is performed and recorded orally as well as published in book form. Caribbean writers have long dealt with this situation specifically in the practical sense of deciding how much 'redundant' information to include for the benefit of outside readers, while not boring local knowledgeable ones (D'Costa 1983: 256–259; 1984). An author could choose, for example, to write of 'a cacique in a tree,' or 'a cacique in a tree, perched on its fragile hanging grass nest,' or 'a cacique in a tree, perched on its fragile hanging grass nest, its bold yellow and black feathers startling against the blue sky and the (red) flowers of the immortelle (tree).'

The particular relationship — specifically the linguistic, cultural and historical ties — between international standard/metropolitan languages such as English, and their 'related' or 'lexically based' creoles, has often been characterized as a 'continuum' (DeCamp 1971; Bickerton 1975; Rickford 1987: 35–38). However, as Carrington (1992) has pointed out, not only does creole reality prove unamenable to such analysis, the model itself — even a 'multi-dimensional' version — encourages 'an interpretation of directionality' (p. 97), i.e. implying that the creole language (and its speakers) are always trying to attain the 'goal' of the standard. He proposes instead images relating to three-dimensional space, e.g. the chocolate-and-vanilla marble cake which 'allows the kinds of blends and swirls that could depict the variable penetration of the upper, middle, and lower layers into their neighbors' (p. 97) or 'an integrated mass of soap bubbles, each of which has the unusual feature of a penetrable skin'; with bubbles of varied and changing shapes and sizes, so that 'the overall shape of the mass would be arbitrary and irregular' (p. 98). While such metaphors are limited, they serve to emphasize that the individuals who inhabit 'creole space' have 'multi-systemic repertoires' and that this space 'coheres because networks of communication overlap' in a way that may be 'neither constant nor systematic' (p. 98).

For Creole speakers, it is often difficult to determine the exact boundaries between Creole and English, and between different varieties and registers of metropolitan English. On the other hand, even Creole speakers who are not very literate are generally familiar with a great deal of English. For English readers, while grammatical and phonological differences between Creole and English are widely evident in writing, perhaps the most confusing area is vocabulary (Winer 1985, 1993: 48–56). The Creole lexicon includes many words which are not part of formal or informal English. These words fall into a number of categories. The first is those whose meaning is basically the same as their English counterparts. Some have become obsolete or dialectal in English, e.g. *pappyshow* 'object of ridicule' (from English 'puppet-show'). Some differ slightly in form, e.g. *flim* 'film' or have been reanalyzed, e.g. *a mice* 'a mouse.' Some Creole words have a much higher frequency of usage (e.g. *fowl* 'chicken'), or a different range of reference than in English, e.g. *silk-cotton tree* refers to only one Caribbean species. In other cases, the Creole words have the same form, but a meaning which differs wholly or partly from that in English, e.g. *fresh* 'gamy, slightly rotten,' *spice* 'cinnamon,' *in flower* 'with buds,' *salt* 'fertilizer'; such form counterparts can lead to serious problems in communication (Winer 1985: 53–56). The largest category of Creole words, those not found in English, can generally be divided into those which, to an English reader, are recognizably foreign — e.g. *congolala*, '*Eclipta alba*, a medicinal plant,' and *chickychong*, 'a type of small kite made from one sheet of paper' — and those that seem foreign overall though made up of English words — e.g. *fore-day morning*, 'the time just before dawn,' and *broughtupsy* 'good breeding, manners.'

One of the most crucial tools of literary language use is a dictionary, and increasingly the gaps in Caribbean English Creole lexicography are being filled. There are available several, from the great pioneer work of the *Dictionary of Jamaican English* (Cassidy and Le Page 1967), to the *Dictionary of Bahamian English* (Holm with Shilling 1982), and the recent pan-Caribbean-oriented *Dictionary of Caribbean English Usage* (Allsopp 1996). For readers of Caribbean literature including Creole lexicon, such reference works can be extremely helpful, but readers must be aware of such possibilities. High purchase prices and lack of continued publicity within the region have worked against such awareness; outside the region they are often astonishingly unknown to readers and researchers. No one dictionary can ever be totally comprehensive, complete, or correct, and it will be a long time, if ever, before disagreements over orthographic choices die out, but all such works can provide an invaluable resource.

Lack of recognition of linguistic differences leads at best to a lack of resonance or depth for the reader, and at worst to limited or distorted comprehension. Because English readers often do not recognize Creole features in Caribbean texts, they often do not understand the text, and yet, by virtue of the nature of the Creole/English overlap, often do not realize that they do not understand it. Of course, any reader's experience and understanding of a text, based on the reader's background knowledge and viewpoints, can be considered a valid interpretation, to some extent. And, of course, authors themselves are not always conscious of all the meaning that can be reasonably derived by readers from their writing.

Nonetheless, without adequate background knowledge of culture-specific assumptions and content — including language — reading can become 'a time-consuming, laborious and unsatisfactory enterprise' (Steffensen 1988: 193). There is ample evidence that lack of appropriate and sufficient background knowledge can cause significant problems in reading in a second language (Steffensen, Joag-dev and Andersen 1979; Carrell 1984; Barnitz 1986; Carrell and Eisterhold 1983; Carrell 1987; Parry 1987). Steffensen (1986), for example, found that the absence of appropriate background knowledge was powerful enough to interfere even with native speakers' understanding of an English text.

Even a deep and genuine interest in the culture represented in the text does not mean the student/reader can accept or even understand some of the basic premises of that culture (Winer and Steffensen 1992: 25).

Add to this general problem the specific one posed to unsuspecting English readers of English/Creole texts by the 'continuum' or, better, the interpenetrating bubbles, of language. These readers may never realize that they are reading two languages at the same time. In fact, it could be argued that there is a third language present. This is *not* an 'interlanguage' of a series of Creole 'approximations' to English, but a 'gestalt language,' a third entity that depends on the reader's knowing *both* Creole and English to be fully understood. To use a limited but perhaps helpful Impressionistic metaphor, if English is orange (< red + yellow) and Creole is green (< blue + yellow), where yellow is the shared overlap, then the combination of English and Creole should be purple (or brown). However, it is still possible to distinguish single-color flakes and swirls, not only of orange and green, but still of red and blue, thus making the gestalt more like confetti that looks purple from a distance than one color.

Whether obstacles or opportunities, how do these shared and unshared features, these unsystematic multi-systemic repertoires, manifest themselves in actual texts, and what implications do the results have for readers? Four Caribbean Creole literary styles are examined here in relationship to these questions:

1. Creole items within an English context, exemplified by Derek Walcott's poem 'Spoiler's Return.'
2. Text style entirely based on Creole oral narrative, exemplified by Olive Senior's story 'Real Old Time T'ing.'
3. Text in English, but with Creole rhythms, i.e. with few or no overt lexical, phonological, or grammatical cues to the underlying Creole discourse, as in Earl Lovelace's *The Dragon Can't Dance*.
4. Hyper-magic realism, in which deliberate word-play, invention, etc. are essential to style and meaning, as in Robert Antoni's novel *Divina Trace*.

## 1.   Creole Items within an English Context

'Spoiler's Return' by Derek Walcott is a poem imagining how The Mighty Spoiler, (Theophilus Phillip) a master calypsonian of the 1940s and 1950s, would comment on contemporary Trinidad society. The poem quotes from and alludes to the 'lords of irony,' both classical/canonical (Rochester, Pope, Arnold, Juvenal) and calypsonian (Spoiler and Atilla) playing 'in Satan tent, next carnival'; it is thus

immediately clear that Walcott is working from a cultural world that encompasses the full range of Creole and metropolitan English culture and literature (in this
case, including classical Latin).

The same is true of language. Some sections are completely in English:

> Hell is a city much like Port of Spain,
> what the rain rots, the sun ripens some more,
> all in due process and within the law,
> as, like a sailor on a spending spree,
> we blow our oil-bloated economy
> on projects from here to eternity.

Some are English but with a heavy cultural load from the local environment:

> and beyond them the firelit mangrove swamps,
> ibises practicing for postage stamps.

(The scarlet *ibis*, a large red bird, and an official symbol of Trinidad and
Tobago, has several times been a featured subject on stamps.)

Common, and striking, is the easy interpenetration of Creole and English
bubbles (or colors). In the following, distinctive Creole elements are marked, and
are clearly juxtaposed with English features, e.g. *sang, chains made us*.

> In all *them* project, all *them* Five-Year-Plan,
> what *happen* to the Brotherhood of Man?
> Around the time I *dead* it wasn't so,
> we sang the Commonwealth of caiso,
> we *was* in chains, but chains made us unite,
> now *who have, good for them*, and *who blight, blight*.

Lexically, *caiso* — as opposed to *calypso* — is clearly Creole. Since most of a
creole's lexicon in "continuum" situations is shared with the lexically related standard
language, it is of course to be expected that many words will be both English
and Creole, e.g. *Five-Year-Plan, the Brotherhood of Man* and *Commonwealth*.

An example of how 'naive' readers can lose both resonance and comprehension can be illustrated in reference to the first lines of the poem:

> I sit high on this bridge in Laventille,
> watching that city where I left no will
> but my own conscience and rum-eaten wit,
> and *limers* passing see me where I sit,
> ghost in brown gabardine, bones in a sack,
> and *bawl*: 'Ay, Spoiler, boy! When you come back?'
> And those *who bold* don't feel they *out of place*
> to peel my *limeskin* back, and see a face
> with eyes as cold as a dead *macajuel* ...

Undergraduate students at Southern Illinois University-Carbondale, in three English classes (an honors poetry seminar, and two sections of a course on Caribbean literature) were asked to interpret individual words and overall meaning for this section. In terms of top-down processing, the most basic problem they displayed was failure to understand the role of the calypsonian as a conscience and voice of justice for the people. Thus several students thought that Spoiler represented a threat to society, either as an agent of Satan ("right-wing" interpretation) or an agent of imperialism ("left-wing" interpretation). The name 'Spoiler' was considered to support either position. Several students thought that Spoiler was a reincarnated slave — the history of the Caribbean envisioned as slavery times and today, with nothing in between. Such misinterpretation is not surprising, given the poem's identification of hell as the place where Spoiler is living, and Satan as a fan of calypso. Much of the overall irony of the poem depends on recognizing the historically low status and scorn heaped by establishment society on the calypsonian; this irony is missed if this recognition is lacking.

In terms of bottom-up processing, most of these readers depended heavily on a strategy of finding cognates, that is, making semantic interpretation of words in terms of their metropolitan English or English-like resemblances. Thus, *macajuel* was taken to be a variant of *mackerel*, thereby reducing the intended shock of a dead snake to the lesser one of a dead fish; *limer* was interpreted as someone who worked in limepits, thereby white from powder, rather than the distinctively Creole *limer* 'idler, talker.' There was little hypothesis-testing to see how these words might stand up with these meanings within the particular text. This combination of inadequate cultural background schema and lack of suspicion of English-appearing words led to frequent misinterpretations, with resonance for any Creole aspects close to zero.

## 2.   Text Style Based on Creole Oral Narrative

Many Caribbean-based stories are increasingly written to appear as if they are simply being told by one person to a group of friends. In the 'purest' forms, as exemplified by the work of Paul Keens-Douglas (e.g. 'Wukhand' 1986), such monologues, printed as poems or stories, are polished versions of the speech of a talented and experienced speaker. In fact, Keens-Douglas's most popular formats are live performances and audio recordings. These are more oriented to Creole speakers, with less apparent support for foreign readers/listeners. Some of the written texts closest to actual speech performance are the vernacular language newspaper columns of social commentary (e.g. Winer 1993: 82–85, 93–103, 127–130).

However, in the more 'literary' orientations of this style, oral performance is a base, and the resulting story is *not* a transcript of an oral narrative.[2] In the following two excerpts, taken from Jamaican writer Olive Senior's story, 'Real Old Time T'ing,' the traditional oral style is clearly dominant. Note here, for example, the typical Creole oral narrative discourse feature of repeating an important phrase ('Sanitary convenience!') and the posing of a rhetorical question to elicit appreciative scornful participatory response from the audience ('So it dont name bath house any more?'). Creole grammar is evident throughout. In addition to the marked features, there are zero-copula predicates, as in 'she [Ø] so hot' and 'she [Ø] down here':

> *Is* the one *name* Patricia *did* start up bout how Papa Sterling *need* a new house for it *look* bad *how* their father *living* in this old *board house* it *don't* even have sanitary convenience. Sanitary convenience! So it *dont name* bath house any more? Then if she [Ø] so hot on sanitary convenience why she [Ø] down here *a buy* up all the old water *goblet* and china *basin* she can find *a talk say* *is* real country *this* and how she just *finding* her roots. (p. 54)

Nonetheless, the narrative style is also colored by English, e.g. the use of *she* where "basilectal" Jamaican would have *(h)im*, and of course *sanitary convenience*. It is also clear that the author is removed, in time as well as place, from an immediate audience.

The following excerpt from the same story exemplifies the difficulty of "untangling" or separating Creole and English.

> So right away everybody *know* something [Ø] going on *in truth* between Papa and Miss Myrtella. But the strange thing is that not a soul *tease* Papa or *say* a word about it. Everybody just *pretend* they dont know what [Ø] going on though they [Ø] watching every move. And *is* like everybody in the district [Ø] holding their breath. They dont want Patricia to get to know bout it for she [Ø] really *vex* with Miss Myrtella and if she ever hear bout the courting she [Ø] bound to try and mash it up. (p. 63)

This is not totally 'natural' speech; this is a literary style, and despite its narrative, story-telling person-to-person intimacy, it is the literary style of the novel or the short story, not that of the dramatic play. For one thing, there are no hesitations, no false starts, no unfinished sentences, no 'mistakes.' Despite obvious Creole grammatical features and lexicon — e.g. *in truth*, *vex*–there are also features that should be considered distinctively "English" — *though*, *their*, *the* rather than *de*. And some elements that might be considered Creole are just as easily English, such as the verbs, which are probably Creole unmarked past but also English historic present. How would/should this narrator in fact speak in "real life" or in a story? Should 'But the strange thing is that not a soul tease Papa' be made more oral/Creole as 'But you know the strange thing? Not a soul tease Papa?' Is the variable interpenetration in this story a result of the author's skill in representing or distilling reality? Or is it the result of compromise of systems to enable a potentially wider audience to understand a highly Creole-marked text?

## 3.    Text in Standard English, with Underlying Creole Rhythms

In most of the writings of Trinidadian author Earl Lovelace, the text appears to be almost entirely in English, though much Creole language and culture are expressed. The apparently English text is in fact infused throughout with the influence of Creole rhythms and oral speech style.[3] Especially when read aloud, some sections, such as the following excerpts from *The Dragon Can't Dance* (1979) show powerful momentum and rhythm built on traditions of Creole oral style, including development through metaphor, repetition, and parallelism. The repetition, in particular, evokes the echoed chorus of the calypsonian:

> Everybody knew him as 'Colts'. Generations of people knew him as a staunch supporter of Colts Football team, relinquishing whatever name he had received at baptism to bear his team's name; and oh, *was to see* all the schoolboys rushing to buy *snowball* from him, shouting 'Colts! Colts! Colts!' as if they were eager to recognize and accept him, and, by some kind of magical rebounding, be themselves recognized and accepted. He had a word he used to say. He used to say, 'Right, man! Right, man!' as an acknowledgement and salutation, with that ease and generosity, as if he knew that he would forever belong here to the earth and to the Savannah and to the fans and the children. 'Right, man!' And he would ask if you wanted your snowball with condensed milk on top of it, or if you wanted green syrup or red syrup or brown. He had a brown syrup that was guava flavoured. That was nice. That was real nice. Some people used to ask for all three, and he used to dip the shaved ice skillfully into the different pans of syrup, dip! dip! dip! flick it up so as not to let syrup leak from the juicy snowball, hand it over with one hand, and receive payment with the other...
>
> And sometimes out of sheer exuberance, out of a sweet admiration at himself, a kind of amazement at his own speed and agility in dispatching so many snowballs — shaving the ice and cupping it and dipping it into at least two pans of syrup and maybe pouring condensed milk atop it, out of his sweet

sense of wonder and of acceptance of the magical clean swiftness and nerve-
lessness of his actions, he would shout as if to steady himself: 'Colts! Colts!'
As if to steady and salute himself, as if to say, Lord, look how I [∅] quick!
Look at my speed! 'Colts!' And some of the people around, sharing in the
marvelling and the admiration, warming to his salute and wanting to join in it,
would chorus, 'Colts! Colts!' and he, Colts, would say it again, accepting their
recognition and salute, 'Colts!' So that there grew in the Savannah on an
evening a song chorused and chanted for Colts, a song to the man and the
football team and the Savannah and the fans and the world. (pp. 84–85)

The use of local referents adds to recognition of the scene as Creole — e.g.
*Savannah, snowball, guava*. The first is a specific place, the Queens Park
Savannah in Port of Spain, and the other two are characteristic of, though not
unique to, the Caribbean, although a case could be made for the locally individual character of such things.

An even clearer example is found in this description of the early years of
the steelbands.

Those were the war days, when every street corner was a garrison; and to be
safe, if you came from Belmont, you didn't let night catch you in St. James;
if your home was Gonzales Place, you didn't go up Laventille; and if you
lived in Morvant, you passed San Juan straight. (p. 54)

Lovelace has 'changed up' the language of a Creole phenomenon to English.
Besides the place names, there are only two linguistic features in this passage
that are distinctively Creole: *go up* [place] 'go up to [place]' and *pass straight*.
If written down in oral Creole, the passage might look like this:

Dem was de war days, an every street corner was a garrison; and if yuh want
to be safe — if yuh belong to Belmont, yuh doh let night catch yuh in St.
James; if yuh livin Gonzales Place, you eh goin up Laventille; and if yuh livin
Morvant, yuh passin San Juan straight.

Is anything lost for Creole readers in this change? Doubtless yes — the feeling
of the full version in oral language — but they can still hear the Creole — the
rhythms, grammar, phonology and vocabulary — resonating clearly underneath
this passage. English speakers who cannot hear this voice will also be missing
something — the recognition of depth and linguistic resonance not visible/audible
on the surface — even if they can recognize that this is not 'just' English.

## 4. Hyper-Magic Realism

In the hyper-magic realism of Robert Antoni's novel *Divina Trace*, deliberate word-play, invention, distortion, and confusion are essential to style (Cobham-Sander 1998). The novel is ostensibly set on the Caribbean island of "Corpus Christi" — nonetheless easily recognizable from its purported history and its place names, and its language, as based on Trinidad. Since large parts of the novel are based on the story of Hanuman, the monkey-god, in the Hindu epic of the Ramayana, it is not surprising to find monkey-games and monkey name-games everywhere. In this paragraph from about mid-point in the novel, some references to monkeys, and to Hamlet's soliloquy 'To be or not to be,' are evident:

> Uakari den Rishymiuka, pigtaile macacaque tween you legs, *alouatta alouatta jeanbaptistelamaracka alouatta!* Sugriva, you now slow-loris, Tara message so nycticebus, both you monkeyhood she pongo proper, both you papio hamadryas good! Sad Sugriva he gray-graylangur — campbelli lowei now he last peg — maurus macaca he fus-fuscata, like he mourning dem 40 pekings drown in Japanese Pearlharbour! 'Wanderloo,' he now sololoquize. 'Tutupia, ono toque? Twoolly tisnoble tabear teasing stone of orangutudinous fortune? Thomasi? Presbytis obscura? Aye, rub de rub! (italics in original, pp. 199–200)

Some linguistic elements are clearly Creole, e.g. *you legs*, *like he mourning*, *dem 40*, the representaiton of pronunciation *de* for *the*. Some are ambiguous, e.g. *she pongo proper*–is *pongo* verb or adjective here?

Some of the monkey names are reasonably straightforward, though they include out-dated synonyms and ambiguous referents.[4] Perhaps the most interesting monkey reference is 'alouatta alouatta.' This doubtless alludes to the French song 'Alouette,' but *Alouatta seniculus insularus* is the indigenous red howler monkey, a species unique to Trinidad. And surely, *jeanbaptistelamaracka* is related to (a different version of? a deliberate distortion of?) the Barbadian-Trinidadian children's counting song: 'eeny-meeny *mackaracka*, R-A dominacka, chickalokka, lollipoppa, om-pom push' (emphasis added). Readers of this paragraph may be dazzled by such linguistic and scientific knowledge, if, in fact, the reader recognizes these words as based on scientific name-forms. The reader may also — understandably — feel thoroughly worn down; perhaps this is the author's warning in 'pongo proper', cf Creole *pong* [pound] 'to subject to verbal abuse.' Indeed, Antoni puts the reader "in a monkey pants," a Trinidadian Creole expression describing a ridiculous and impossible situation.

The extent to which Antoni plays tricks on the reader borders on the perverse, as in the monkey-name passage above. A small example: he uses the Creole word *rockstone* (p. 154), but also the word *boulderstone* (p. 264), a word that is not Creole, and not English. A Creole reader would recognize its non-Creole nature immediately, and might then view it either as a clever play on and extension of *rockstone*, or as a mistake, an error in Creole. An English reader would probably not recognize this, possibly assuming that a *boulderstone* is simply a larger kind of *rockstone*. Virtually every page holds traps of this sort, lulling readers into a false sense of stable insecurity. On page 71, for example, are found the real Creole words *mappapire, macajuel, oui fute, fight up, chapelet, oui, crapo, forceripe, bamsee, Bazil, callaloo, samaan, La Divina Pastora* and *clearskin*, but also made-up forms — *most daybreak, mangrove banyan* and *Papamoi*.

How can the reader trust this? A survey of the reviews of *Divina Trace* reveals that at least the initial response of (presumed) English readers was that unfamiliar words must simply be 'dialect.'

> Like Faulkner, Antoni is a master of the voice, the telling of a story as if it were part of an oral rather than a written tradition. The method has its dangers. Readers of Antoni, like readers of Faulkner, will either 'hear' the individual rhythms and tones of the voices and appreciate, or not hear and lose patience. The difficulty with *Divina Trace* will likely be even more severe than with Faulkner's works, if only because most readers in the United States are more familiar with southern speech patterns than with West Indian. (Lemon 1993: 155)

> A reader ... eventually just feels *buried*. Partly it's a problem constitutional to dialect books — 'Yes Doodoo, now de burden of passing on dis story must fall pon you. Because Evalina not here not more to push she foot long de road again, and you is firstborn Domingo manchild, beget by de firstborn Dominago manchild, beget by dis wadjank-cacashat who is Satan self, who defile Papa God own sweet saint of heaven to beget dis diab-crapostory hand down to you ...' — and partly it's the fault of the swollen diameter of Antoni's mythic purpose, when in fact all he has to tell is a small story. (*Kirkus Reviews* 1991: 1483)

## Conclusion

Membership in any type of discourse community of readers requires specific levels of competence for various texts. But the particular characteristics of the Creole-English matrix make a special demand: simply put, that the English reader be aware and suspicious of the underlying *language* of the text, a language that may look like a duck, walk like a duck, and even quack like a duck, but may not be any kind of duck at all.

The choices that Caribbean authors make involve factors of comprehensibility, related to awareness of audience, as well as a complicated and perhaps not always conscious dialectic between the oral and the literary, and a sense of sheer linguistic play. While Caribbean authors are generally very aware of their audience's potential limitations, however they choose to write, it may be that English readers are not. This has some rather concrete implications. For example, in the study of Caribbean literature by metropolitan English readers, the supply of appropriate background knowledge — both cultural and linguistic — is essential in order to ensure comprehension and some resonance. Only to some extent can English readers be considered part of the same literary discourse community. What kinds of understanding and resonance are lost or muted, when recognition of Creole elements does not occur within the reader?

Further research in this area might well focus on the relationship between orality and literary forms. For this, a great deal more work is needed on the fundamentals of creole discourse style. That is, not simply the use of Creole elements, but the style and linguistic choices of Creole narrative.

## Acknowledgments

I am very grateful to Rhonda Cobham-Sander for letting me read and be inspired by her work in progress on Antoni's *Divina Trace* and for reading Lovelace aloud; to Hans E.A. Boos for help with monkey-names and monkey-games; and to Agnes He, John Singler and Clarisse Zimra for their comments. All errors of omission and commission are of course the author's.

## Notes

1. The deliberate use of geographically or temporally local words is very evident in historical novels, particularly romances and mysteries, where use of such lexicon can be quite aggressive, e.g.

   > A middle-aged gentleman with well-grayed hair and pleasant face... dressed in a green wool houpelande to his knees, split front and back for ease of riding, with lamb's wool budge at its cuffs and collar, his hood with its trailing liripipe laid to one side. (Frazer 1992: 5–6)

2. For examples of recorded and transcribed oral Creole narratives for Trinidad see Winer (1993: Section 7).

3. In a review of a work by a Caribbean-Canadian author, Hahnel (1995: 36) notes that "Caribbean speech rhythms animate Palmer's descriptions." The small segment she quotes can be used to illustrate this point, but also to illustrate that there are real differences between authentic oral speech and literary speech:

   > Pastor Paul was a kind-face man. Old. About sixty with a soft voice. He wasn't married and you could tell because his clothes always had a shine on them. You know when you press black on the right side... how it picks up a shine? Just so

his clothes always looked... it was as though the sun was always shining in him and somehow it shone through his clothes.

In what ways has this narration been modified for literary form? For example, should the last lines here be more realistically rendered

> Pastor Paul was a kind-face man. Old. About sixty with a soft voice. He eh married and you coulda tell because his clothes always have a shine on it. You know how when you press black on the right side... how it pick up a shine. Just so he clothes always lookin / He clothes always lookin so... like the sun always shinin inside a he and shinin through he clothes.

4.  To wit: *uakari* (*Cacajao rubicundus*, the red uakari; *C. calvus*, the white or bald uakari, *C. melanocephalus*, the black-headed uakari, Upper Amazon Basin); *pigtail macacaque* (*Macaca nemestrina*, the pigtail macaque, India-Philippines); *alouatta* (see below); *slow-loris* (*Nyctibeus coucang*, the slow loris, India-Sri Lanka); *nycticebus* (*Nyctibeus coucang*, the slow loris, India-Sri Lanka); *pongo* (*Pongo pygmaeus*, the orangutan); *papio hamadryas* (*Papio hamadryas*, the Sacred or Hamadryad baboon, Egypt-Ethiopia); *gray-graylangur* (*Presbytis entellus*, the gray or Hanuman langur, India); *campbelli lowei* (*Cercopithecus lowei* → *C. campbelli*, Campbells's monkey, W. Africa); *maurus macaca he fus-fuscata* (*Macaca maurus*, the Moor macaque, Celebes, and *Macaca fuscata*, the Japanese macaque); *Macaca sinica* (the toque macaque, Sri Lanka); *Twoolly* (*Lagothrix lagotricha*, the common woolly monkey); *Thomasi* (*Presbytis thomasi*, Indonesia-Sumatra; *Cercopithecus thomasi* → *C. lhoesti*, L'Hoest's monkey, E. Africa; *Cheirogaleus medius* → *C. thomasi*, the fat-tailed dwarf lemur, Madagascar; *Galagoides thomasi* → *G. demidoff*, the African galago; *Saguinus thomasi* → *S. labiatus*, the white-lipped tamarin, S. America; *Presbytis obscura* (→ *Trachypithecus obscurus*) the spectacled or dusky leaf-monkey/langur, Malaysia); *Aye* (*Daubentonia madagascariensis*, the aye-aye, Madagascar) (Corbet and Hill 1991).

# References

Allsopp, Richard. 1996. *Dictionary of Caribbean English usage.* Oxford: Oxford University Press.

Antoni, Robert. 1992. *Divina Trace.* Woodstock, NY: Overlook Press.

Barnitz, J. 1986. "Toward understanding the effects of cross-cultural schemata and discourse structure on second language reading comprehension." *Journal of Reading Behavior* 18: 95–116.

Bickerton, Derek. 1975. *Dynamics of a Creole System.* Cambridge: Cambridge University Press.

Carrell, Patricia L. 1984. "The effects of rhetorical organization on ESL readers." *TESOL Quarterly* 18: 441–69.

———. 1987. "Content and formal schemata in ESL reading." *TESOL Quarterly* 21:461–81.

Carrell, Patricia L. and Joan Carson Eisterhold. 1983. "Schema theory and ESL reading." *TESOL Quarterly* 17: 553–74.

Carrington, Lawrence D. 1992. "Images of Creole space." *Journal of Pidgin and Creole Languages* 7: 93–9.

Cassidy, F. G. and R. Le Page. 1967. *Dictionary of Jamaican English*. Cambridge University Press.

Cobham-Sander, Rhonda. 1998. "Of boloms, mirrors, and monkeymen: What's real and what's not in Robert Antoni's *Divina Trace*." *Annals of Scholarship* 12.1–2:49–74. (This issue was guest-edited by Kamau Brathwaite and Timothy J. Reiss, and entitled, *Sisyphus and El Dorado: Magical and Other realisms in Caribbean Literature*.)

Corbet, G. B. and J. E. Hill. 1991. *A World List of Mammalian Species*. 3rd ed. Oxford: Oxford University Press.

D'Costa, Jean. 1983. "The West Indian novelist and language: A search for a literary medium." In Lawrence D. Carrington (ed.), in collaboration with Dennis Craig and Ramon Todd Dandaré, *Studies in Caribbean Language*. St. Augustine, Trinidad: Society for Caribbean Linguistics, 252–265.

D'Costa, Jean. 1984. "Expression and communication: Literary challenges to the Caribbean polydialectal writers." *Journal of Commonwealth Literature* 19: 123–41.

De Camp, David. 1971. "Toward a generative analysis of a post-creole speech continuum." In Dell Hymes (ed.), *Pidginization and Creolization of Languages*. Cambridge: Cambridge University Press, 349–370.

Frazer, Margaret. 1992. *The Novice's Tale*. New York: Berkley Publishing.

Groves, Colin p. 1993. "Order Primates." In Don E. Wilson and DeAnn M. Reeder (eds.), *Mammalian Species of the World: A Taxonomy and Geographical Reference*, 2nd ed. Washington, DC: Smithsonian Institution Press, 243–77.

Hahnel, Lori. 1995. "Brief review of Hazelle Palmer's *Tales from the gardens and beyond*." *Books in Canada* November:36.

Holm, John A., with Allison Shilling. 1982. *Dictionary of Bahamian English*. Cold Spring, NY: Lexik House.

Keens-Douglas, Paul. 1986. "Wukhand." In Paula Burnett (ed.), *The Penguin book of Caribbean Verse*, 58–60. Harmondsworth: Penguin.

Kingston, Maxine Hong. 1975. *The Woman Warrior*. New York: Vintage Books.

*Kirkus Reviews*. 1991. "Review of Antoni's *Divina trace*." Dec. 1, No. 5923, p. 1483.

Lemon, Lee. 1993. "Review of Antoni's Divina trace [et al.]." *Prairie Schooner*, Spring, 671:154–7.

Lovelace, Earl. 1979. *The Dragon Can't Dance*. London: Andrê Deutsch.

Parry, Kate J. 1987. "Reading in a second culture." In J. Devine, P. L. Carrell, & D. E. Eskey (eds.), *Research in Reading in English as a Second Language*. Washington, DC: TESOL, 59–70.

Rickford, John R. 1987. *Dimensions of a Creole Continuum*. Stanford, CA: Stanford University Press.

Senior, Olive. 1986. "Real Old Time T'ing." In *Summer Lightning and Other Stories*. Essex: Longman, 54–66.

Steffensen, Margaret S. 1986. "Register, cohesion, and cross-cultural reading comprehension." *Applied Linguistics* 7: 71–85.

————. 1988. "The dialogue journal: A method of improving cross-cultural reading comprehension." *Reading in a Foreign Language* 51: 193–203.

Steffensen, Margaret S., Chitra Joag-dev and R. C. Andersen. 1979. "A cross-cultural perspective on reading comprehension." *Reading Research Quarterly* 51:10–29.

Tanizaki, Junichiro. 1957. *The Makioka Sisters*. Translated by Edward Seidensticker. New York: Grosset & Dunlap.

Walcott, Derek. 1986 [1982]. "Spoiler's return." In Paula Burnett (ed.), *The Penguin Book of Caribbean Verse*. Harmondsworth: Penguin, 249–54.

Winer, Lise. 1985. "Trini Talk: Learning an English creole as a second language." In Ian F. Hancock (ed.), *Diversity and Development in English-Related Creoles*. Ann Arbor, MI: Karoma Press, 44–67.

————. 1993. *Trinidad and Tobago*. Varieties of English Around the World, vol. 6. Amsterdam: John Benjamins.

Winer, Lise and Margaret Steffensen. 1992. "Cross-cultural peer dialogue journals in ESOL teacher education." *TESOL Journal* 13:23–7.

# Name Index

# Language Index

# Subject Index